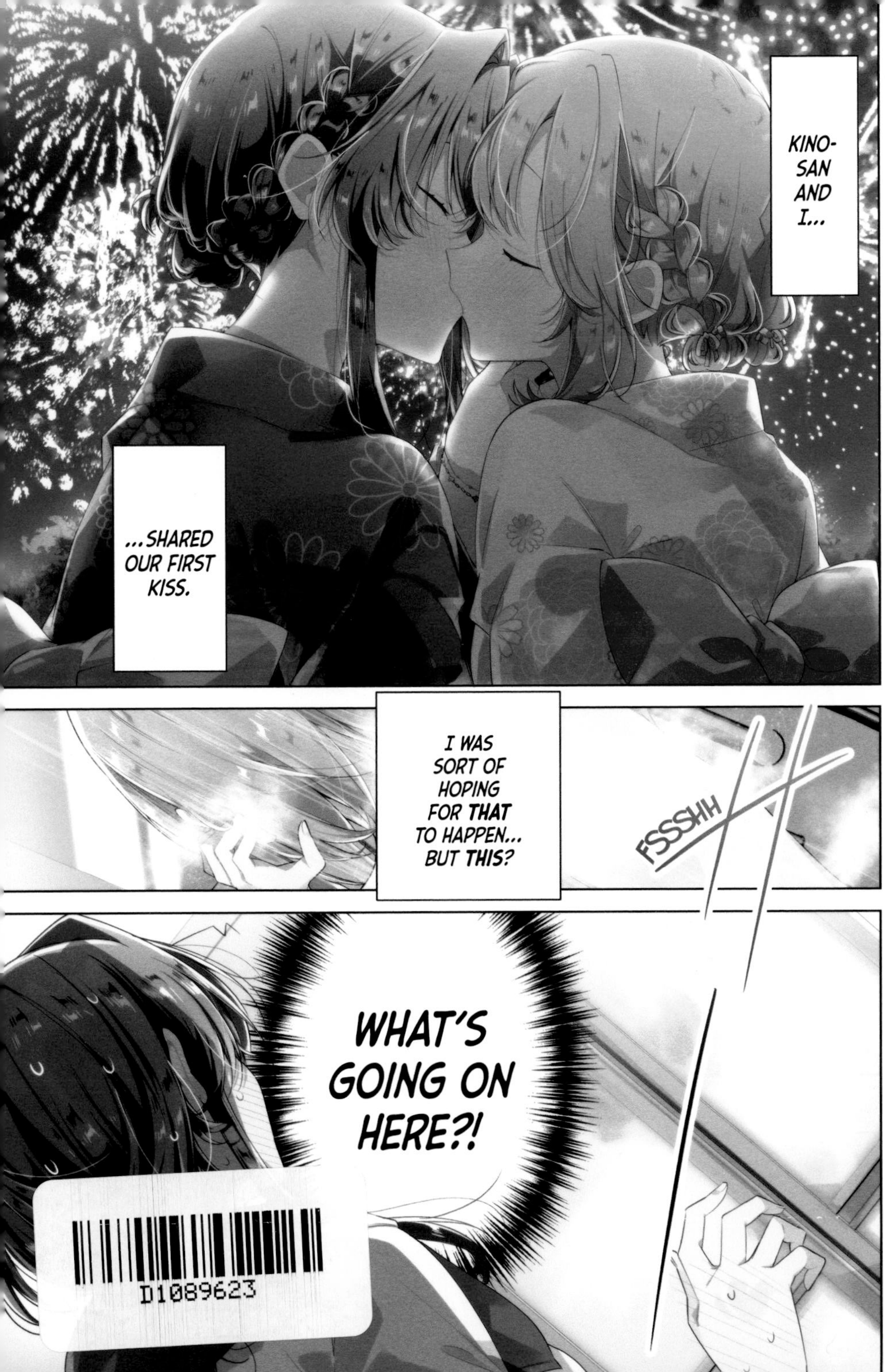
KINO-SAN AND I...
...SHARED OUR FIRST KISS.
FSSSHH
I WAS SORT OF HOPING FOR THAT TO HAPPEN... BUT THIS?
WHAT'S GOING ON HERE?!

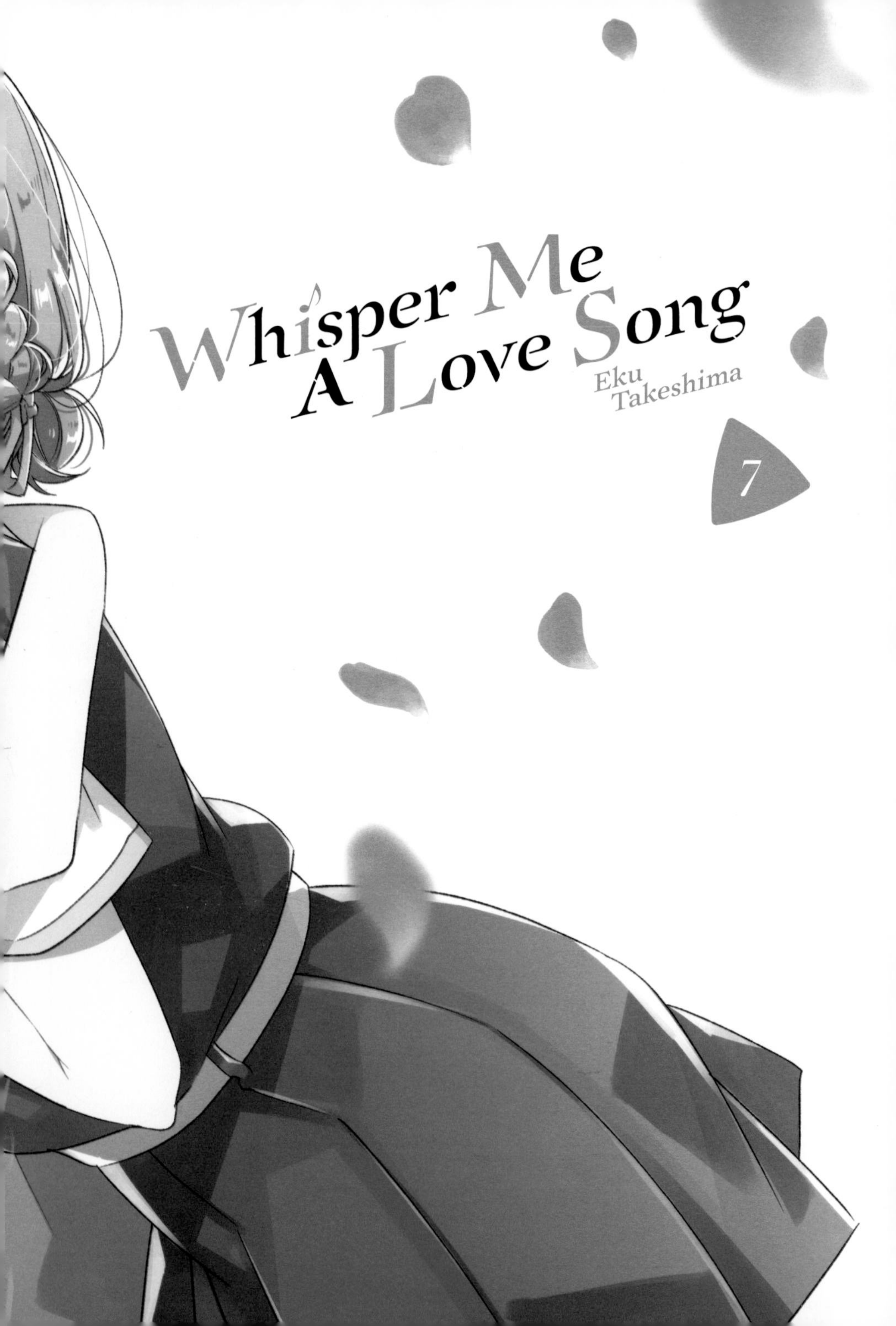

Whisper Me A Love Song

Eku Takeshima

7

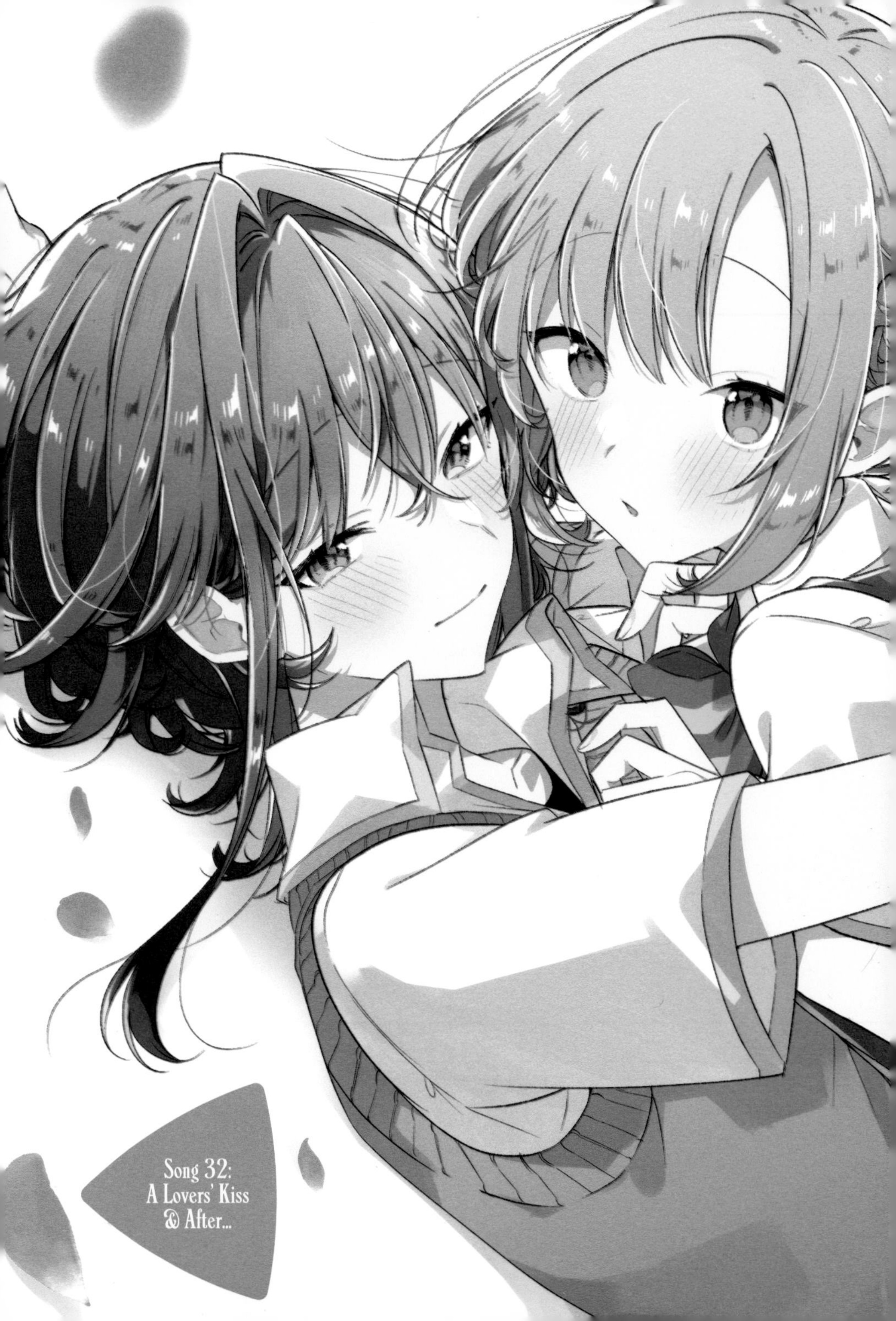
Song 32:
A Lovers' Kiss
& After...

7

contents

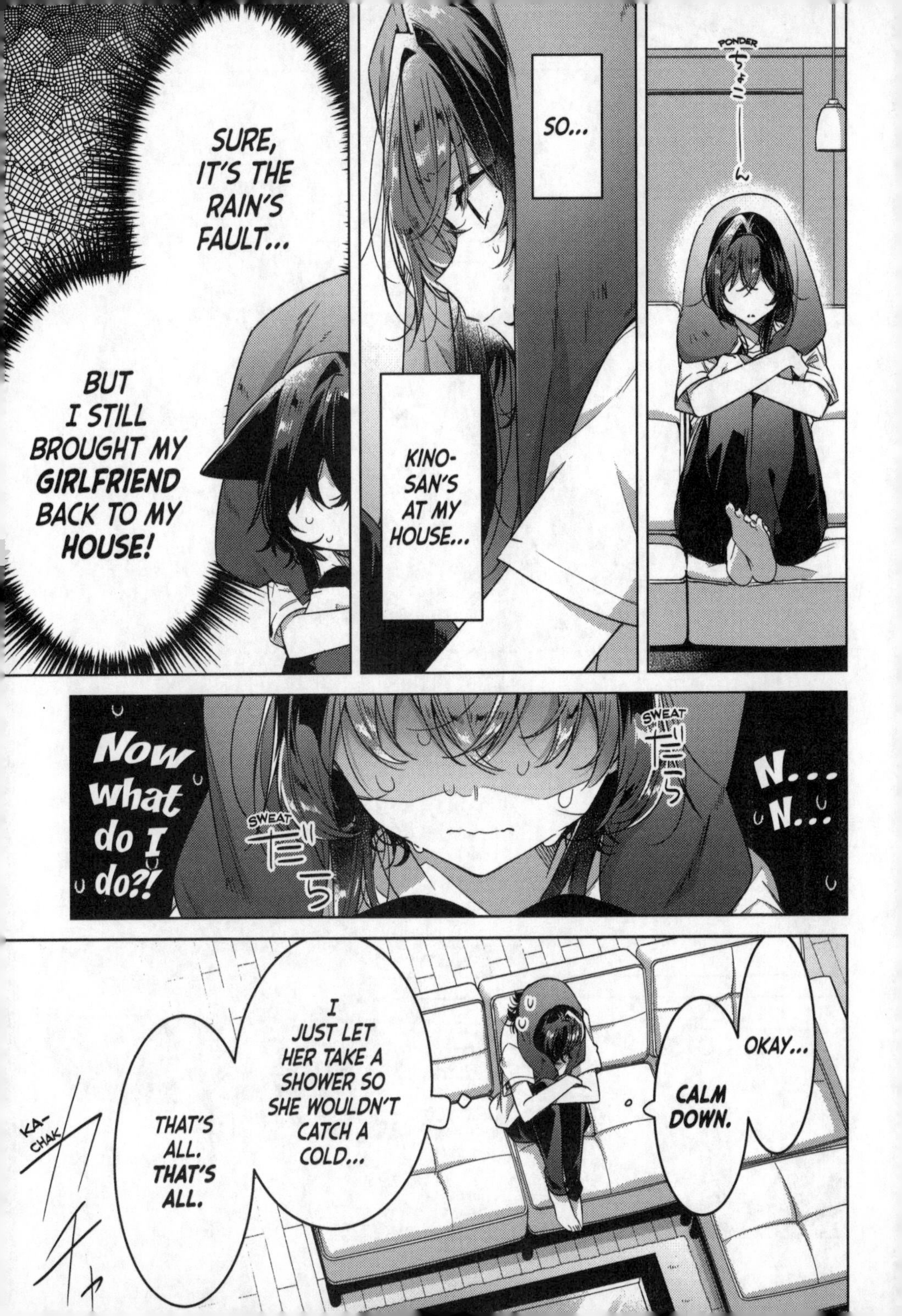

PONDER
SO...
KINO-SAN'S AT MY HOUSE...
SURE, IT'S THE RAIN'S FAULT...
BUT I STILL BROUGHT MY GIRLFRIEND BACK TO MY HOUSE!
N... N...
SWEAT
SWEAT
Now what do I do?!
OKAY...
CALM DOWN.
I JUST LET HER TAKE A SHOWER SO SHE WOULDN'T CATCH A COLD...
THAT'S ALL. THAT'S ALL.
KA-CHAK

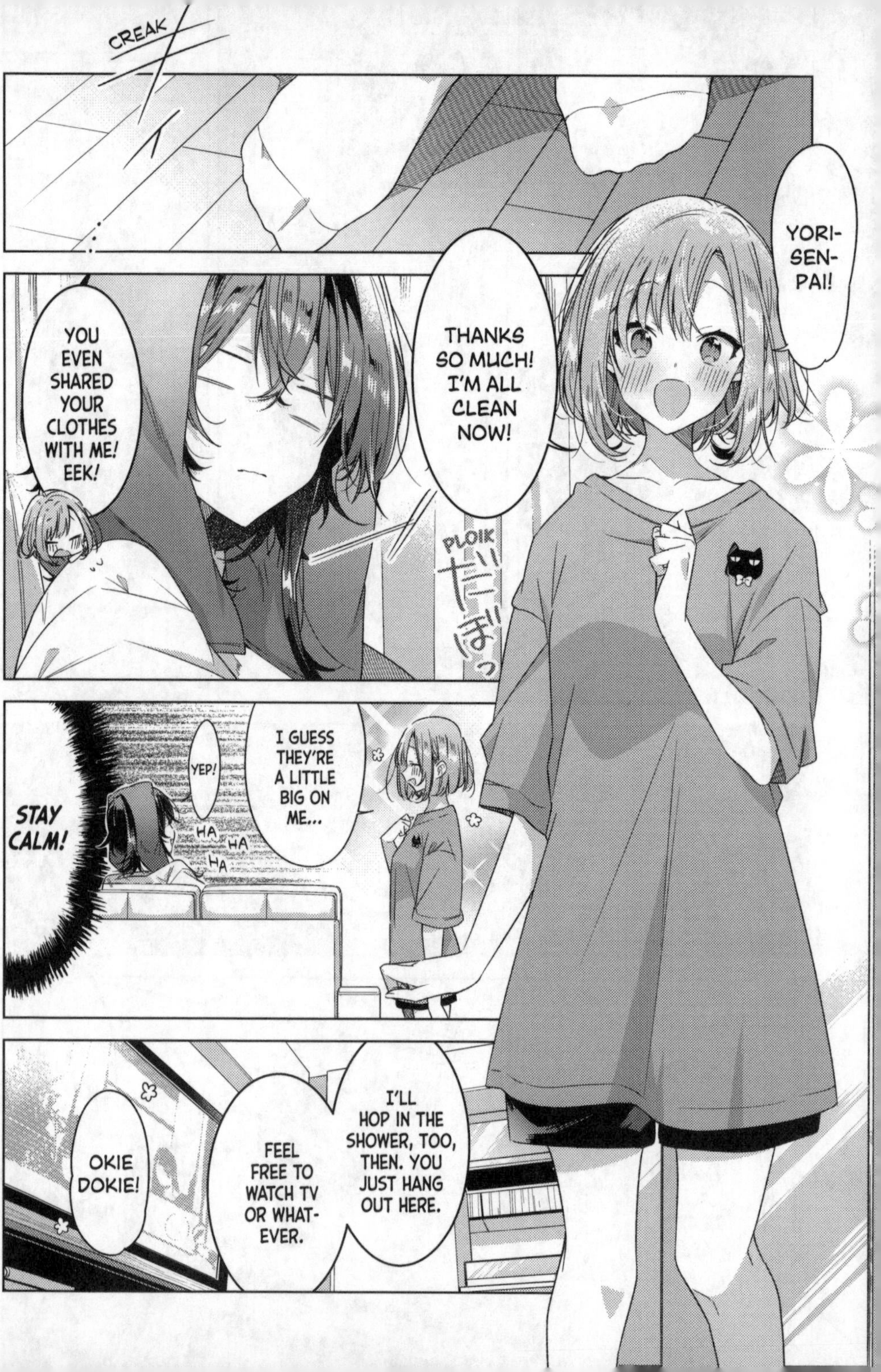
CREAK
...
YORI-SENPAI!
THANKS SO MUCH! I'M ALL CLEAN NOW!
PLOIK
だぼっ
YOU EVEN SHARED YOUR CLOTHES WITH ME! EEK!
I GUESS THEY'RE A LITTLE BIG ON ME...
YEP!
STAY CALM!
HA HA HA
I'LL HOP IN THE SHOWER, TOO, THEN. YOU JUST HANG OUT HERE.
FEEL FREE TO WATCH TV OR WHAT-EVER.
OKIE DOKIE!

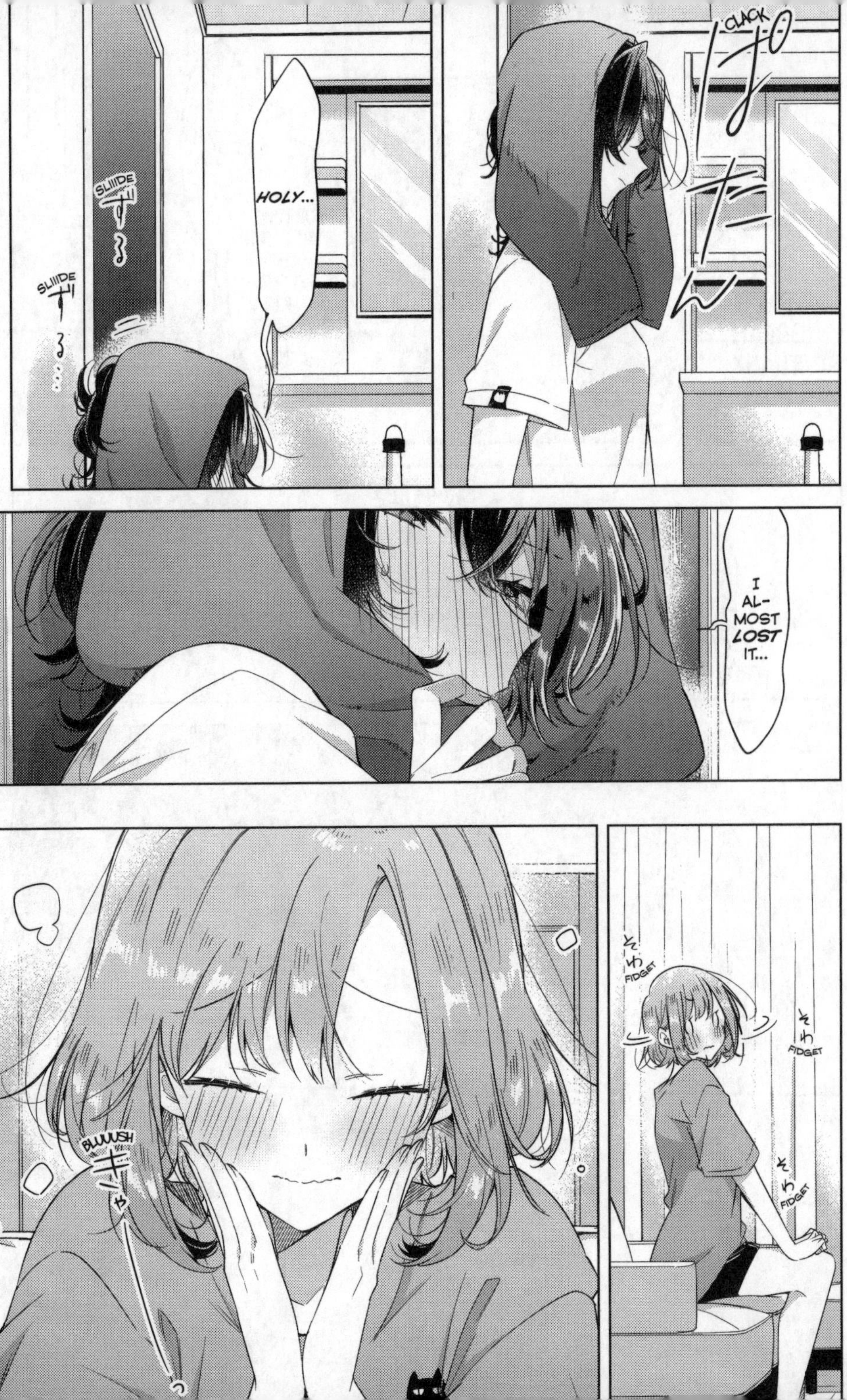

CLACK
HOLY...
SLIIIDE
SLIIIDE
I AL-MOST LOST IT...
FIDGET
FIDGET
FIDGET
BLUUUSH

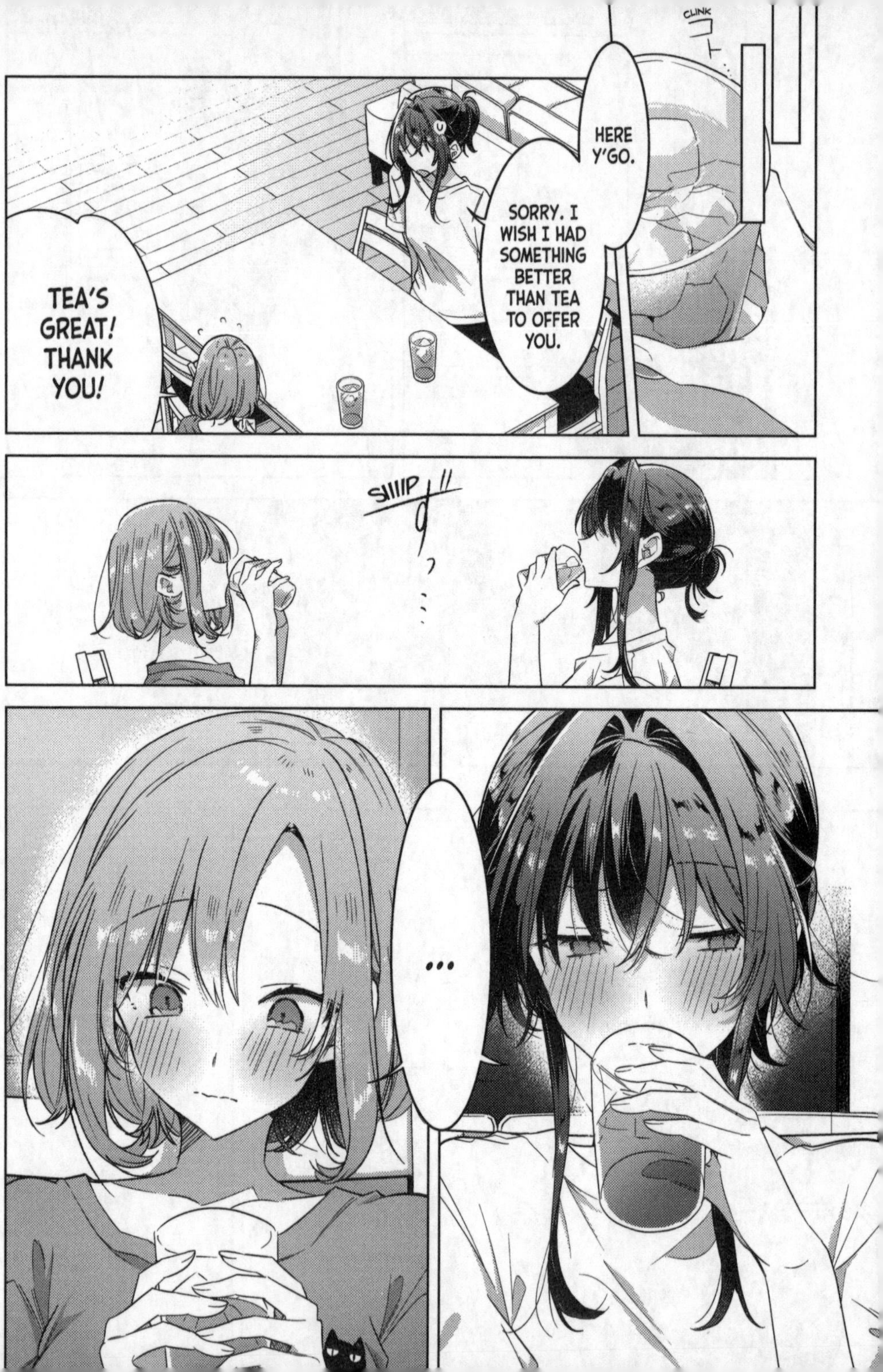
CLINK
HERE Y'GO.
SORRY. I WISH I HAD SOMETHING BETTER THAN TEA TO OFFER YOU.
TEA'S GREAT! THANK YOU!
SIIIIP
...

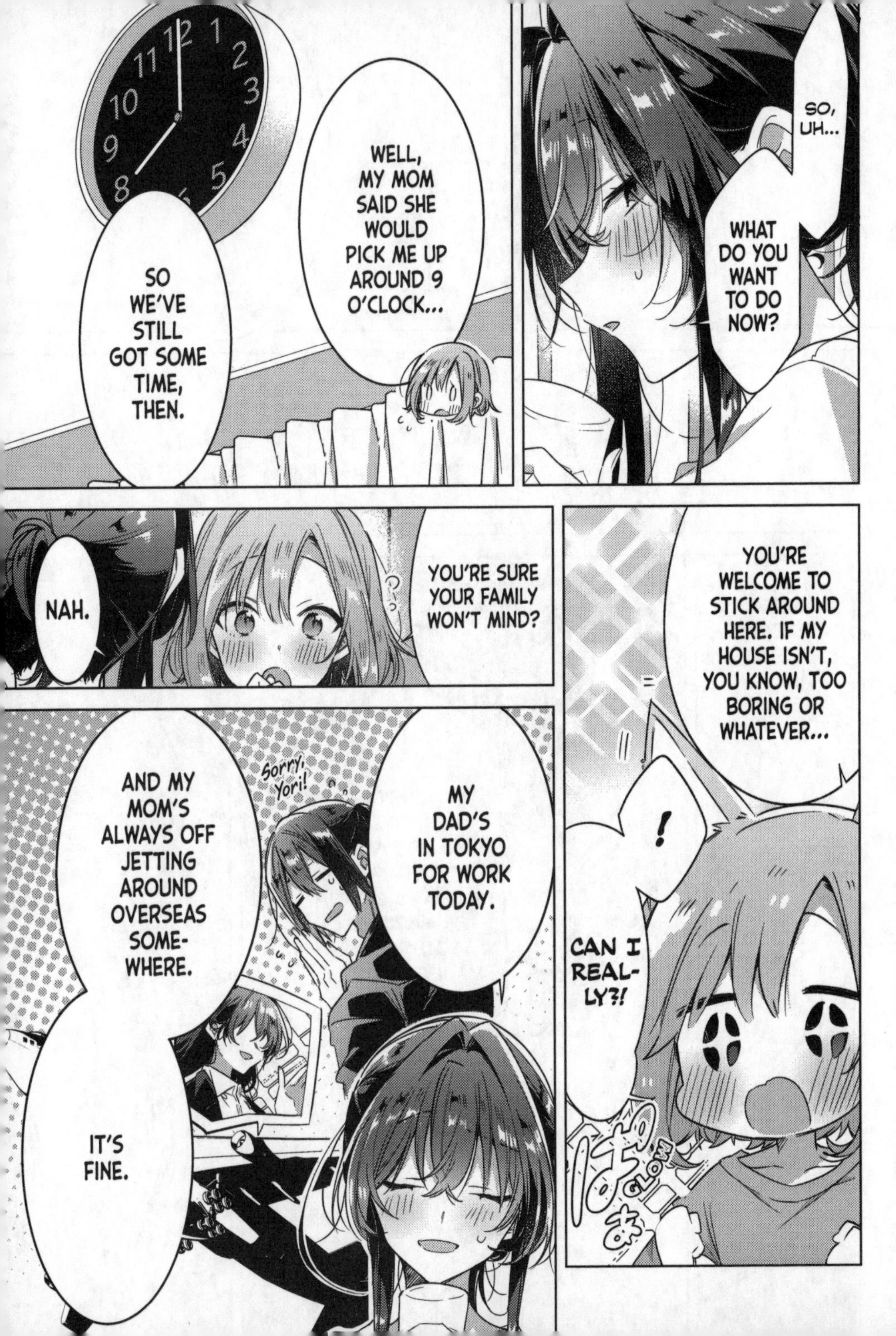
SO, UH...
WHAT DO YOU WANT TO DO NOW?
WELL, MY MOM SAID SHE WOULD PICK ME UP AROUND 9 O'CLOCK...
SO WE'VE STILL GOT SOME TIME, THEN.
YOU'RE WELCOME TO STICK AROUND HERE. IF MY HOUSE ISN'T, YOU KNOW, TOO BORING OR WHATEVER...
!
CAN I REAL-LY?!
GLOW
YOU'RE SURE YOUR FAMILY WON'T MIND?
NAH.
MY DAD'S IN TOKYO FOR WORK TODAY.
Sorry, Yori!
AND MY MOM'S ALWAYS OFF JETTING AROUND OVERSEAS SOME-WHERE.
IT'S FINE.

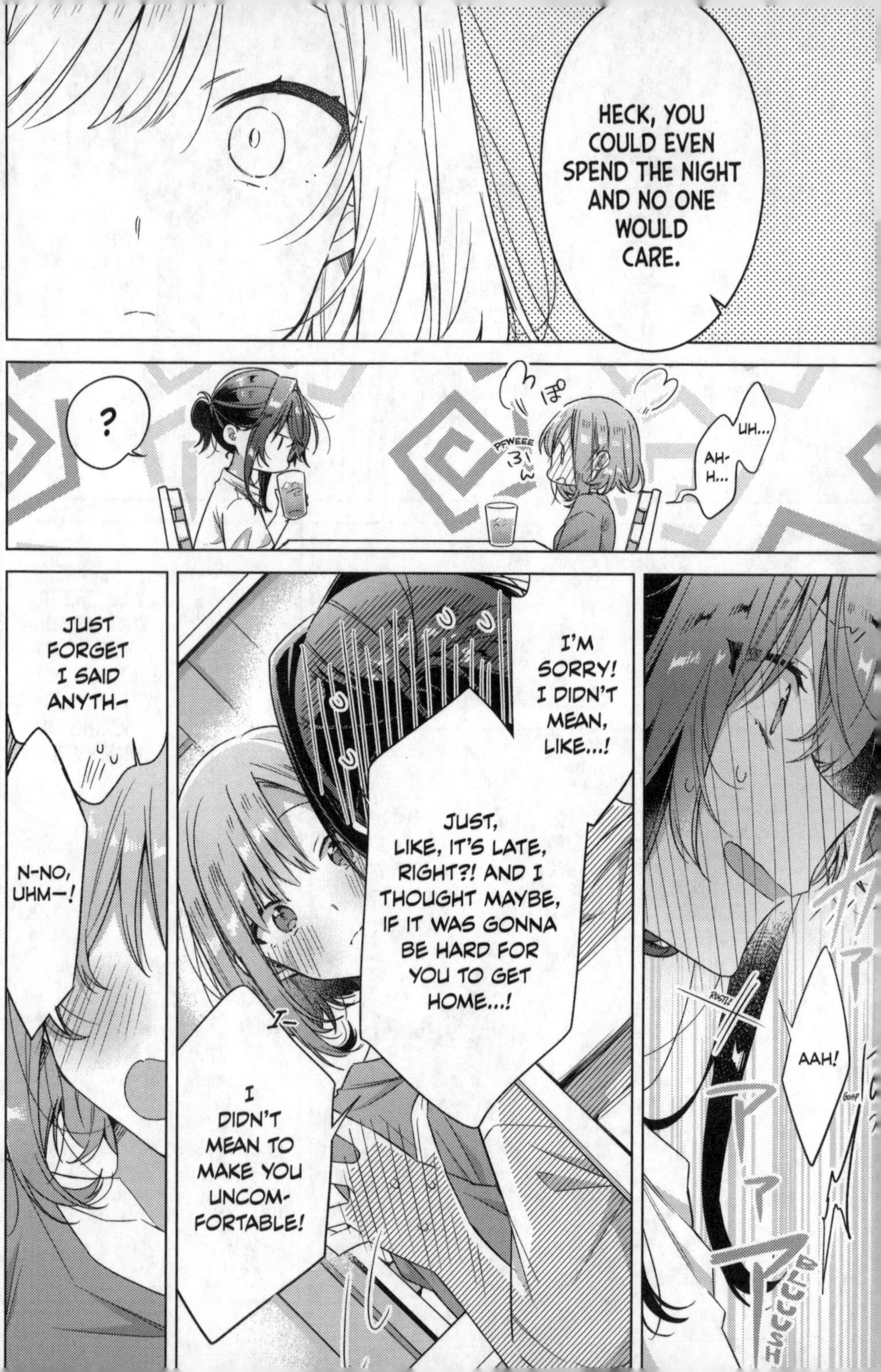
HECK, YOU COULD EVEN SPEND THE NIGHT AND NO ONE WOULD CARE.
UH...
AH-H...
ぽ
PFWEEE
?
AAH!
RUSTLE
GASP
I'M SORRY! I DIDN'T MEAN, LIKE...!
JUST, LIKE, IT'S LATE, RIGHT?! AND I THOUGHT MAYBE, IF IT WAS GONNA BE HARD FOR YOU TO GET HOME...!
I–
I DIDN'T MEAN TO MAKE YOU UNCOM-FORTABLE!
JUST FORGET I SAID ANYTH-
N-NO, UHM—!

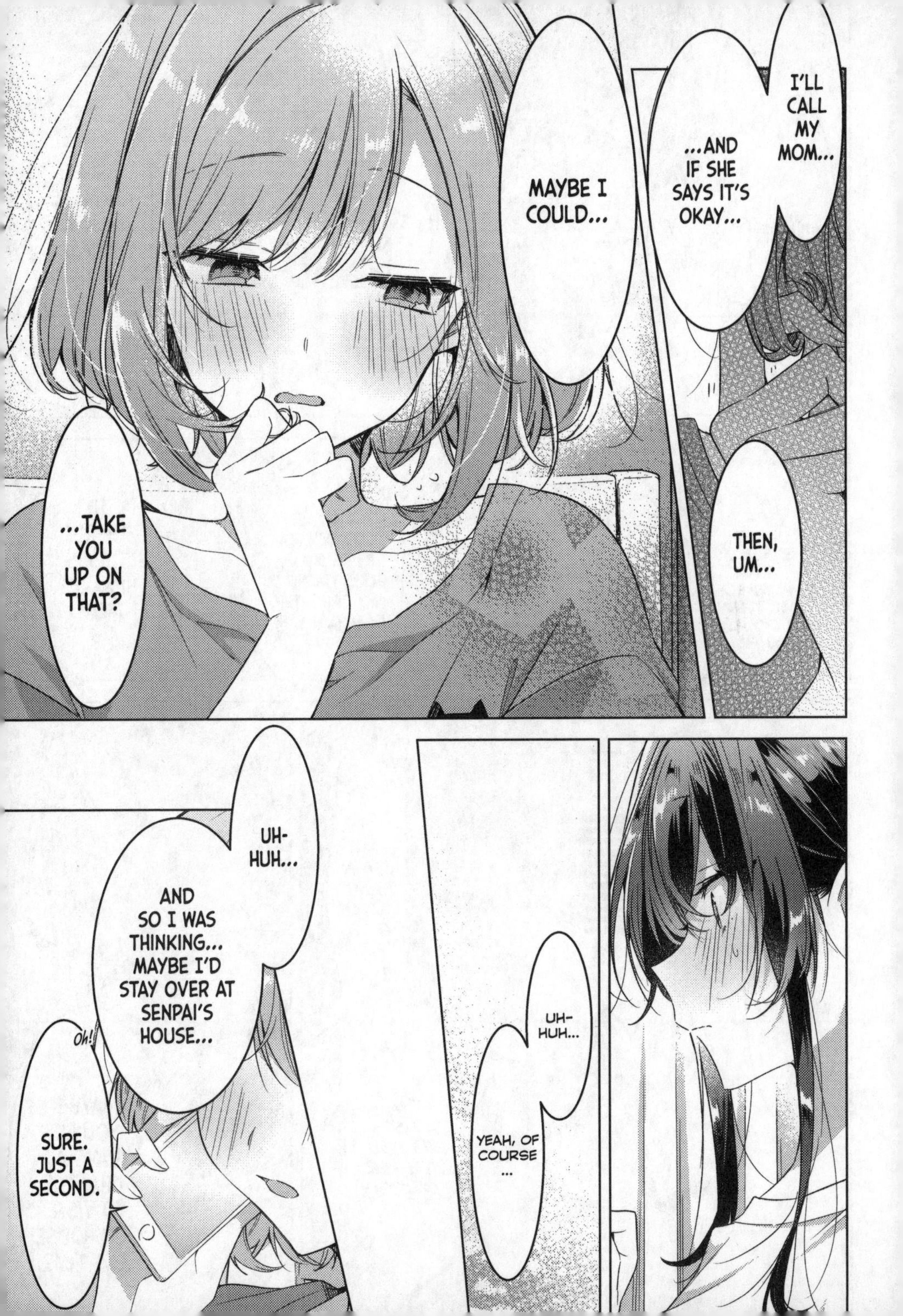
I'LL CALL MY MOM...
...AND IF SHE SAYS IT'S OKAY...
THEN, UM...
MAYBE I COULD...
...TAKE YOU UP ON THAT?
UH-HUH...
YEAH, OF COURSE ...
UH-HUH...
AND SO I WAS THINKING... MAYBE I'D STAY OVER AT SENPAI'S HOUSE...
Oh!
SURE. JUST A SECOND.

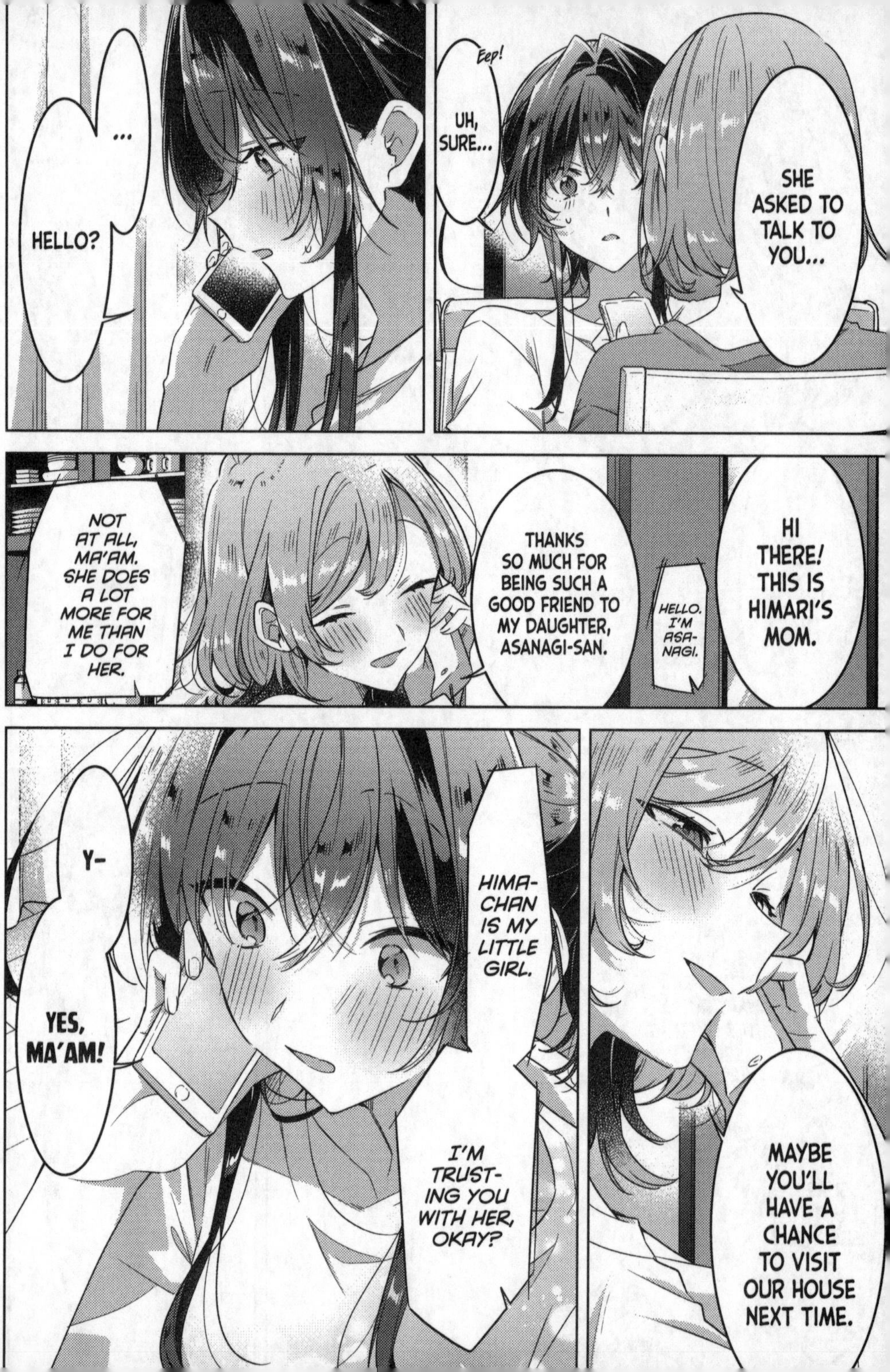
SHE ASKED TO TALK TO YOU...
Eep!
UH, SURE...
...
HELLO?
HI THERE! THIS IS HIMARI'S MOM.
HELLO. I'M ASA-NAGI.
THANKS SO MUCH FOR BEING SUCH A GOOD FRIEND TO MY DAUGHTER, ASANAGI-SAN.
NOT AT ALL, MA'AM. SHE DOES A LOT MORE FOR ME THAN I DO FOR HER.
MAYBE YOU'LL HAVE A CHANCE TO VISIT OUR HOUSE NEXT TIME.
HIMA-CHAN IS MY LITTLE GIRL.
I'M TRUST-ING YOU WITH HER, OKAY?
Y-
YES, MA'AM!

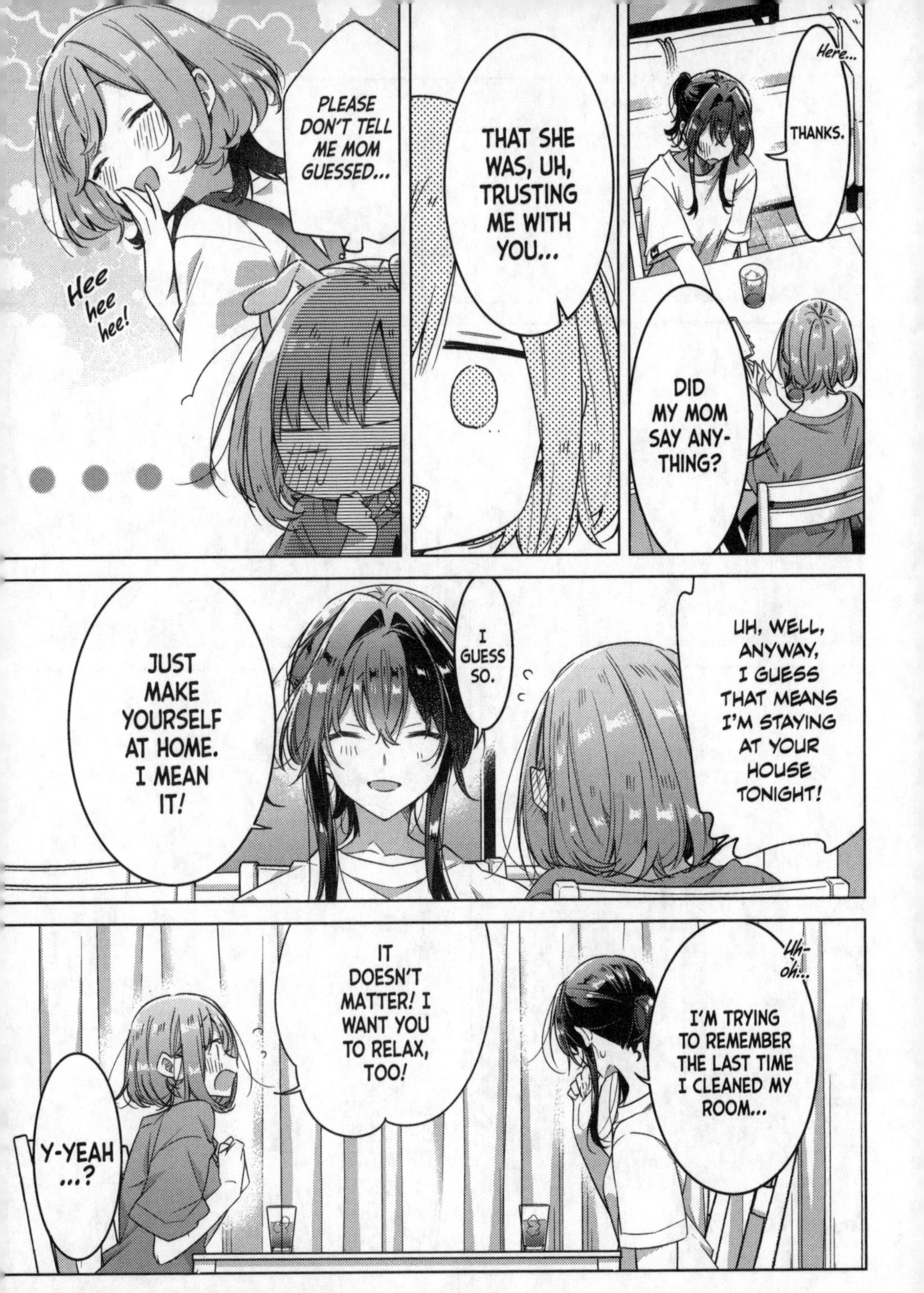
Here...
THANKS.
DID MY MOM SAY ANYTHING?
THAT SHE WAS, UH, TRUSTING ME WITH YOU...
PLEASE DON'T TELL ME MOM GUESSED...
Hee hee hee!
UH, WELL, ANYWAY, I GUESS THAT MEANS I'M STAYING AT YOUR HOUSE TONIGHT!
I GUESS SO.
JUST MAKE YOURSELF AT HOME. I MEAN IT!
Uh-oh...
I'M TRYING TO REMEMBER THE LAST TIME I CLEANED MY ROOM...
IT DOESN'T MATTER! I WANT YOU TO RELAX, TOO!
Y-YEAH ...?

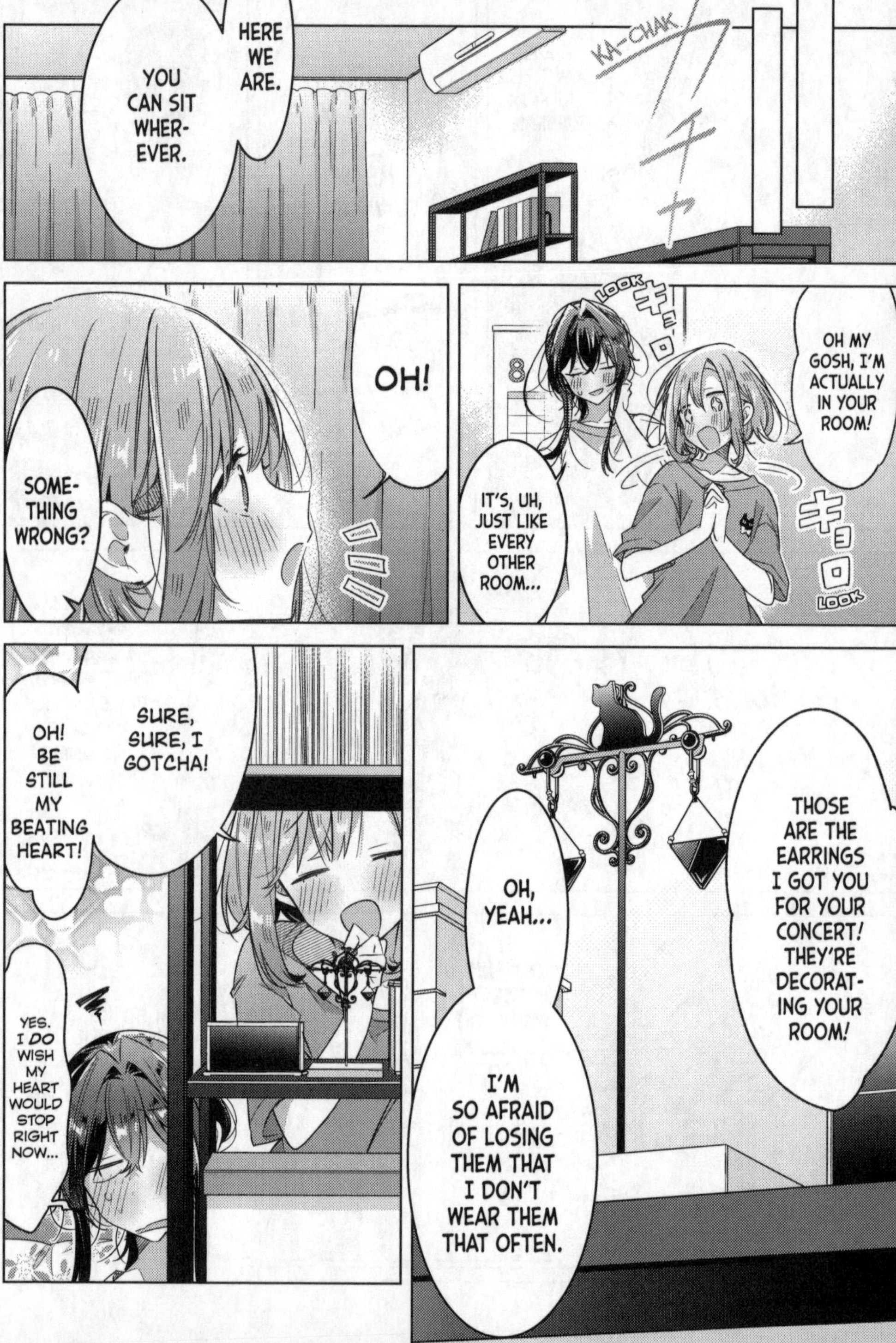
KA-CHAK
HERE WE ARE.
YOU CAN SIT WHEREVER.
LOOK
OH MY GOSH, I'M ACTUALLY IN YOUR ROOM!
IT'S, UH, JUST LIKE EVERY OTHER ROOM...
LOOK
OH!
SOMETHING WRONG?
THOSE ARE THE EARRINGS I GOT YOU FOR YOUR CONCERT! THEY'RE DECORATING YOUR ROOM!
OH, YEAH...
I'M SO AFRAID OF LOSING THEM THAT I DON'T WEAR THEM THAT OFTEN.
SURE, SURE, I GOTCHA!
OH! BE STILL MY BEATING HEART!
YES. I *DO* WISH MY HEART WOULD STOP RIGHT NOW...

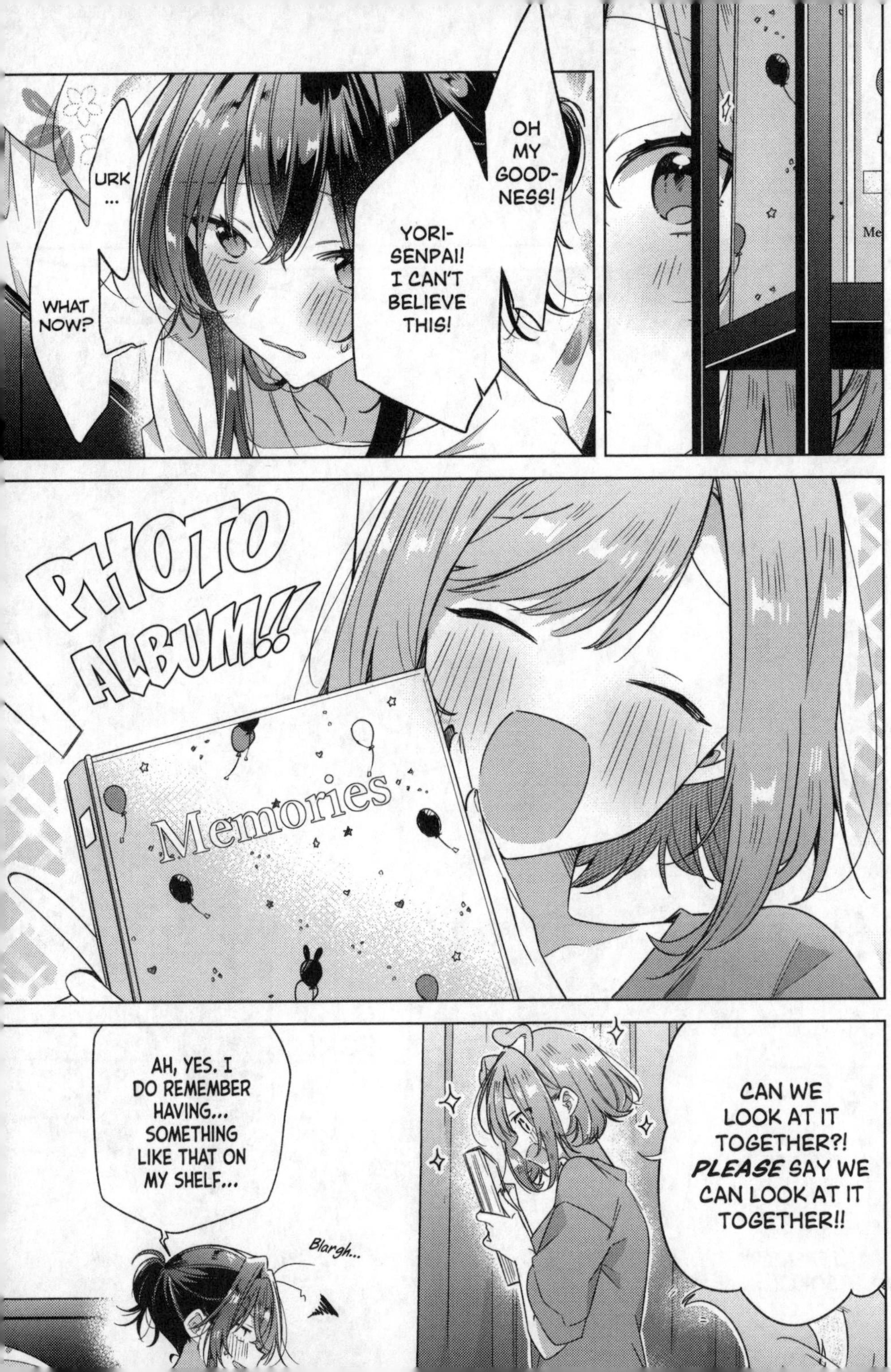
OH MY GOODNESS!
YORI-SENPAI! I CAN'T BELIEVE THIS!
URK ...
WHAT NOW?
PHOTO ALBUM!!
Memories
CAN WE LOOK AT IT TOGETHER?! *PLEASE* SAY WE CAN LOOK AT IT TOGETHER!!
AH, YES. I DO REMEMBER HAVING... SOMETHING LIKE THAT ON MY SHELF...
Blargh...

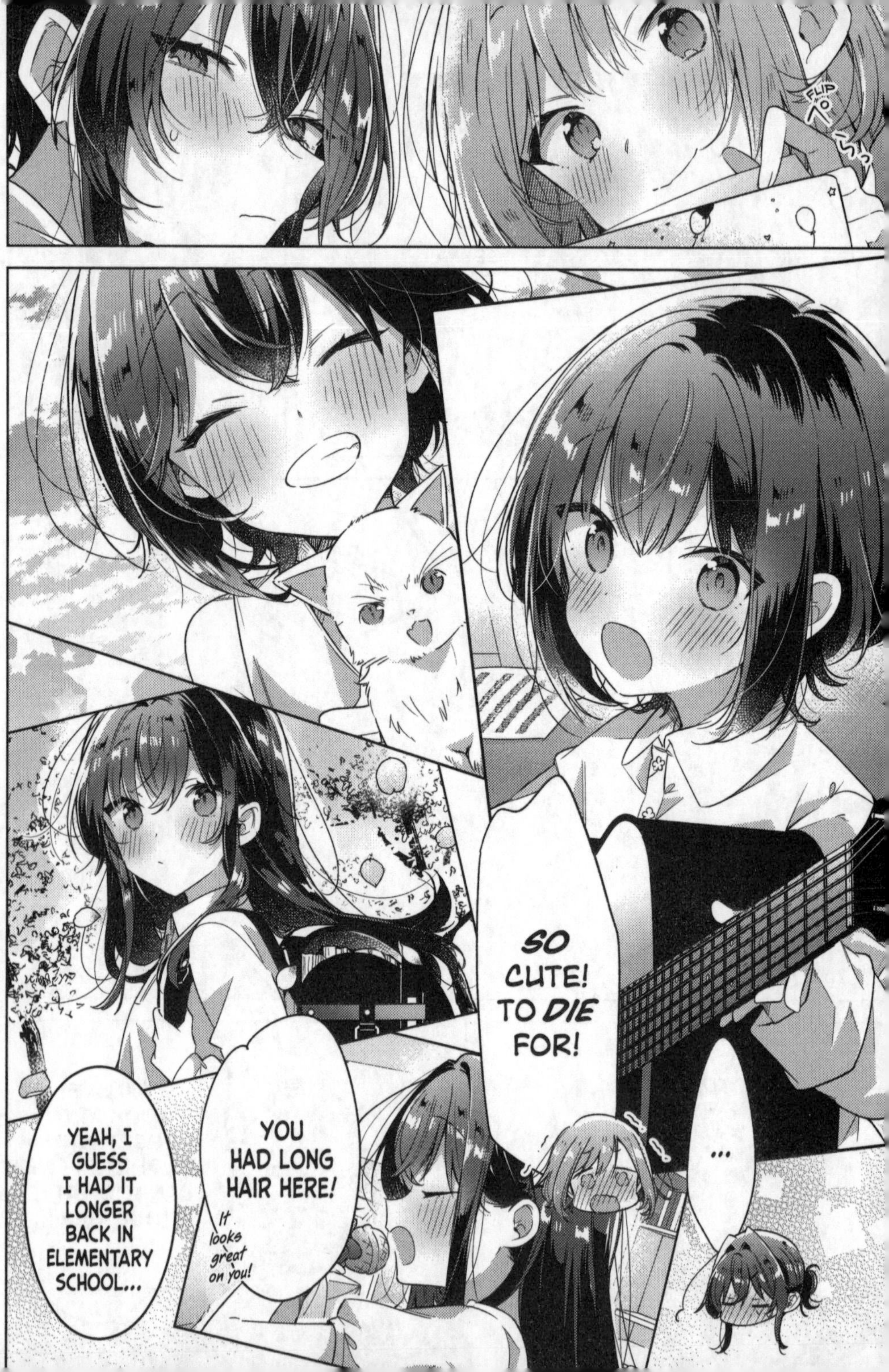
FLIP
ぺらっ
SO CUTE! TO DIE FOR!
...
YOU HAD LONG HAIR HERE!
It looks great on you!
YEAH, I GUESS I HAD IT LONGER BACK IN ELEMENTARY SCHOOL...

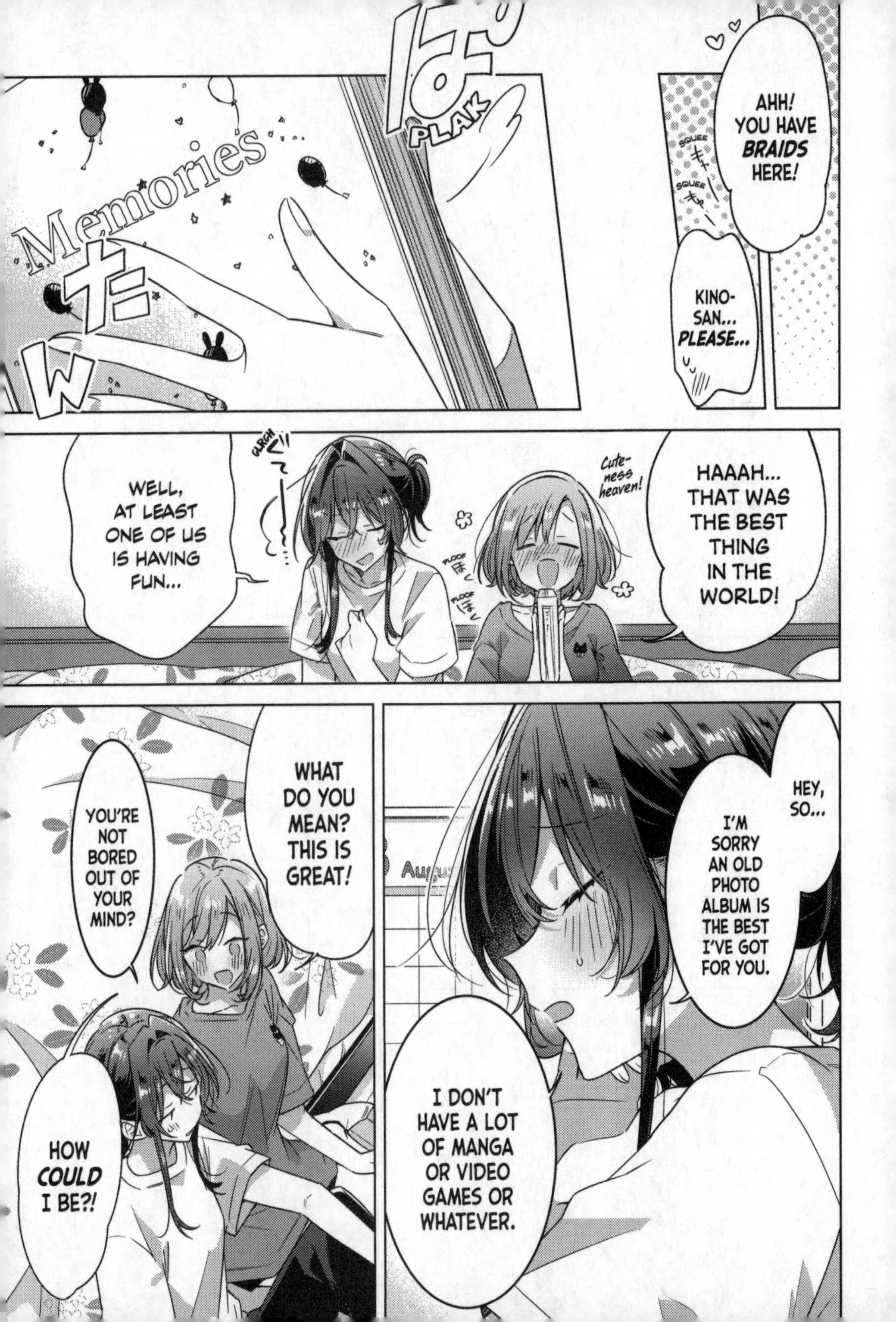
AHH! YOU HAVE BRAIDS HERE!
SQUEE
SQUEE
KINO-SAN... PLEASE...
PLAK
Memories
W
HAAAH... THAT WAS THE BEST THING IN THE WORLD!
Cute-ness heaven!
PLOOF
PLOOF
GLRCH
WELL, AT LEAST ONE OF US IS HAVING FUN...
HEY, SO...
I'M SORRY AN OLD PHOTO ALBUM IS THE BEST I'VE GOT FOR YOU.
I DON'T HAVE A LOT OF MANGA OR VIDEO GAMES OR WHATEVER.
WHAT DO YOU MEAN? THIS IS GREAT!
YOU'RE NOT BORED OUT OF YOUR MIND?
HOW COULD I BE?!

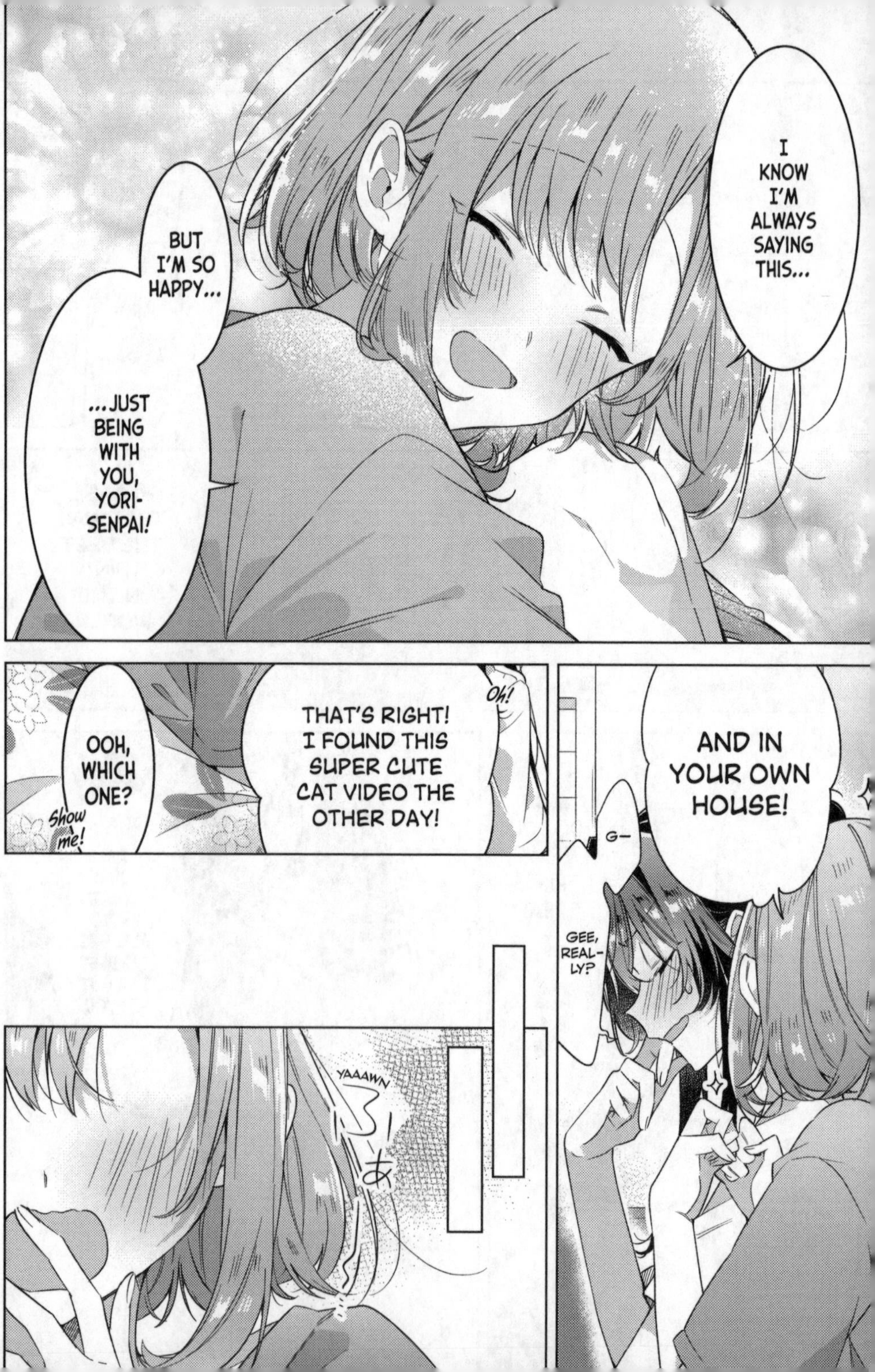
I KNOW I'M ALWAYS SAYING THIS...
BUT I'M SO HAPPY...
...JUST BEING WITH YOU, YORI-SENPAI!
AND IN YOUR OWN HOUSE!
G—
GEE, REAL-LY?
Oh!
THAT'S RIGHT! I FOUND THIS SUPER CUTE CAT VIDEO THE OTHER DAY!
OOH, WHICH ONE?
Show me!
YAAAWN

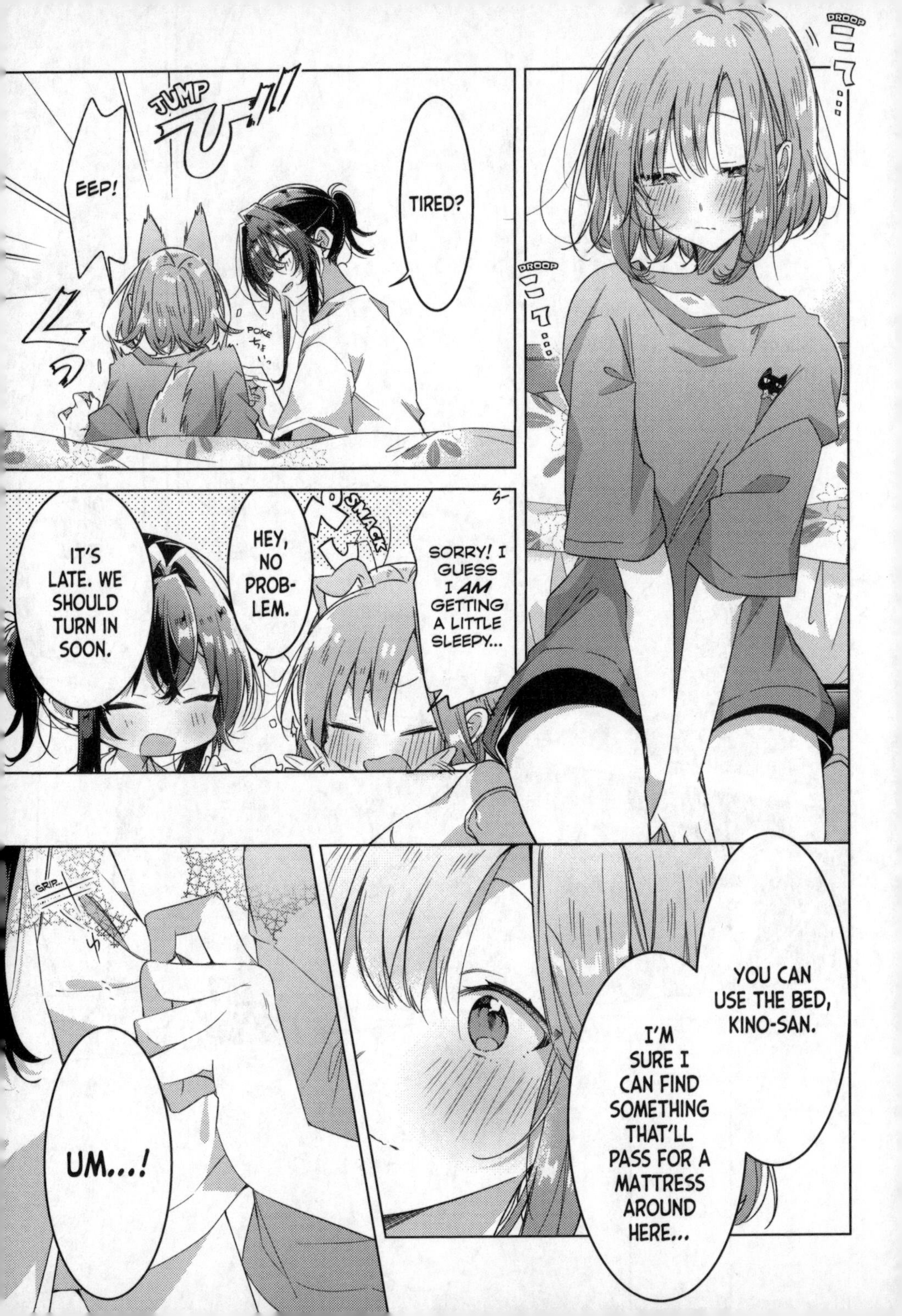
DROOP
DROOP
TIRED?
JUMP
EEP!
POKE
SORRY! I GUESS I *AM* GETTING A LITTLE SLEEPY...
SMACK
HEY, NO PROB-LEM.
IT'S LATE. WE SHOULD TURN IN SOON.
YOU CAN USE THE BED, KINO-SAN.
I'M SURE I CAN FIND SOMETHING THAT'LL PASS FOR A MATTRESS AROUND HERE...
GRIP...
UM...!

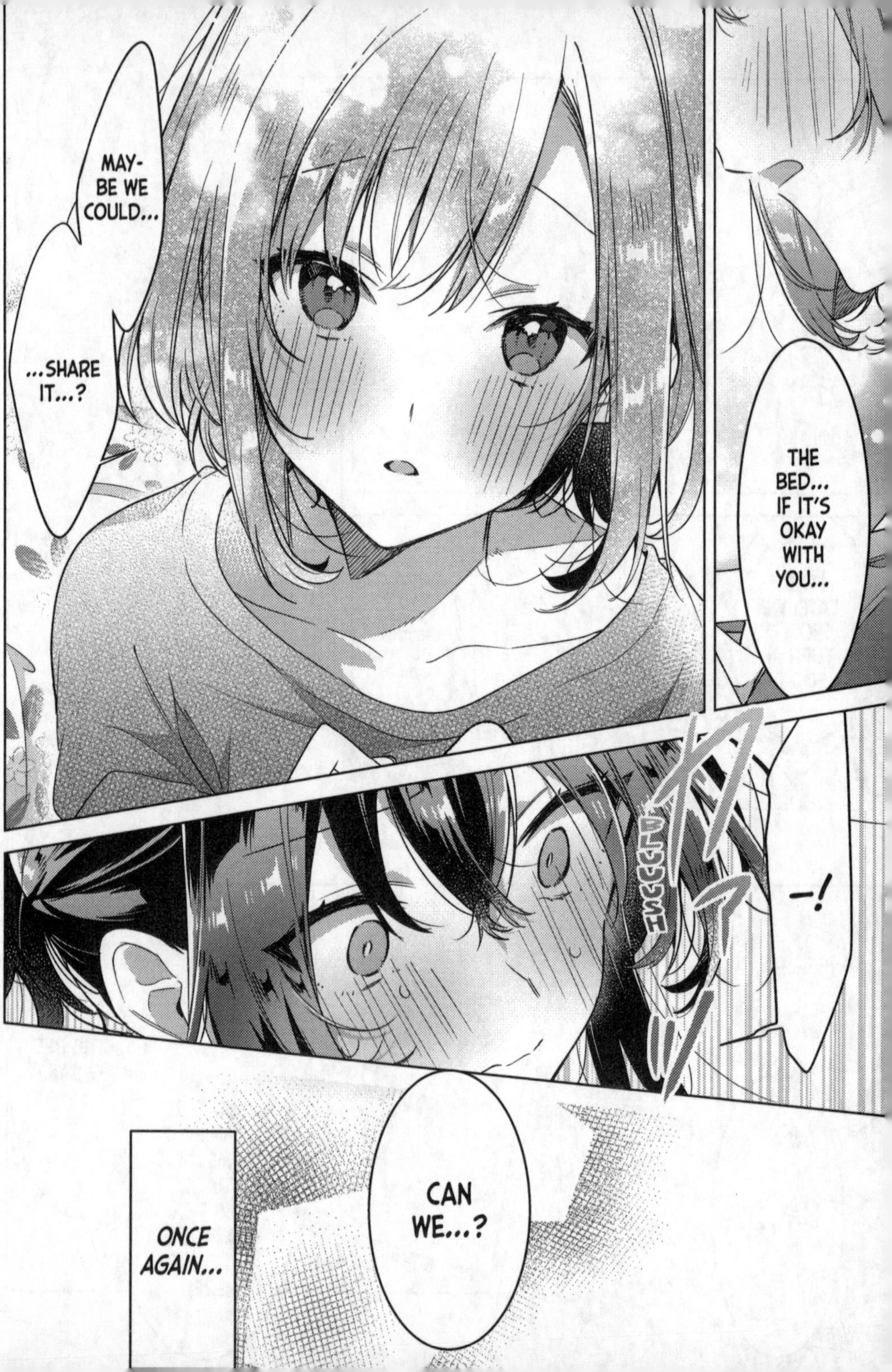
THE BED... IF IT'S OKAY WITH YOU...
MAY-BE WE COULD...
...SHARE IT...?
FLUSH
—!
CAN WE...?
ONCE AGAIN...

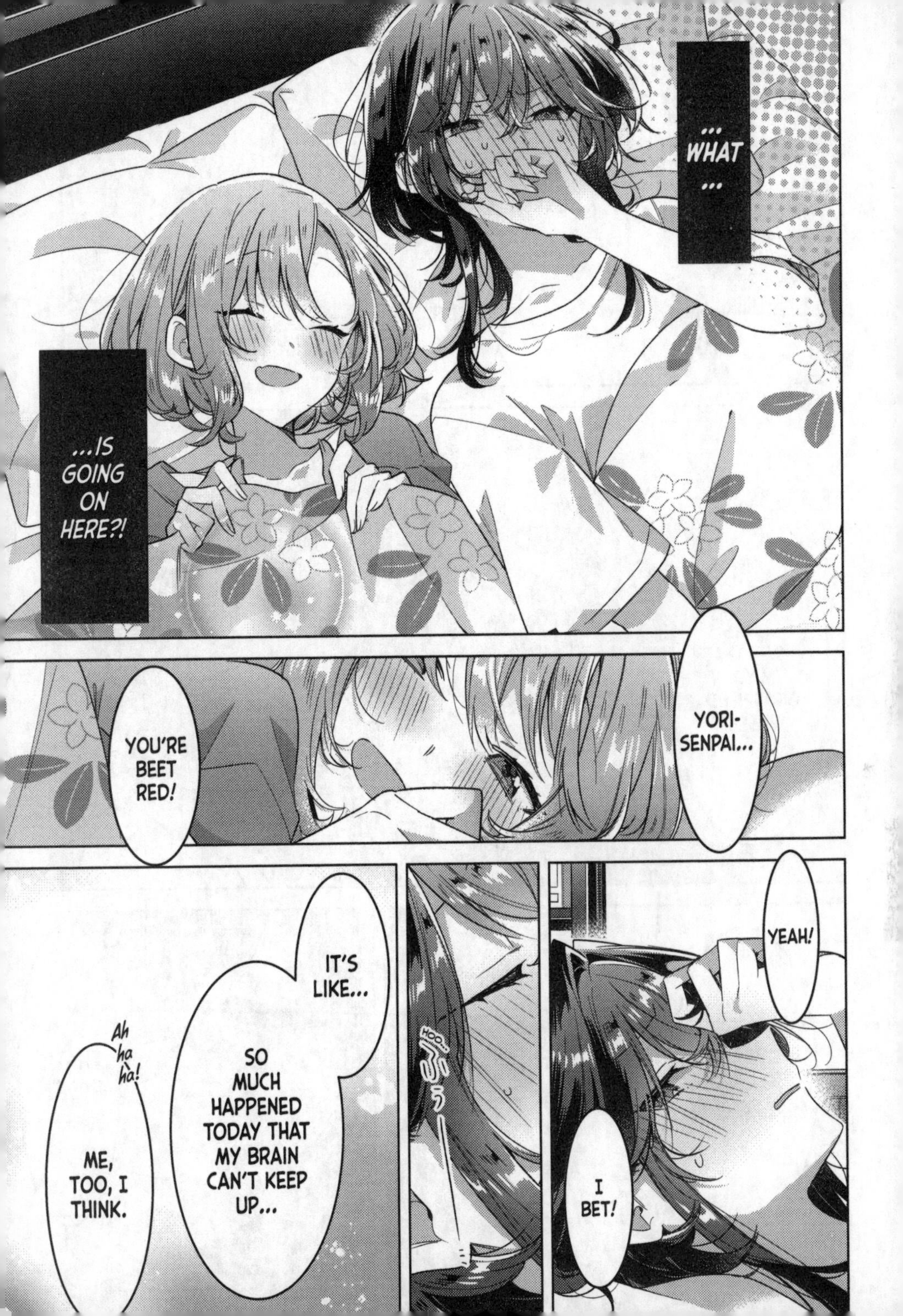
...WHAT...
...IS GOING ON HERE?!
YORI-SENPAI...
YOU'RE BEET RED!
YEAH!
I BET!
HOO...
IT'S LIKE...
SO MUCH HAPPENED TODAY THAT MY BRAIN CAN'T KEEP UP...
Ah ha ha!
ME, TOO, I THINK.

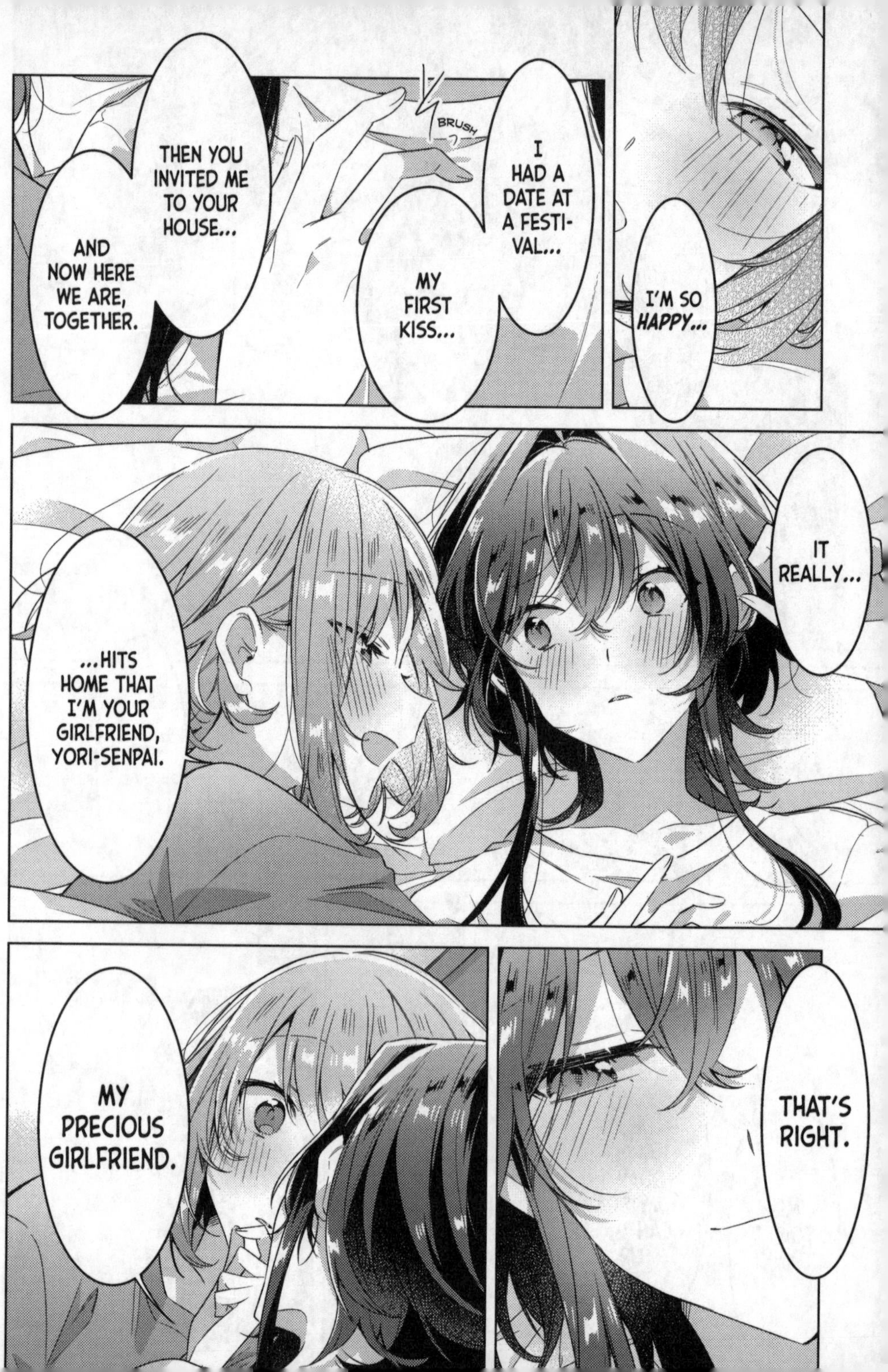
I'M SO HAPPY...
I HAD A DATE AT A FESTIVAL...
BRUSH
MY FIRST KISS...
THEN YOU INVITED ME TO YOUR HOUSE...
AND NOW HERE WE ARE, TOGETHER.
IT REALLY...
...HITS HOME THAT I'M YOUR GIRLFRIEND, YORI-SENPAI.
THAT'S RIGHT.
MY PRECIOUS GIRLFRIEND.

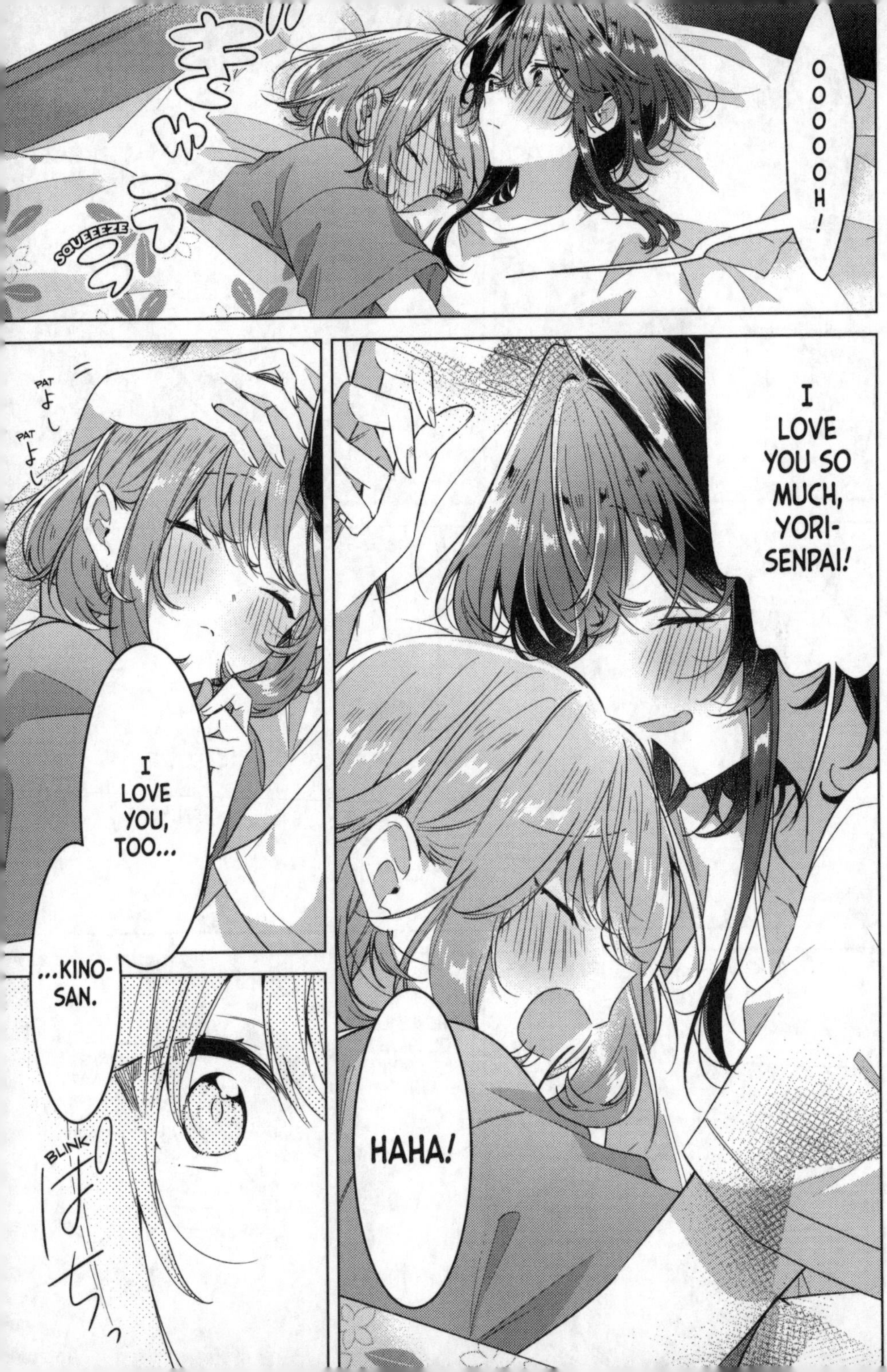
OOOOOOH!
ぎゅううう
SQUEEEZE
I LOVE YOU SO MUCH, YORI-SENPAI!
HAHA!
PAT よし
PAT よし
I LOVE YOU, TOO...
...KINO-SAN.
BLINK
ぱちっ

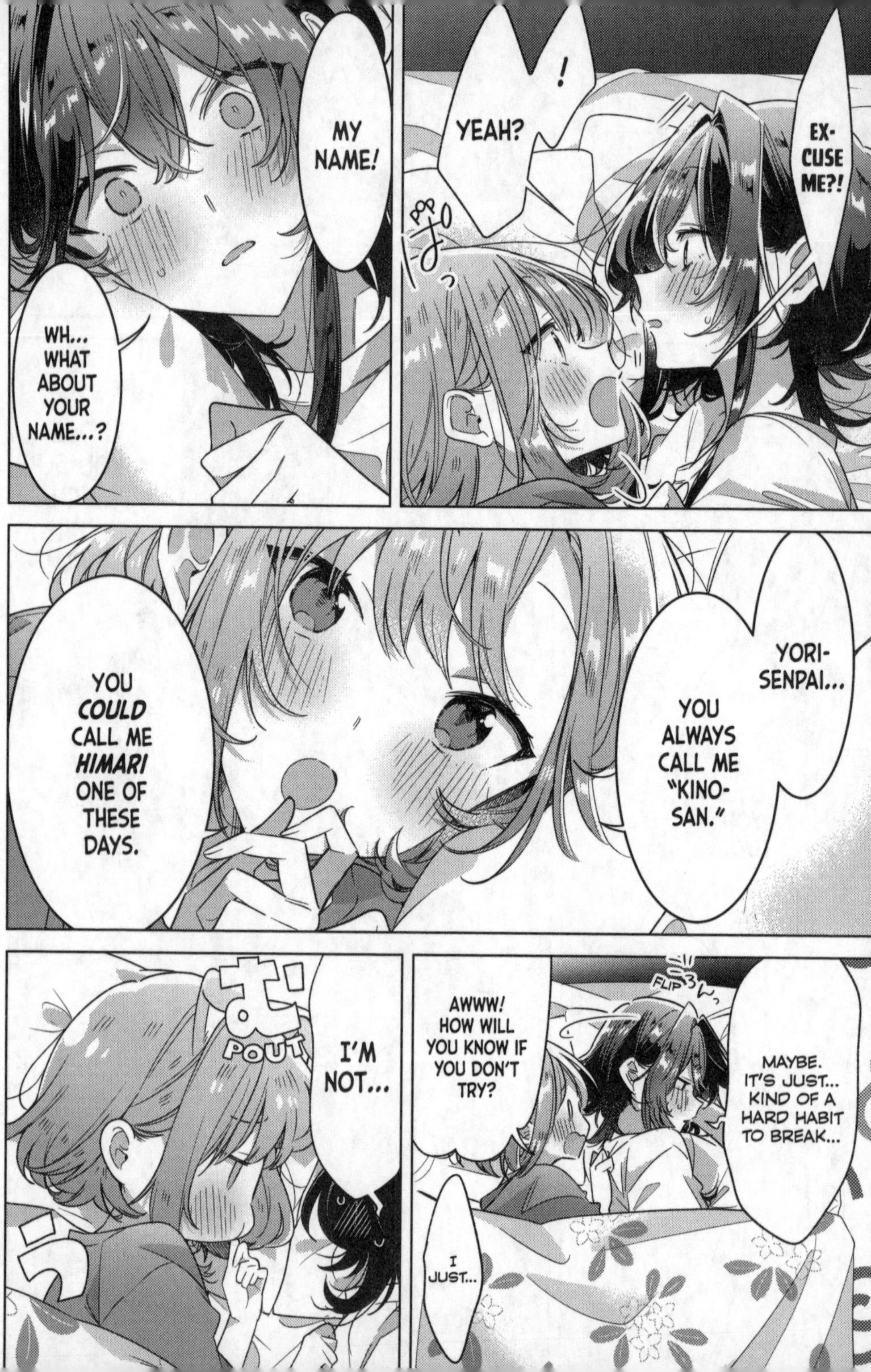
EX-CUSE ME?!
!
YEAH?
MY NAME!
WH... WHAT ABOUT YOUR NAME...?
YORI-SENPAI...
YOU ALWAYS CALL ME "KINO-SAN."
YOU COULD CALL ME HIMARI ONE OF THESE DAYS.
FLIP
MAYBE. IT'S JUST... KIND OF A HARD HABIT TO BREAK...
AWWW! HOW WILL YOU KNOW IF YOU DON'T TRY?
I JUST...
I'M NOT...
POUT

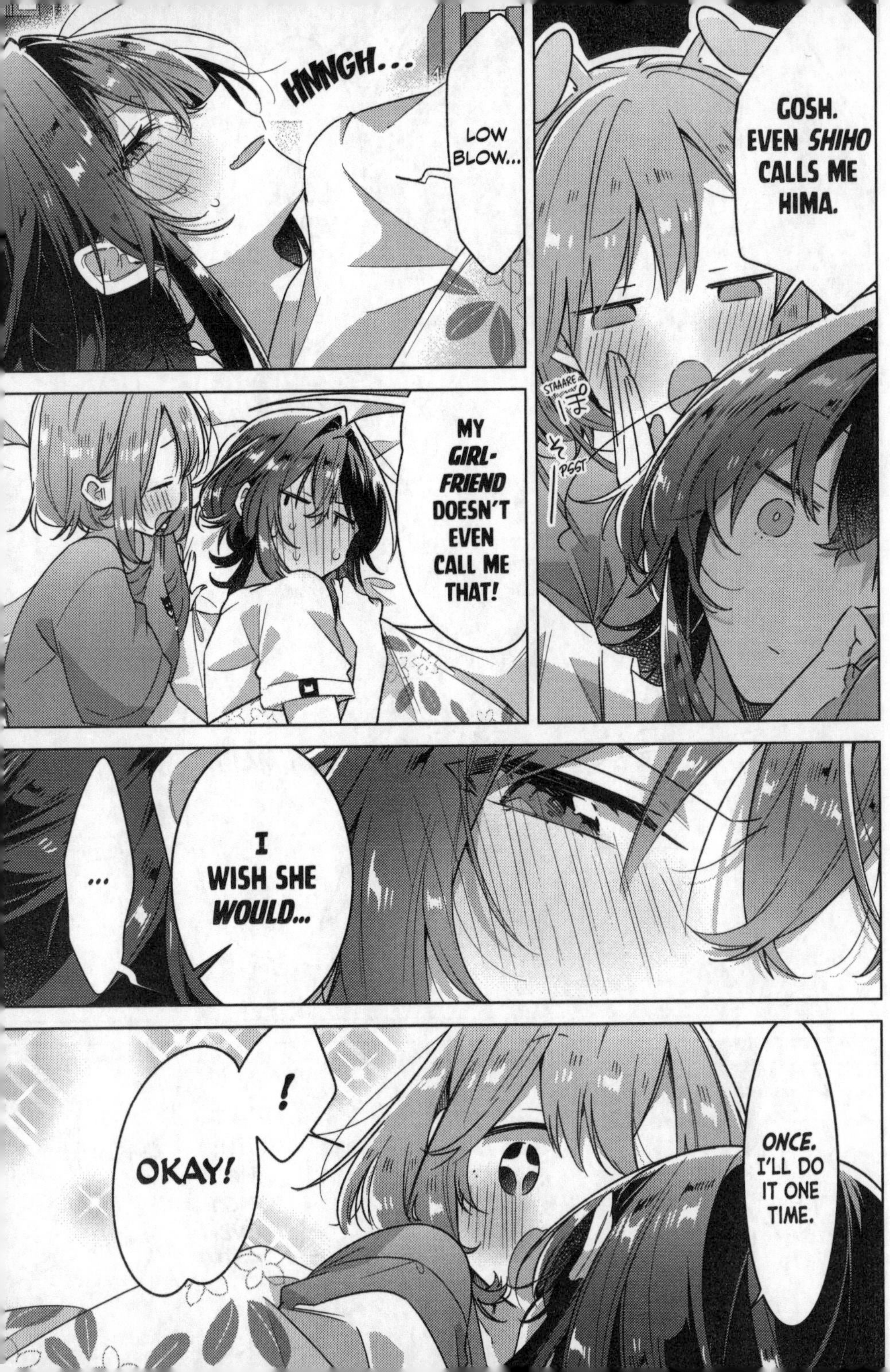
GOSH. EVEN *SHIHO* CALLS ME HIMA.
STAARE
PSST
HNNGH...
LOW BLOW...
MY *GIRL-FRIEND* DOESN'T EVEN CALL ME THAT!
I WISH SHE *WOULD*...
...
ONCE. I'LL DO IT ONE TIME.
!
OKAY!

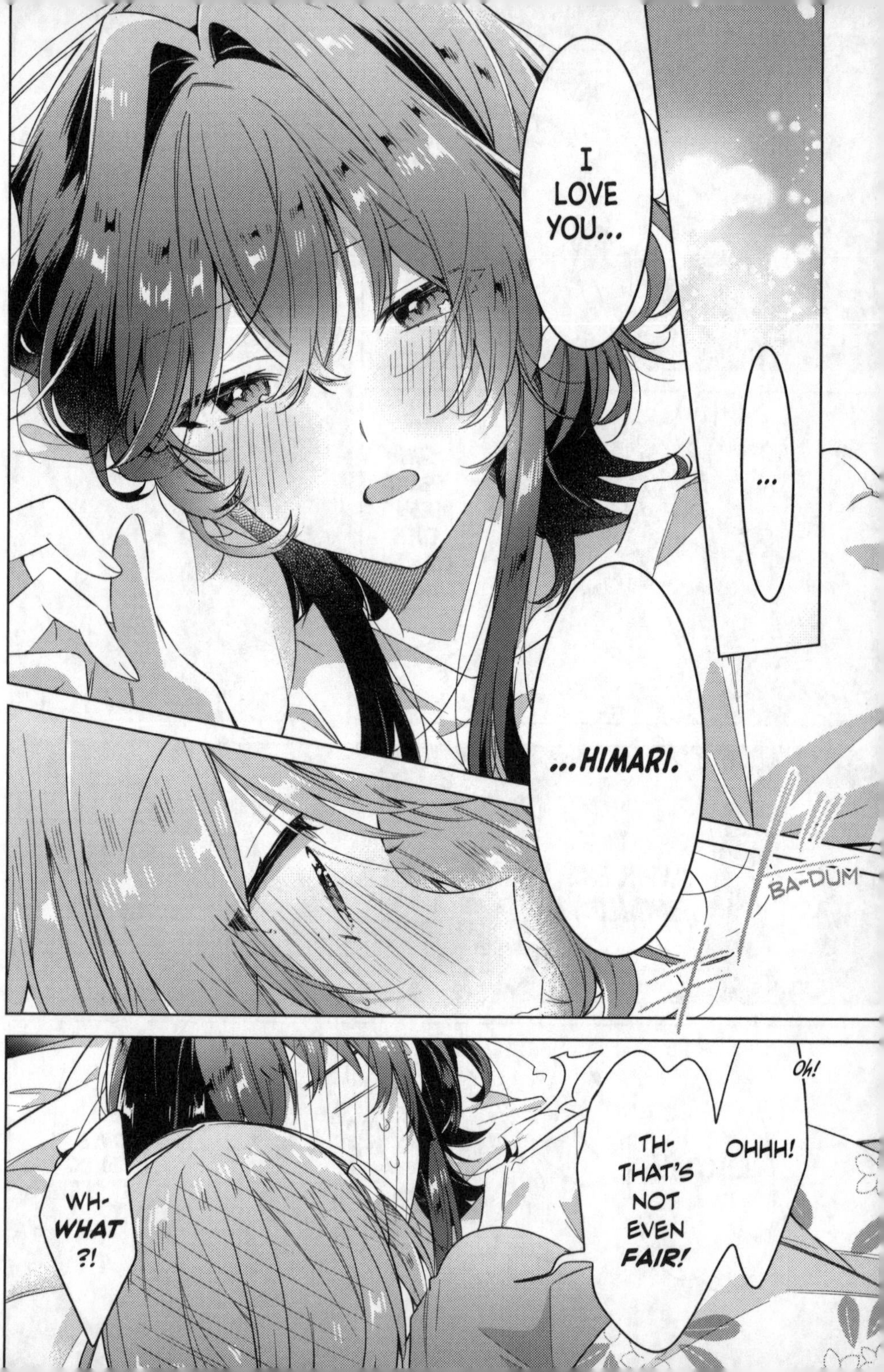

I LOVE YOU...
...
...HIMARI.
BA-DUM
Oh!
OHHH!
TH-THAT'S NOT EVEN FAIR!
WH-WHAT?!

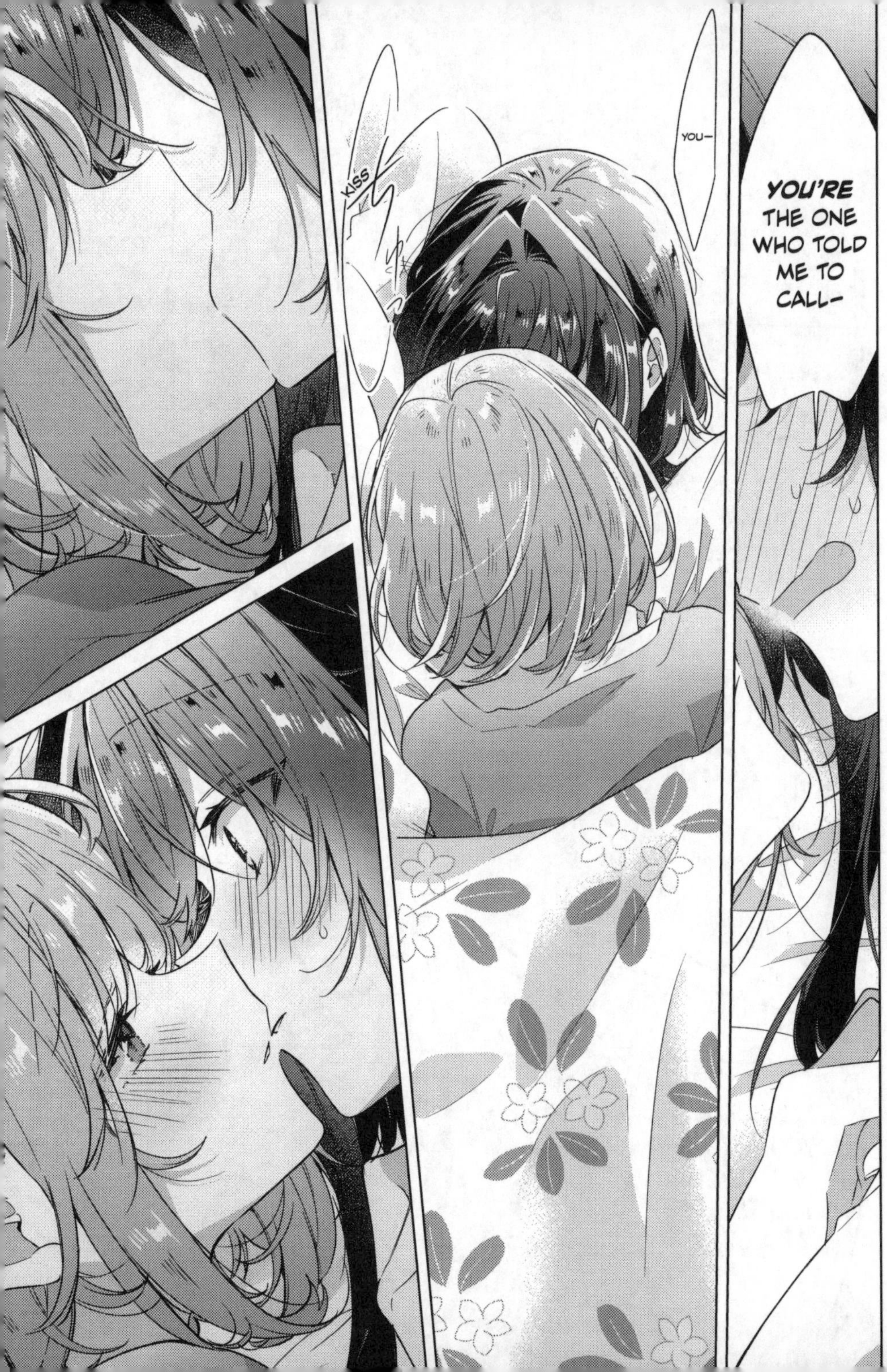
YOU'RE THE ONE WHO TOLD ME TO CALL–
YOU–
KISS

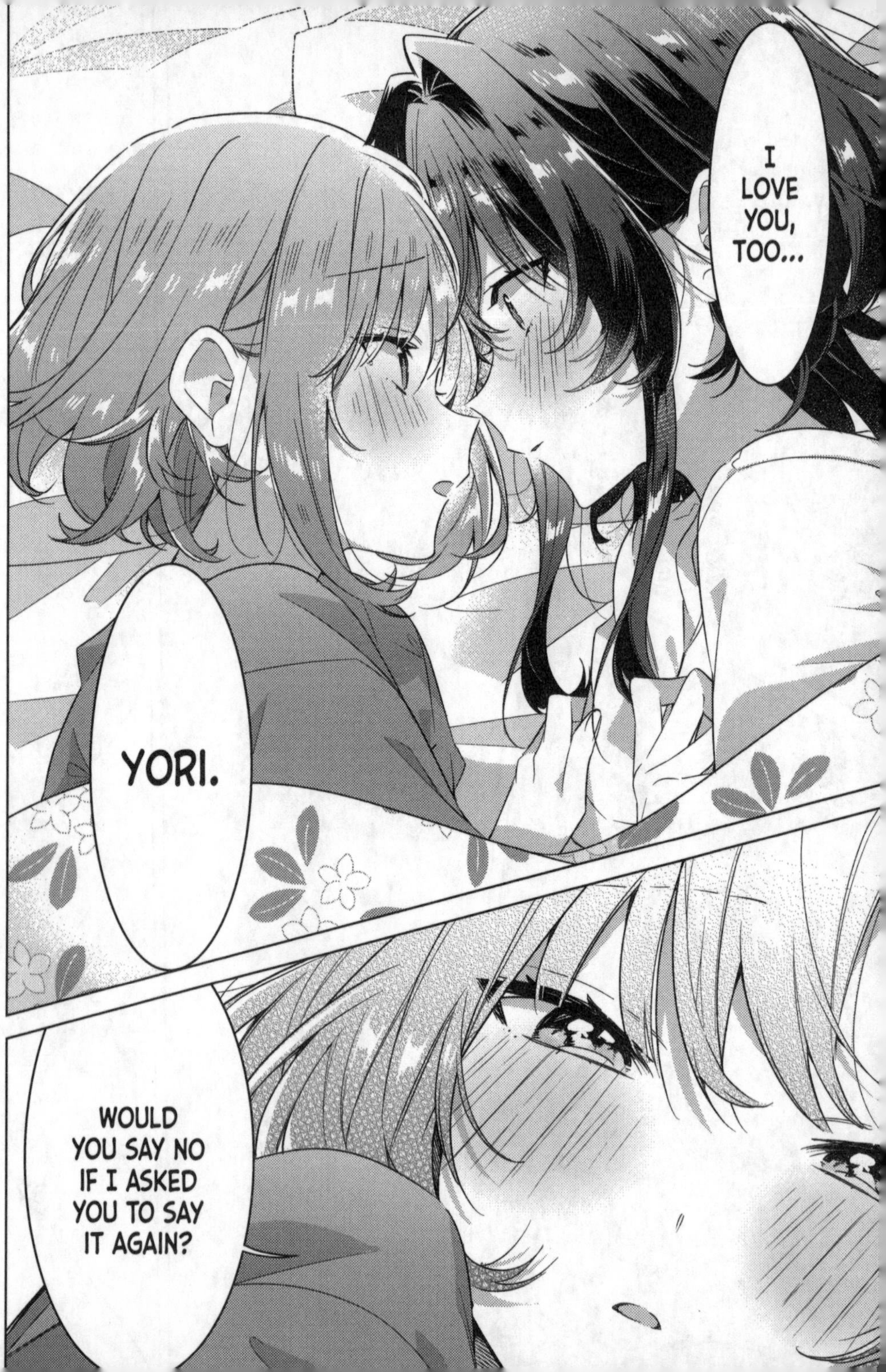
I LOVE YOU, TOO...
YORI.
WOULD YOU SAY NO IF I ASKED YOU TO SAY IT AGAIN?

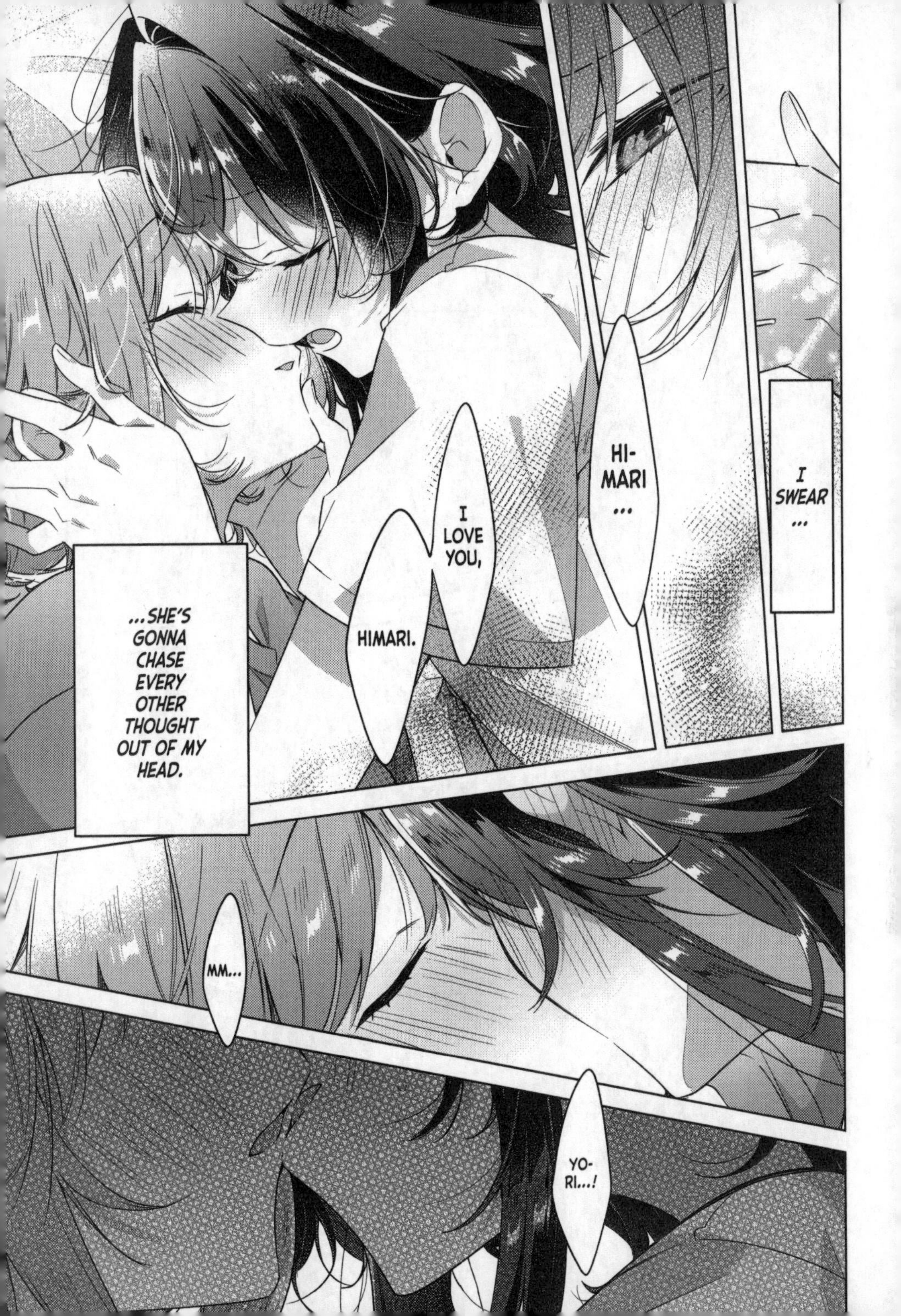
I SWEAR...
HI-MARI...
I LOVE YOU, HIMARI.
...SHE'S GONNA CHASE EVERY OTHER THOUGHT OUT OF MY HEAD.
MM...
YO-RI...!

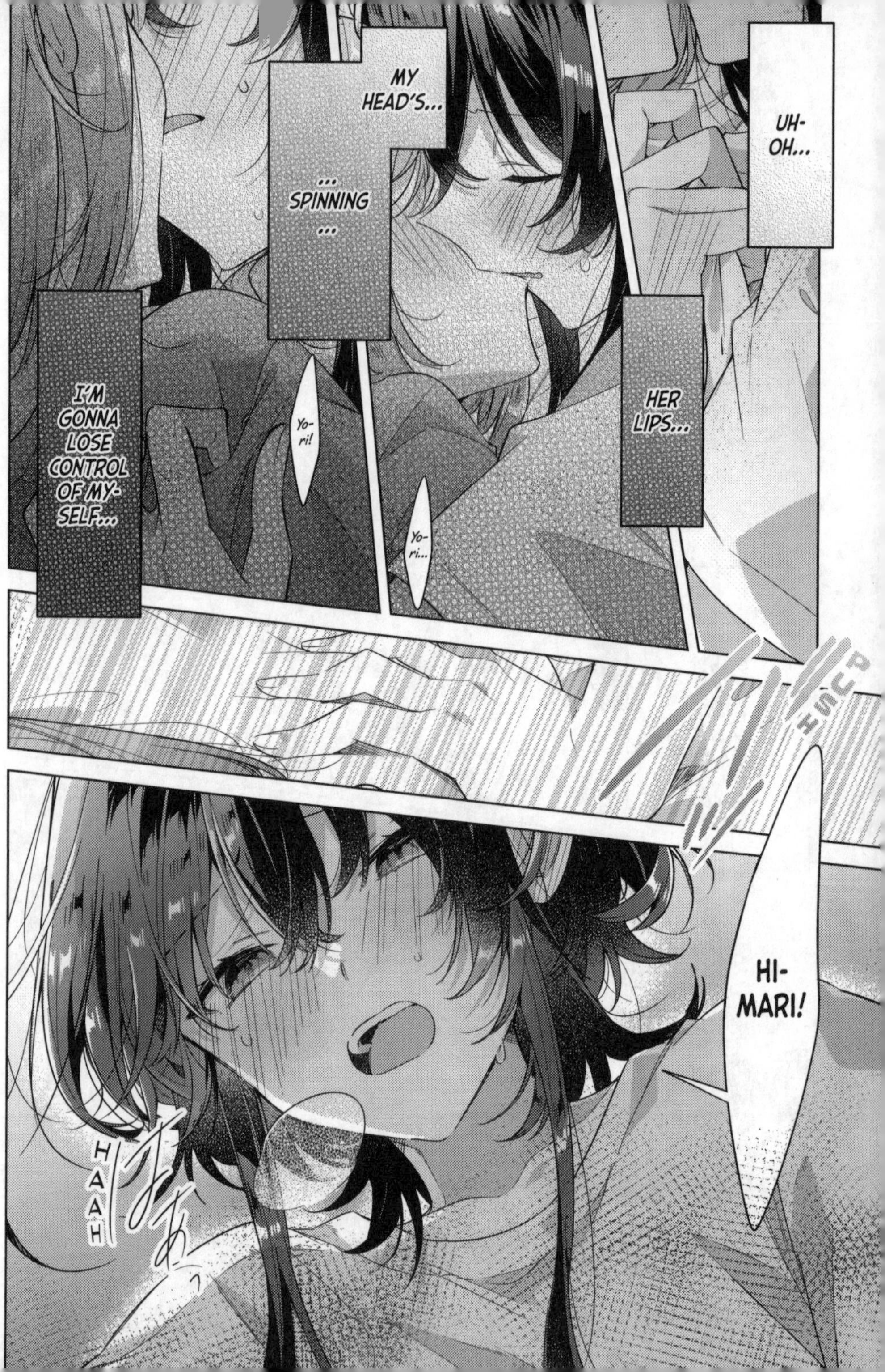
UH-OH...
HER LIPS...
MY HEAD'S...
... SPINNING ...
Yo-ri!
Yo-ri...
I'M GONNA LOSE CONTROL OF MY-SELF...
HI-MARI!
HAAH

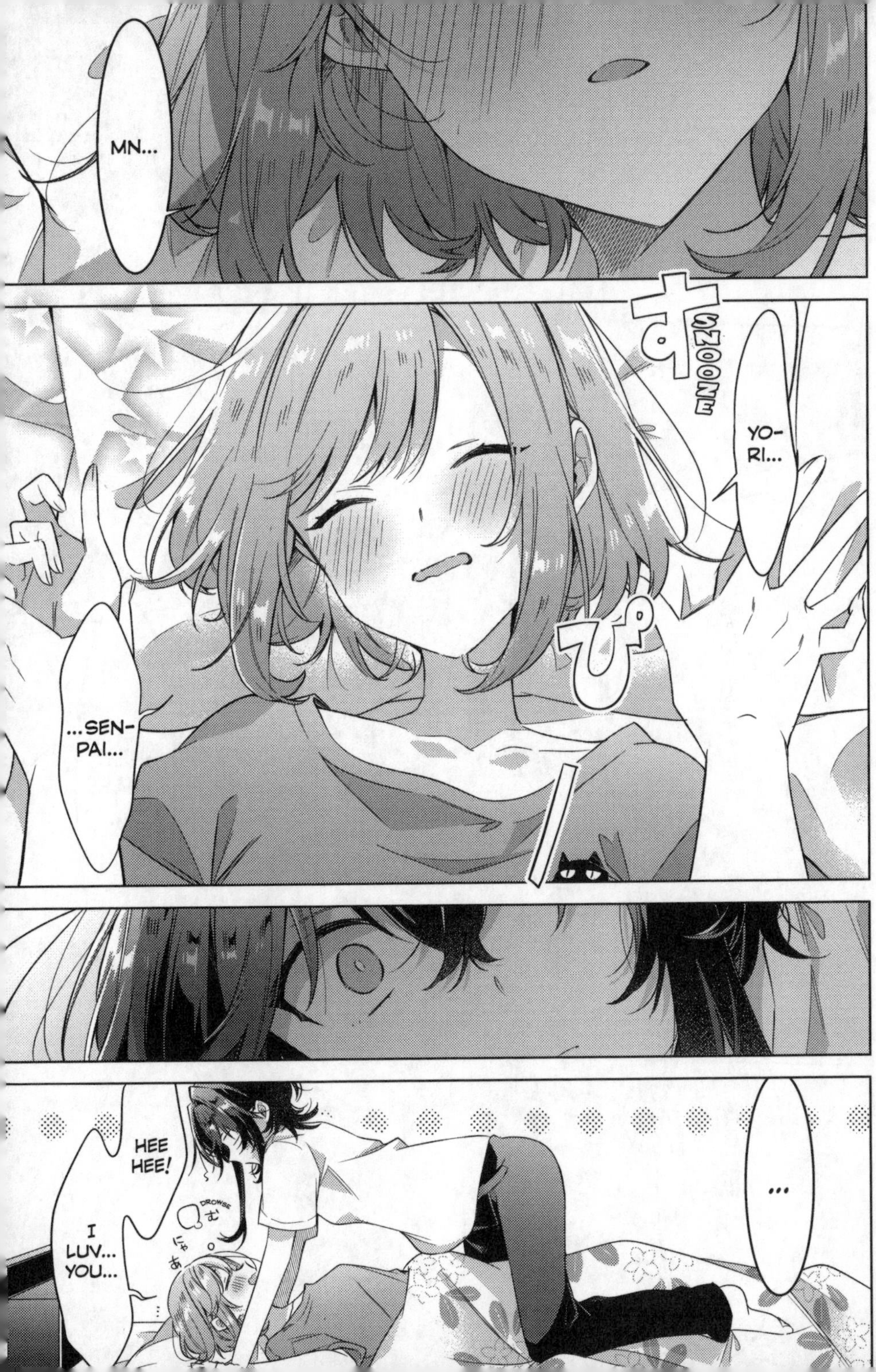
MN...
す SNOOZE
YO-RI...
...SEN-PAI...
...
HEE HEE!
DROWSE む
I LUV... YOU...

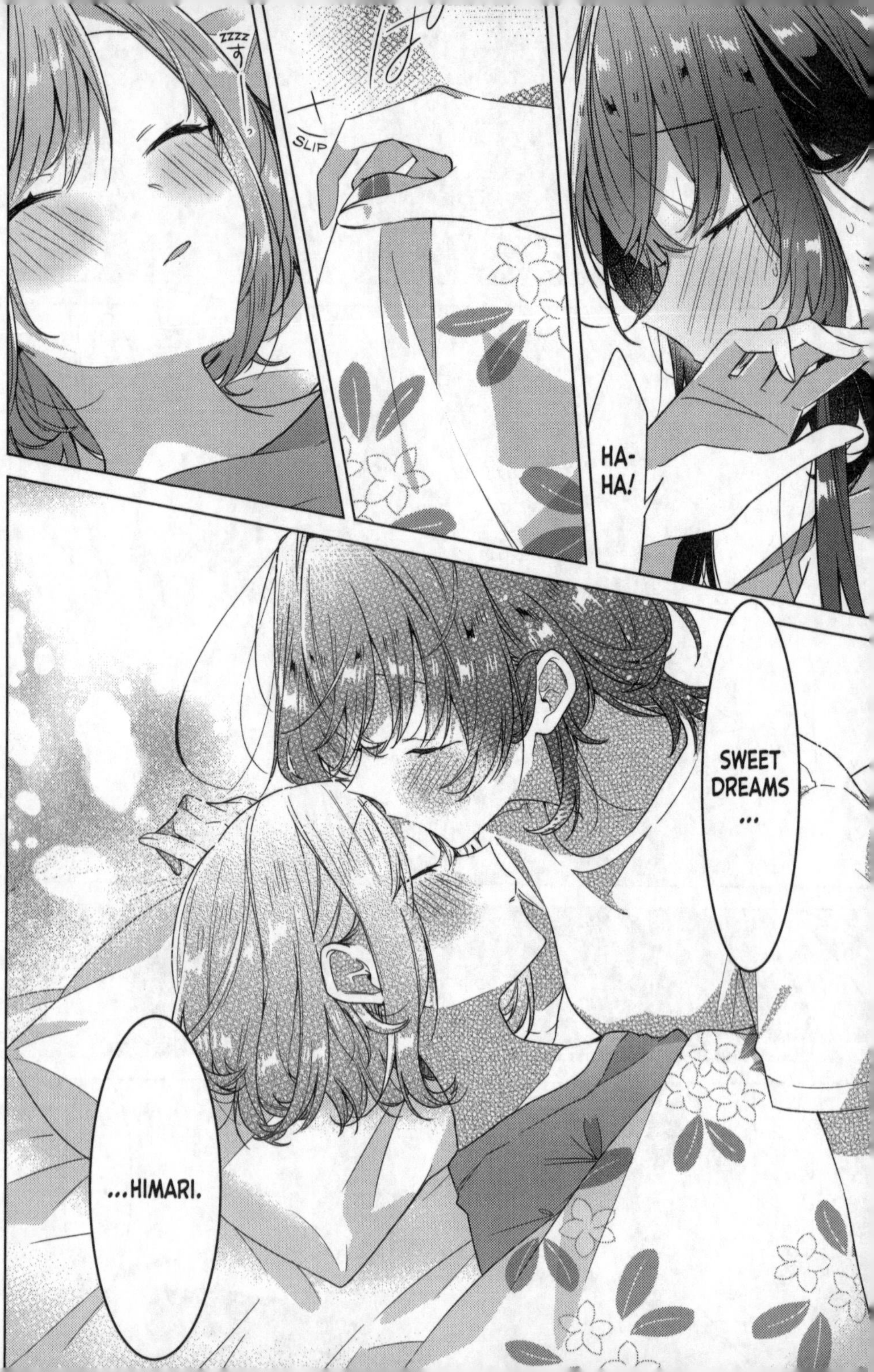
HA-HA!
SLIP
ZZZZ
す
SWEET DREAMS ...
...HIMARI.

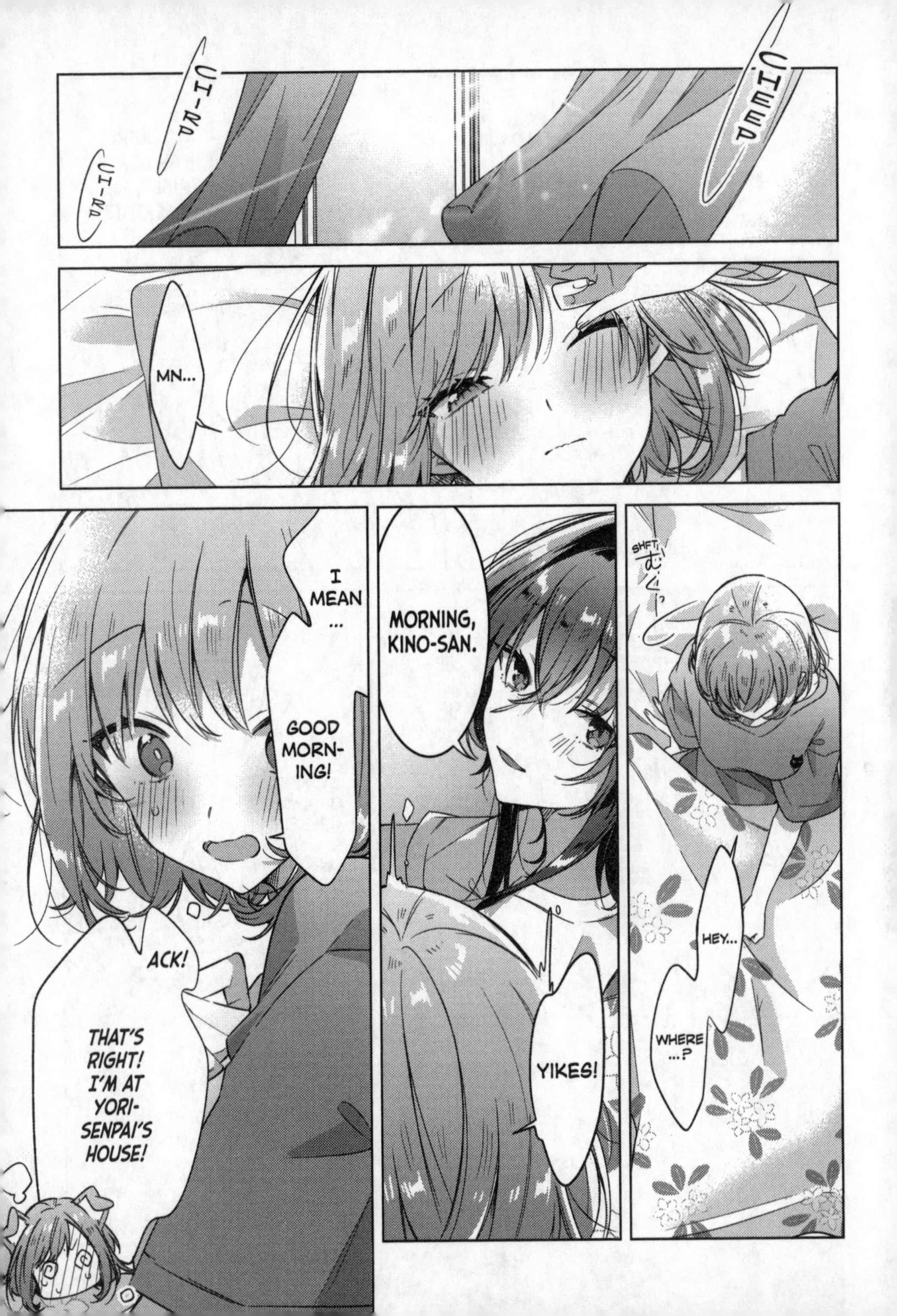
CHEEP
CHI-RP
CHI-RP
MN...
SHFT
むくっ
HEY...
WHERE ...?
MORNING, KINO-SAN.
YIKES!
I MEAN ...
GOOD MORN-ING!
ACK!
THAT'S RIGHT! I'M AT YORI-SENPAI'S HOUSE!

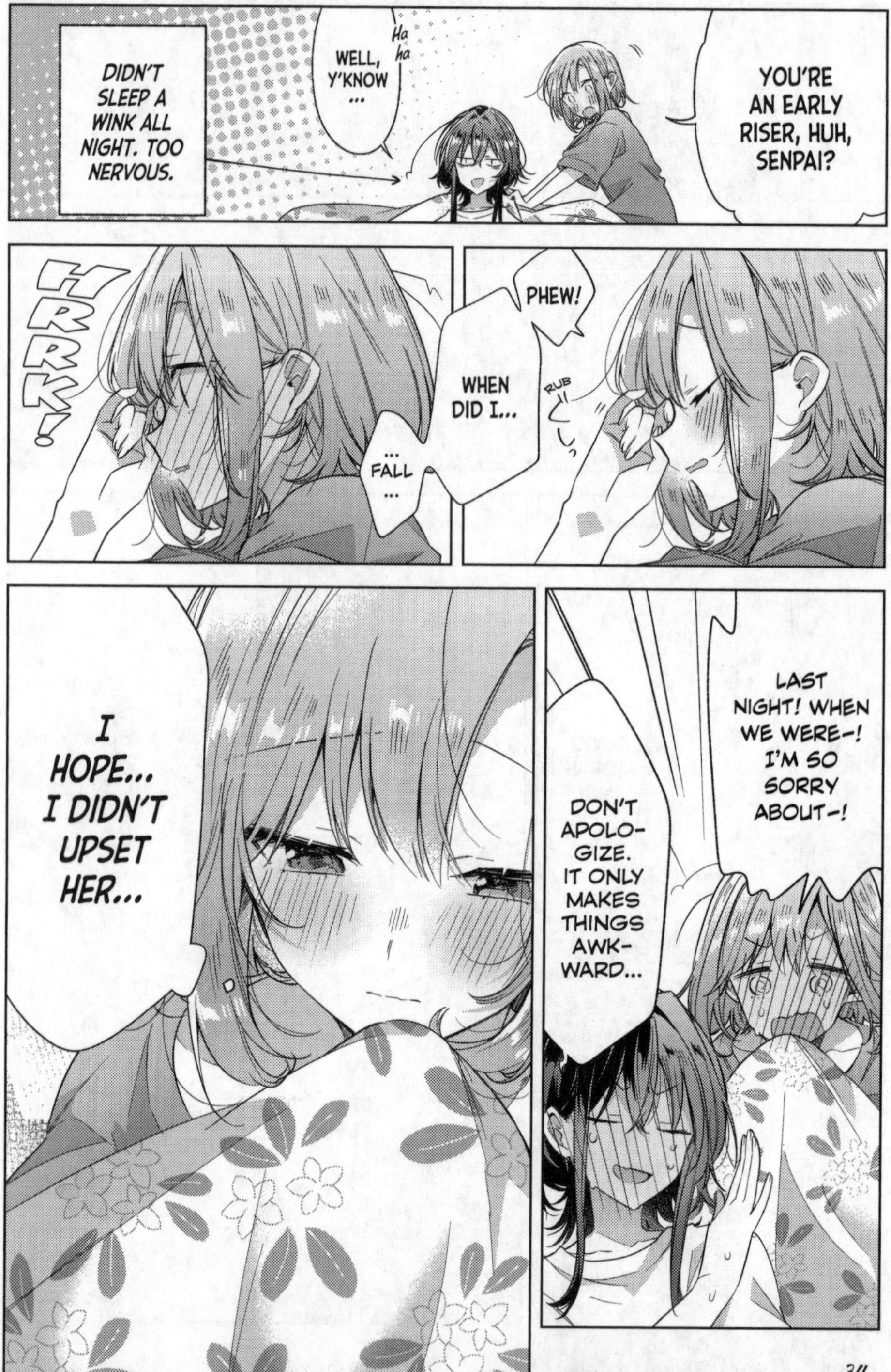
YOU'RE AN EARLY RISER, HUH, SENPAI?
Ha ha
WELL, Y'KNOW ...
DIDN'T SLEEP A WINK ALL NIGHT. TOO NERVOUS.
PHEW!
RUB
WHEN DID I...
... FALL ...
HRRK!
LAST NIGHT! WHEN WE WERE-! I'M SO SORRY ABOUT-!
DON'T APOLO-GIZE. IT ONLY MAKES THINGS AWK-WARD...
I HOPE... I DIDN'T UPSET HER...

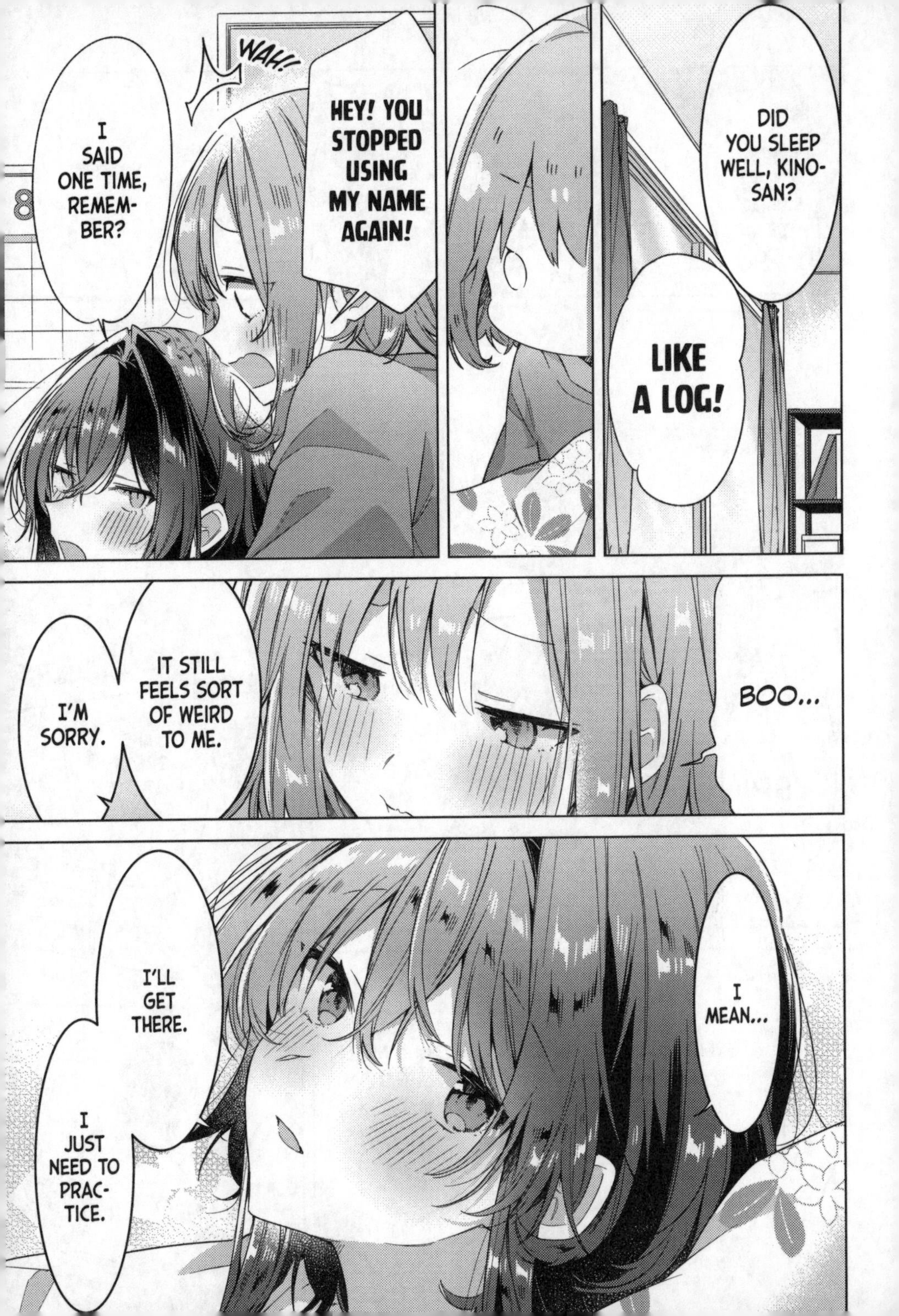
DID YOU SLEEP WELL, KINO-SAN?
LIKE A LOG!
WAH!
HEY! YOU STOPPED USING MY NAME AGAIN!
I SAID ONE TIME, REMEMBER?
BOO...
IT STILL FEELS SORT OF WEIRD TO ME.
I'M SORRY.
I MEAN...
I'LL GET THERE.
I JUST NEED TO PRACTICE.

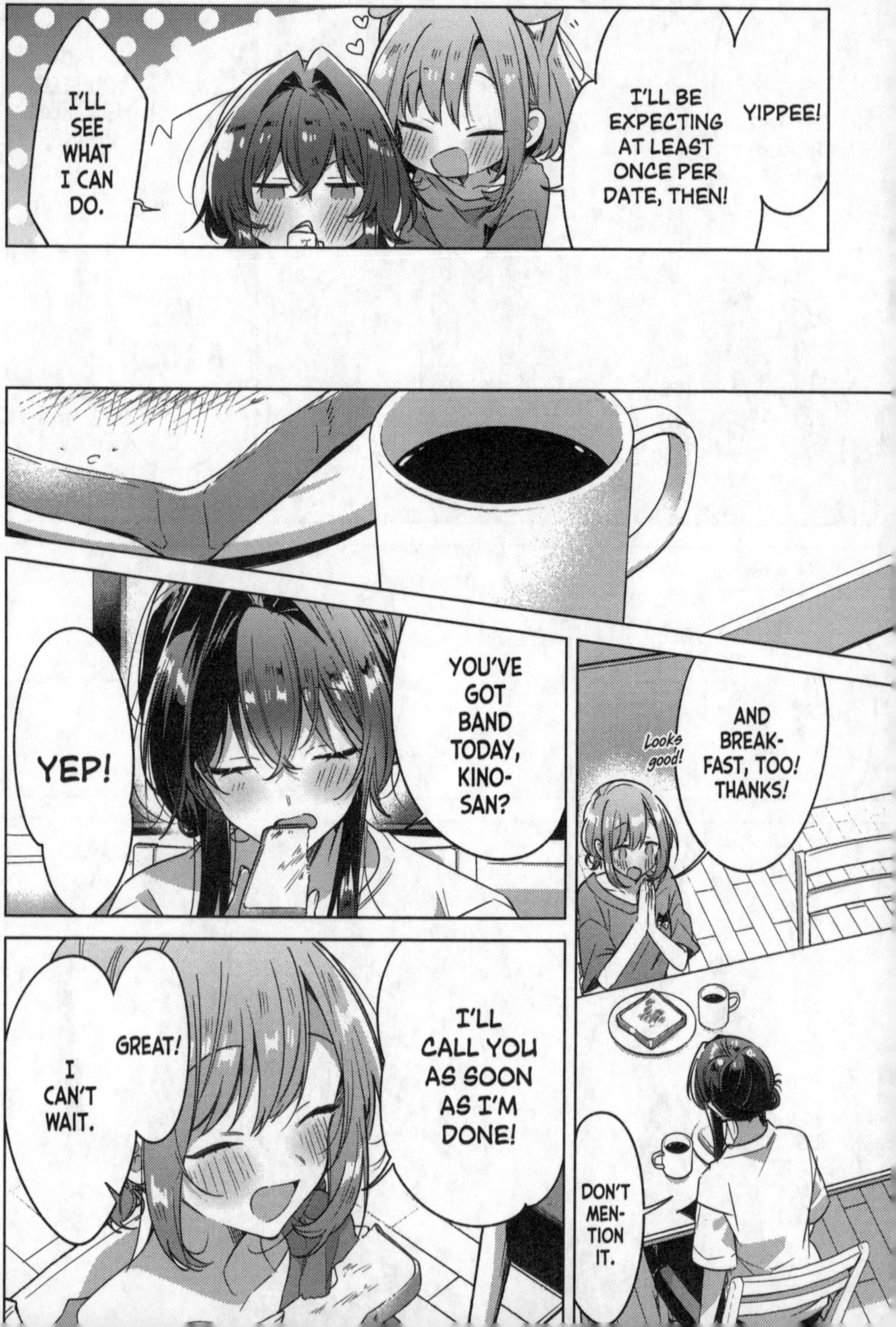
YIPPEE!
I'LL BE EXPECTING AT LEAST ONCE PER DATE, THEN!
I'LL SEE WHAT I CAN DO.
Looks good!
AND BREAK-FAST, TOO! THANKS!
DON'T MEN-TION IT.
YOU'VE GOT BAND TODAY, KINO-SAN?
YEP!
I'LL CALL YOU AS SOON AS I'M DONE!
GREAT!
I CAN'T WAIT.

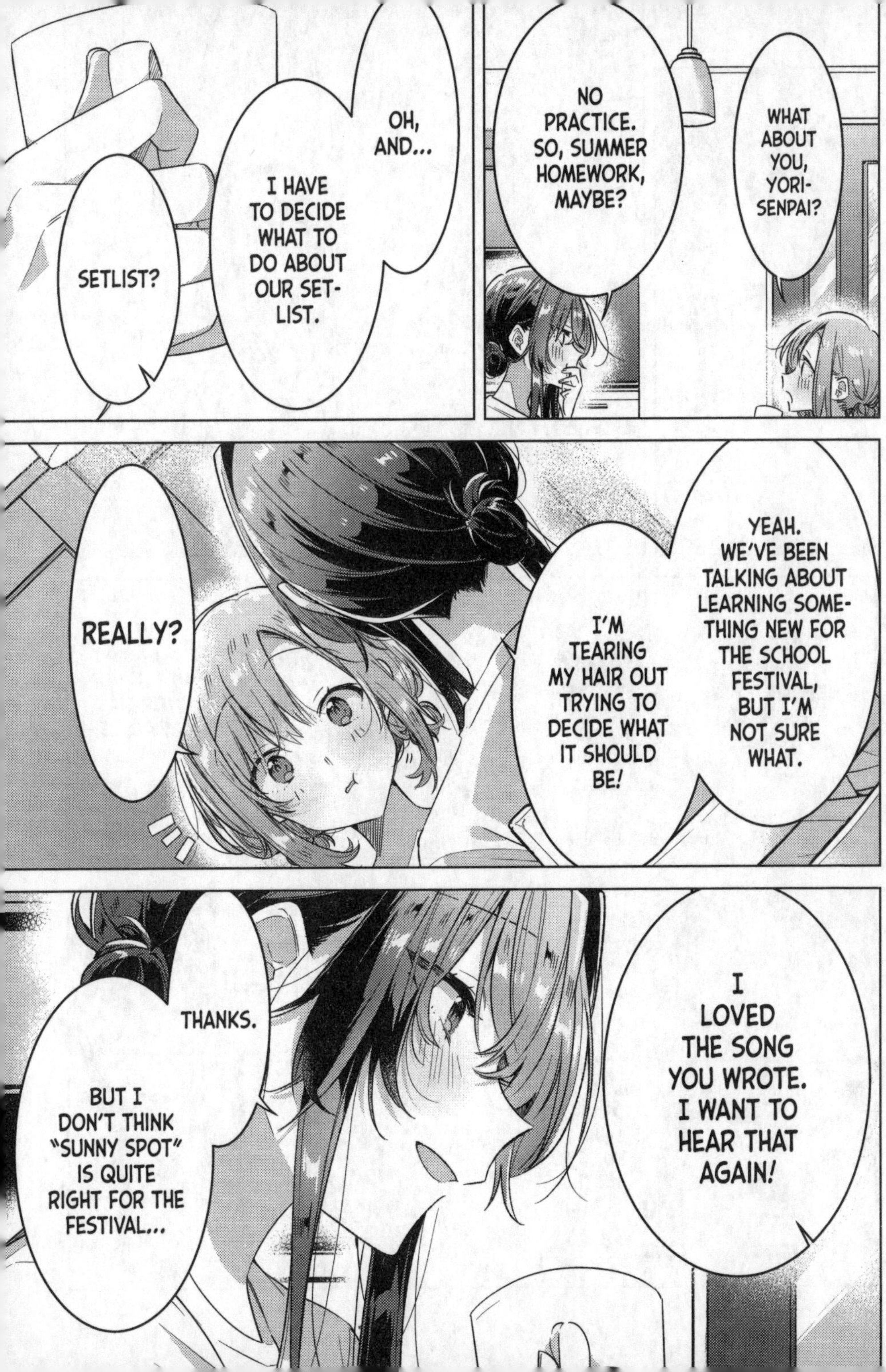
WHAT ABOUT YOU, YORI-SENPAI?
NO PRACTICE. SO, SUMMER HOMEWORK, MAYBE?
OH, AND...
I HAVE TO DECIDE WHAT TO DO ABOUT OUR SET-LIST.
SETLIST?
YEAH. WE'VE BEEN TALKING ABOUT LEARNING SOME-THING NEW FOR THE SCHOOL FESTIVAL, BUT I'M NOT SURE WHAT.
I'M TEARING MY HAIR OUT TRYING TO DECIDE WHAT IT SHOULD BE!
REALLY?
I LOVED THE SONG YOU WROTE. I WANT TO HEAR THAT AGAIN!
THANKS.
BUT I DON'T THINK "SUNNY SPOT" IS QUITE RIGHT FOR THE FESTIVAL...

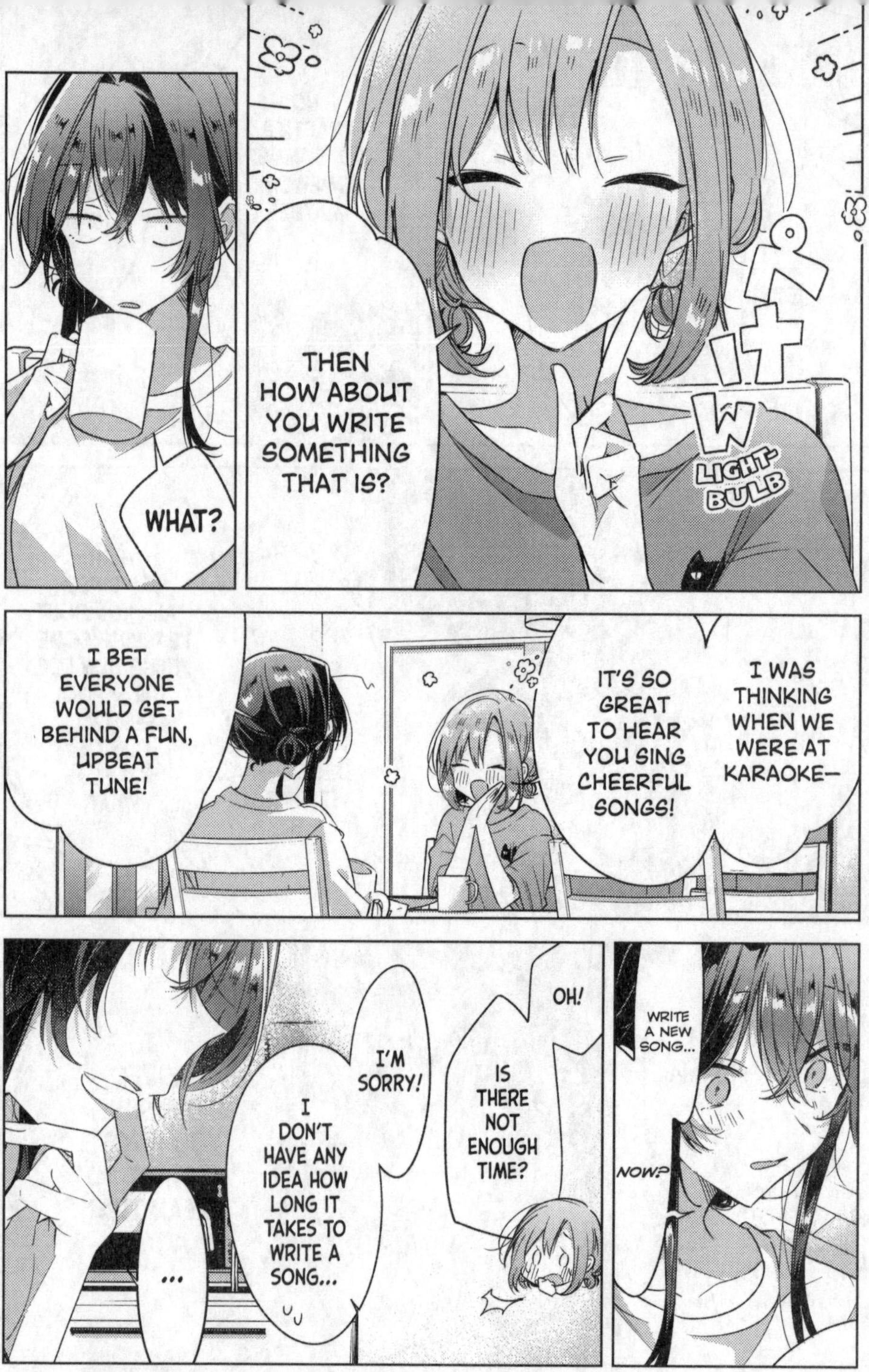
THEN HOW ABOUT YOU WRITE SOMETHING THAT IS?
LIGHT-BULB
WHAT?
I WAS THINKING WHEN WE WERE AT KARAOKE—
IT'S SO GREAT TO HEAR YOU SING CHEERFUL SONGS!
I BET EVERYONE WOULD GET BEHIND A FUN, UPBEAT TUNE!
WRITE A NEW SONG...
NOW?
OH!
IS THERE NOT ENOUGH TIME?
I'M SORRY!
I DON'T HAVE ANY IDEA HOW LONG IT TAKES TO WRITE A SONG...
...

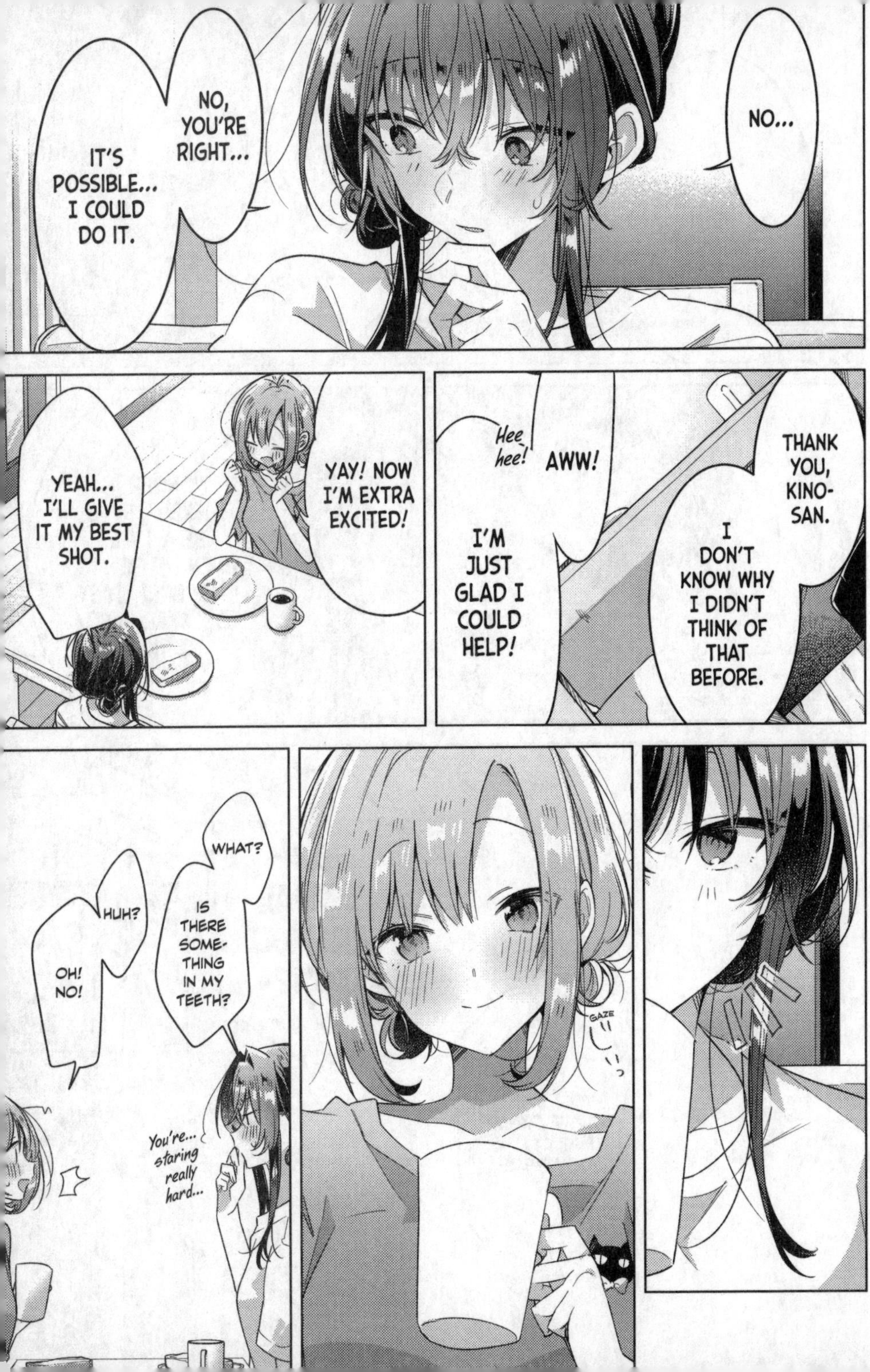
NO...
NO, YOU'RE RIGHT...
IT'S POSSIBLE... I COULD DO IT.
THANK YOU, KINO-SAN.
I DON'T KNOW WHY I DIDN'T THINK OF THAT BEFORE.
AWW!
Hee hee!
I'M JUST GLAD I COULD HELP!
YAY! NOW I'M EXTRA EXCITED!
YEAH... I'LL GIVE IT MY BEST SHOT.
GAZE
WHAT?
IS THERE SOME-THING IN MY TEETH?
HUH?
OH! NO!
You're... staring really hard...

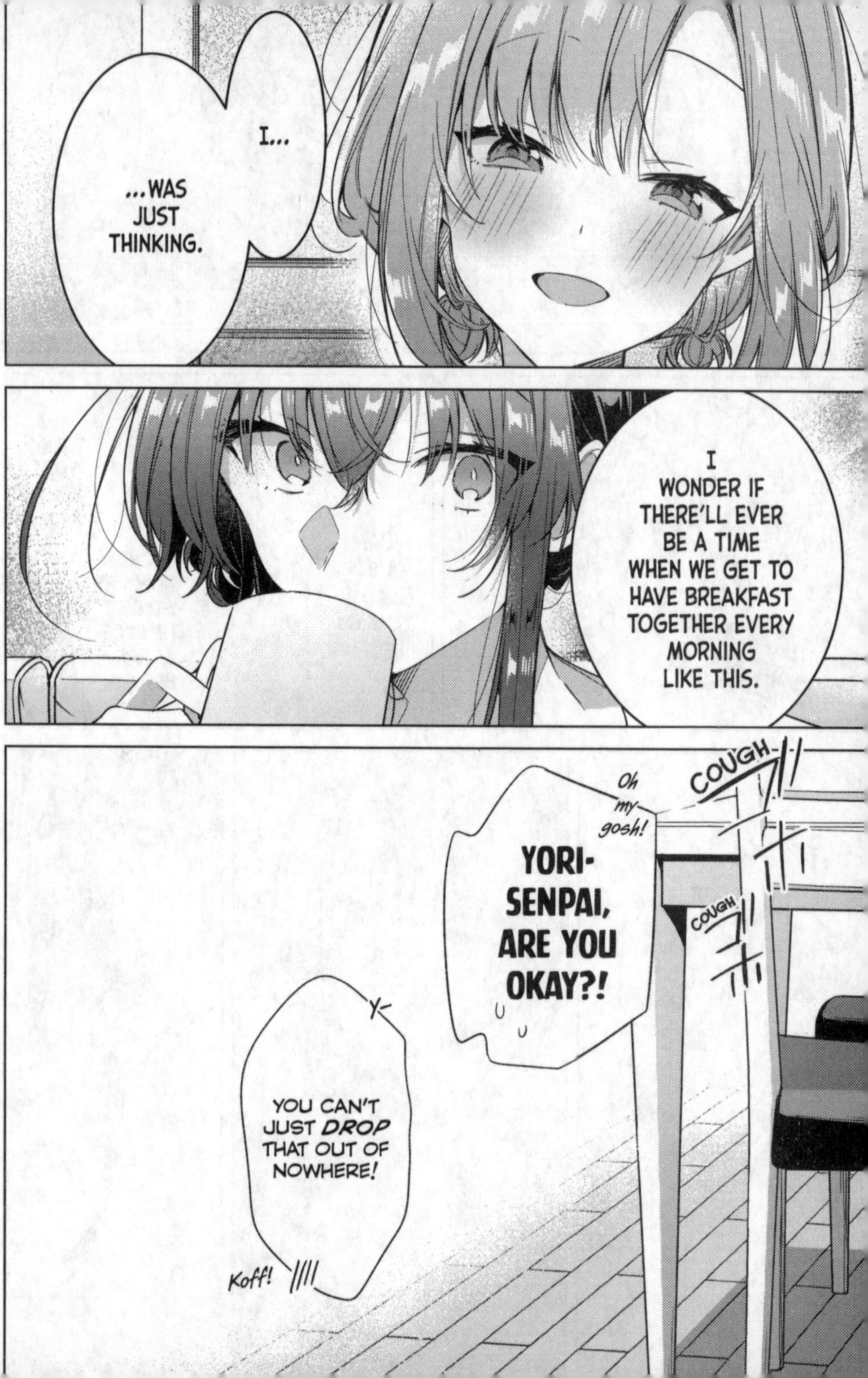
I...
...WAS JUST THINKING.
I WONDER IF THERE'LL EVER BE A TIME WHEN WE GET TO HAVE BREAKFAST TOGETHER EVERY MORNING LIKE THIS.
COUGH
Oh my gosh!
YORI-SENPAI, ARE YOU OKAY?!
COUGH
YOU CAN'T JUST DROP THAT OUT OF NOWHERE!
Koff!

Whisper Me A Love Song
Eku Takeshima

Whisper Me
A Love Song

Eku
Takeshima

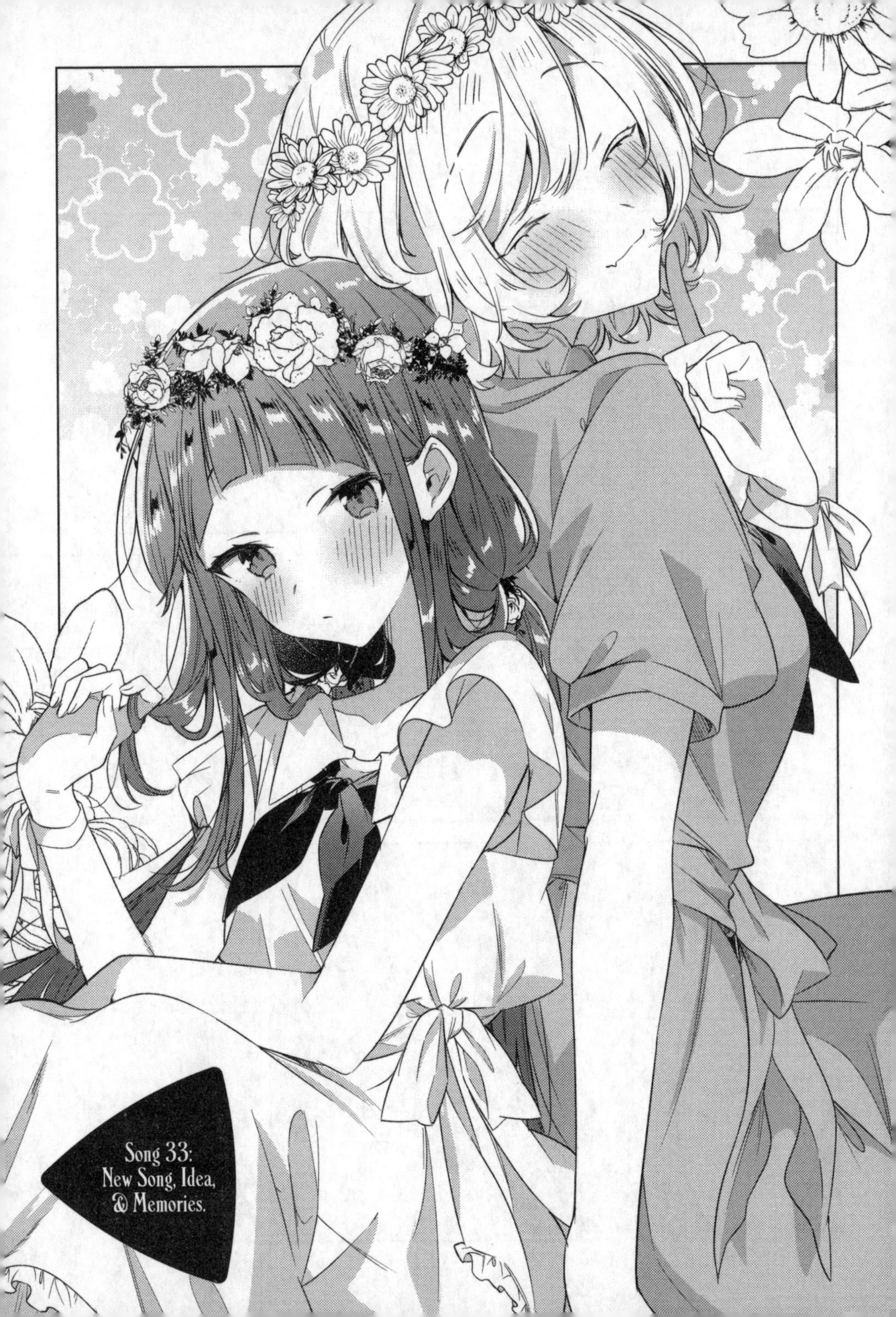
Song 33:
New Song, Idea,
& Memories.

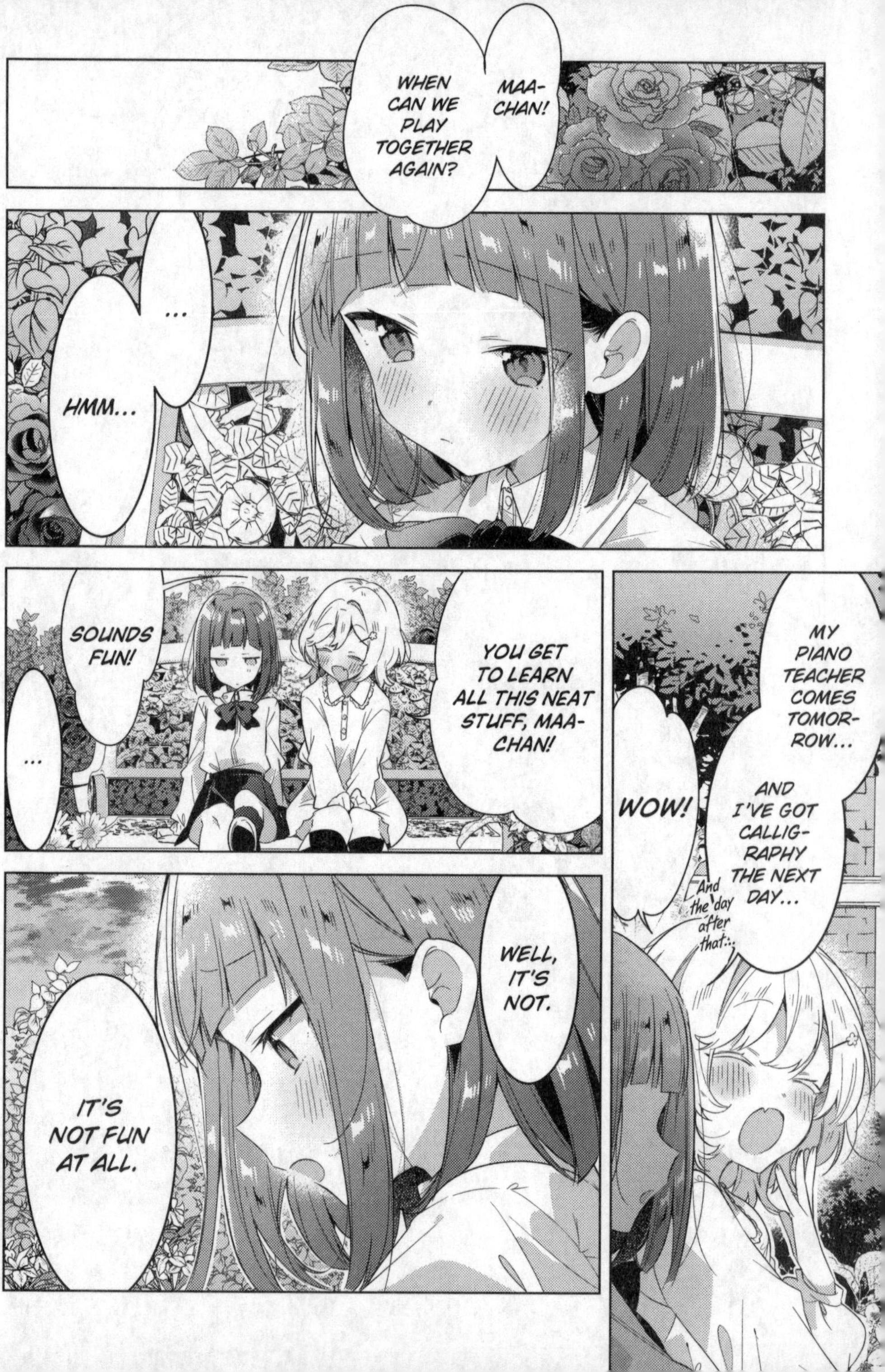
MAA-CHAN! WHEN CAN WE PLAY TOGETHER AGAIN?
... HMM...
MY PIANO TEACHER COMES TOMORROW...
AND I'VE GOT CALLIGRAPHY THE NEXT DAY...
And the day after that...
WOW!
YOU GET TO LEARN ALL THIS NEAT STUFF, MAA-CHAN!
SOUNDS FUN! ...
WELL, IT'S NOT.
IT'S NOT FUN AT ALL.

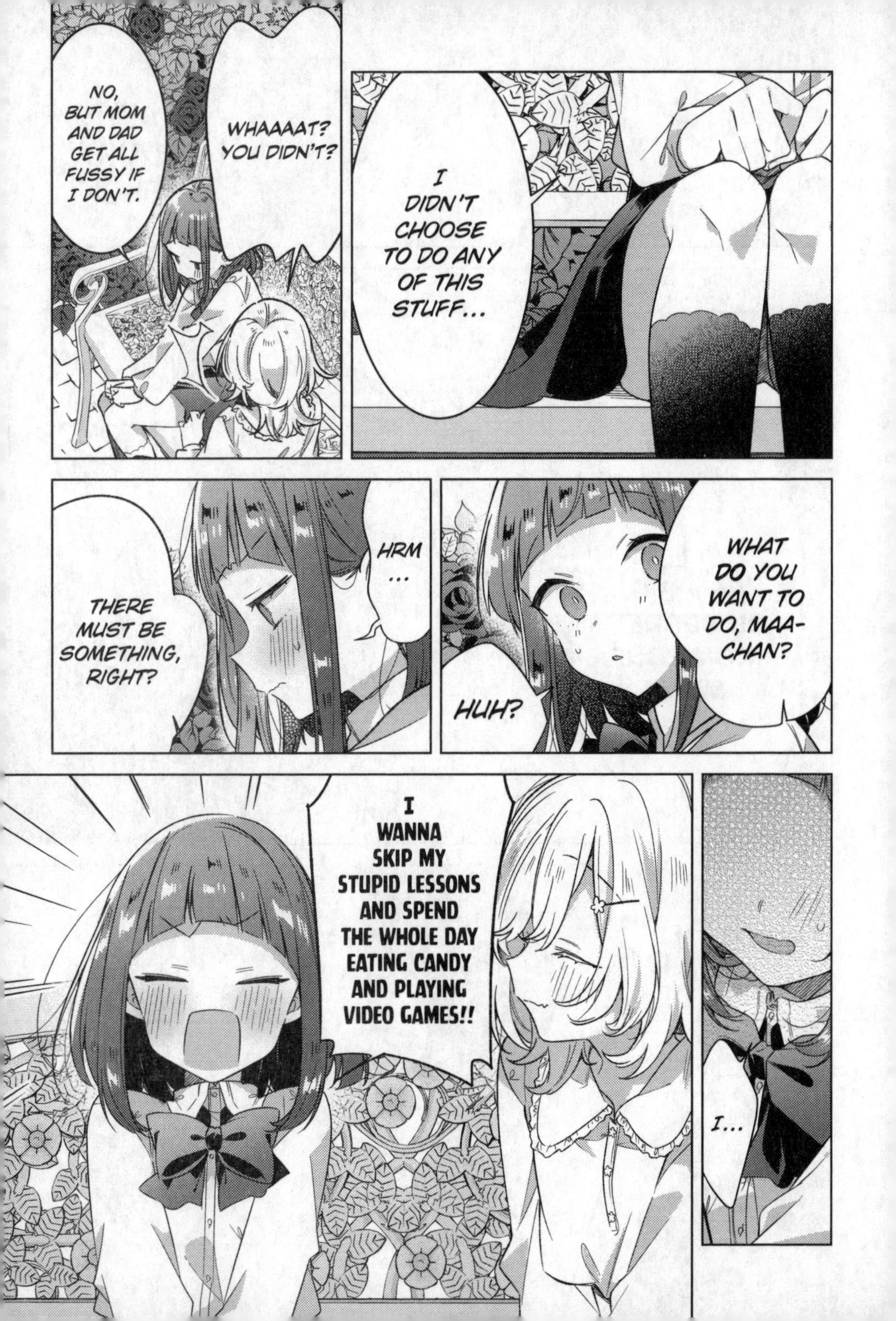
I DIDN'T CHOOSE TO DO ANY OF THIS STUFF...
WHAAAAT? YOU DIDN'T?
NO, BUT MOM AND DAD GET ALL FUSSY IF I DON'T.
WHAT DO YOU WANT TO DO, MAA-CHAN?
HUH?
HRM ...
THERE MUST BE SOMETHING, RIGHT?
I...
I WANNA SKIP MY STUPID LESSONS AND SPEND THE WHOLE DAY EATING CANDY AND PLAYING VIDEO GAMES!!

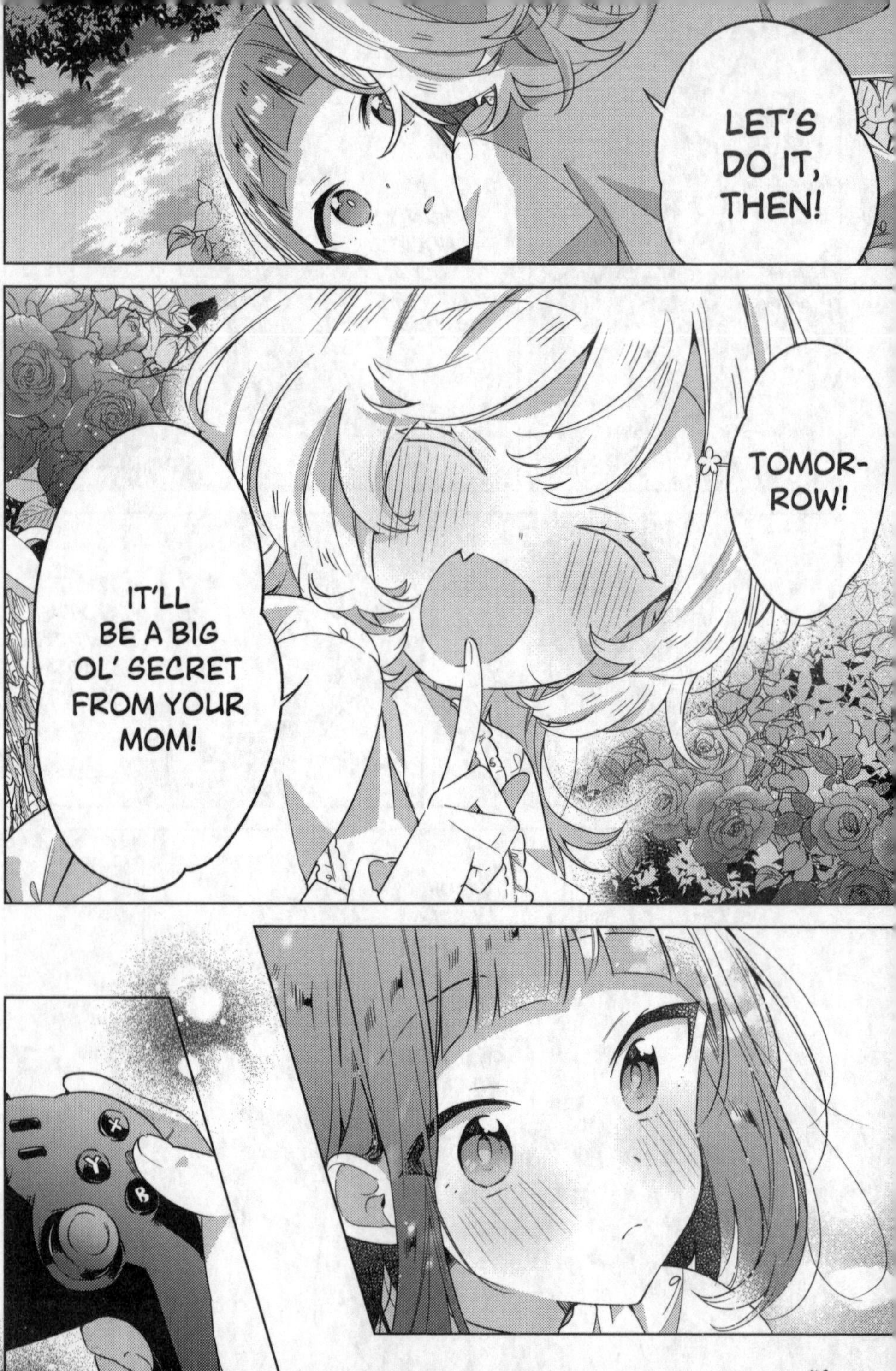
LET'S DO IT, THEN!
TOMOR-ROW!
IT'LL BE A BIG OL' SECRET FROM YOUR MOM!

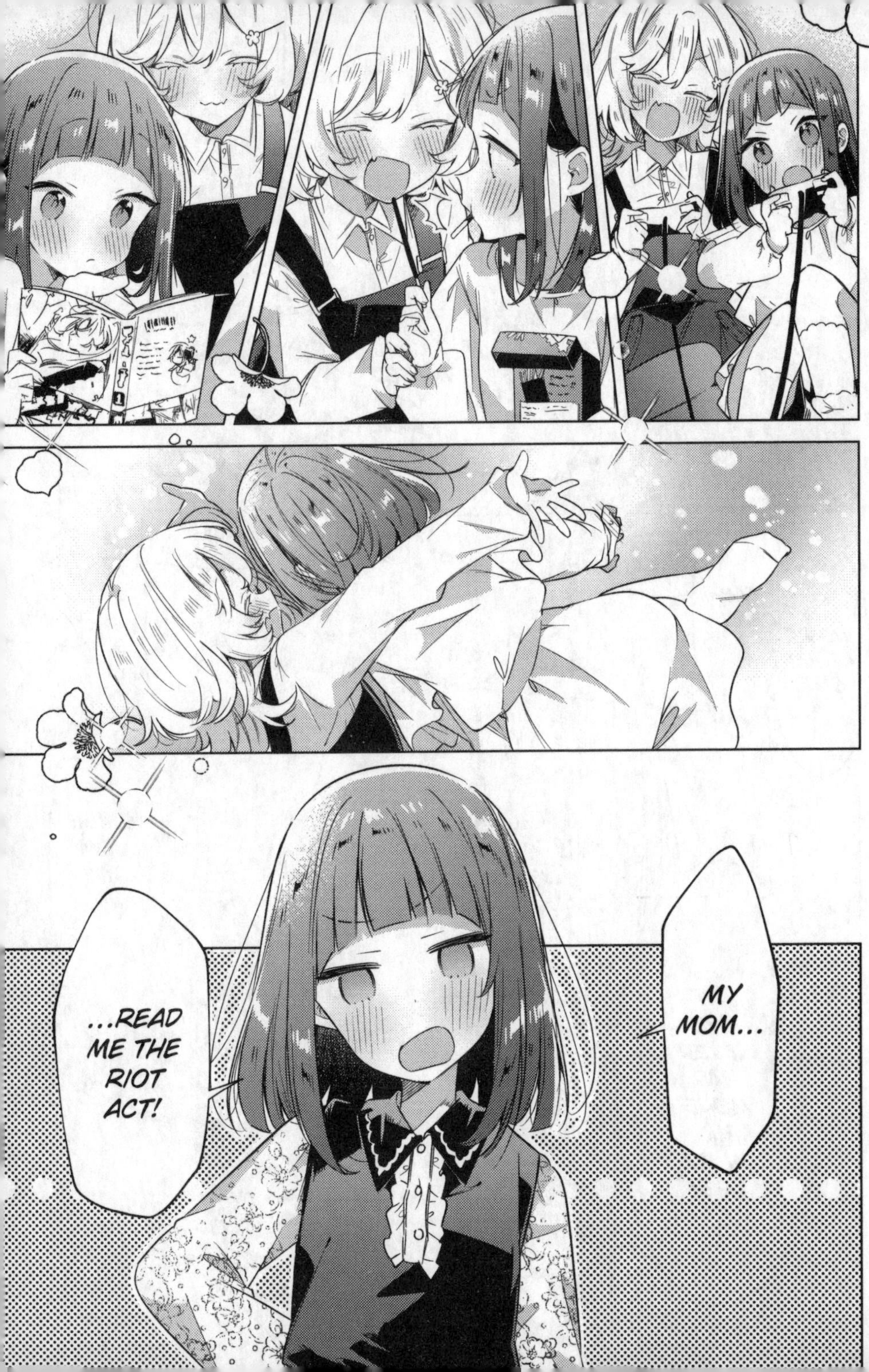
MY MOM...
...READ ME THE RIOT ACT!

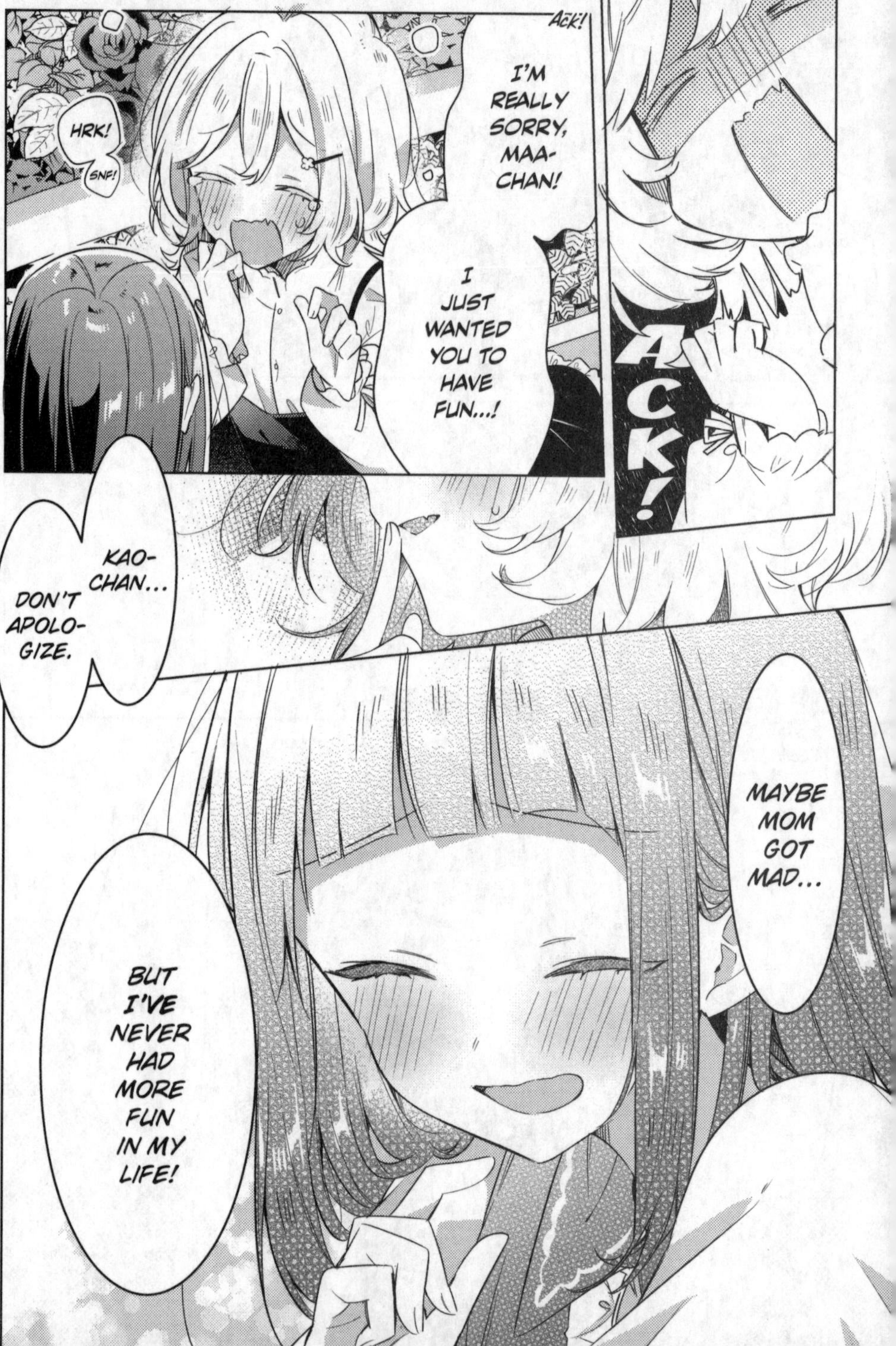
ACK!
Ack!
I'M REALLY SORRY, MAA-CHAN!
I JUST WANTED YOU TO HAVE FUN...!
HRK!
SNF!
KAO-CHAN... DON'T APOLO-GIZE.
MAYBE MOM GOT MAD...
BUT I'VE NEVER HAD MORE FUN IN MY LIFE!

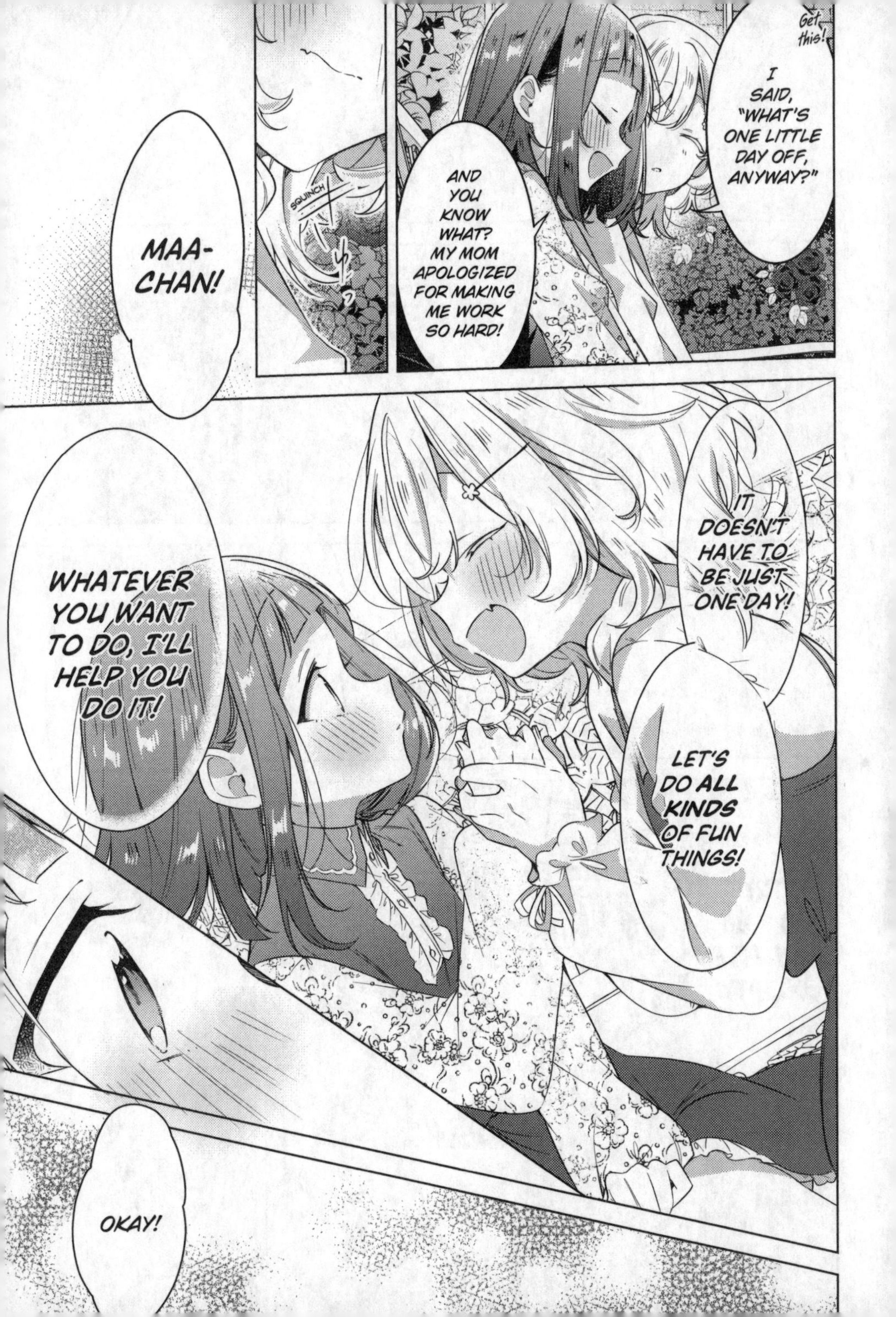
Get this!
I SAID, "WHAT'S ONE LITTLE DAY OFF, ANYWAY?"
AND YOU KNOW WHAT? MY MOM APOLOGIZED FOR MAKING ME WORK SO HARD!
SQUINCH
MAA-CHAN!
IT DOESN'T HAVE TO BE JUST ONE DAY!
LET'S DO ALL KINDS OF FUN THINGS!
WHATEVER YOU WANT TO DO, I'LL HELP YOU DO IT!
OKAY!

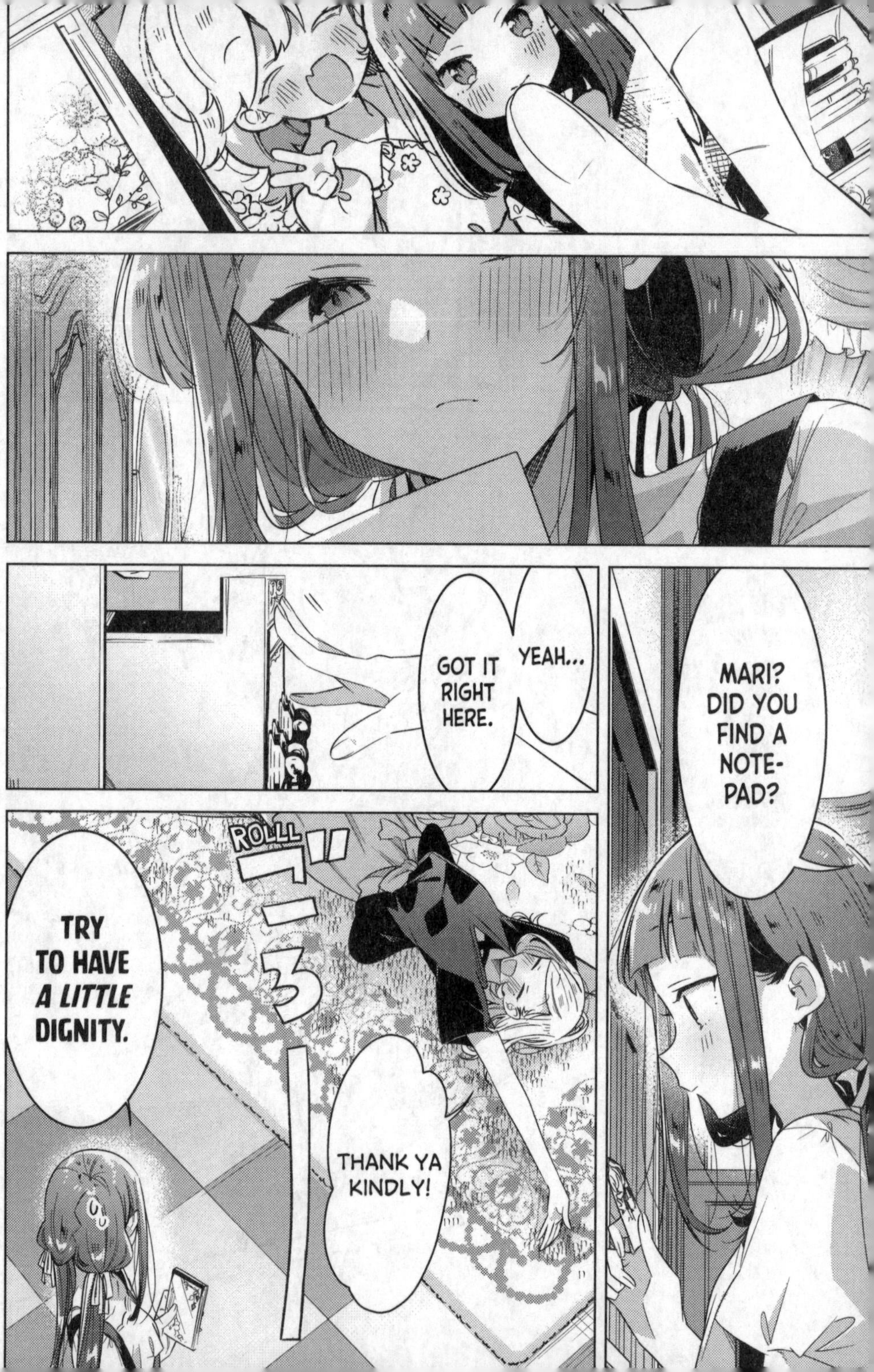
MARI? DID YOU FIND A NOTE-PAD?
YEAH...
GOT IT RIGHT HERE.
ROLLL
THANK YA KINDLY!
TRY TO HAVE *A LITTLE* DIGNITY.

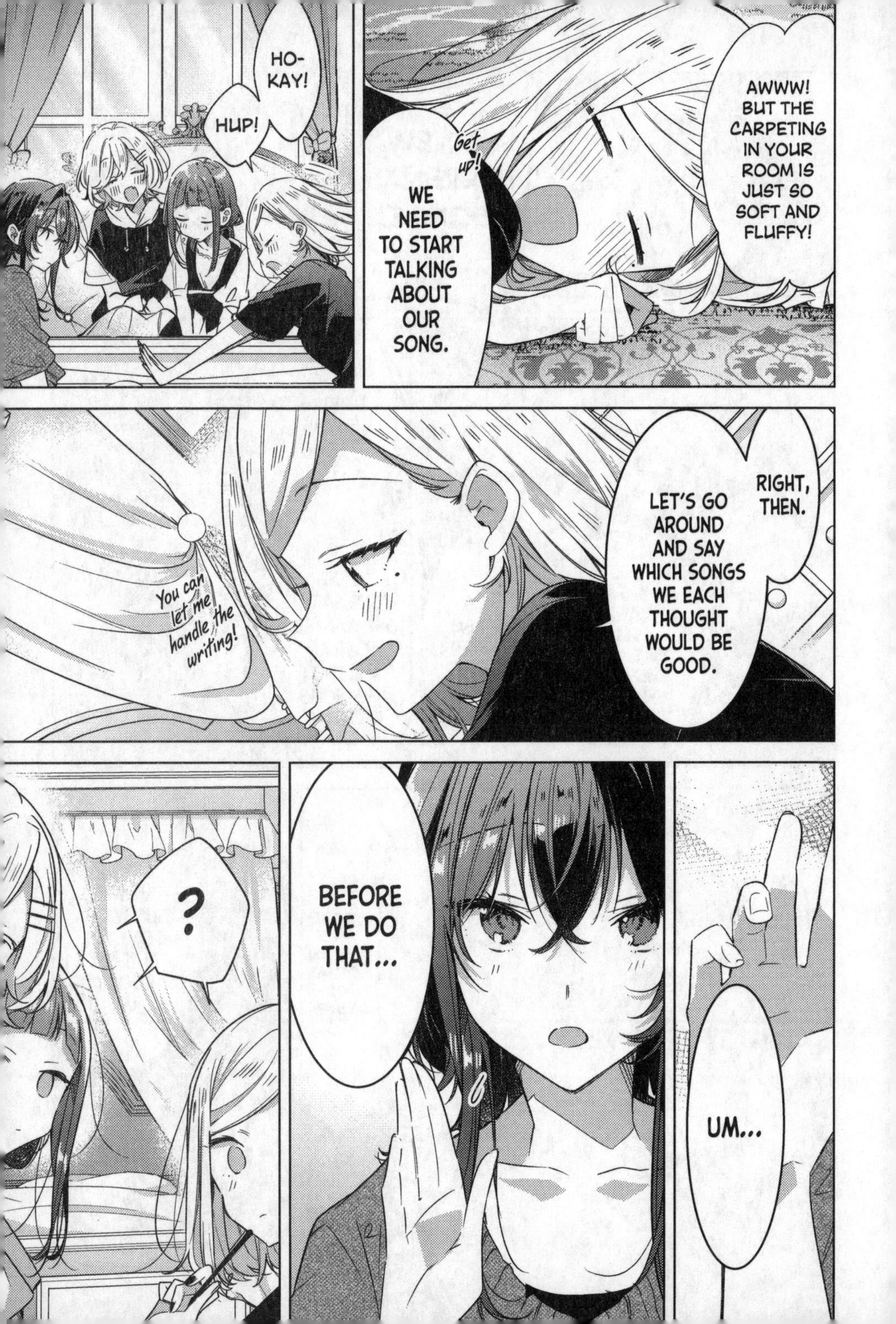
AWWW! BUT THE CARPETING IN YOUR ROOM IS JUST SO SOFT AND FLUFFY!
Get up!
WE NEED TO START TALKING ABOUT OUR SONG.
HO-KAY!
HUP!
RIGHT, THEN.
LET'S GO AROUND AND SAY WHICH SONGS WE EACH THOUGHT WOULD BE GOOD.
You can let me handle the writing!
UM...
BEFORE WE DO THAT...
?

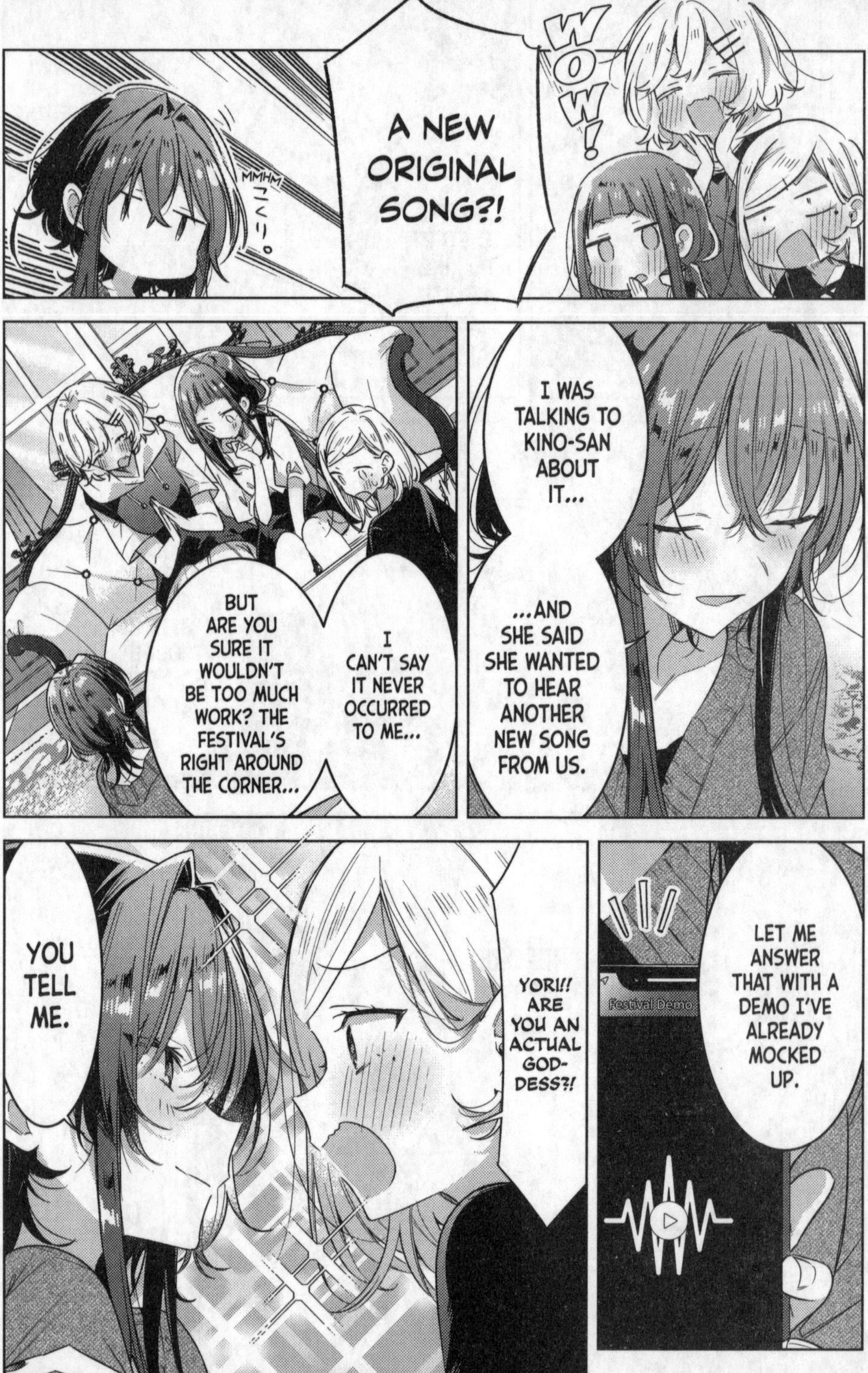
WOW!
A NEW ORIGINAL SONG?!
MMHM
こくり。
I WAS TALKING TO KINO-SAN ABOUT IT...
...AND SHE SAID SHE WANTED TO HEAR ANOTHER NEW SONG FROM US.
I CAN'T SAY IT NEVER OCCURRED TO ME...
BUT ARE YOU SURE IT WOULDN'T BE TOO MUCH WORK? THE FESTIVAL'S RIGHT AROUND THE CORNER...
LET ME ANSWER THAT WITH A DEMO I'VE ALREADY MOCKED UP.
Festival Demo
YORI!! ARE YOU AN ACTUAL GOD-DESS?!
YOU TELL ME.

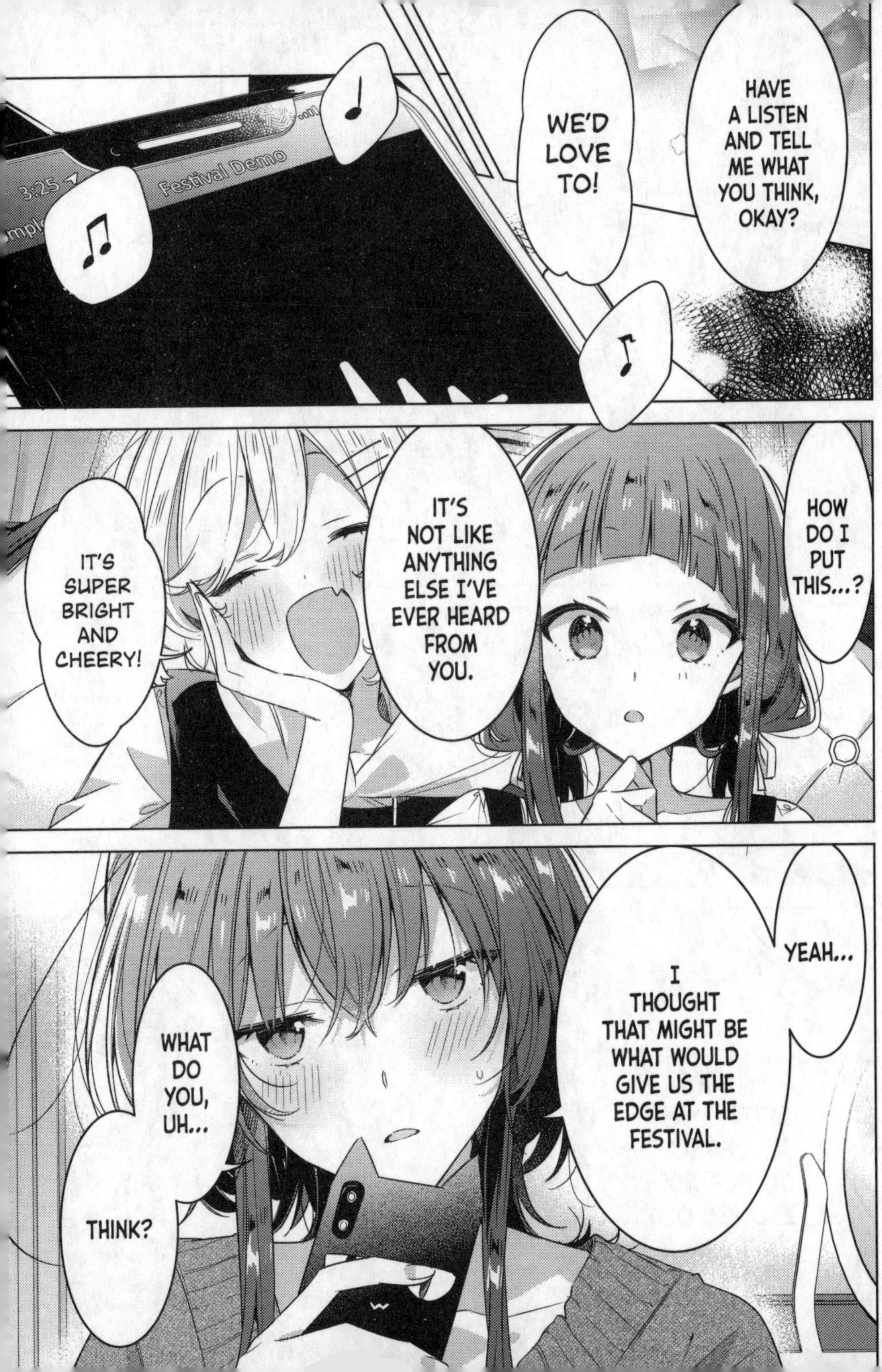
3:25
Festival Demo
HAVE A LISTEN AND TELL ME WHAT YOU THINK, OKAY?
WE'D LOVE TO!
HOW DO I PUT THIS...?
IT'S NOT LIKE ANYTHING ELSE I'VE EVER HEARD FROM YOU.
IT'S SUPER BRIGHT AND CHEERY!
YEAH...
I THOUGHT THAT MIGHT BE WHAT WOULD GIVE US THE EDGE AT THE FESTIVAL.
WHAT DO YOU, UH...
THINK?

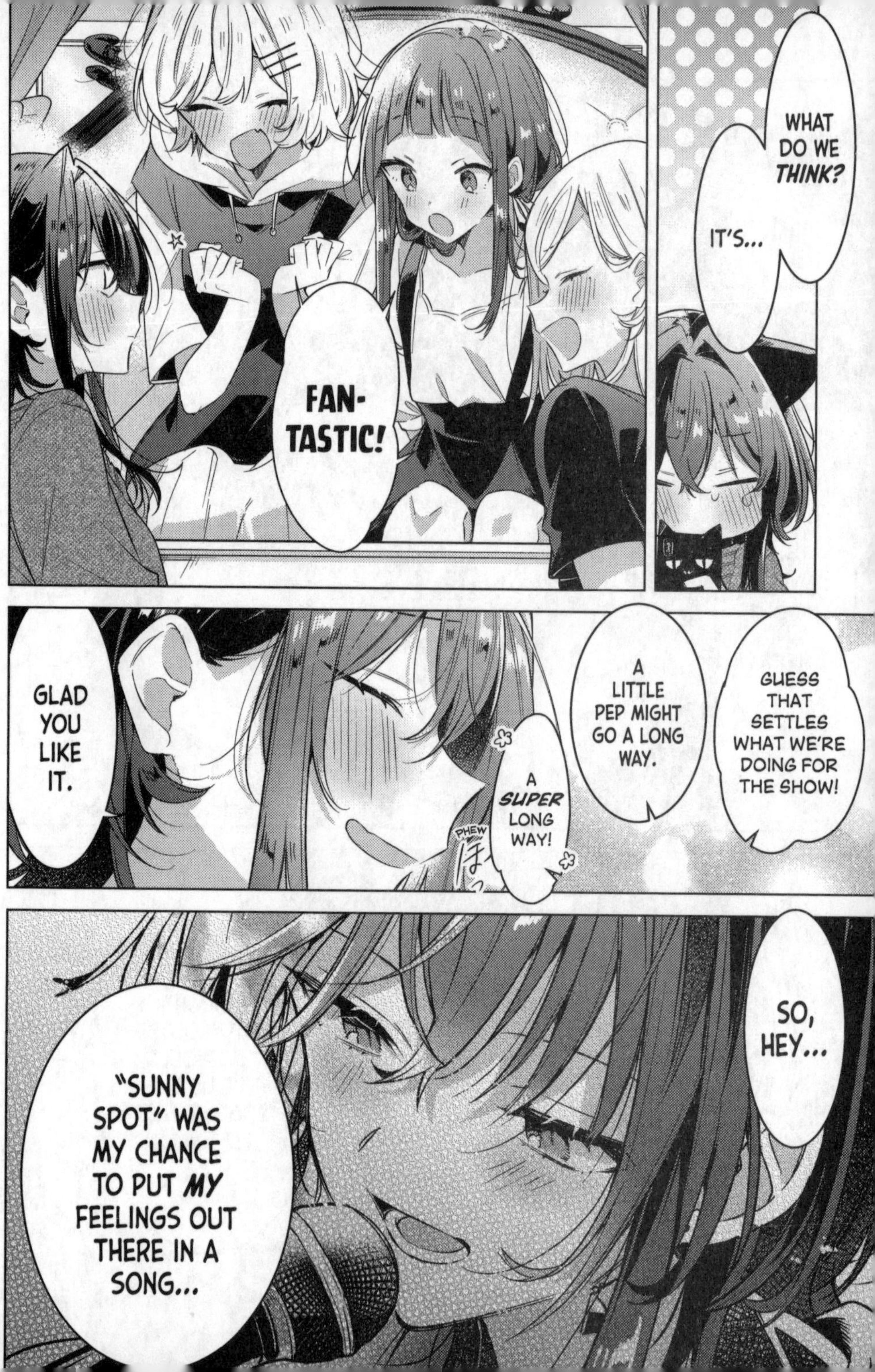
WHAT DO WE *THINK?*
IT'S...
FAN-TASTIC!
GUESS THAT SETTLES WHAT WE'RE DOING FOR THE SHOW!
A LITTLE PEP MIGHT GO A LONG WAY.
A *SUPER* LONG WAY!
PHEW
GLAD YOU LIKE IT.
SO, HEY...
"SUNNY SPOT" WAS MY CHANCE TO PUT *MY* FEELINGS OUT THERE IN A SONG...

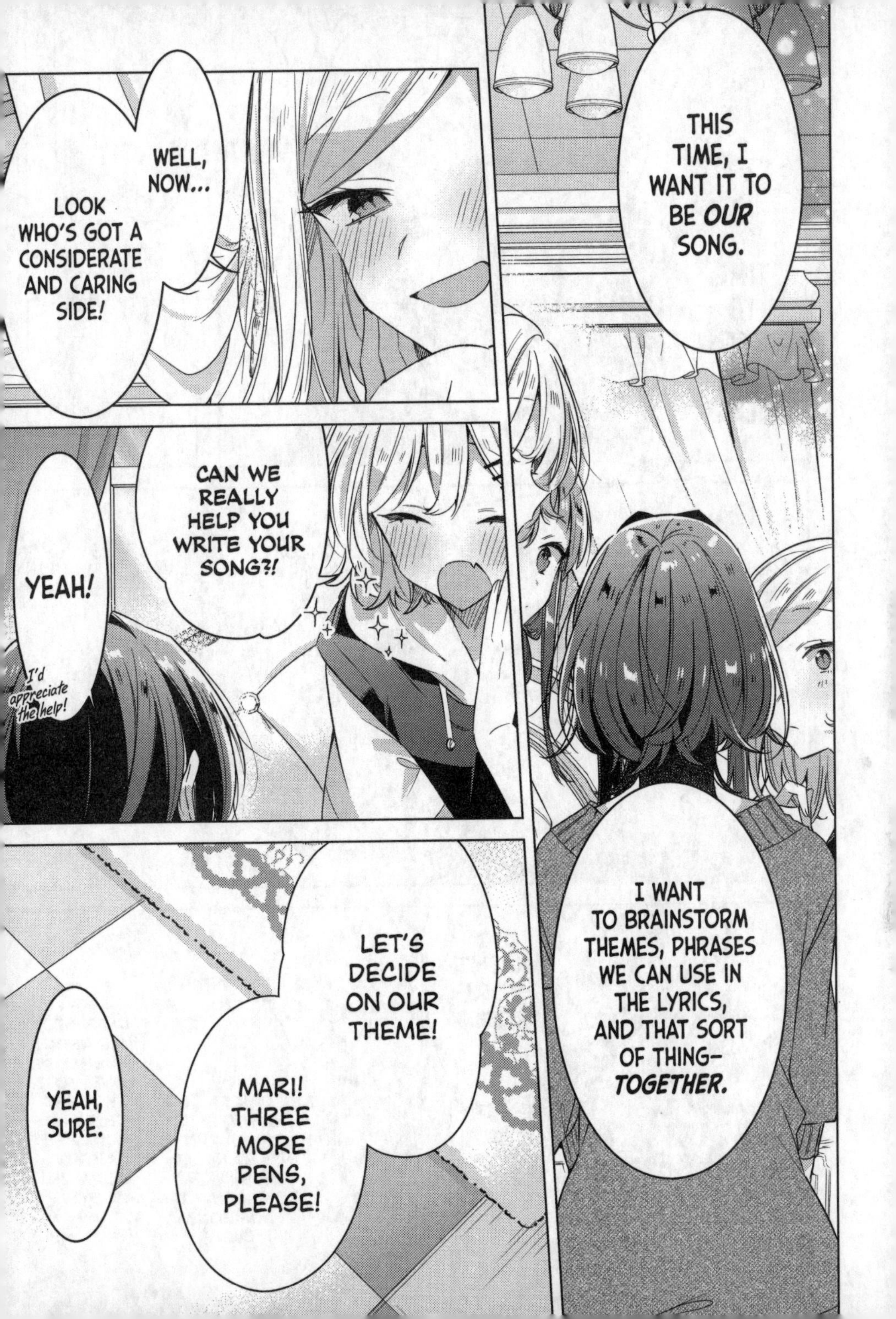
THIS TIME, I WANT IT TO BE *OUR* SONG.
I WANT TO BRAINSTORM THEMES, PHRASES WE CAN USE IN THE LYRICS, AND THAT SORT OF THING—*TOGETHER.*
WELL, NOW...
LOOK WHO'S GOT A CONSIDERATE AND CARING SIDE!
CAN WE REALLY HELP YOU WRITE YOUR SONG?!
YEAH!
I'd appreciate the help!
LET'S DECIDE ON OUR THEME!
MARI! THREE MORE PENS, PLEASE!
YEAH, SURE.

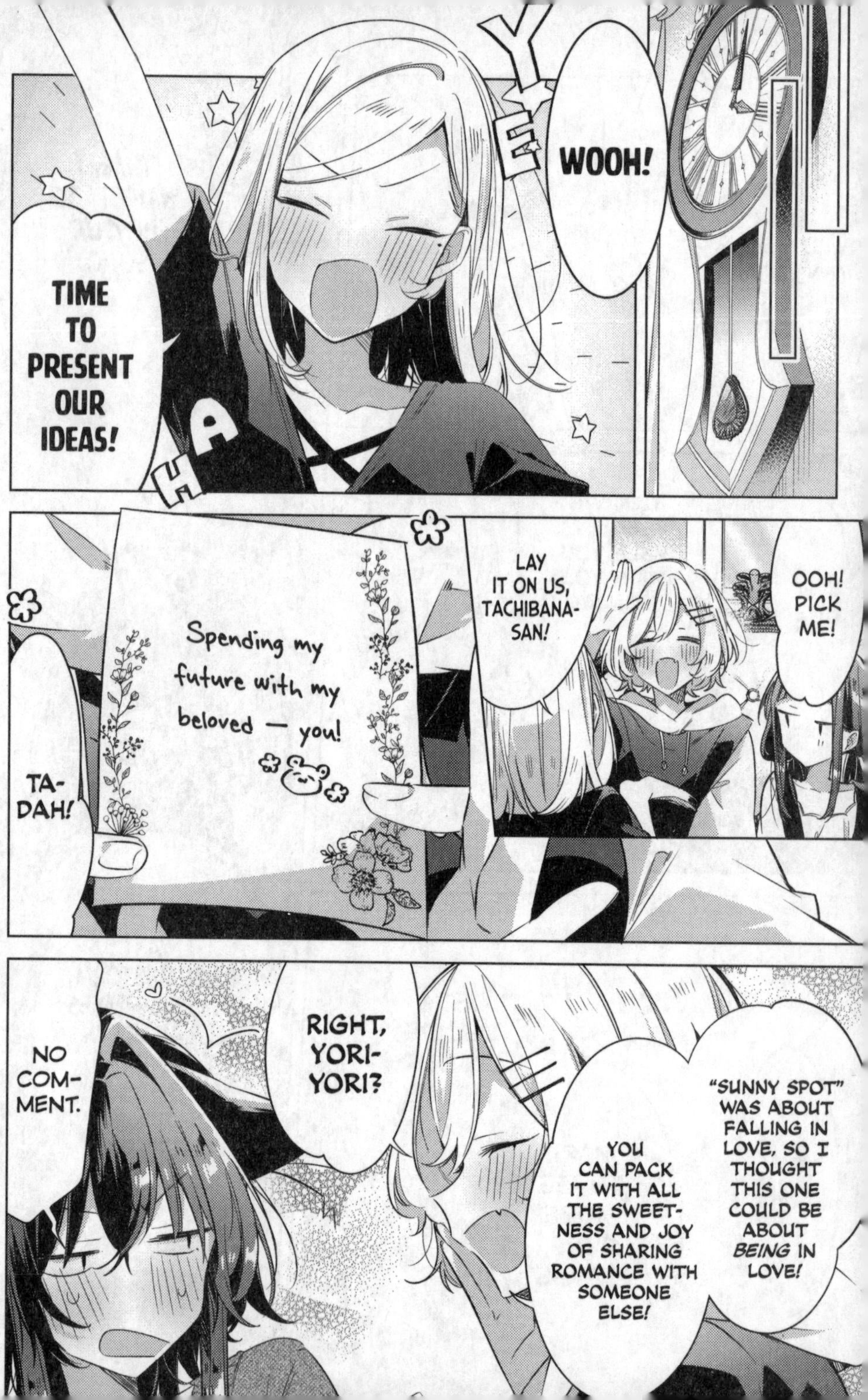
YE
WOOH!
TIME TO PRESENT OUR IDEAS!
HA
OOH! PICK ME!
LAY IT ON US, TACHIBANA-SAN!
Spending my future with my beloved — you!
TA-DAH!
"SUNNY SPOT" WAS ABOUT FALLING IN LOVE, SO I THOUGHT THIS ONE COULD BE ABOUT *BEING* IN LOVE!
YOU CAN PACK IT WITH ALL THE SWEETNESS AND JOY OF SHARING ROMANCE WITH SOMEONE ELSE!
RIGHT, YORI-YORI?
NO COMMENT.

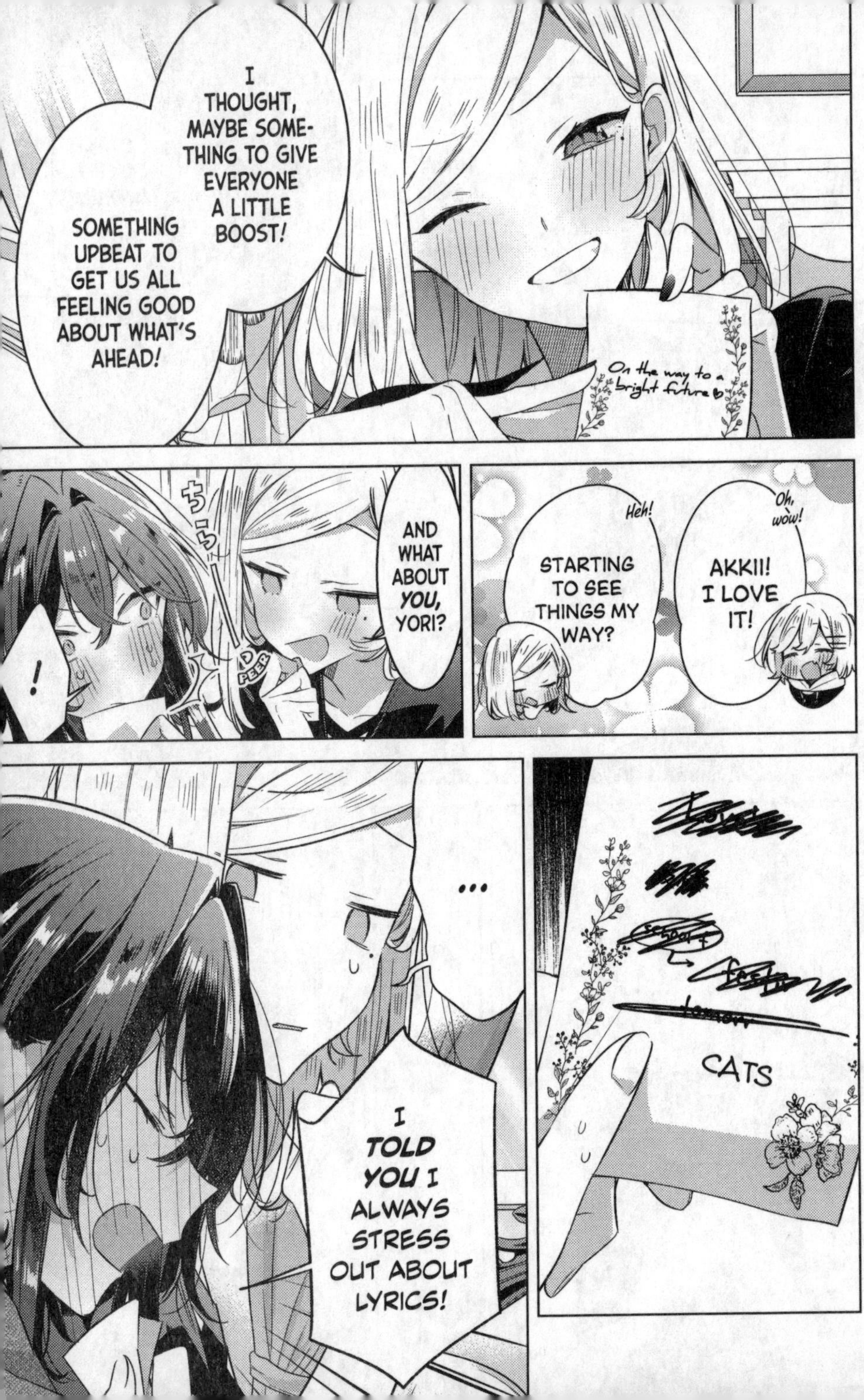
I THOUGHT, MAYBE SOMETHING TO GIVE EVERYONE A LITTLE BOOST!
SOMETHING UPBEAT TO GET US ALL FEELING GOOD ABOUT WHAT'S AHEAD!
On the way to a bright future♡
Oh, wow!
AKKII! I LOVE IT!
Heh!
STARTING TO SEE THINGS MY WAY?
AND WHAT ABOUT *YOU*, YORI?
ちら
PEEP
!
CATS
...
I *TOLD YOU* I ALWAYS STRESS OUT ABOUT LYRICS!

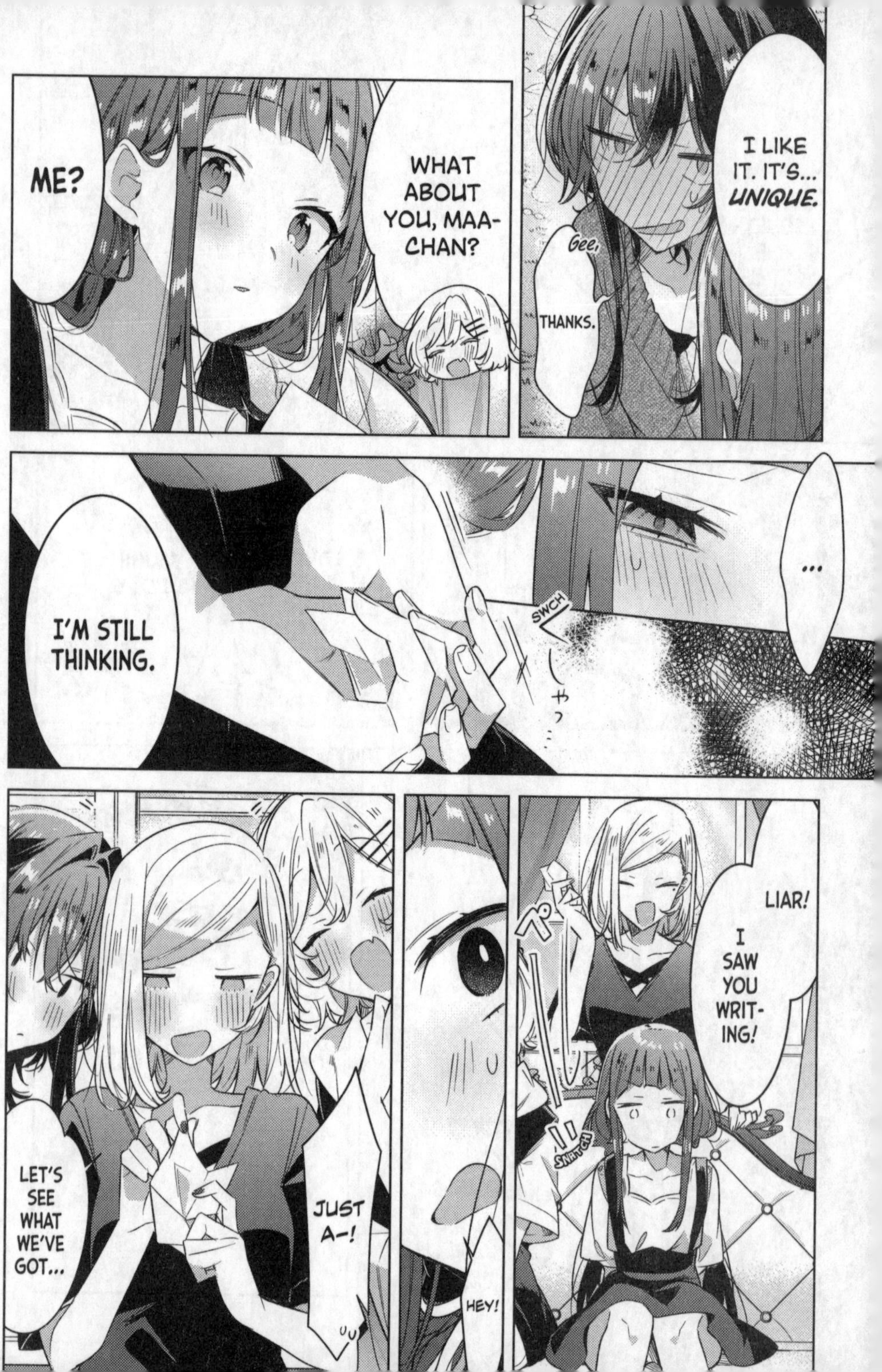
I LIKE IT. IT'S... UNIQUE.
Gee,
THANKS.
WHAT ABOUT YOU, MAA-CHAN?
ME?
...
SWCH
I'M STILL THINKING.
LIAR!
I SAW YOU WRITING!
SNATCH
JUST A-!
HEY!
LET'S SEE WHAT WE'VE GOT...

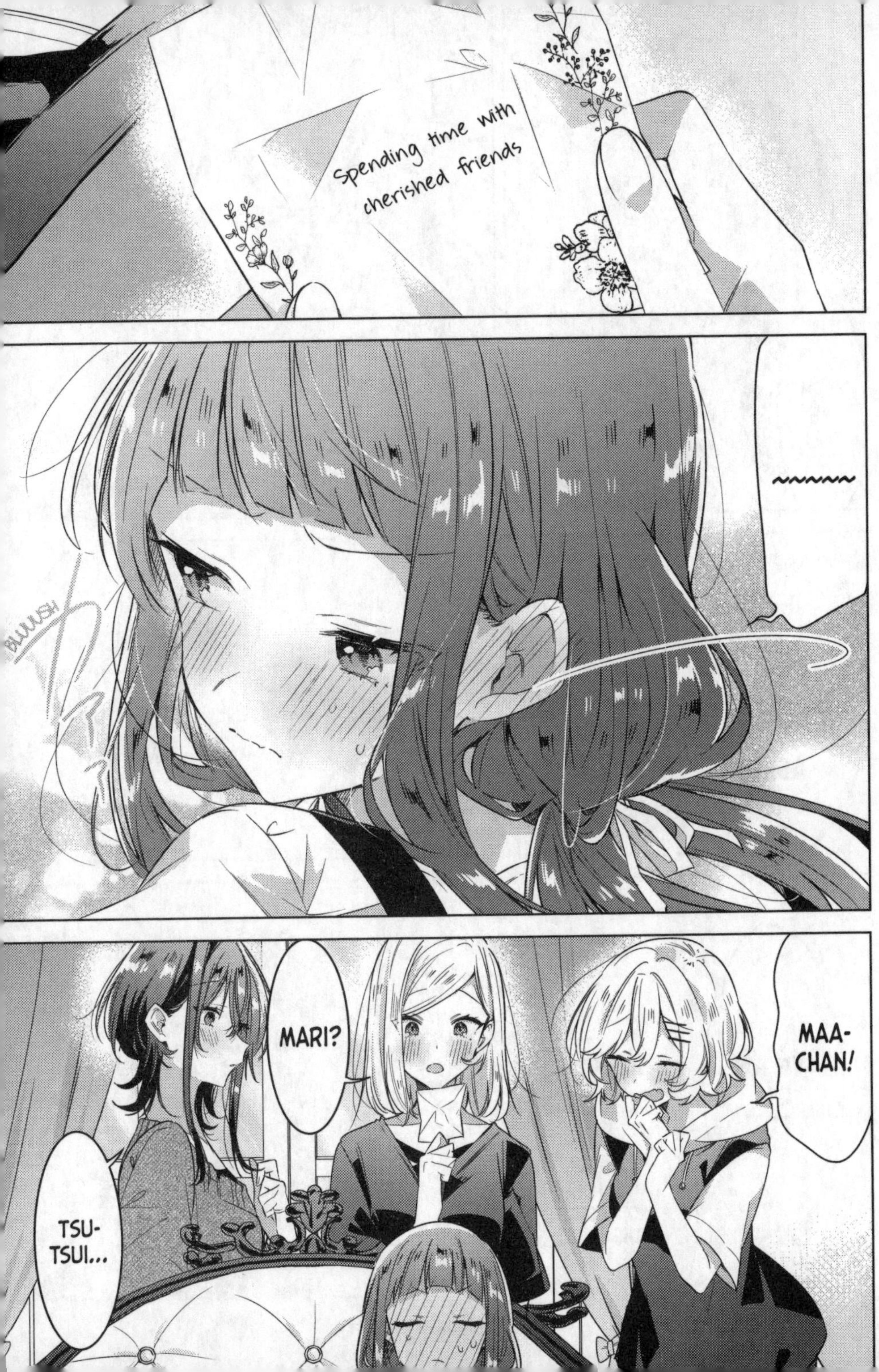
Spending time with cherished friends
~~~~~~
BLUUUSH
MAA-CHAN!
MARI?
TSU-TSUI...
~~~~~~

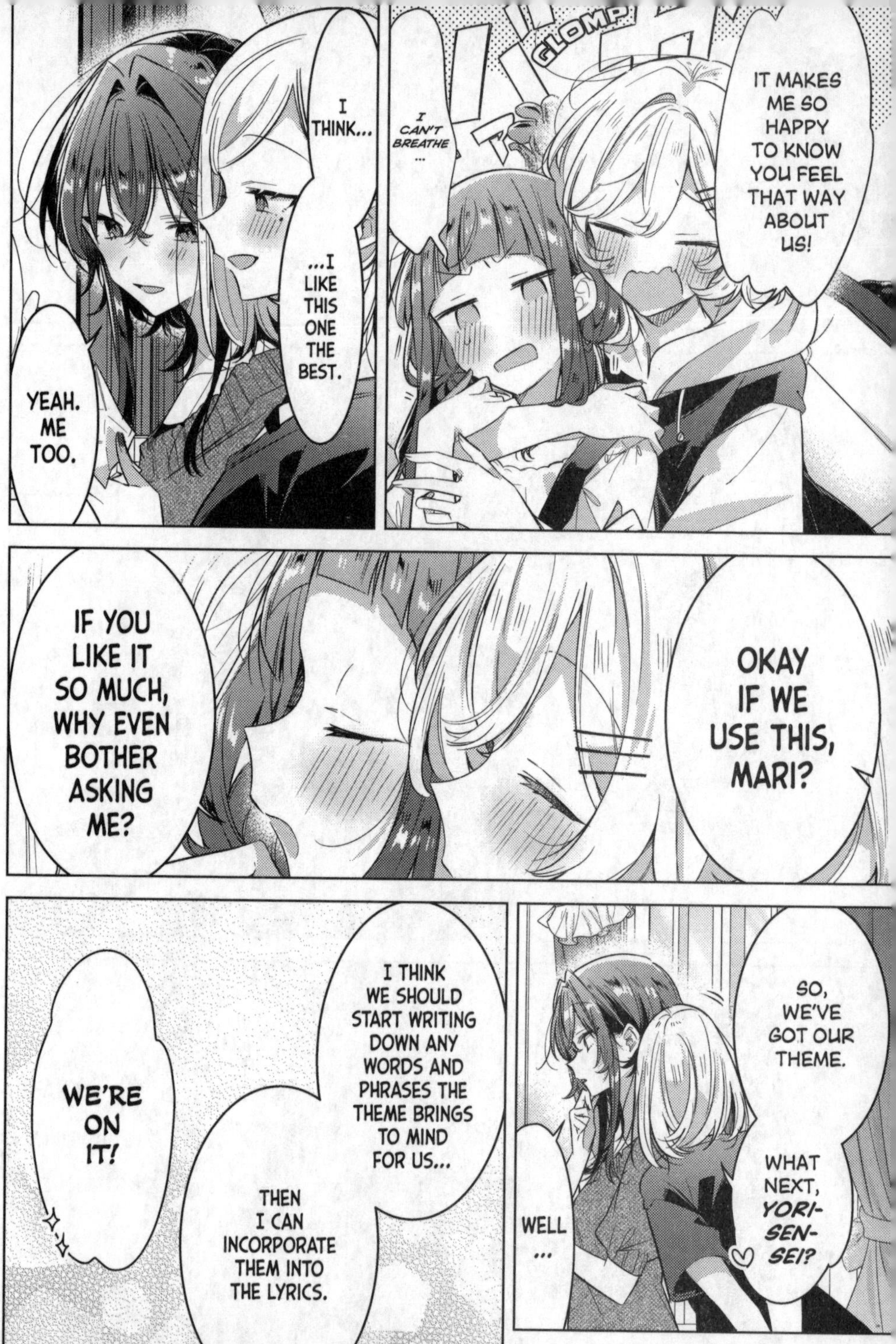
GLOMP
IT MAKES ME SO HAPPY TO KNOW YOU FEEL THAT WAY ABOUT US!
I CAN'T BREATHE ...
I THINK...
...I LIKE THIS ONE THE BEST.
YEAH. ME TOO.
OKAY IF WE USE THIS, MARI?
IF YOU LIKE IT SO MUCH, WHY EVEN BOTHER ASKING ME?
SO, WE'VE GOT OUR THEME.
WHAT NEXT, YORI-SENSEI?
WELL ...
I THINK WE SHOULD START WRITING DOWN ANY WORDS AND PHRASES THE THEME BRINGS TO MIND FOR US...
THEN I CAN INCORPORATE THEM INTO THE LYRICS.
WE'RE ON IT!

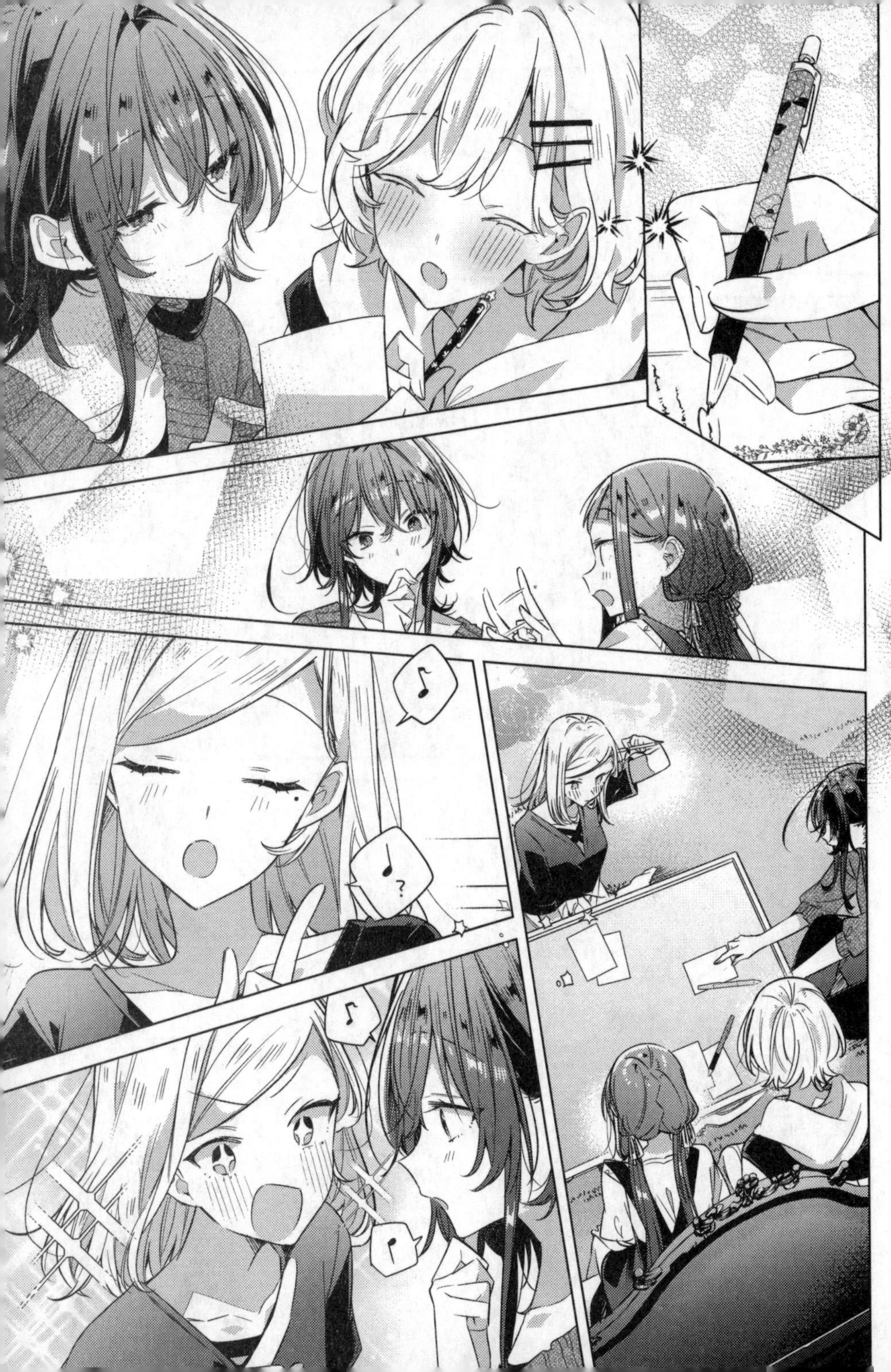
♪
♪?
♪
♪

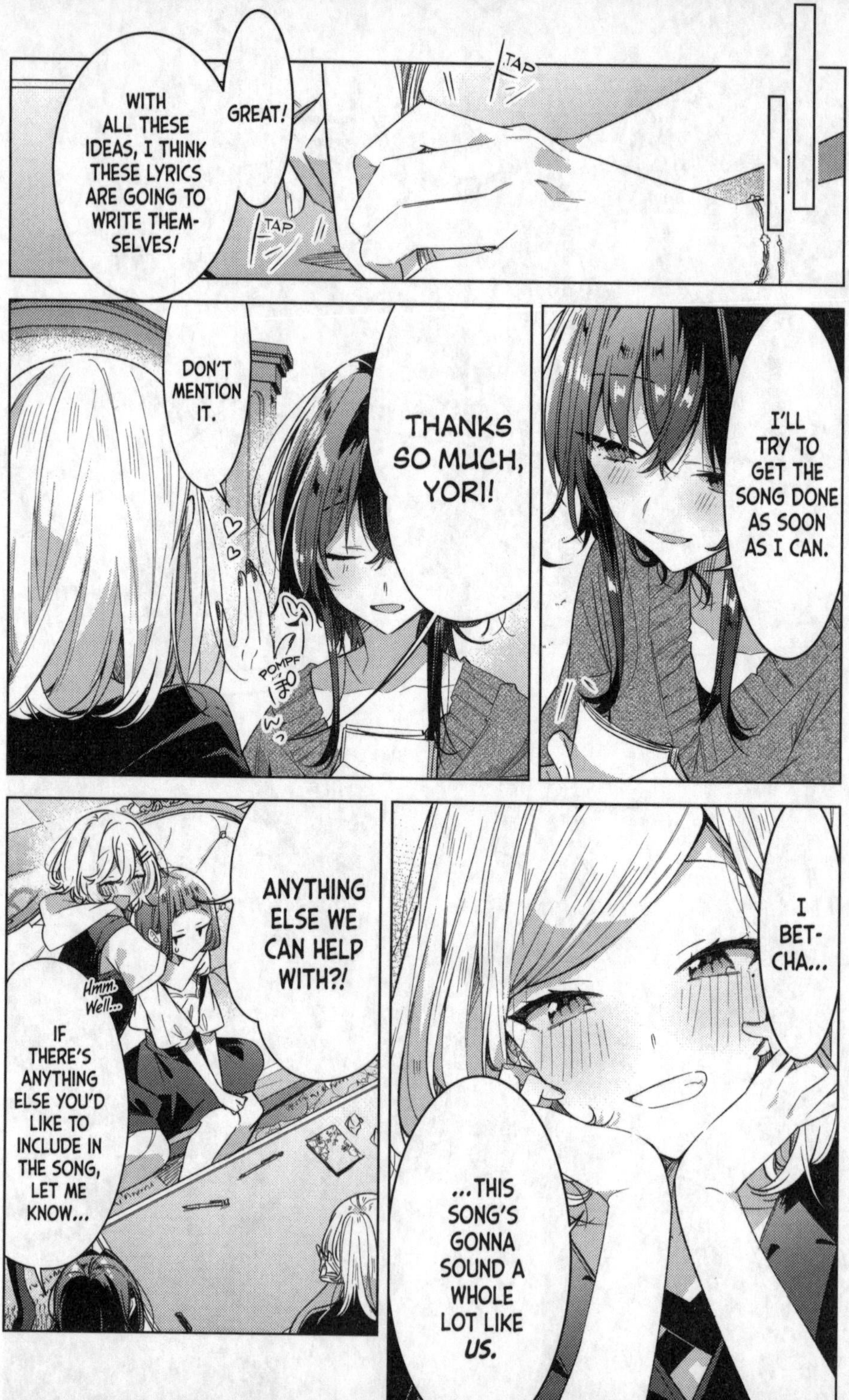
TAP
GREAT!
WITH ALL THESE IDEAS, I THINK THESE LYRICS ARE GOING TO WRITE THEM-SELVES!
TAP
I'LL TRY TO GET THE SONG DONE AS SOON AS I CAN.
THANKS SO MUCH, YORI!
DON'T MENTION IT.
POMPF
I BET-CHA...
...THIS SONG'S GONNA SOUND A WHOLE LOT LIKE *US*.
ANYTHING ELSE WE CAN HELP WITH?!
Hmm. Well...
IF THERE'S ANYTHING ELSE YOU'D LIKE TO INCLUDE IN THE SONG, LET ME KNOW...

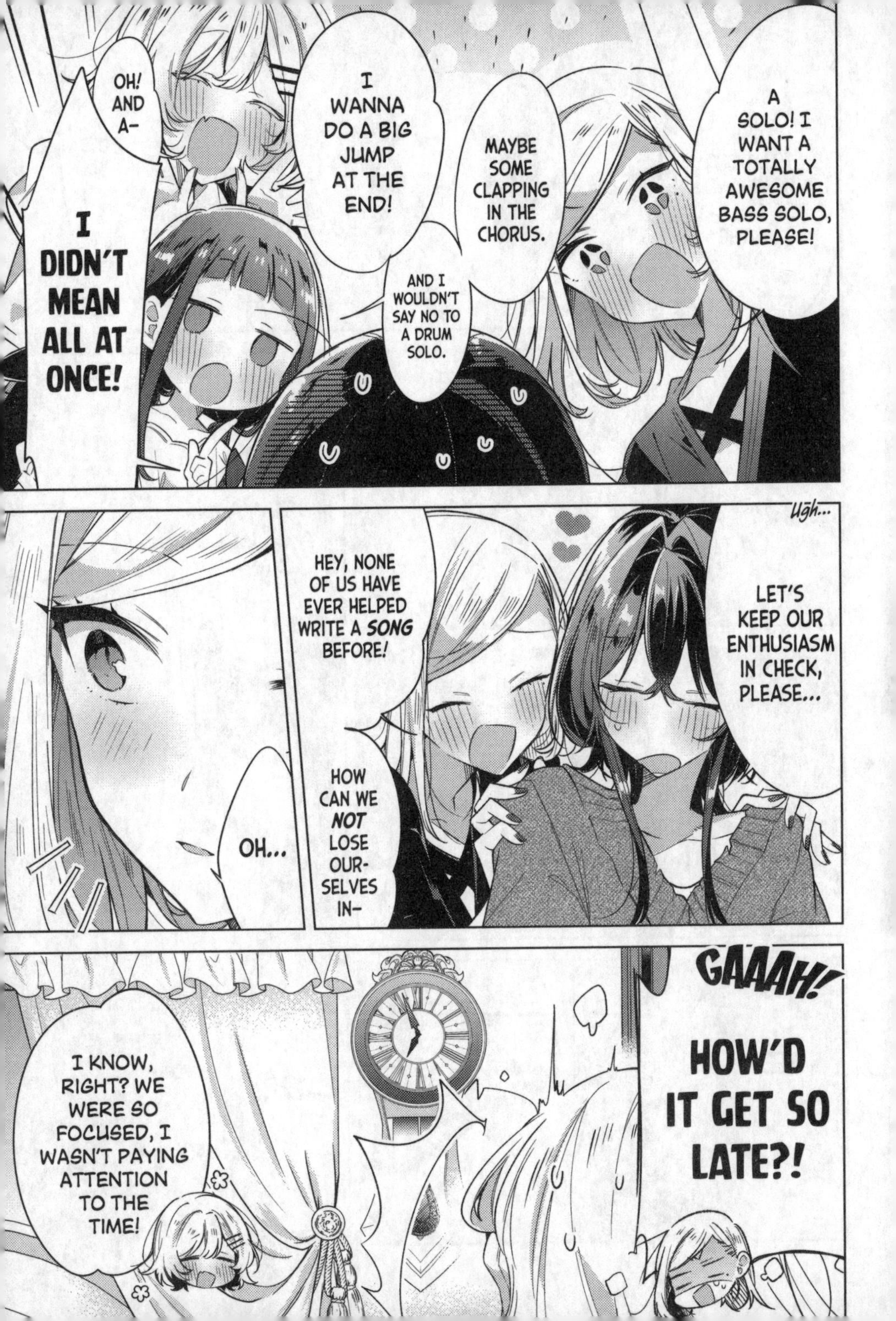
A SOLO! I WANT A TOTALLY AWESOME BASS SOLO, PLEASE!
MAYBE SOME CLAPPING IN THE CHORUS.
AND I WOULDN'T SAY NO TO A DRUM SOLO.
I WANNA DO A BIG JUMP AT THE END!
OH! AND A-
I DIDN'T MEAN ALL AT ONCE!
Ugh...
LET'S KEEP OUR ENTHUSIASM IN CHECK, PLEASE...
HEY, NONE OF US HAVE EVER HELPED WRITE A *SONG* BEFORE!
HOW CAN WE *NOT* LOSE OUR-SELVES IN-
OH...
GAAAH!
HOW'D IT GET SO LATE?!
I KNOW, RIGHT? WE WERE SO FOCUSED, I WASN'T PAYING ATTENTION TO THE TIME!

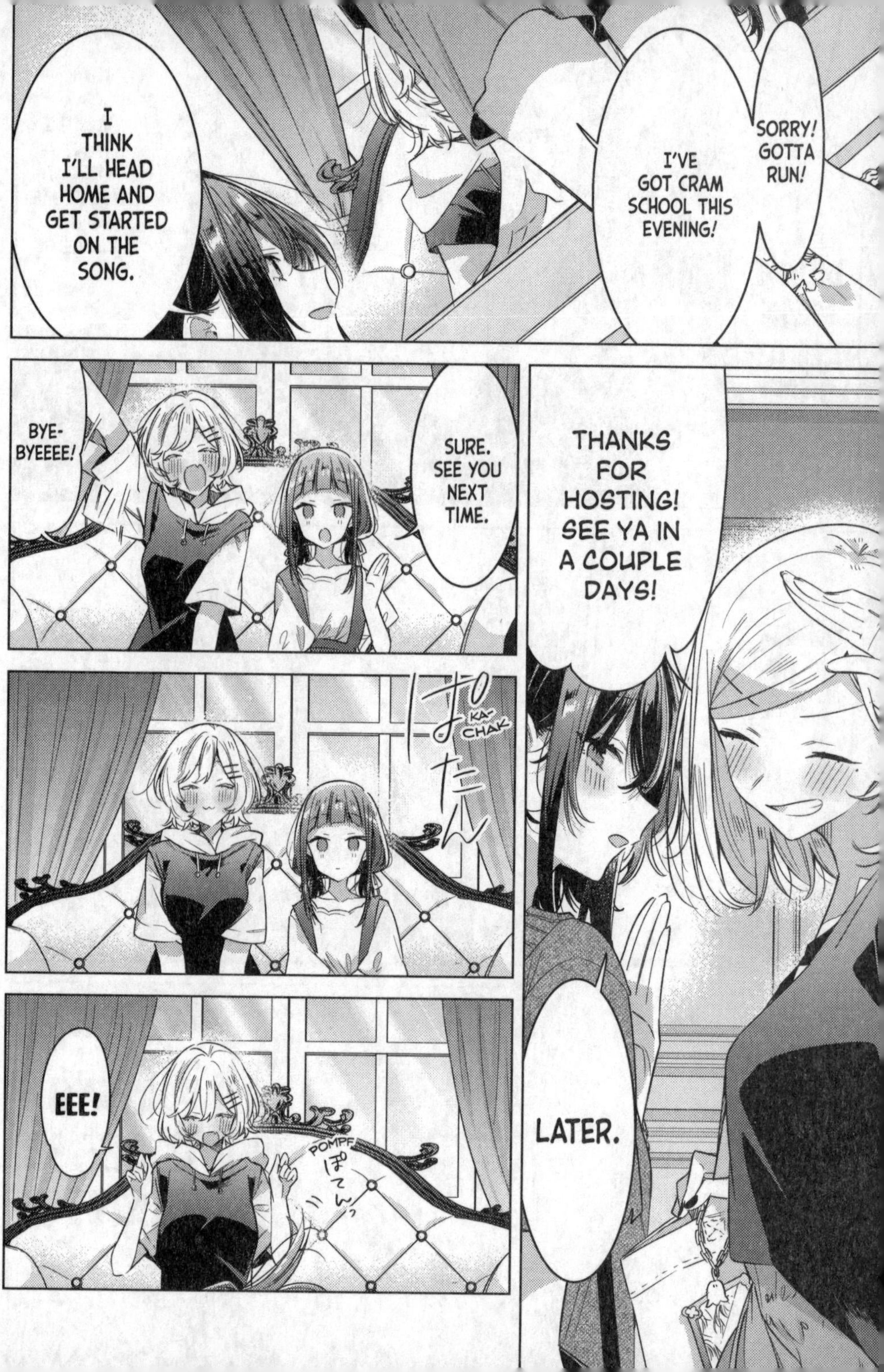
SORRY! GOTTA RUN!
I'VE GOT CRAM SCHOOL THIS EVENING!
I THINK I'LL HEAD HOME AND GET STARTED ON THE SONG.
THANKS FOR HOSTING! SEE YA IN A COUPLE DAYS!
LATER.
SURE. SEE YOU NEXT TIME.
BYE-BYEEEE!
KA-CHAK
EEE!
POMPF

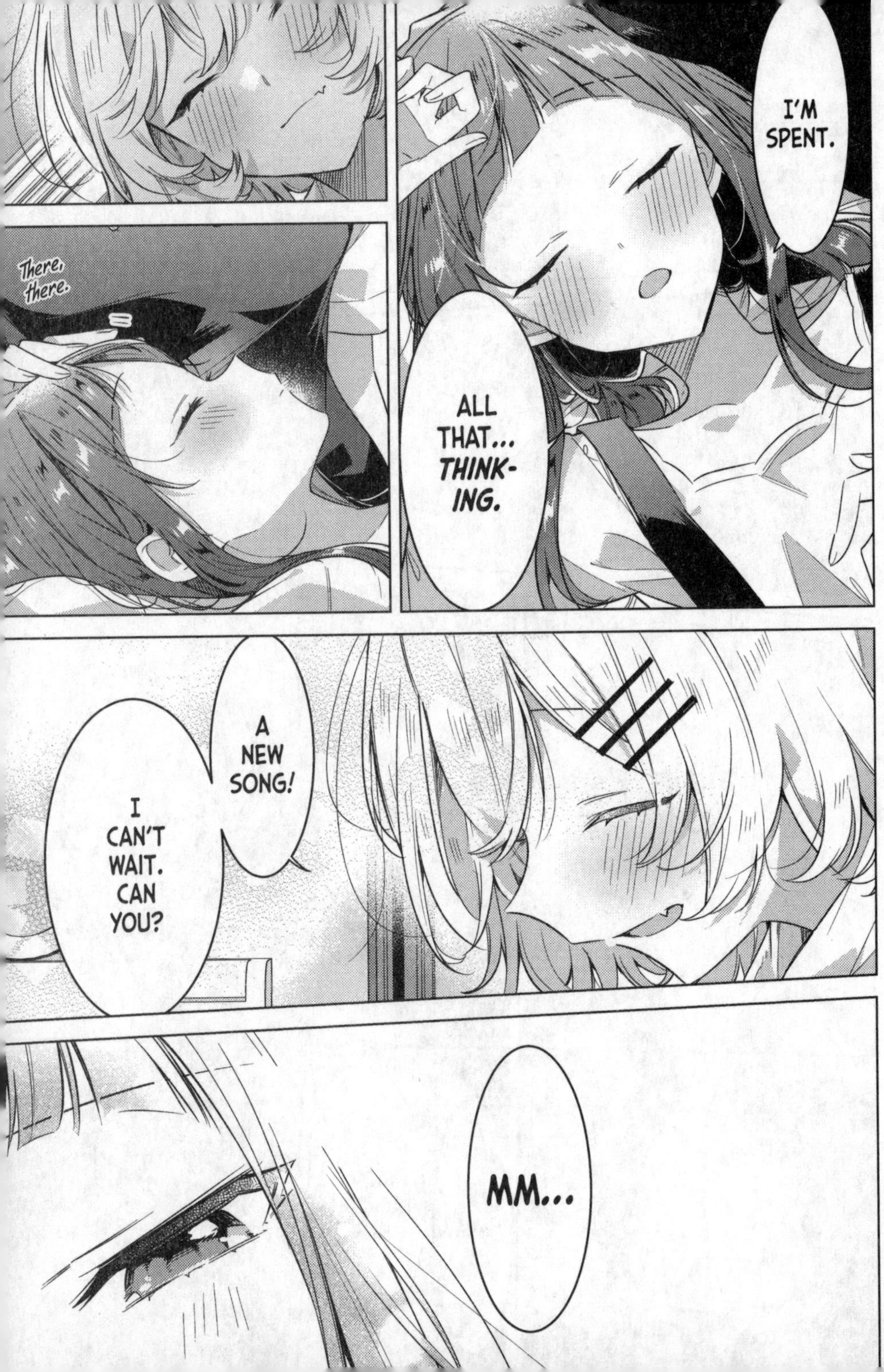
I'M SPENT.
ALL THAT... *THINKING.*
There, there.
A NEW SONG!
I CAN'T WAIT. CAN YOU?
MM...

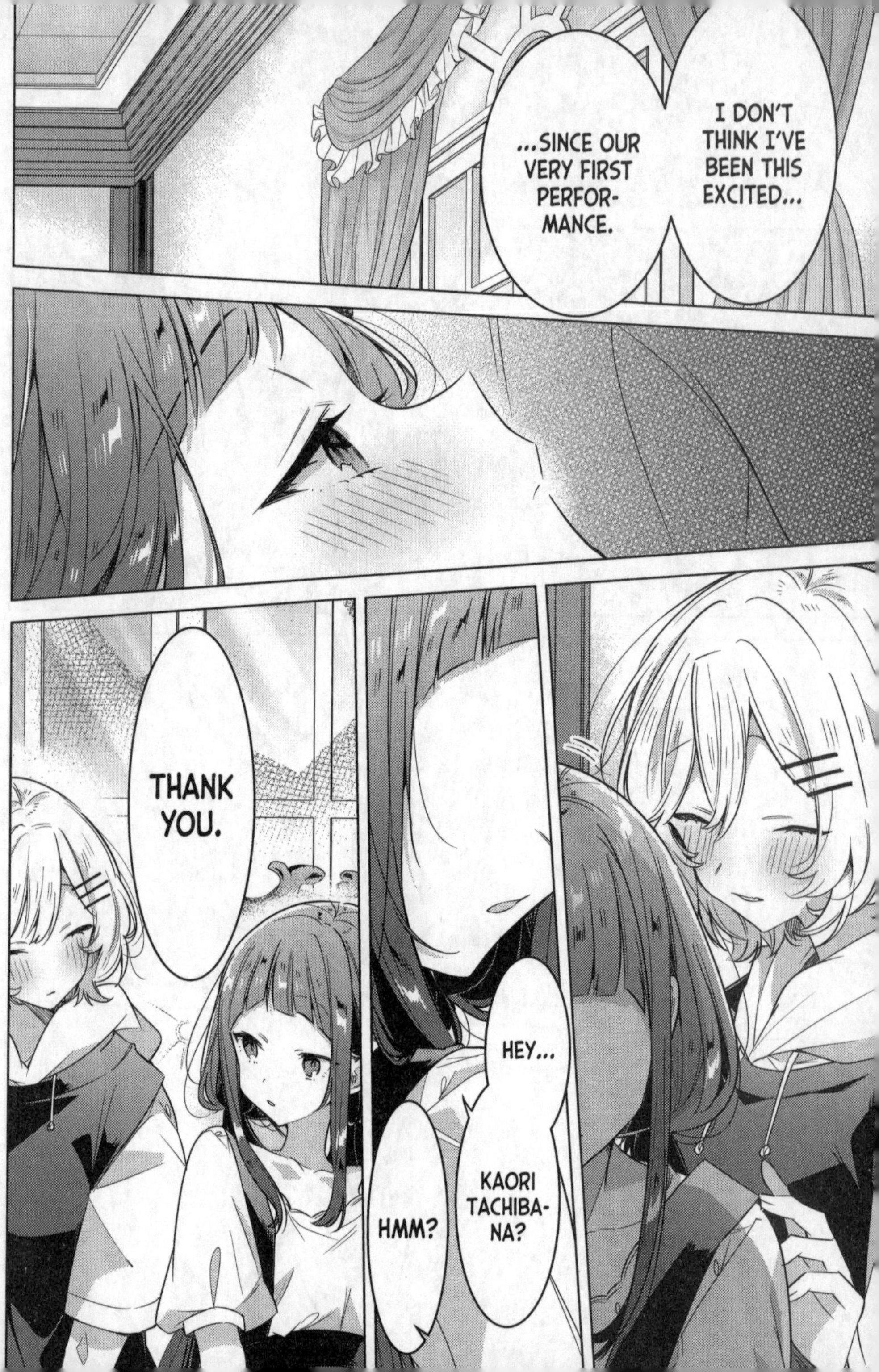
I DON'T THINK I'VE BEEN THIS EXCITED...
...SINCE OUR VERY FIRST PERFOR-MANCE.
HEY...
KAORI TACHIBA-NA?
HMM?
THANK YOU.

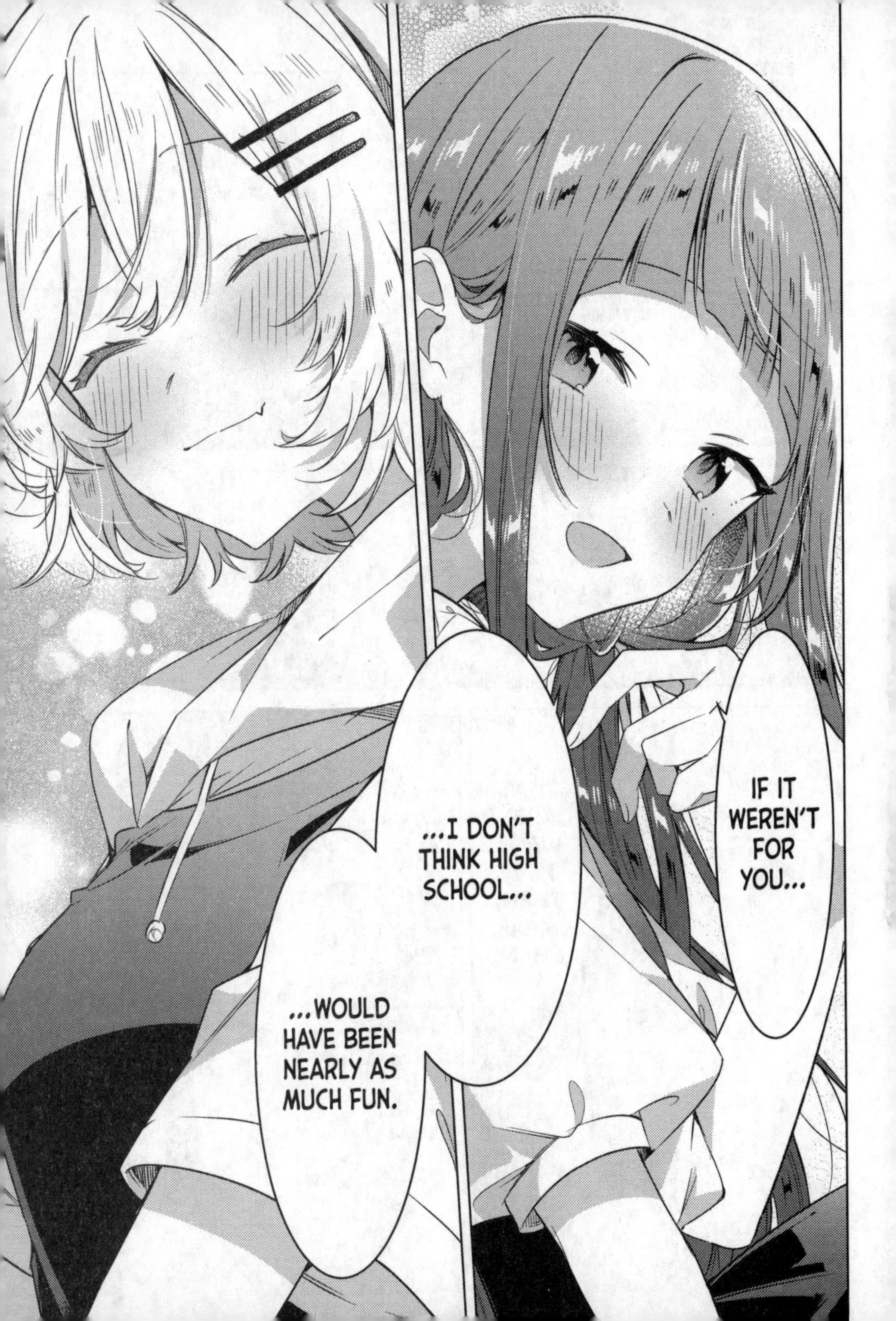
IF IT WEREN'T FOR YOU...
...I DON'T THINK HIGH SCHOOL...
...WOULD HAVE BEEN NEARLY AS MUCH FUN.

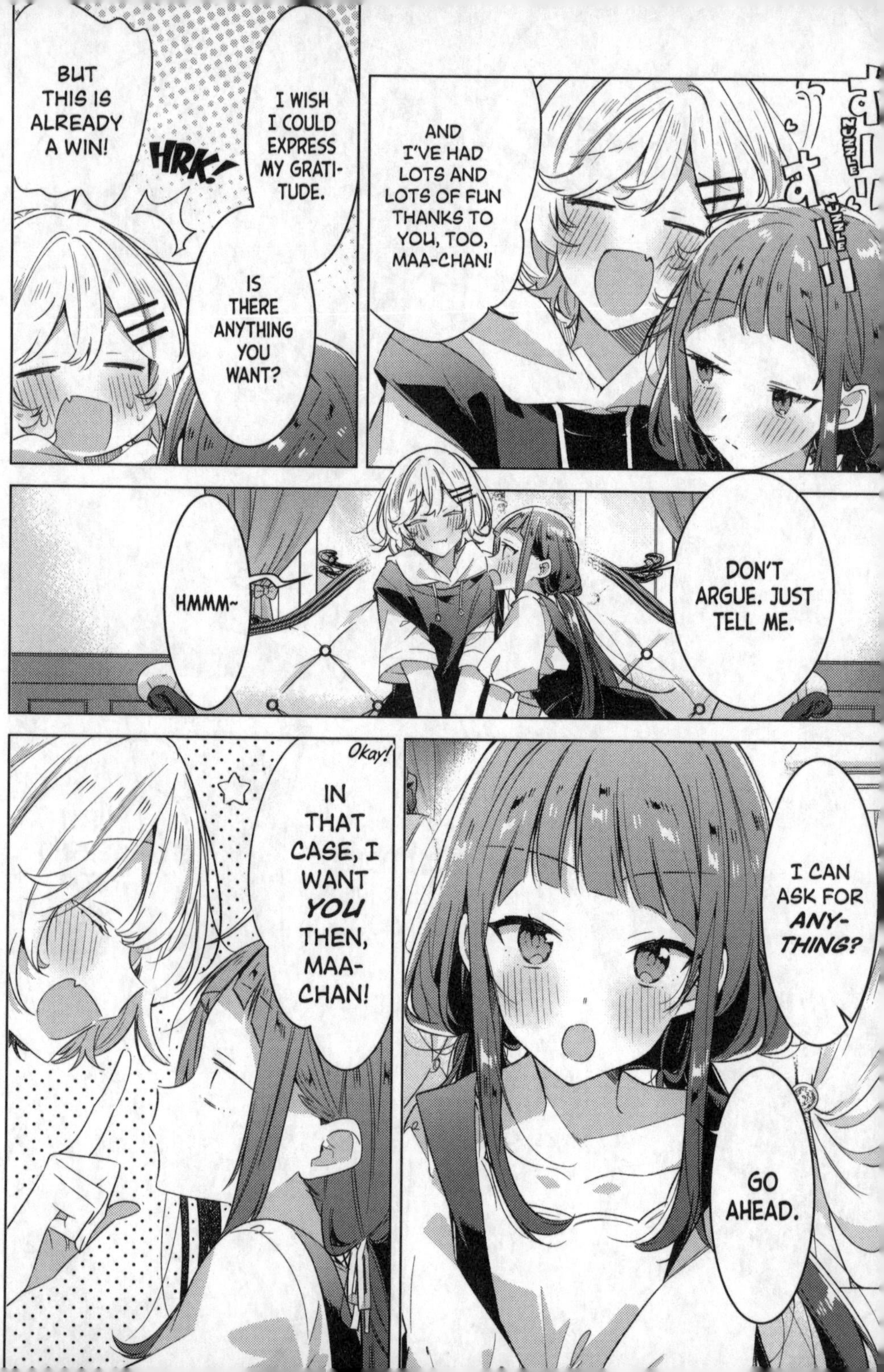
AND I'VE HAD LOTS AND LOTS OF FUN THANKS TO YOU, TOO, MAA-CHAN!
I WISH I COULD EXPRESS MY GRATI-TUDE.
IS THERE ANYTHING YOU WANT?
HRK!
BUT THIS IS ALREADY A WIN!
DON'T ARGUE. JUST TELL ME.
HMMM~
I CAN ASK FOR *ANY-THING?*
GO AHEAD.
Okay!
IN THAT CASE, I WANT *YOU* THEN, MAA-CHAN!

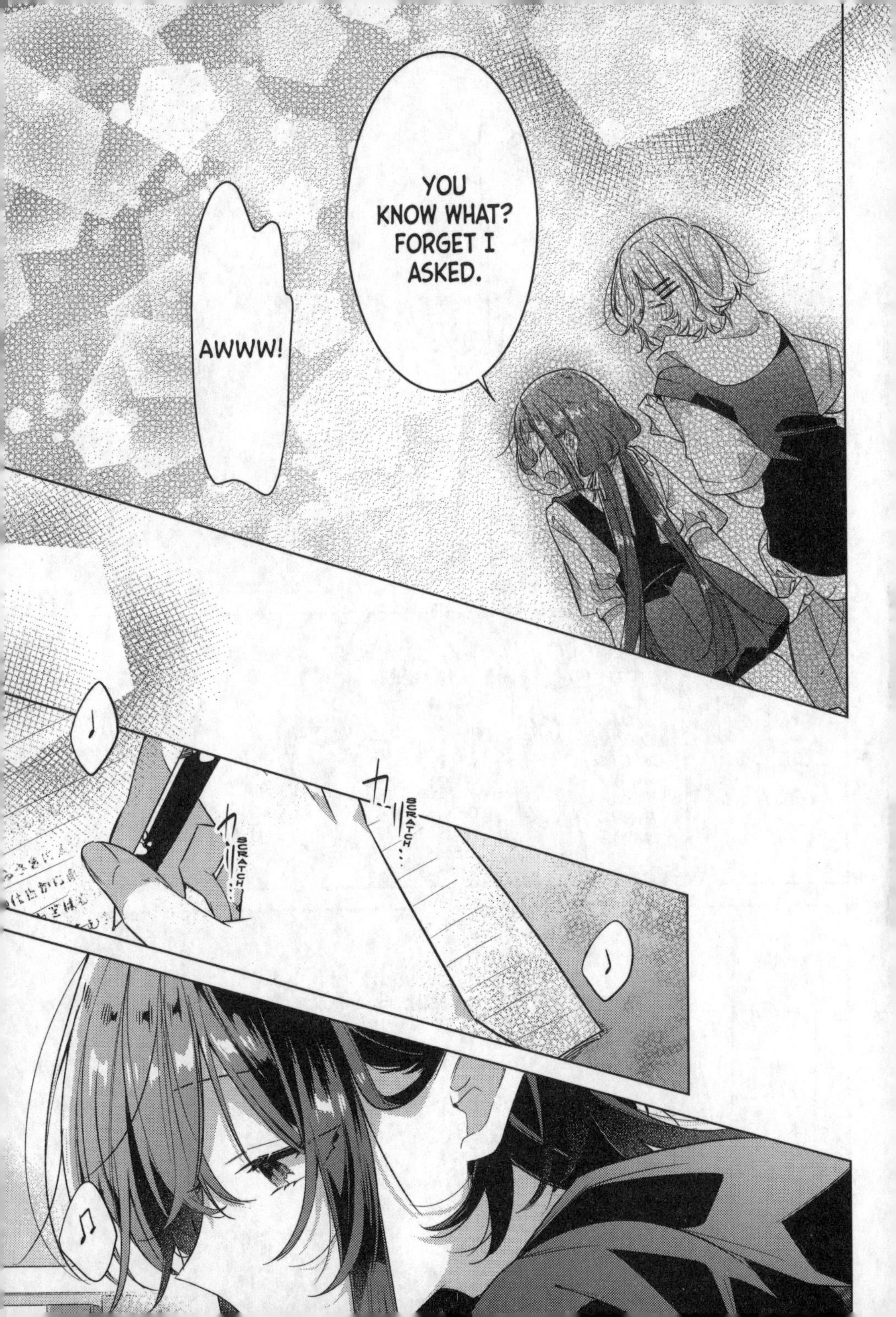
YOU KNOW WHAT? FORGET I ASKED.
AWWW!
SCRATCH...
SCRATCH...

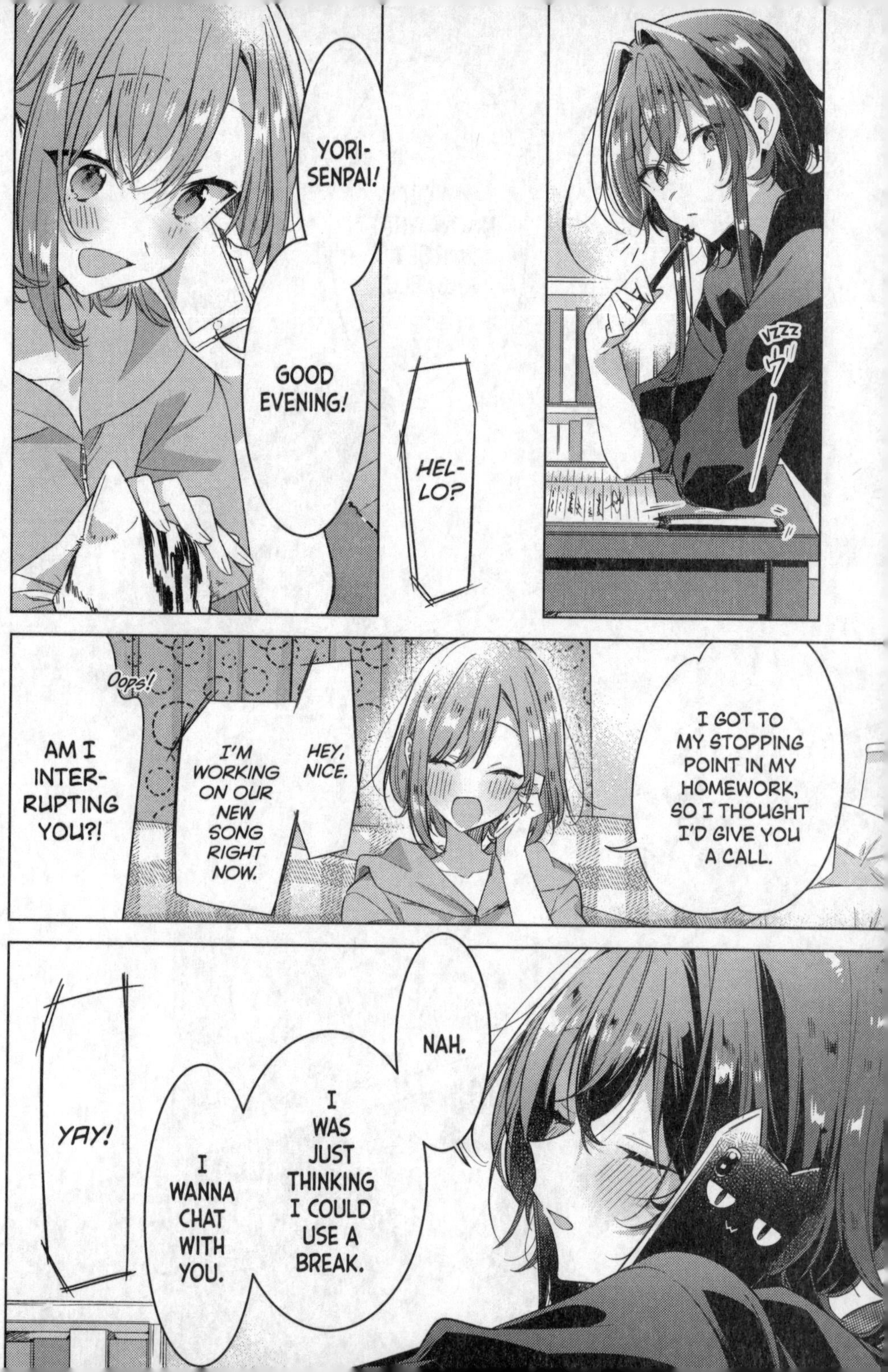
VZZZ
HEL-LO?
YORI-SENPAI!
GOOD EVENING!
I GOT TO MY STOPPING POINT IN MY HOMEWORK, SO I THOUGHT I'D GIVE YOU A CALL.
HEY, NICE.
I'M WORKING ON OUR NEW SONG RIGHT NOW.
Oops!
AM I INTERRUPTING YOU?!
NAH.
I WAS JUST THINKING I COULD USE A BREAK.
I WANNA CHAT WITH YOU.
YAY!

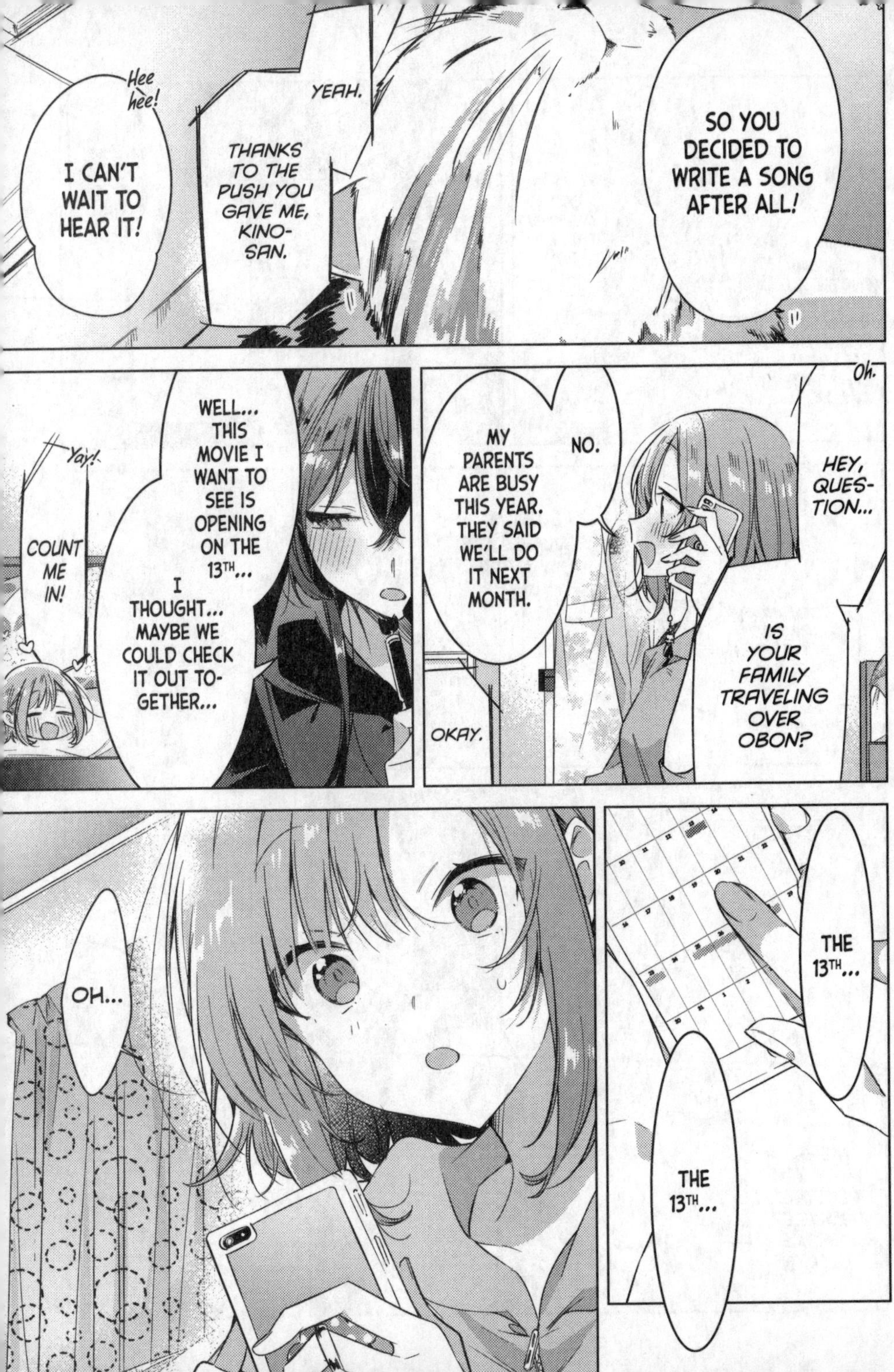
SO YOU DECIDED TO WRITE A SONG AFTER ALL!
YEAH.
THANKS TO THE PUSH YOU GAVE ME, KINO-SAN.
Hee hee!
I CAN'T WAIT TO HEAR IT!
Oh.
HEY, QUESTION...
IS YOUR FAMILY TRAVELING OVER OBON?
NO.
MY PARENTS ARE BUSY THIS YEAR. THEY SAID WE'LL DO IT NEXT MONTH.
OKAY.
WELL... THIS MOVIE I WANT TO SEE IS OPENING ON THE 13TH...
I THOUGHT... MAYBE WE COULD CHECK IT OUT TOGETHER...
Yay!
COUNT ME IN!
THE 13TH...
THE 13TH...
OH...

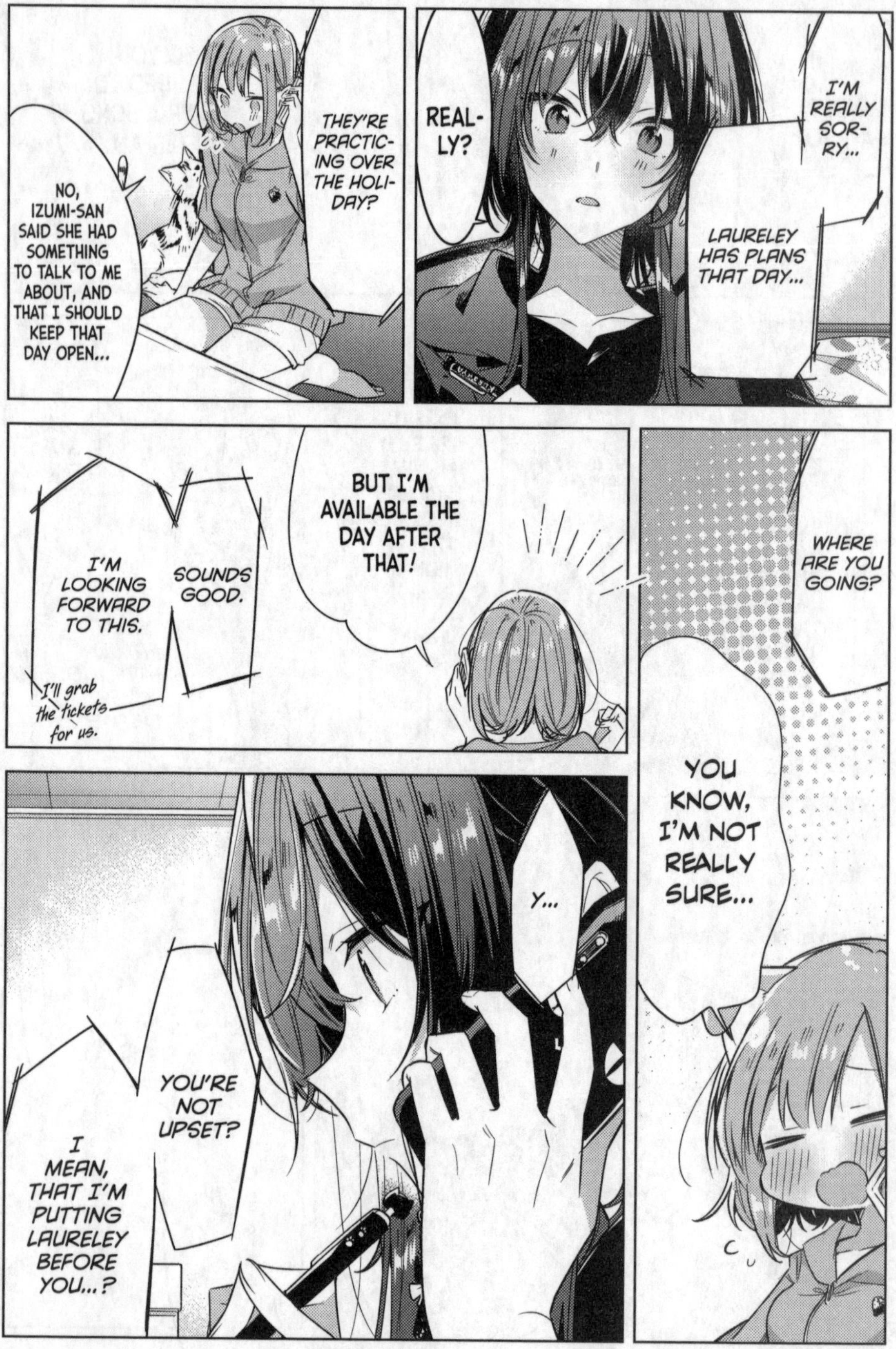
I'M REALLY SORRY...
LAURELEY HAS PLANS THAT DAY...
REALLY?
THEY'RE PRACTICING OVER THE HOLIDAY?
NO, IZUMI-SAN SAID SHE HAD SOMETHING TO TALK TO ME ABOUT, AND THAT I SHOULD KEEP THAT DAY OPEN...
WHERE ARE YOU GOING?
BUT I'M AVAILABLE THE DAY AFTER THAT!
SOUNDS GOOD.
I'M LOOKING FORWARD TO THIS.
I'll grab the tickets for us.
YOU KNOW, I'M NOT REALLY SURE...
Y...
YOU'RE NOT UPSET?
I MEAN, THAT I'M PUTTING LAURELEY BEFORE YOU...?

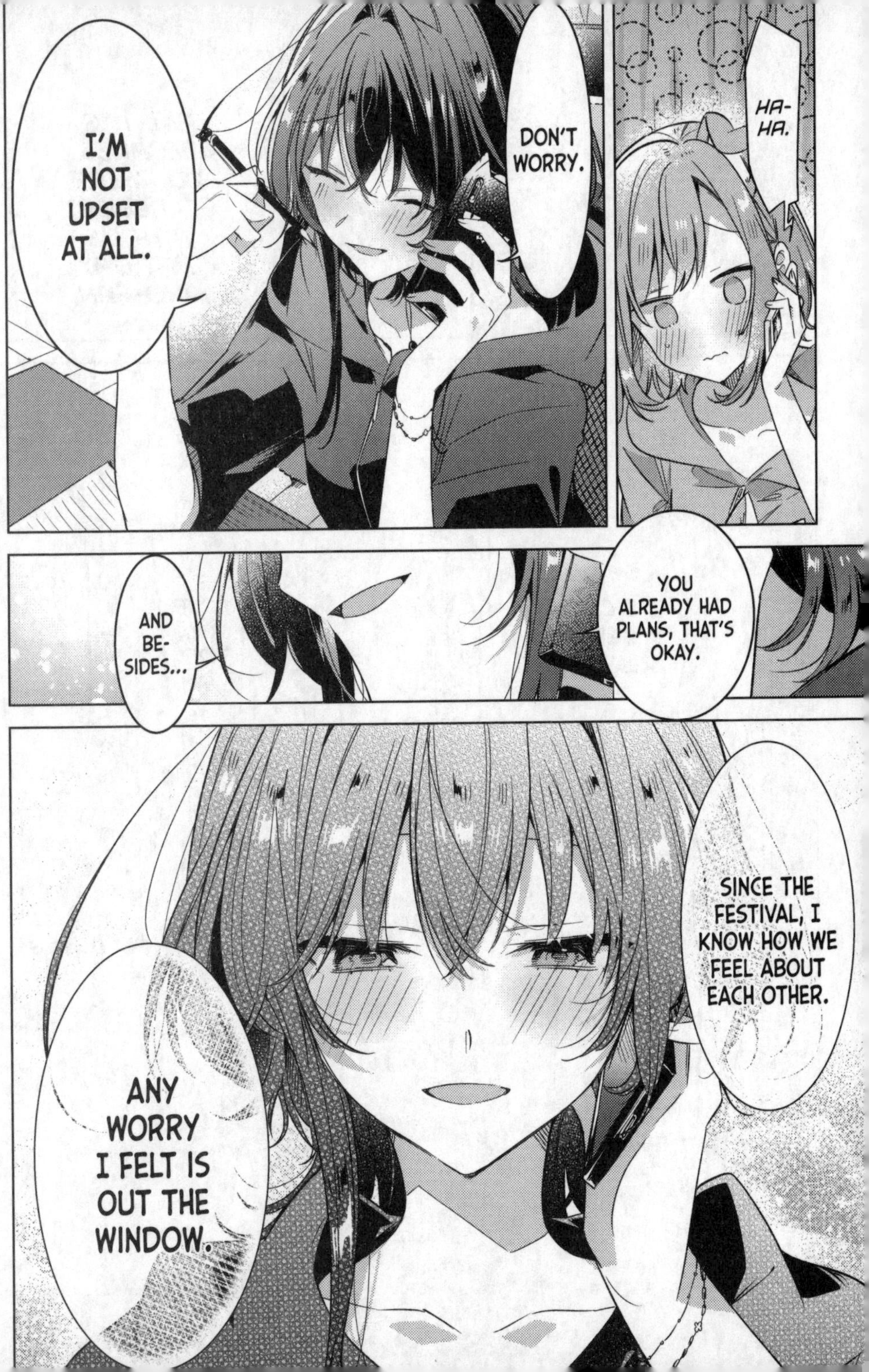
HA-HA.
DON'T WORRY.
I'M NOT UPSET AT ALL.
YOU ALREADY HAD PLANS, THAT'S OKAY.
AND BE-SIDES...
SINCE THE FESTIVAL, I KNOW HOW WE FEEL ABOUT EACH OTHER.
ANY WORRY I FELT IS OUT THE WINDOW.

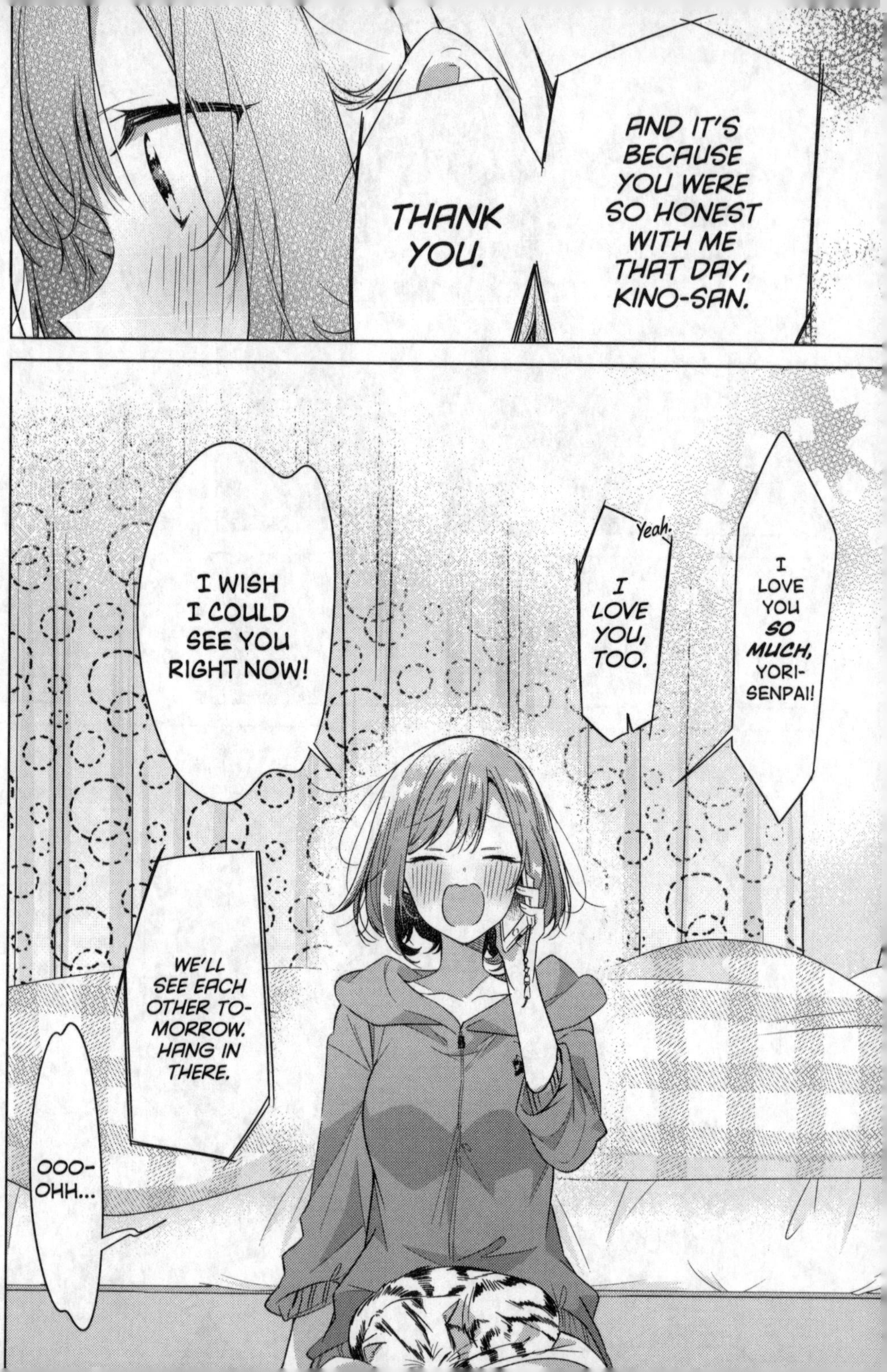
AND IT'S BECAUSE YOU WERE SO HONEST WITH ME THAT DAY, KINO-SAN.
THANK YOU.
I LOVE YOU SO MUCH, YORI-SENPAI!
Yeah.
I LOVE YOU, TOO.
I WISH I COULD SEE YOU RIGHT NOW!
WE'LL SEE EACH OTHER TO-MORROW. HANG IN THERE.
OOO-OHH...

Whisper Me
A Love Song

Eku Takeshima

Whisper Me
A Love Song
Eku
Takeshima

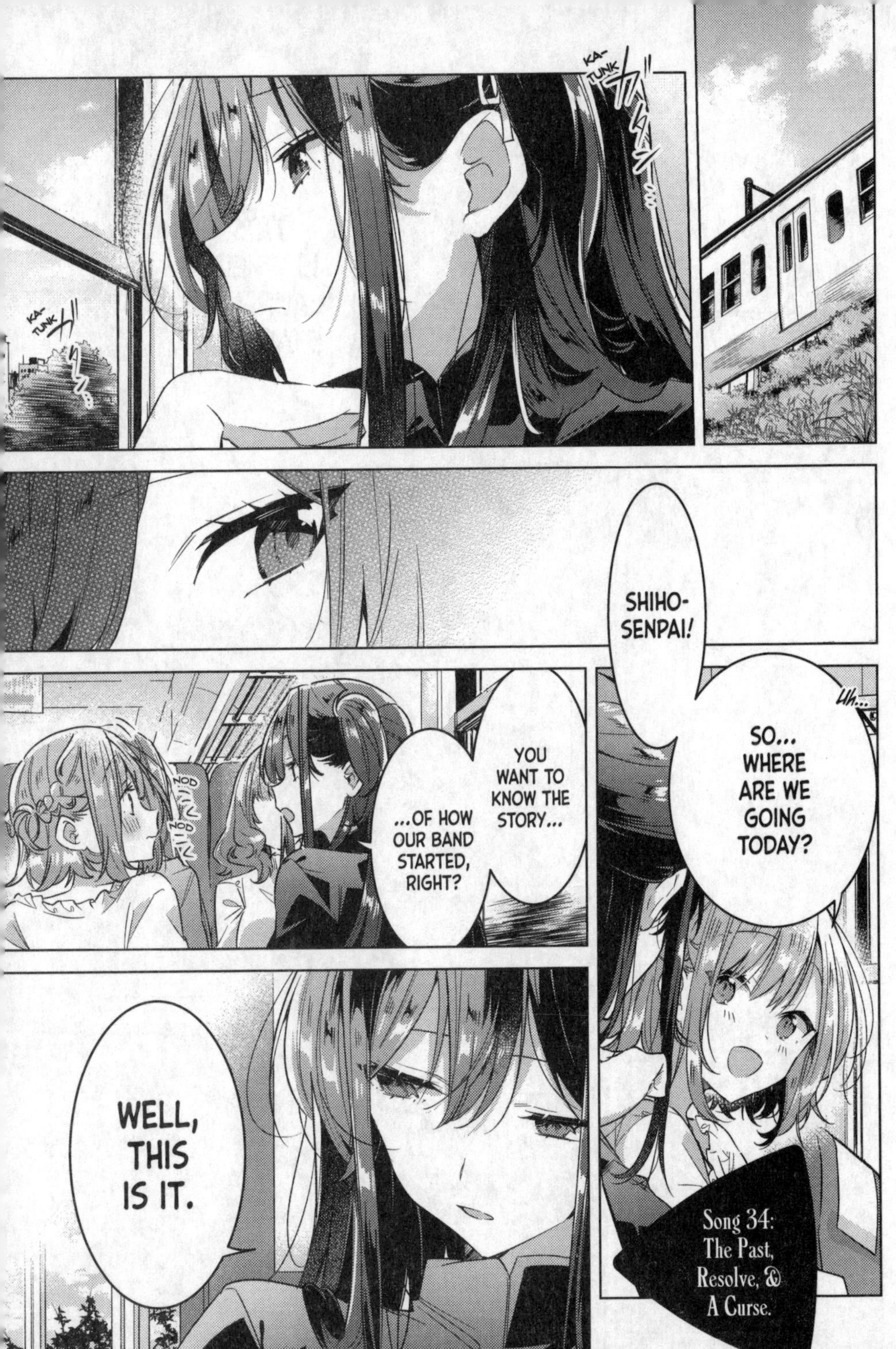
KA-TUNK
KA-TUNK
SHIHO-SENPAI!
Uh...
SO... WHERE ARE WE GOING TODAY?
Song 34: The Past, Resolve, & A Curse.
YOU WANT TO KNOW THE STORY...
...OF HOW OUR BAND STARTED, RIGHT?
NOD NOD
WELL, THIS IS IT.

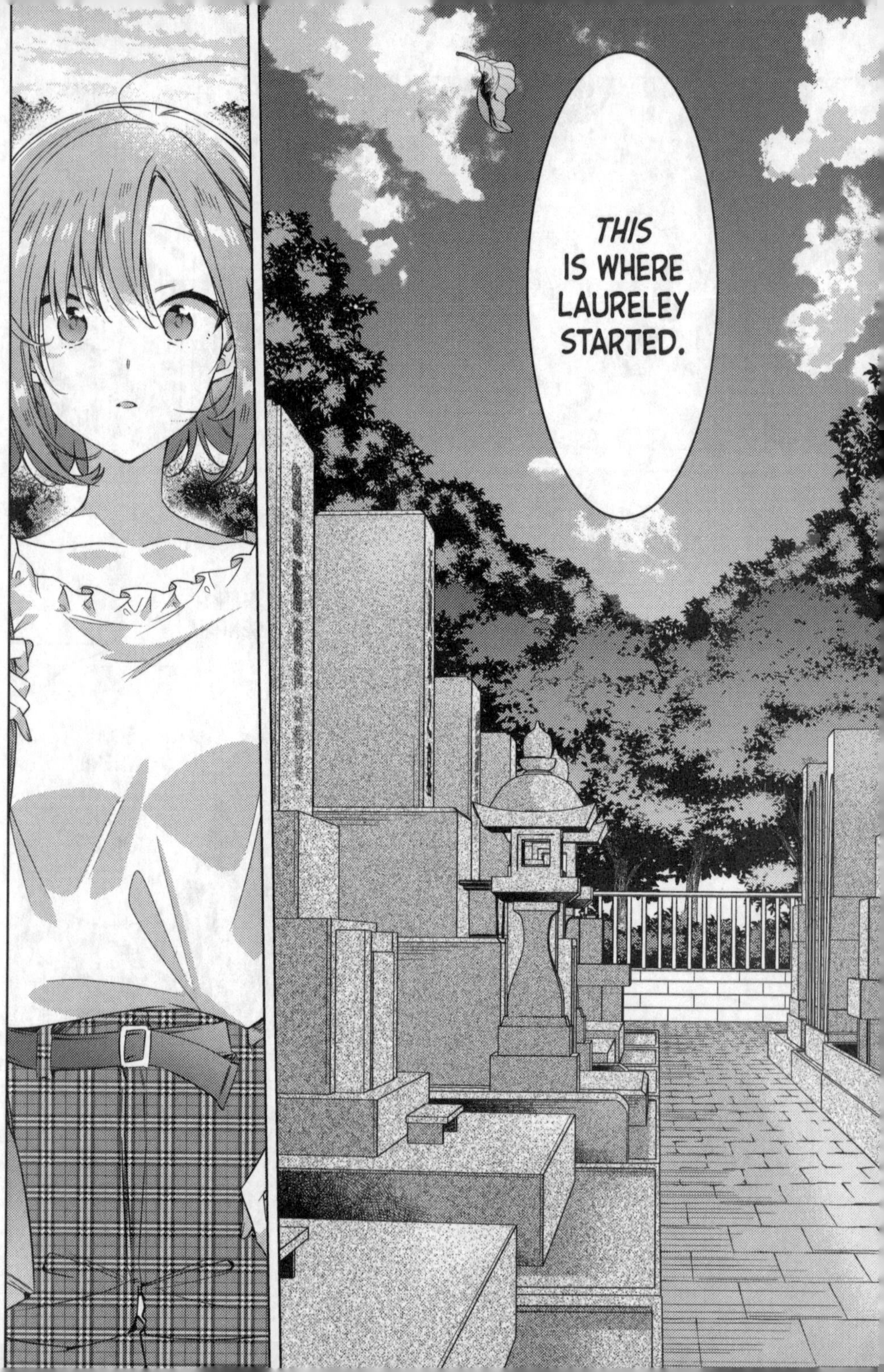
THIS IS WHERE LAURELEY STARTED.

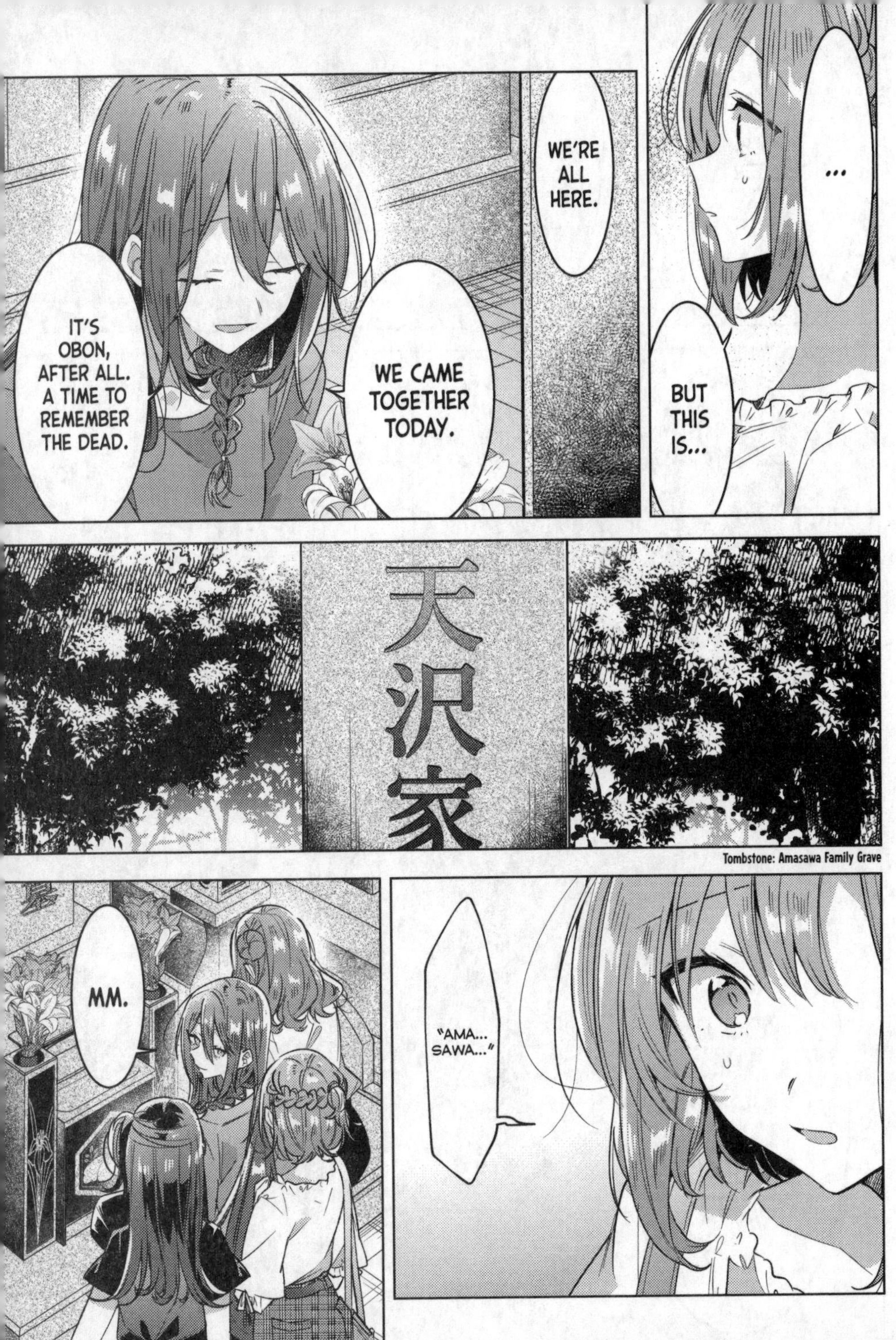
...
BUT THIS IS...
WE'RE ALL HERE.
WE CAME TOGETHER TODAY.
IT'S OBON, AFTER ALL. A TIME TO REMEMBER THE DEAD.
天沢家
"AMA... SAWA..."
MM.
Tombstone: Amasawa Family Grave

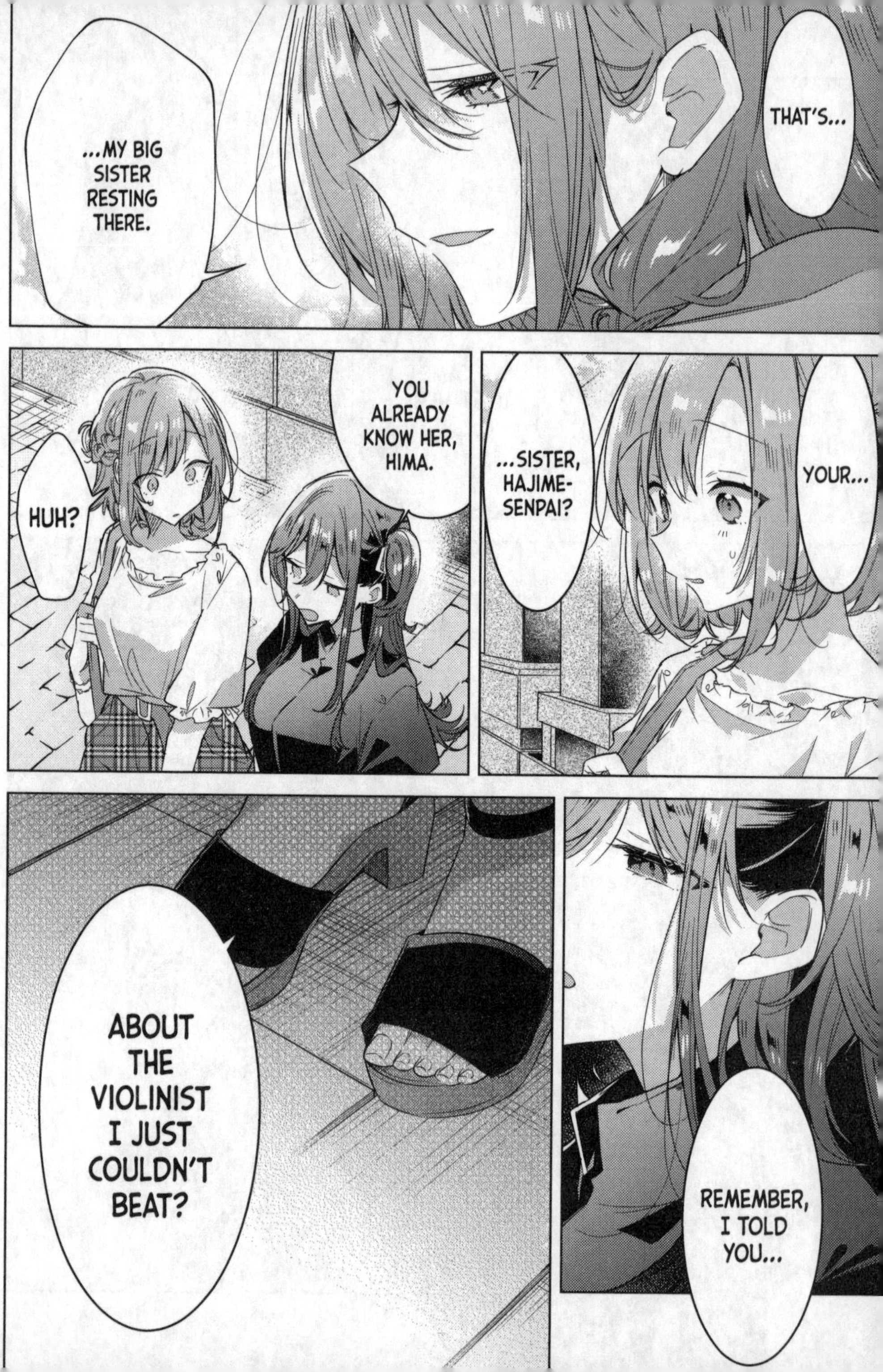
THAT'S...
...MY BIG SISTER RESTING THERE.
YOUR...
...SISTER, HAJIME-SENPAI?
YOU ALREADY KNOW HER, HIMA.
HUH?
REMEMBER, I TOLD YOU...
ABOUT THE VIOLINIST I JUST COULDN'T BEAT?

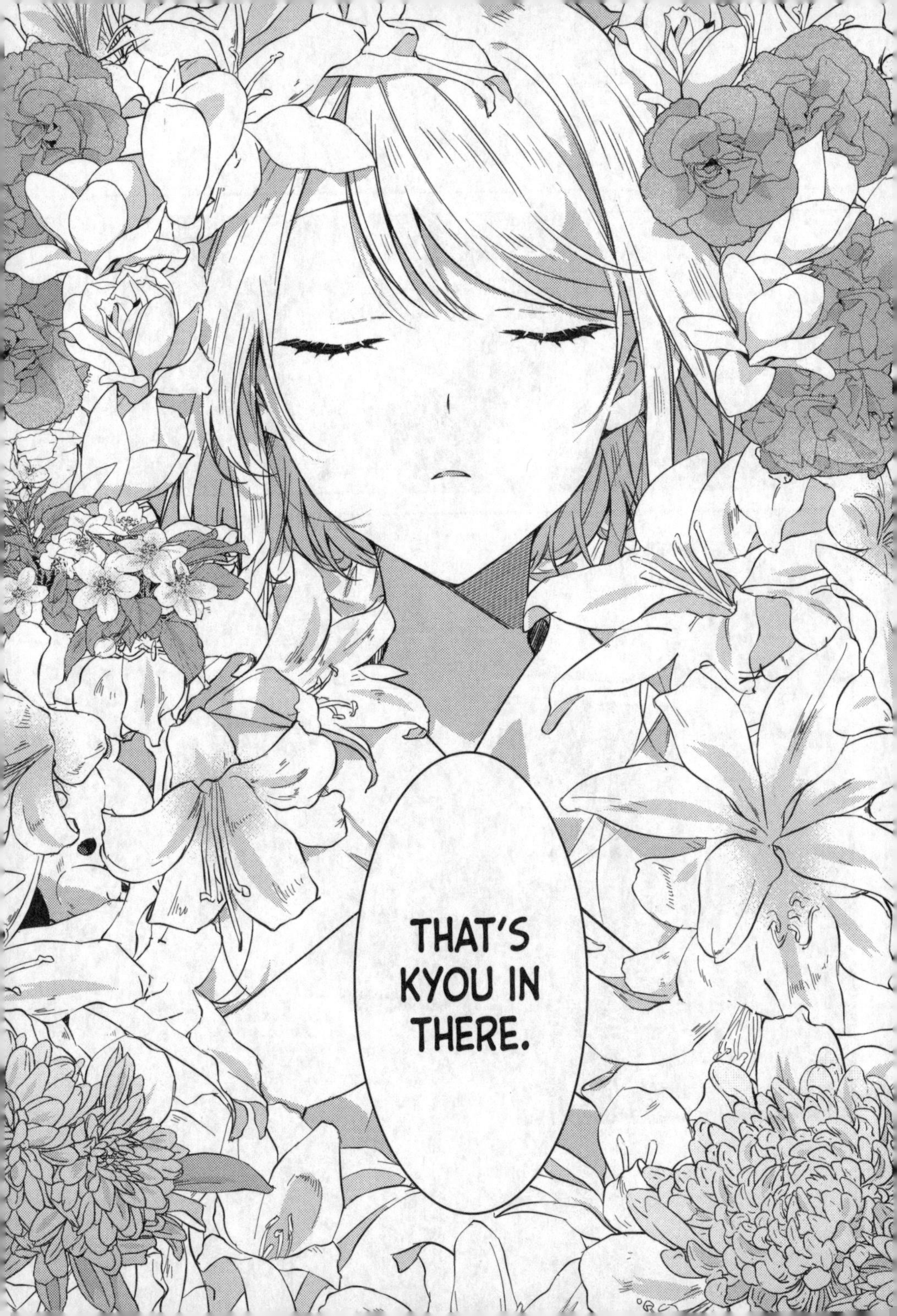
THAT'S KYOU IN THERE.

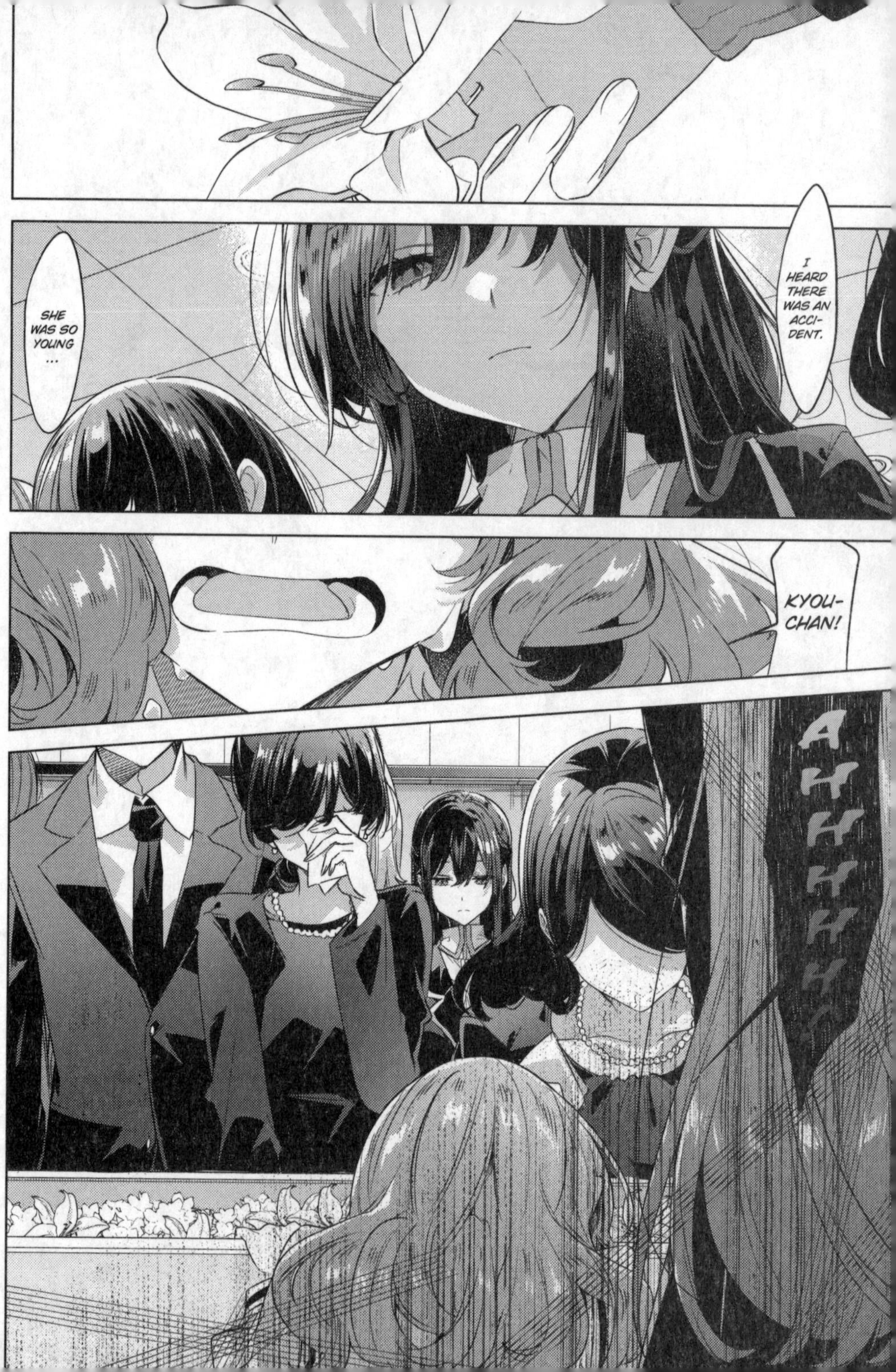
I HEARD THERE WAS AN ACCI-DENT.
SHE WAS SO YOUNG...
KYOU-CHAN!
AHHHHHH

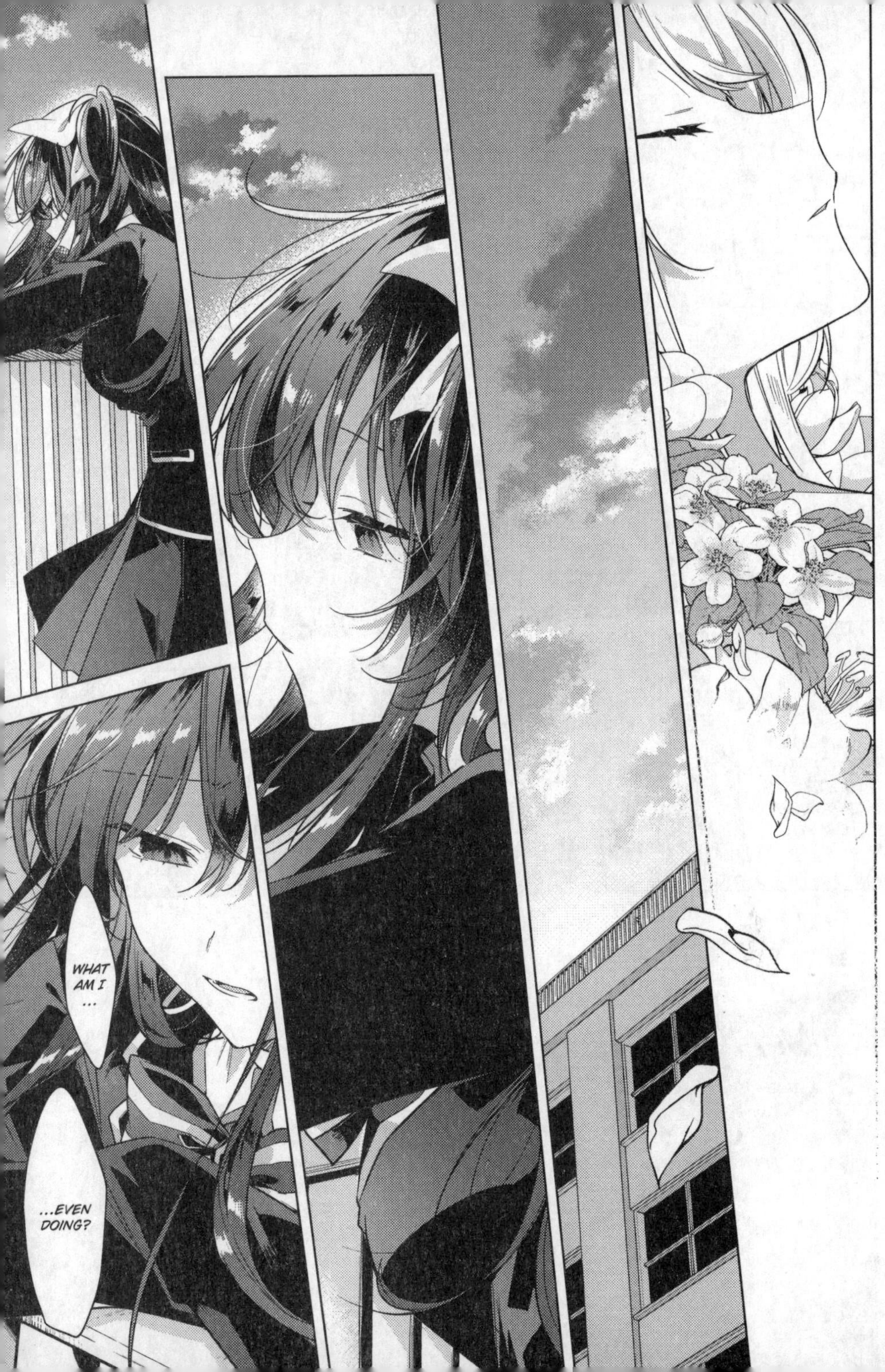
WHAT AM I ...
...EVEN DOING?

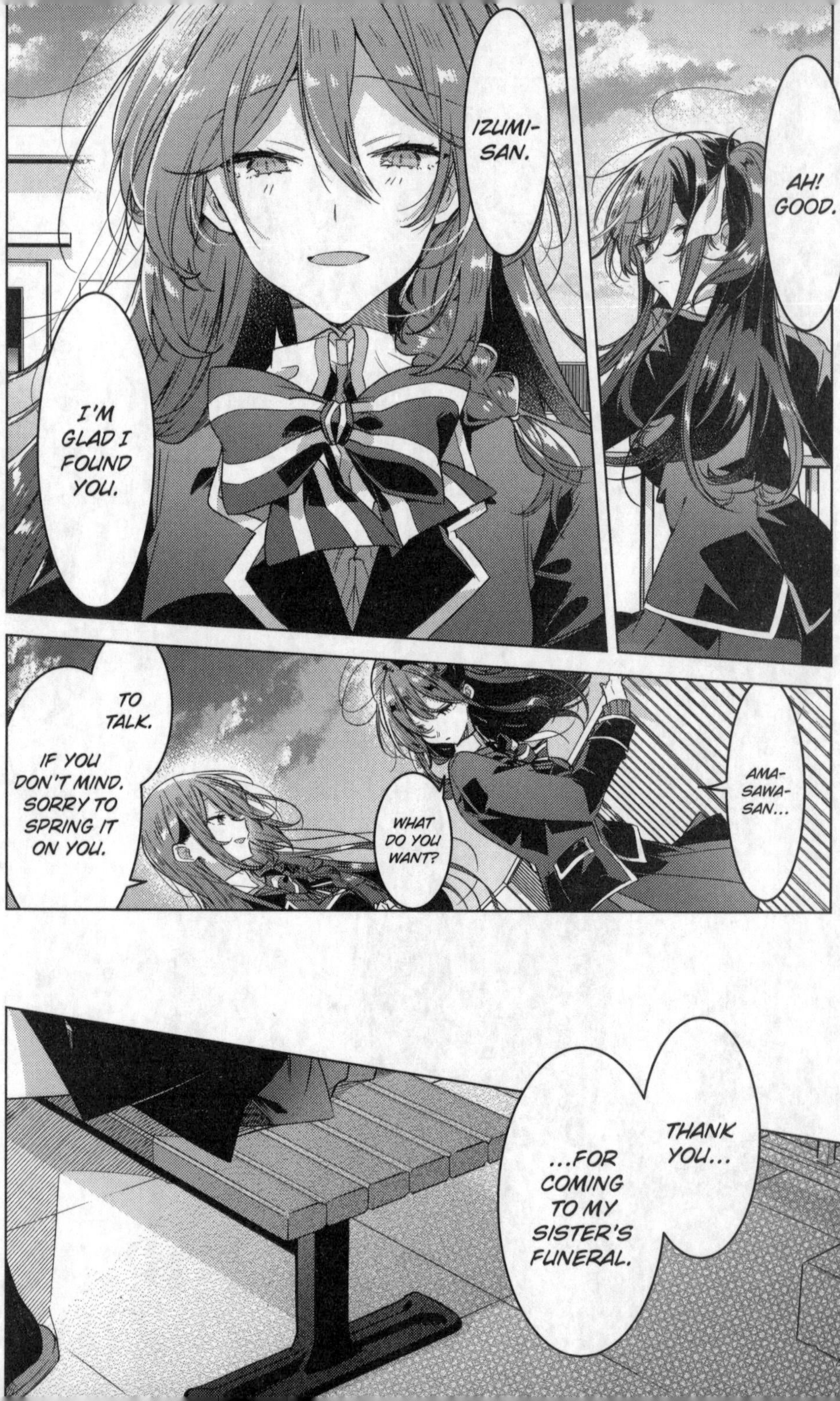
AH! GOOD.
IZUMI-SAN.
I'M GLAD I FOUND YOU.
AMA-SAWA-SAN...
WHAT DO YOU WANT?
TO TALK.
IF YOU DON'T MIND. SORRY TO SPRING IT ON YOU.
THANK YOU...
...FOR COMING TO MY SISTER'S FUNERAL.

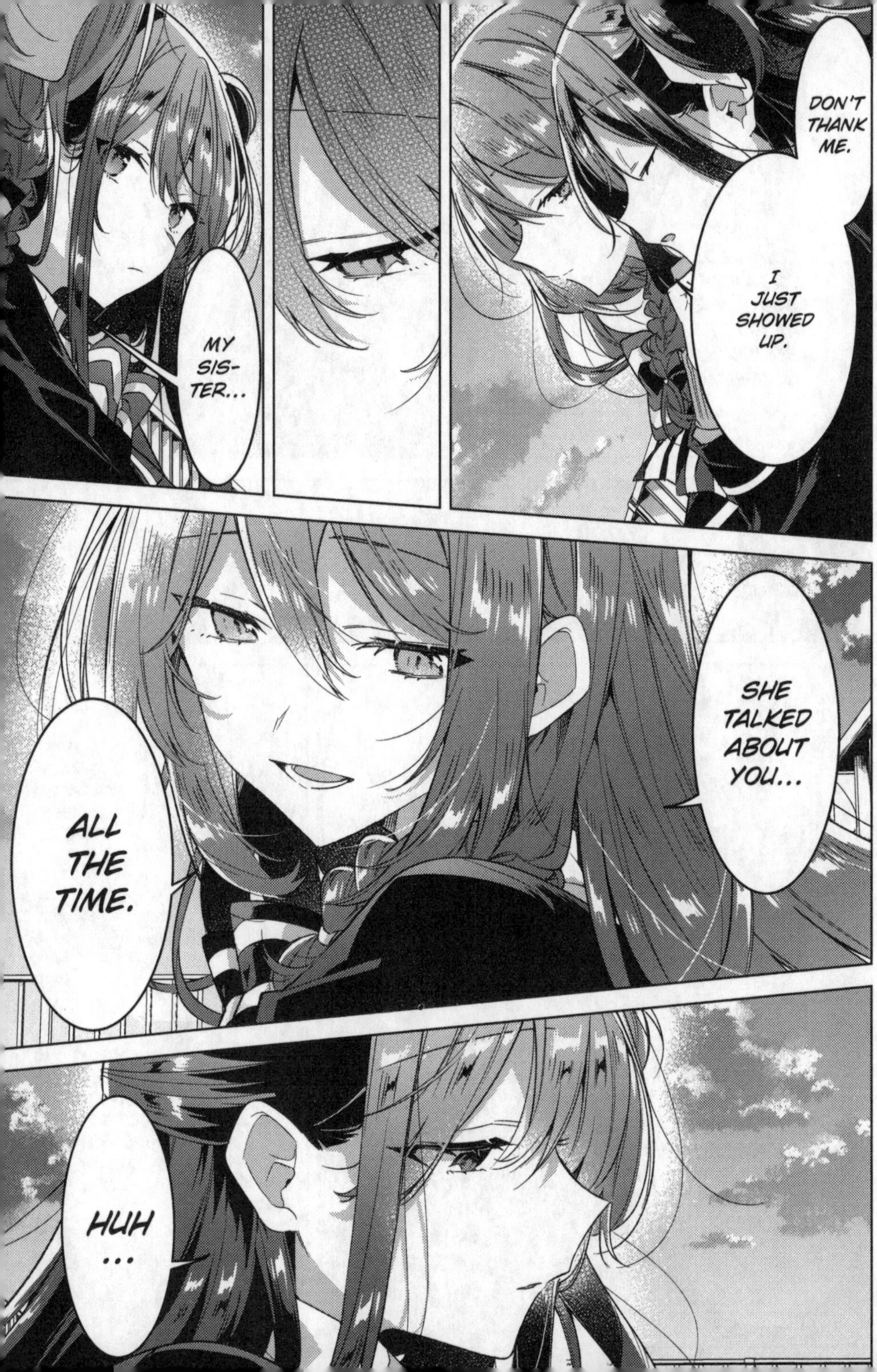
DON'T THANK ME.
I JUST SHOWED UP.
MY SIS-TER...
SHE TALKED ABOUT YOU...
ALL THE TIME.
HUH...

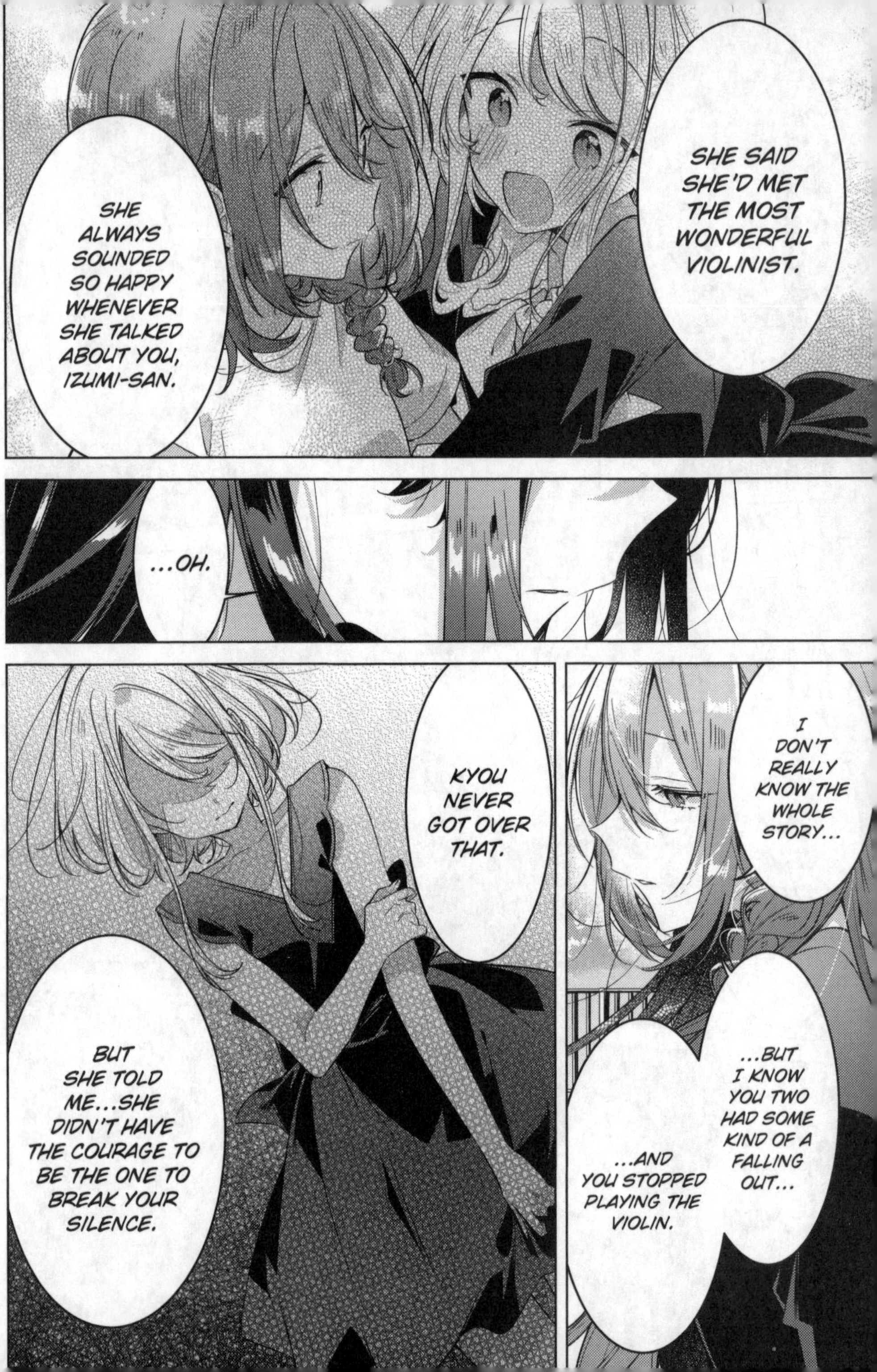
SHE SAID SHE'D MET THE MOST WONDERFUL VIOLINIST.
SHE ALWAYS SOUNDED SO HAPPY WHENEVER SHE TALKED ABOUT YOU, IZUMI-SAN.
...OH.
I DON'T REALLY KNOW THE WHOLE STORY...
...BUT I KNOW YOU TWO HAD SOME KIND OF A FALLING OUT...
...AND YOU STOPPED PLAYING THE VIOLIN.
KYOU NEVER GOT OVER THAT.
BUT SHE TOLD ME...SHE DIDN'T HAVE THE COURAGE TO BE THE ONE TO BREAK YOUR SILENCE.

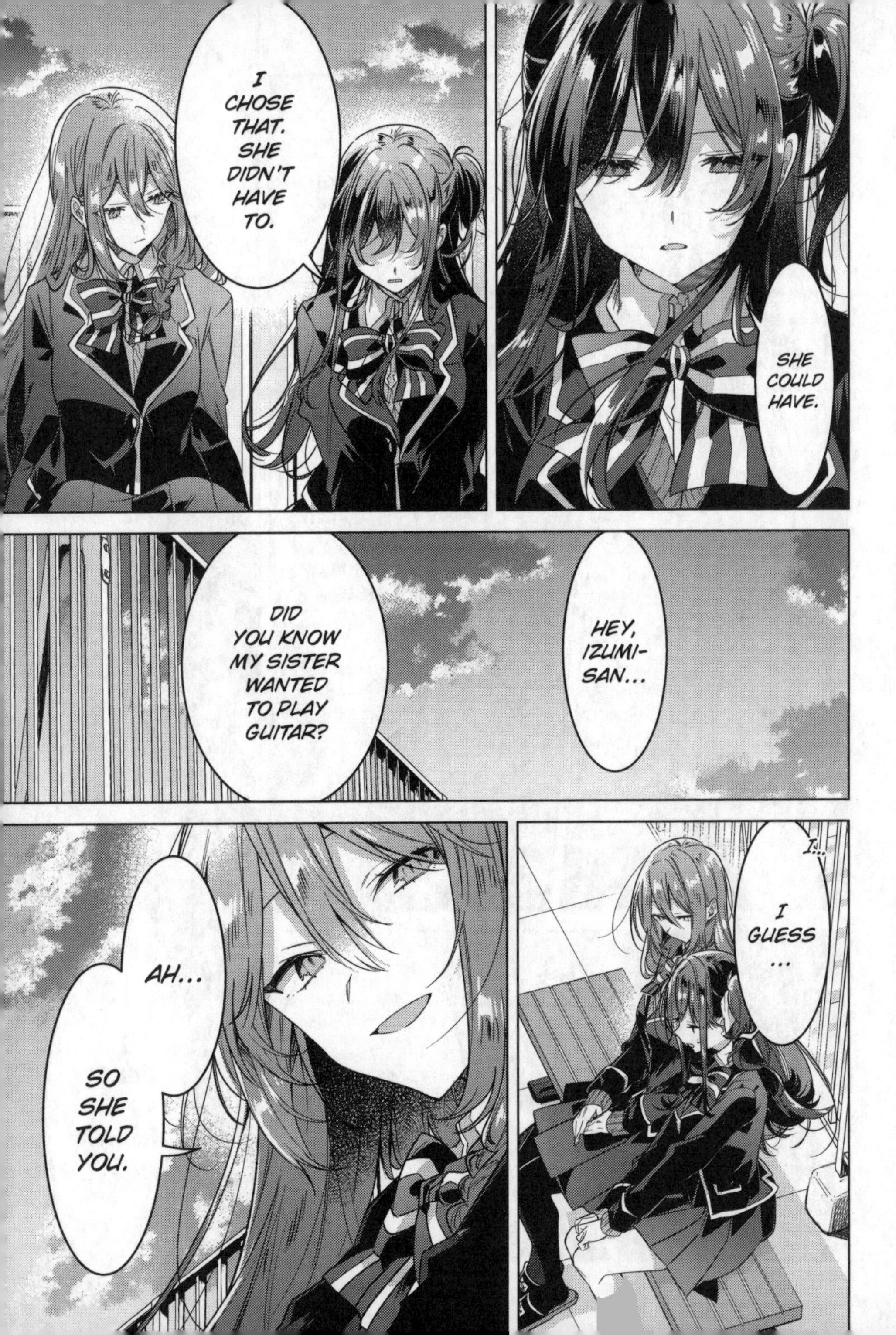
SHE COULD HAVE.
I CHOSE THAT. SHE DIDN'T HAVE TO.
HEY, IZUMI-SAN...
DID YOU KNOW MY SISTER WANTED TO PLAY GUITAR?
I...
I GUESS...
AH...
SO SHE TOLD YOU.

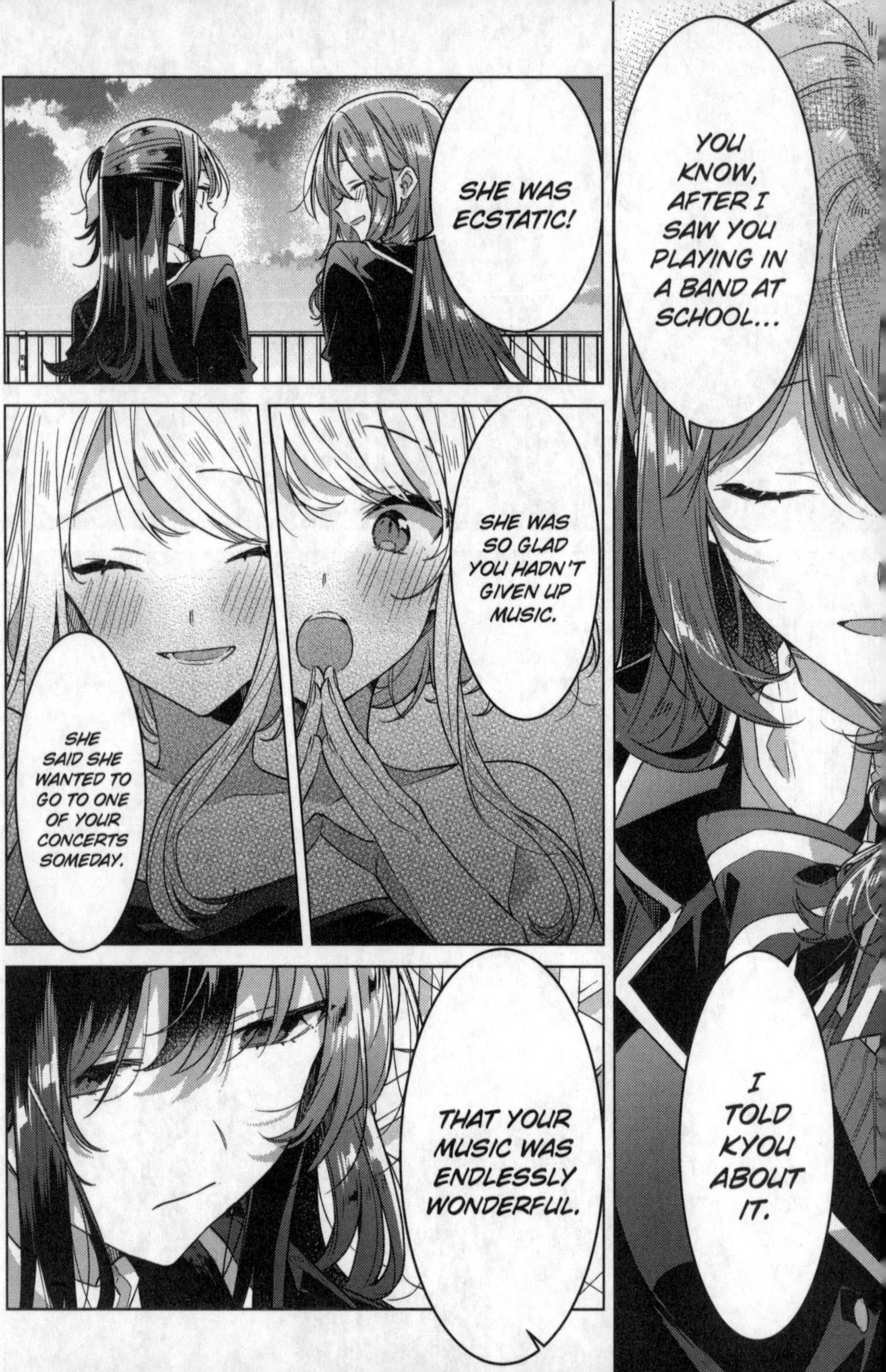
YOU KNOW, AFTER I SAW YOU PLAYING IN A BAND AT SCHOOL...
I TOLD KYOU ABOUT IT.
SHE WAS ECSTATIC!
SHE WAS SO GLAD YOU HADN'T GIVEN UP MUSIC.
SHE SAID SHE WANTED TO GO TO ONE OF YOUR CONCERTS SOMEDAY.
THAT YOUR MUSIC WAS ENDLESSLY WONDERFUL.

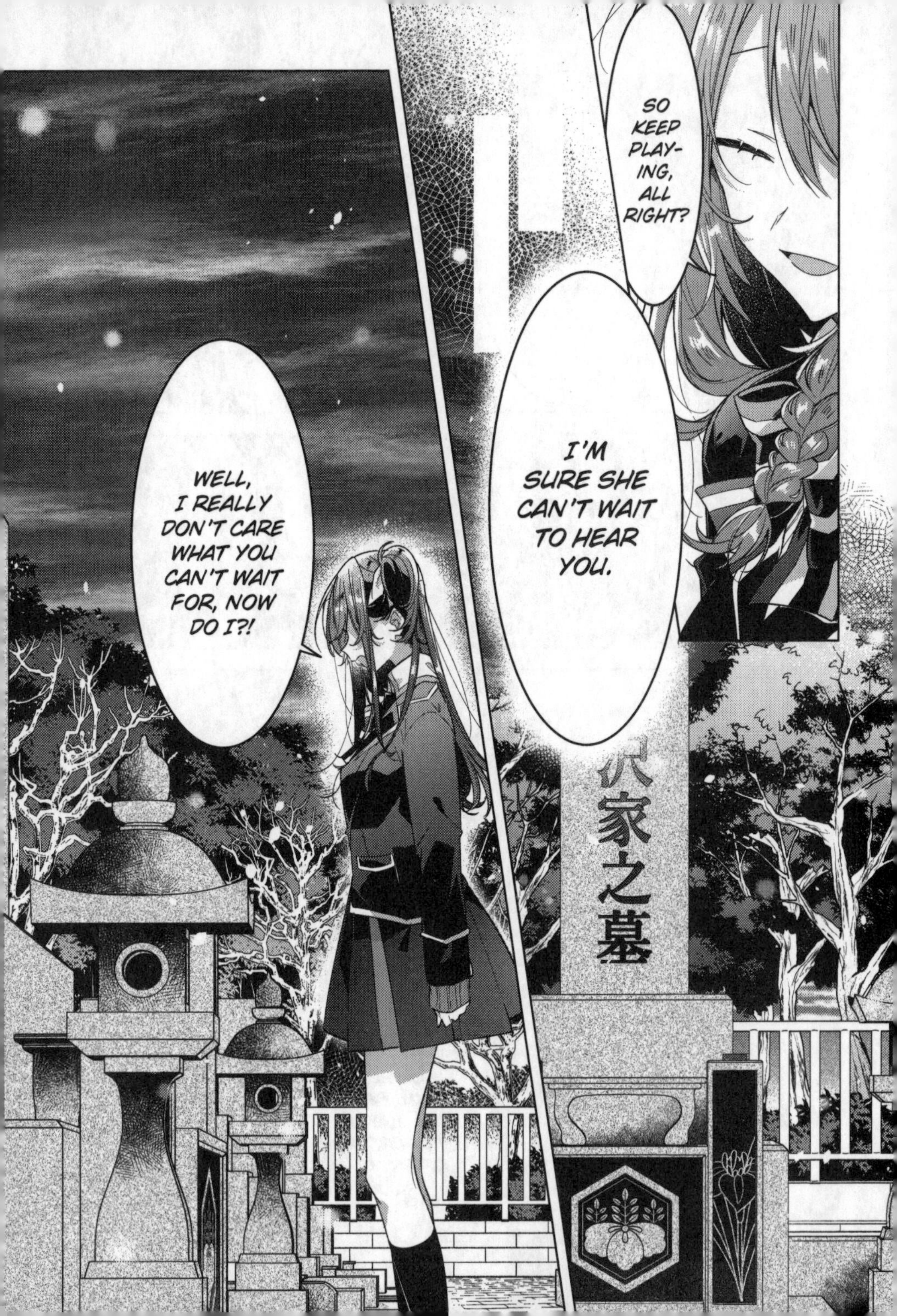
SO KEEP PLAY-ING, ALL RIGHT?
I'M SURE SHE CAN'T WAIT TO HEAR YOU.
家之墓
WELL, I REALLY DON'T CARE WHAT YOU CAN'T WAIT FOR, NOW DO I?!

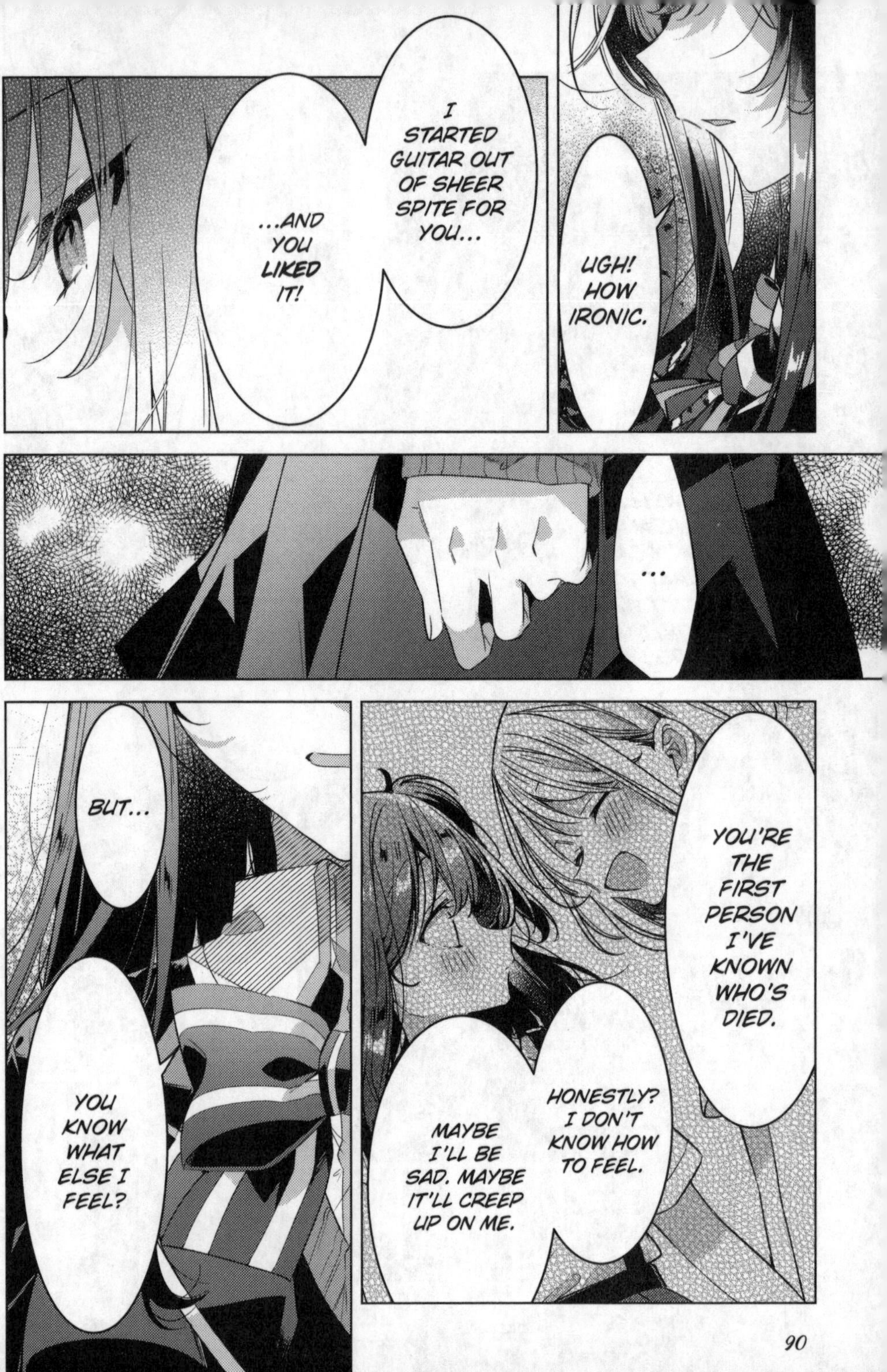
UGH! HOW IRONIC.
I STARTED GUITAR OUT OF SHEER SPITE FOR YOU...
...AND YOU LIKED IT!
...
YOU'RE THE FIRST PERSON I'VE KNOWN WHO'S DIED.
HONESTLY? I DON'T KNOW HOW TO FEEL.
MAYBE I'LL BE SAD. MAYBE IT'LL CREEP UP ON ME.
BUT...
YOU KNOW WHAT ELSE I FEEL?

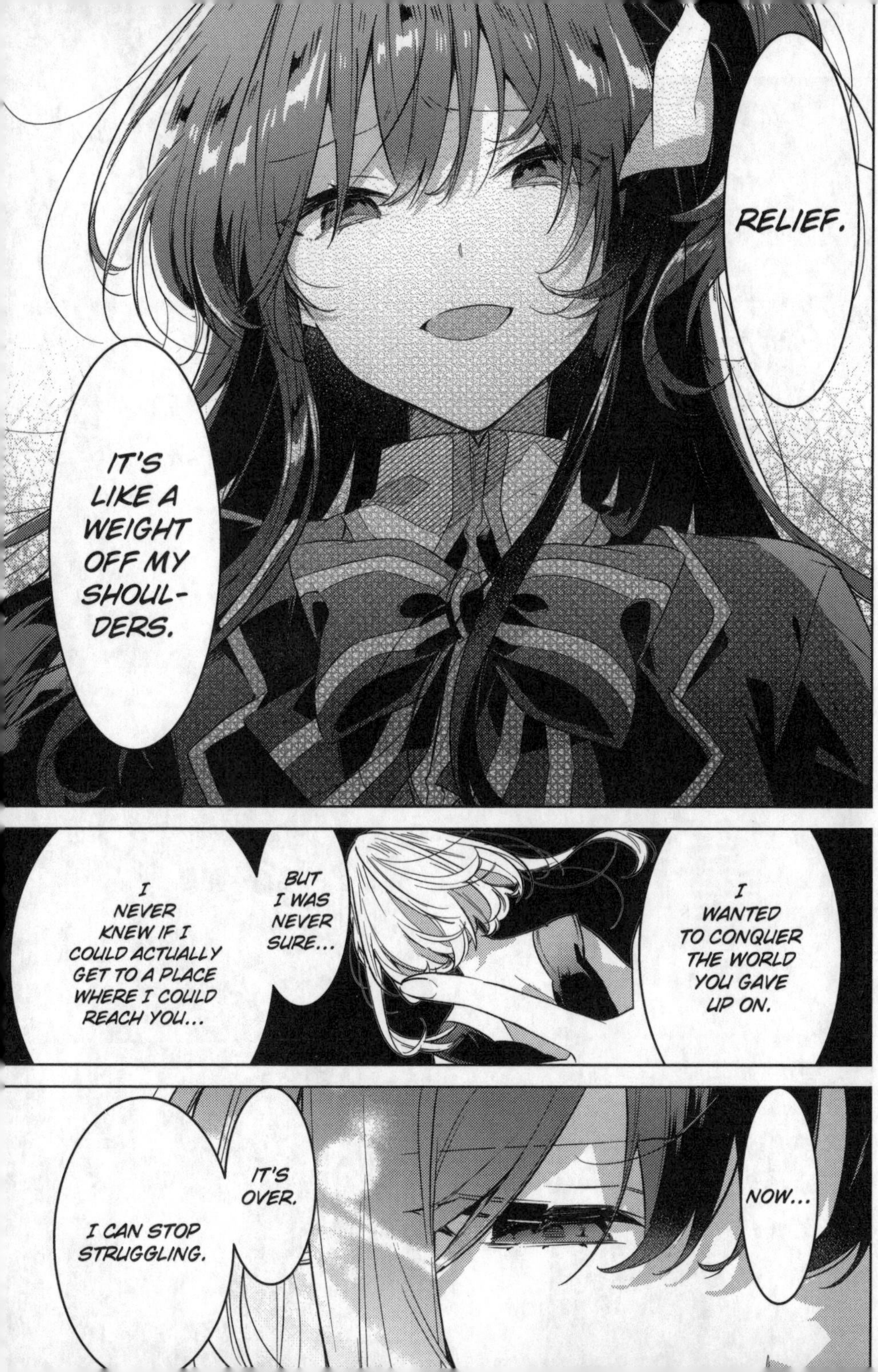
RELIEF.
IT'S LIKE A WEIGHT OFF MY SHOUL-DERS.
I WANTED TO CONQUER THE WORLD YOU GAVE UP ON.
BUT I WAS NEVER SURE...
I NEVER KNEW IF I COULD ACTUALLY GET TO A PLACE WHERE I COULD REACH YOU...
NOW...
IT'S OVER.
I CAN STOP STRUGGLING.

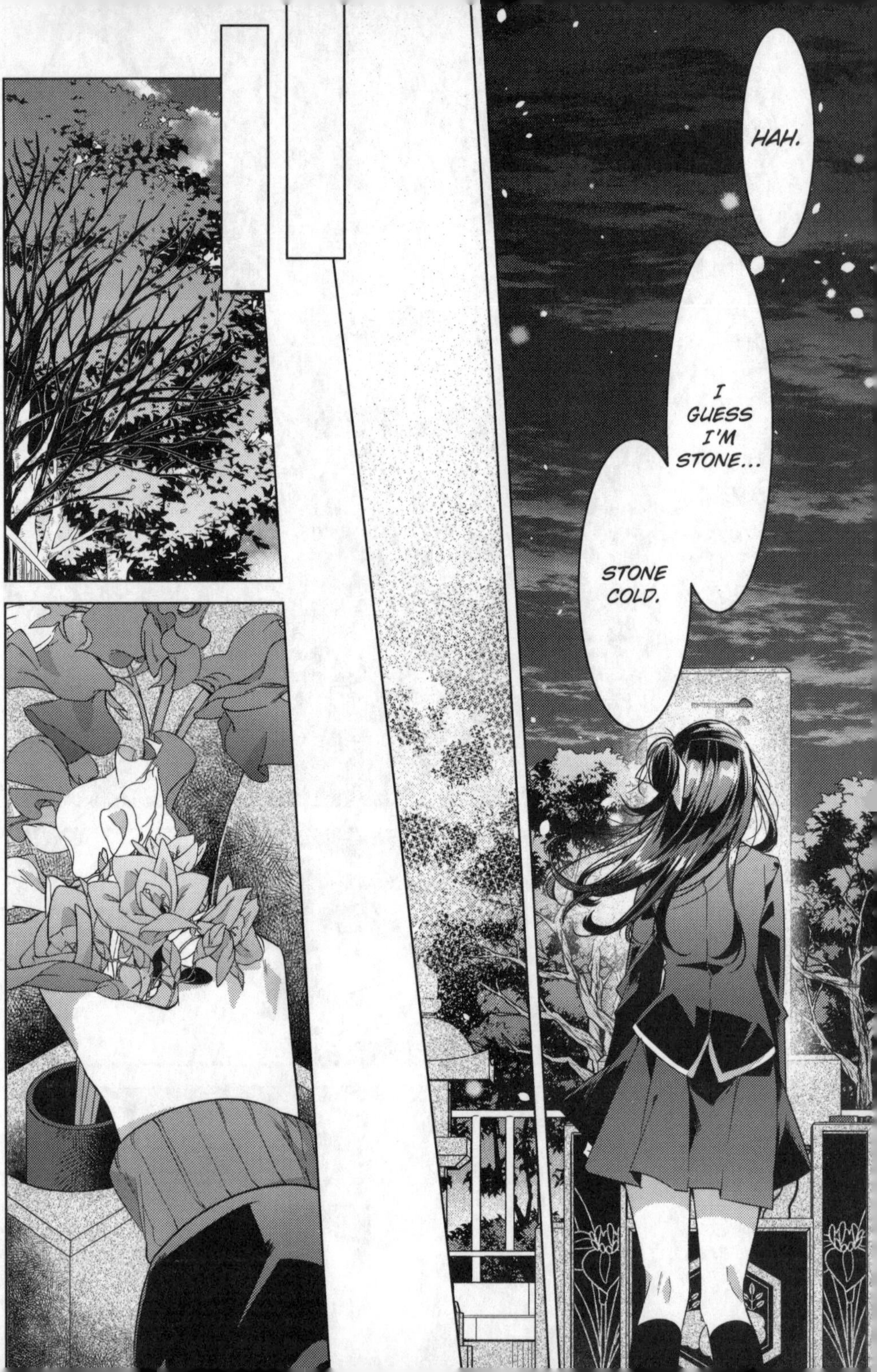
HAH.
I GUESS I'M STONE...
STONE COLD.

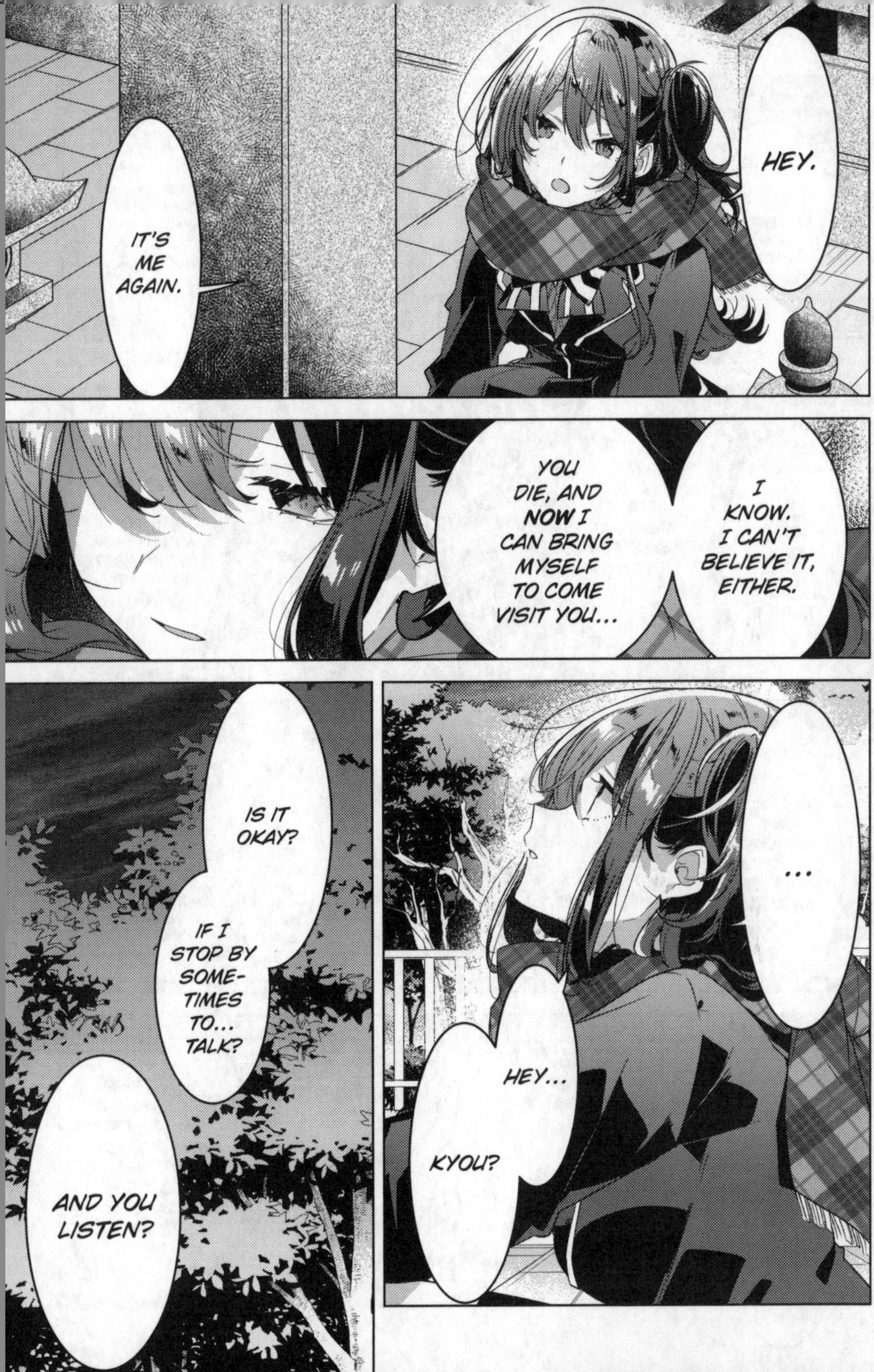
HEY.
IT'S ME AGAIN.
YOU DIE, AND NOW I CAN BRING MYSELF TO COME VISIT YOU...
I KNOW. I CAN'T BELIEVE IT, EITHER.
...
HEY...
KYOU?
IS IT OKAY?
IF I STOP BY SOME-TIMES TO... TALK?
AND YOU LISTEN?

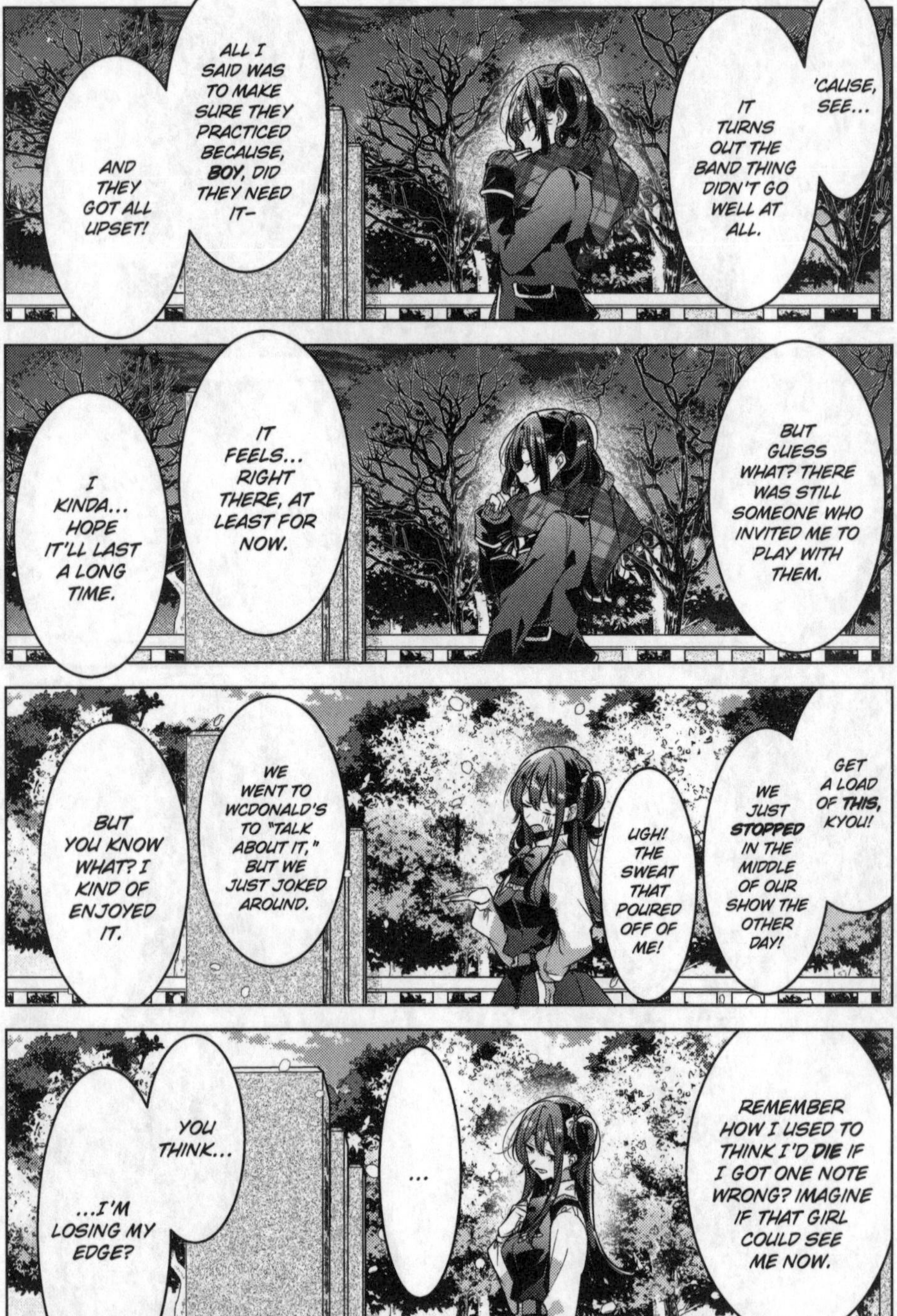
'CAUSE, SEE...
IT TURNS OUT THE BAND THING DIDN'T GO WELL AT ALL.
ALL I SAID WAS TO MAKE SURE THEY PRACTICED BECAUSE, **BOY**, DID THEY NEED IT-
AND THEY GOT ALL UPSET!
BUT GUESS WHAT? THERE WAS STILL SOMEONE WHO INVITED ME TO PLAY WITH THEM.
IT FEELS... RIGHT THERE, AT LEAST FOR NOW.
I KINDA... HOPE IT'LL LAST A LONG TIME.
GET A LOAD OF **THIS**, KYOU!
WE JUST **STOPPED** IN THE MIDDLE OF OUR SHOW THE OTHER DAY!
UGH! THE SWEAT THAT POURED OFF OF ME!
WE WENT TO WCDONALD'S TO "TALK ABOUT IT," BUT WE JUST JOKED AROUND.
BUT YOU KNOW WHAT? I KIND OF ENJOYED IT.
REMEMBER HOW I USED TO THINK I'D **DIE** IF I GOT ONE NOTE WRONG? IMAGINE IF THAT GIRL COULD SEE ME NOW.
...
YOU THINK...
...I'M LOSING MY EDGE?

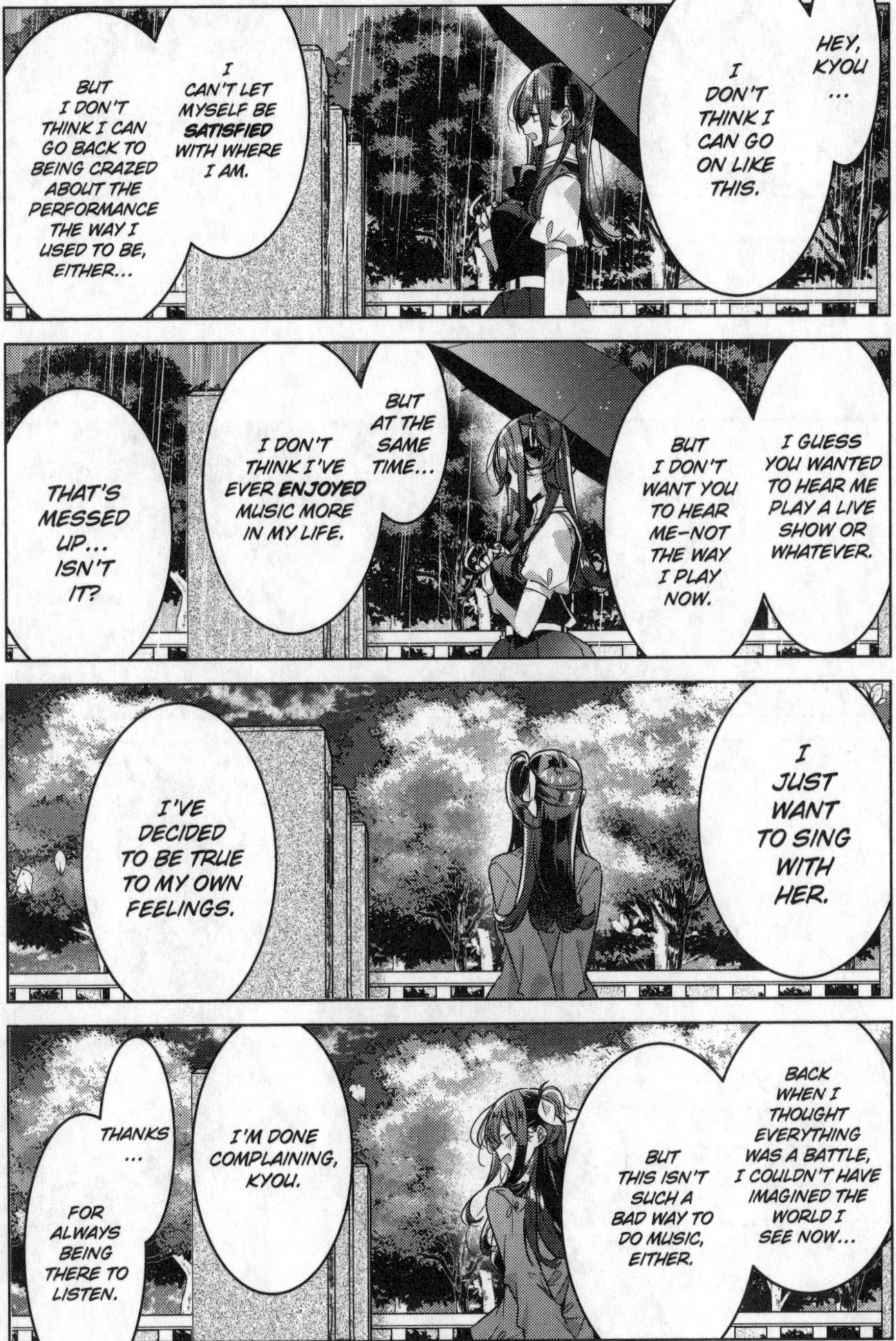
HEY, KYOU...
I DON'T THINK I CAN GO ON LIKE THIS.
I CAN'T LET MYSELF BE **SATISFIED** WITH WHERE I AM.
BUT I DON'T THINK I CAN GO BACK TO BEING CRAZED ABOUT THE PERFORMANCE THE WAY I USED TO BE, EITHER...
I GUESS YOU WANTED TO HEAR ME PLAY A LIVE SHOW OR WHATEVER.
BUT I DON'T WANT YOU TO HEAR ME—NOT THE WAY I PLAY NOW.
BUT AT THE SAME TIME...
I DON'T THINK I'VE EVER **ENJOYED** MUSIC MORE IN MY LIFE.
THAT'S MESSED UP... ISN'T IT?
I JUST WANT TO SING WITH HER.
I'VE DECIDED TO BE TRUE TO MY OWN FEELINGS.
BACK WHEN I THOUGHT EVERYTHING WAS A BATTLE, I COULDN'T HAVE IMAGINED THE WORLD I SEE NOW...
BUT THIS ISN'T SUCH A BAD WAY TO DO MUSIC, EITHER.
I'M DONE COMPLAINING, KYOU.
THANKS...
FOR ALWAYS BEING THERE TO LISTEN.

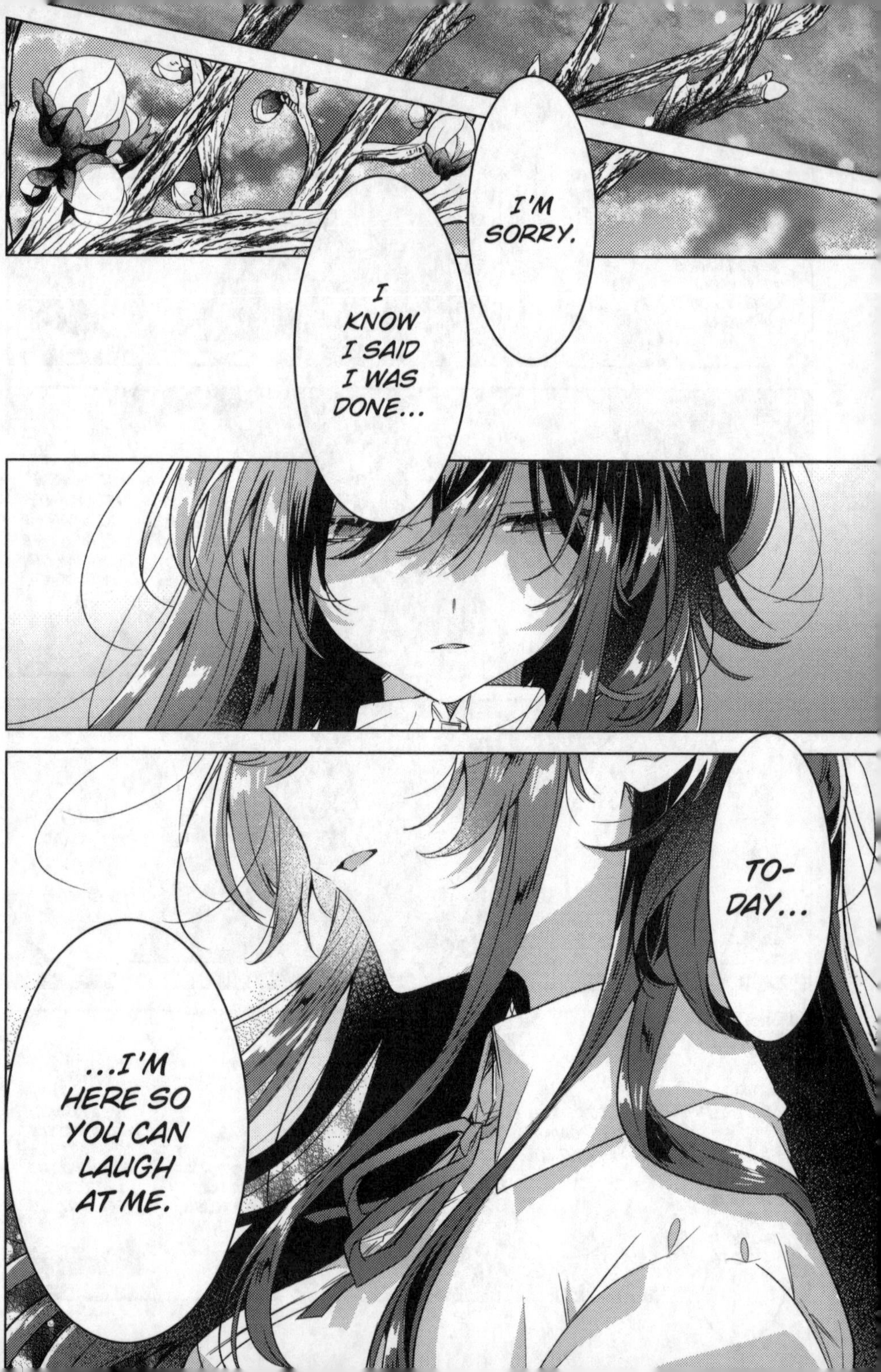
I'M SORRY.
I KNOW I SAID I WAS DONE...
TO-DAY...
...I'M HERE SO YOU CAN LAUGH AT ME.

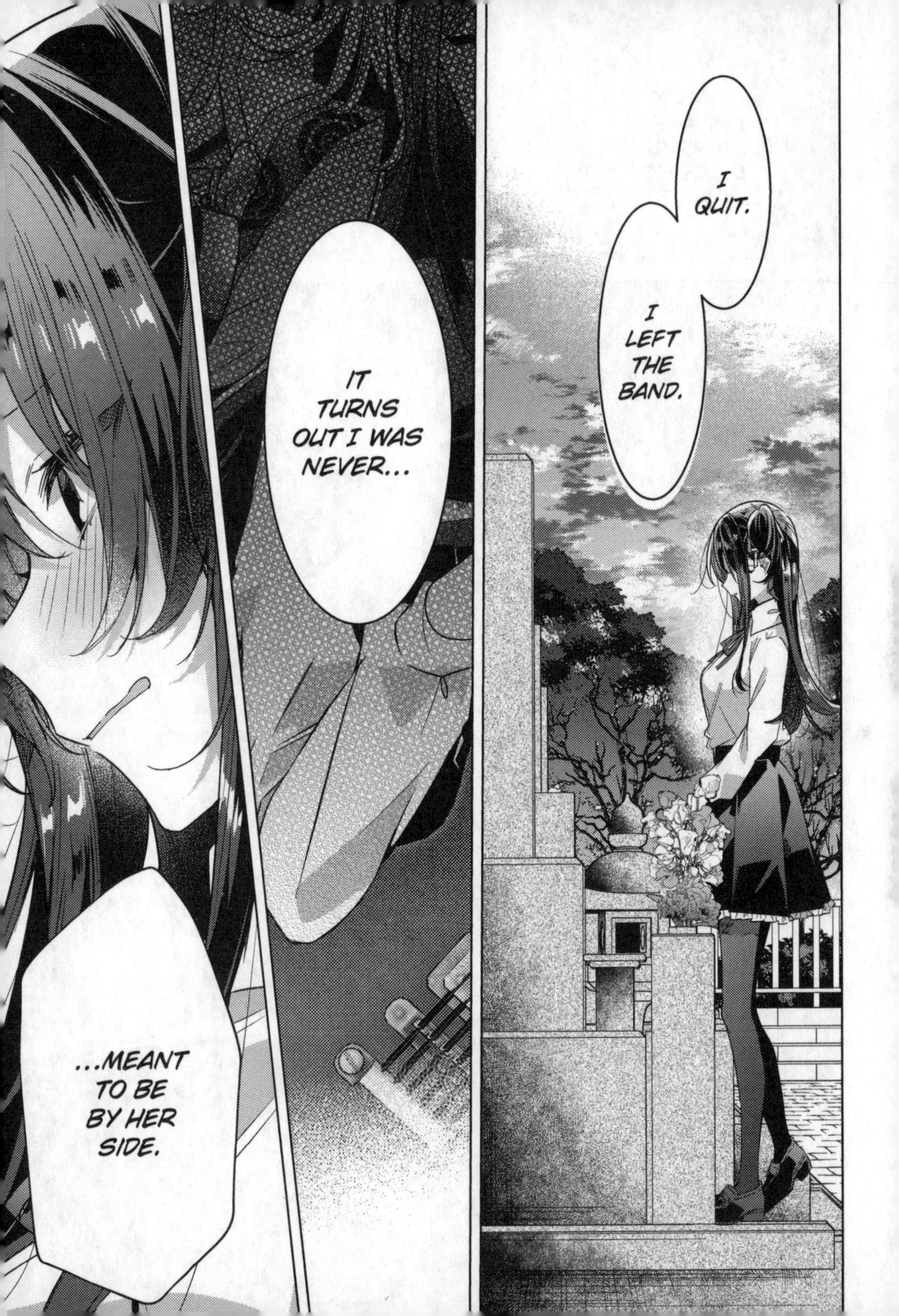
I QUIT.
I LEFT THE BAND.
IT TURNS OUT I WAS NEVER...
...MEANT TO BE BY HER SIDE.

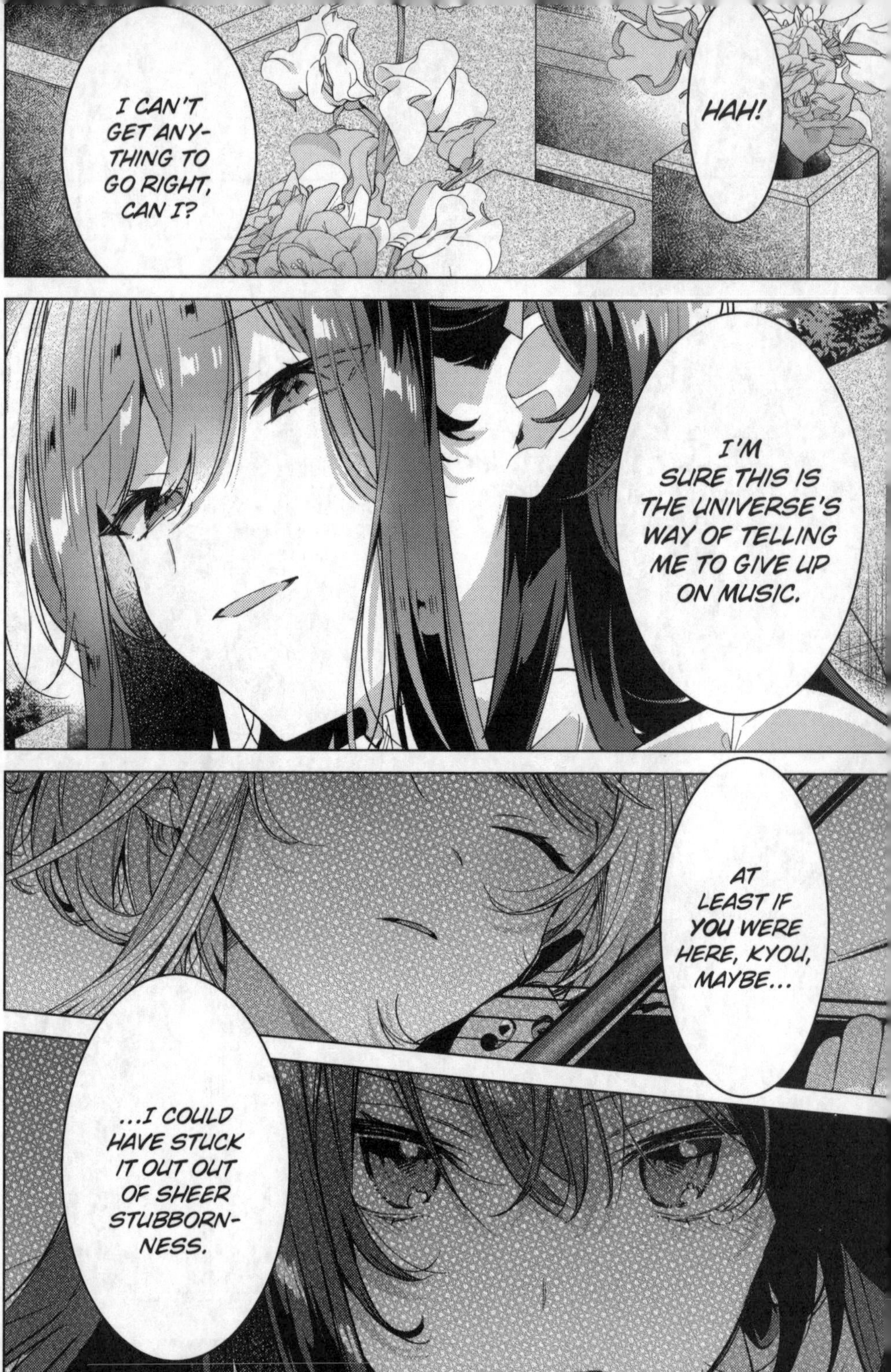
HAH!
I CAN'T GET ANY-THING TO GO RIGHT, CAN I?
I'M SURE THIS IS THE UNIVERSE'S WAY OF TELLING ME TO GIVE UP ON MUSIC.
AT LEAST IF YOU WERE HERE, KYOU, MAYBE...
...I COULD HAVE STUCK IT OUT OUT OF SHEER STUBBORN-NESS.

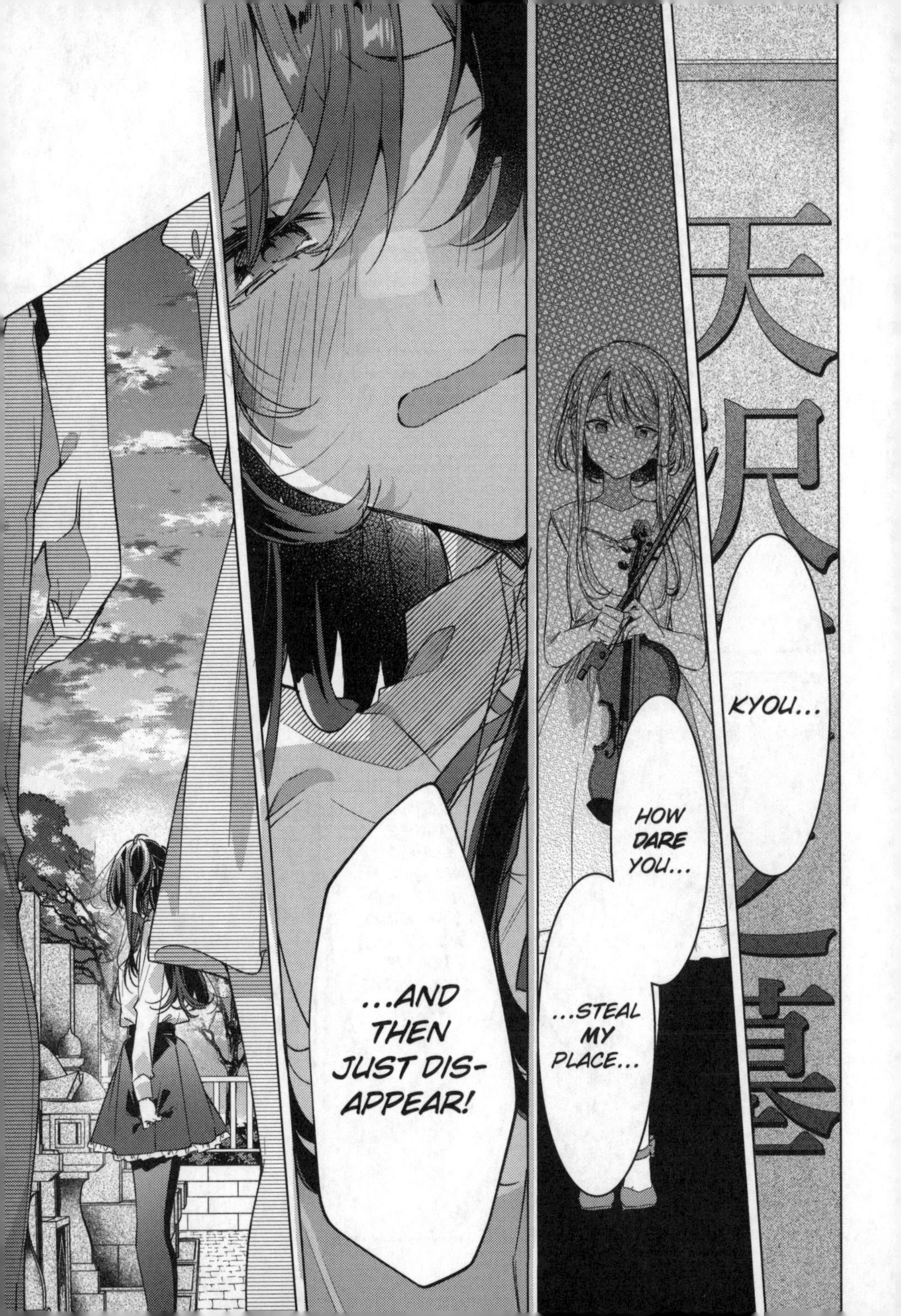
KYOU…
HOW DARE YOU…
…STEAL MY PLACE…
…AND THEN JUST DIS-APPEAR!

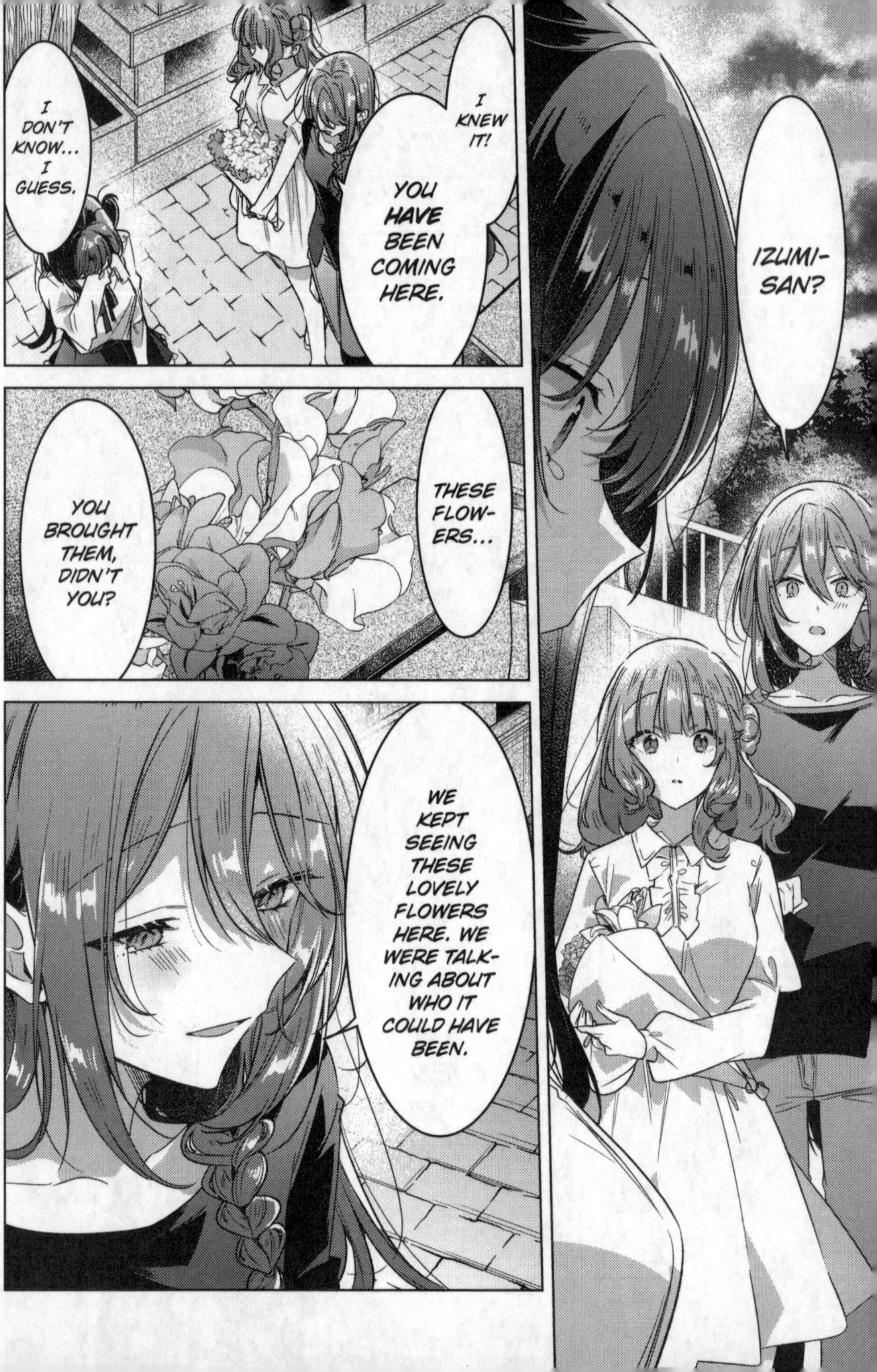
IZUMI-SAN?
I KNEW IT! YOU HAVE BEEN COMING HERE.
I DON'T KNOW... I GUESS.
THESE FLOW-ERS...
YOU BROUGHT THEM, DIDN'T YOU?
WE KEPT SEEING THESE LOVELY FLOWERS HERE. WE WERE TALK-ING ABOUT WHO IT COULD HAVE BEEN.

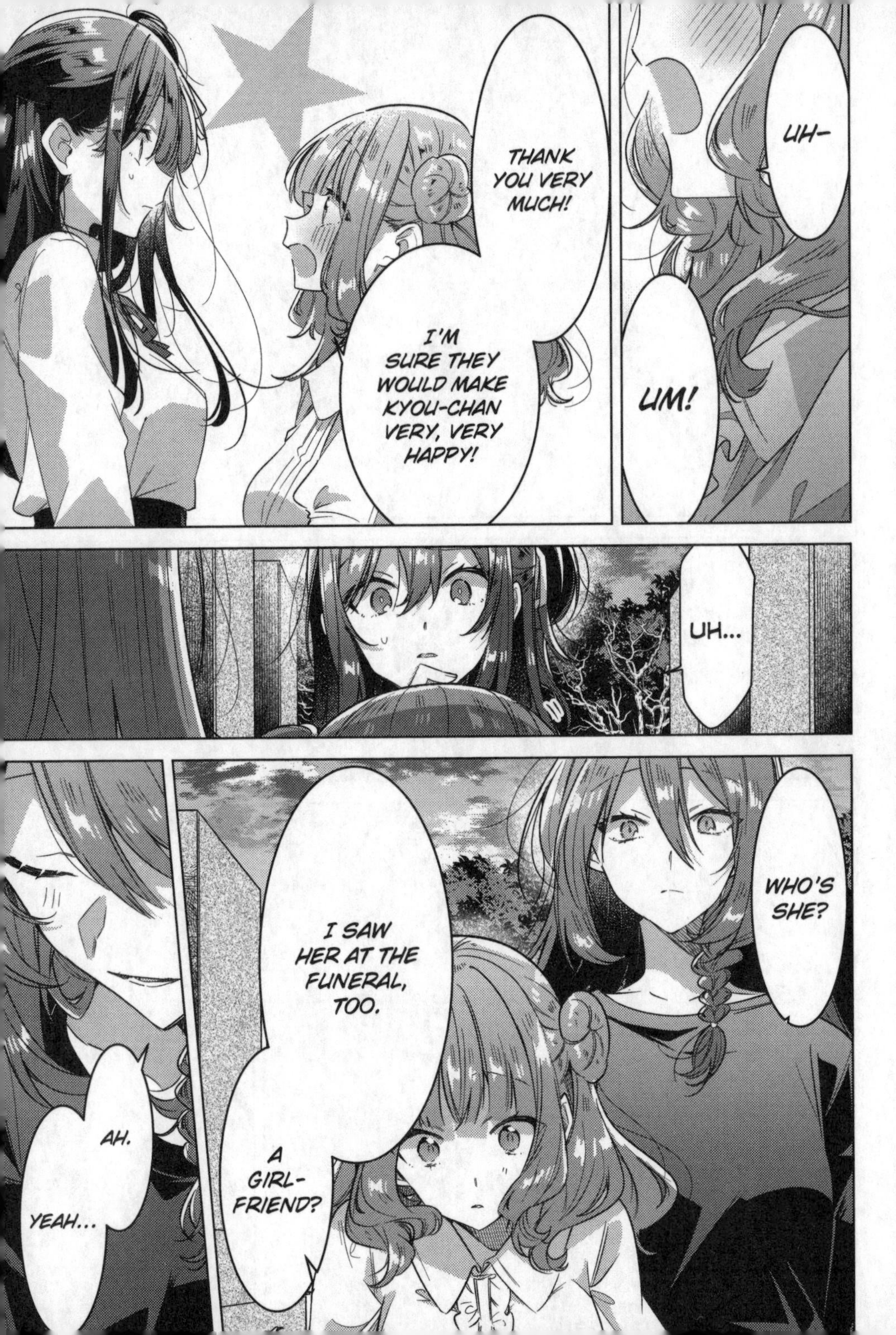
UH-
UM!
THANK YOU VERY MUCH!
I'M SURE THEY WOULD MAKE KYOU-CHAN VERY, VERY HAPPY!
UH...
WHO'S SHE?
I SAW HER AT THE FUNERAL, TOO.
A GIRL-FRIEND?
AH.
YEAH...

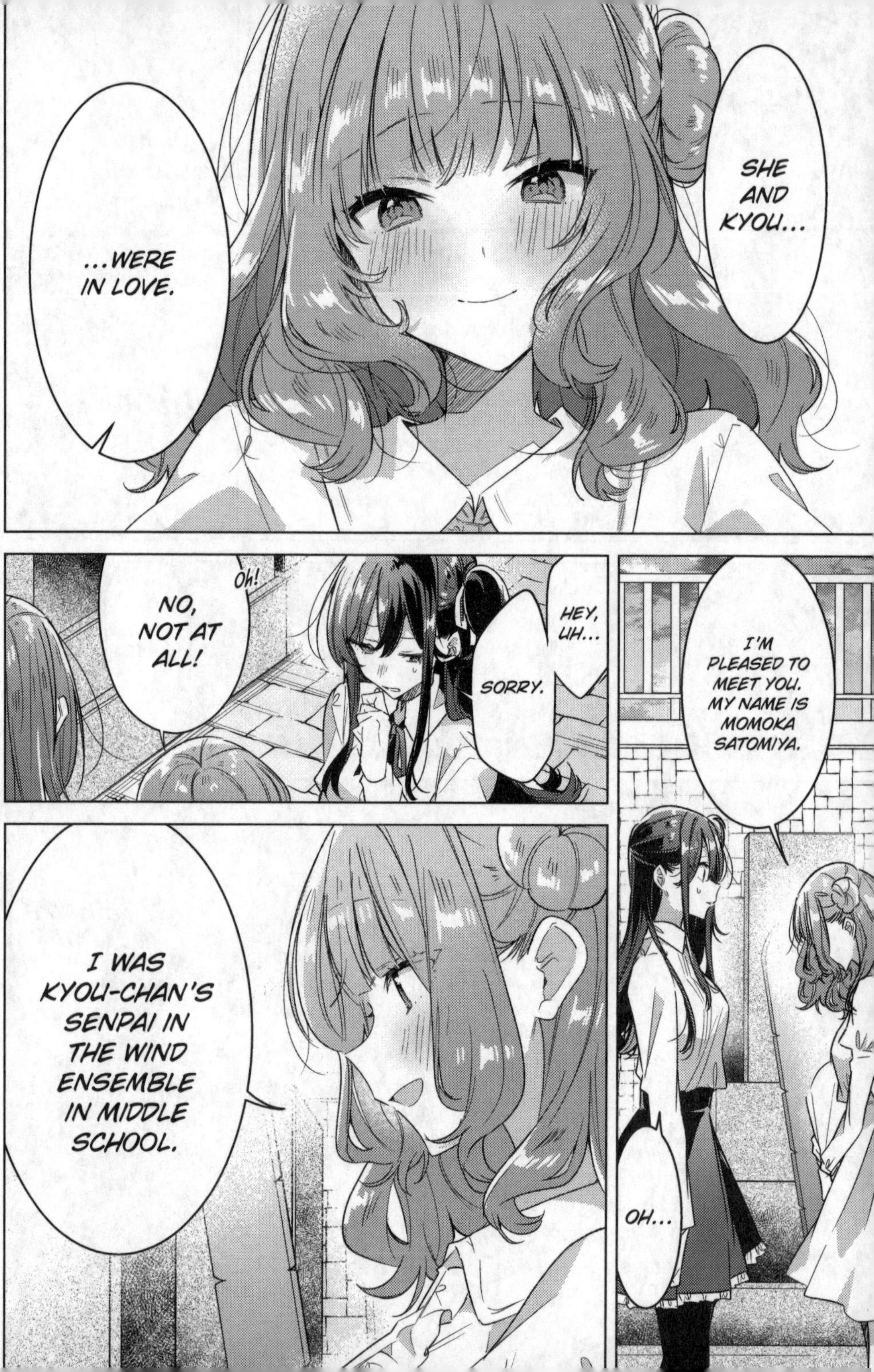
SHE AND KYOU...
...WERE IN LOVE.
I'M PLEASED TO MEET YOU. MY NAME IS MOMOKA SATOMIYA.
OH...
HEY, UH...
SORRY.
Oh!
NO, NOT AT ALL!
I WAS KYOU-CHAN'S SENPAI IN THE WIND ENSEMBLE IN MIDDLE SCHOOL.

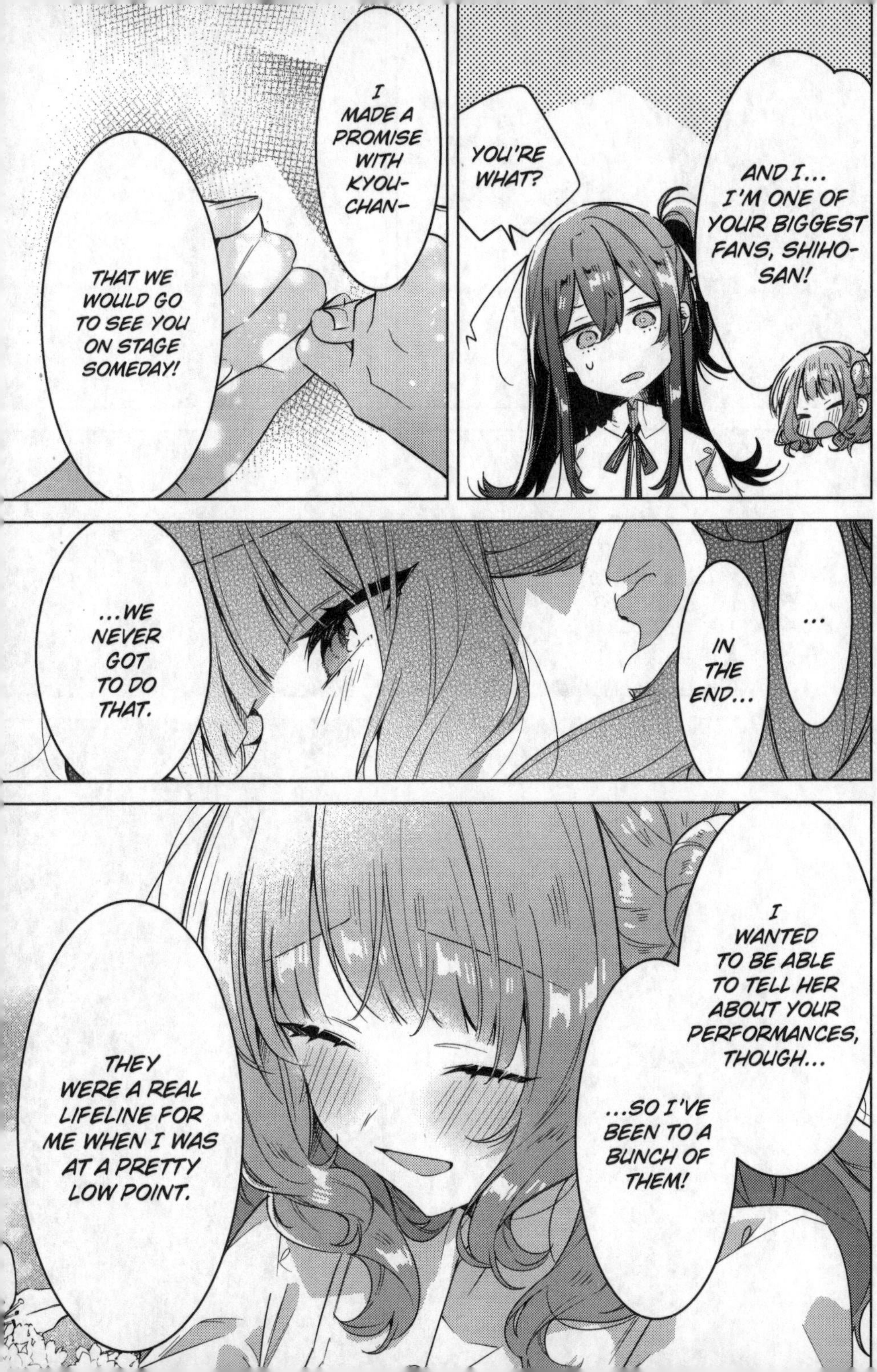
AND I... I'M ONE OF YOUR BIGGEST FANS, SHIHO-SAN!
YOU'RE WHAT?
I MADE A PROMISE WITH KYOU-CHAN-
THAT WE WOULD GO TO SEE YOU ON STAGE SOMEDAY!
...
IN THE END...
...WE NEVER GOT TO DO THAT.
I WANTED TO BE ABLE TO TELL HER ABOUT YOUR PERFORMANCES, THOUGH...
...SO I'VE BEEN TO A BUNCH OF THEM!
THEY WERE A REAL LIFELINE FOR ME WHEN I WAS AT A PRETTY LOW POINT.

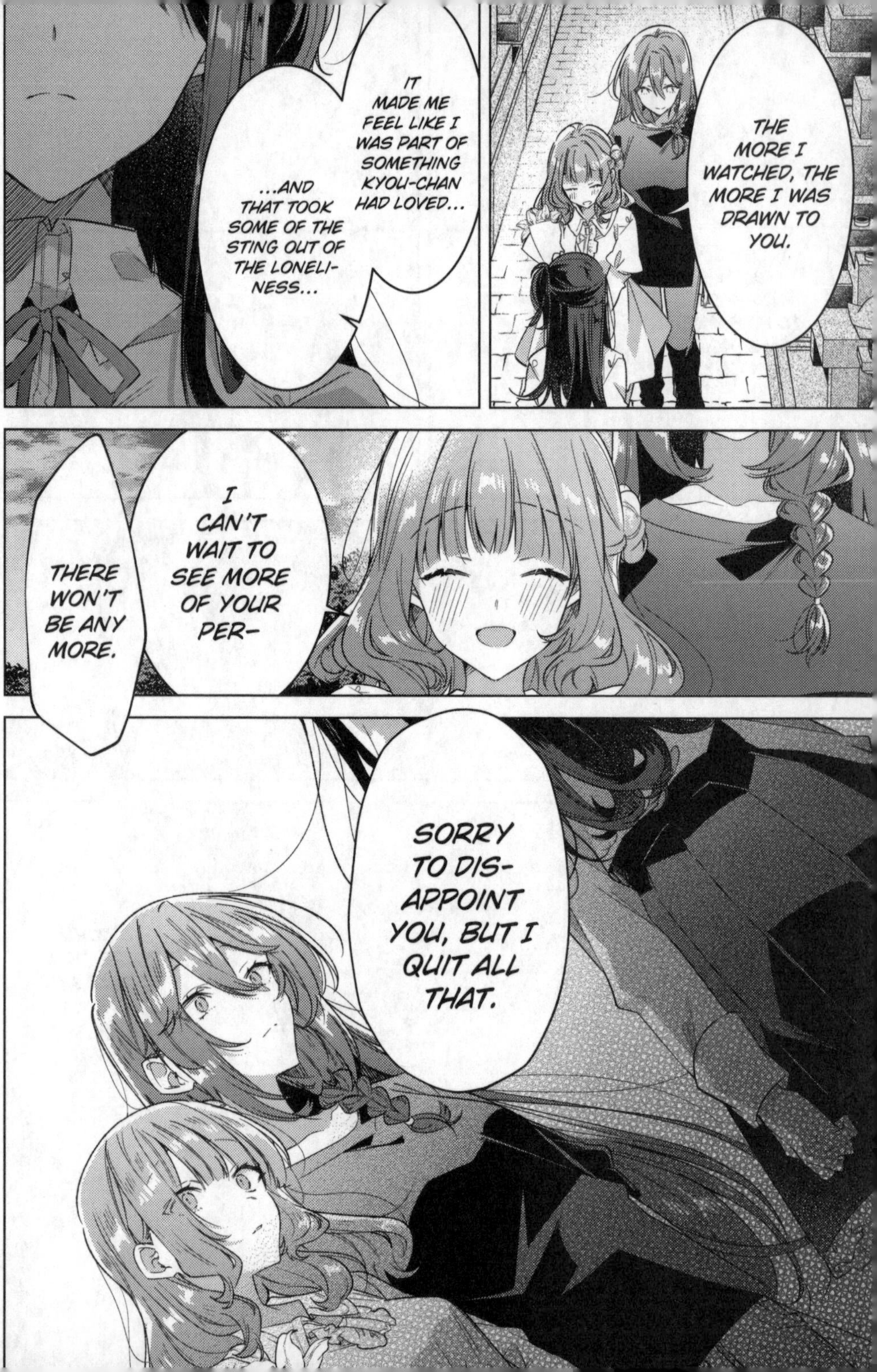
THE MORE I WATCHED, THE MORE I WAS DRAWN TO YOU.
IT MADE ME FEEL LIKE I WAS PART OF SOMETHING KYOU-CHAN HAD LOVED...
...AND THAT TOOK SOME OF THE STING OUT OF THE LONELI-NESS...
I CAN'T WAIT TO SEE MORE OF YOUR PER-
THERE WON'T BE ANY MORE.
SORRY TO DIS-APPOINT YOU, BUT I QUIT ALL THAT.

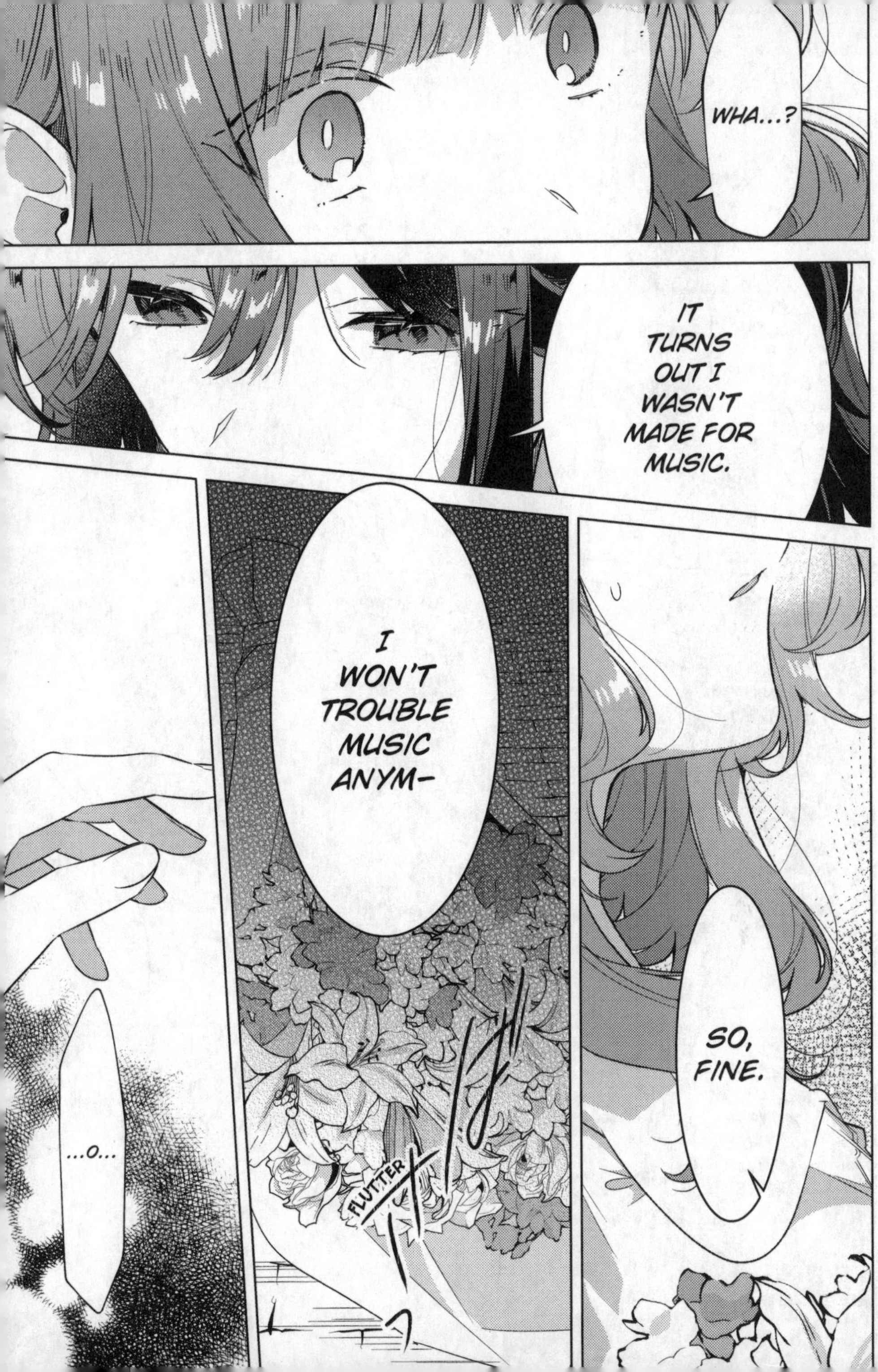
WHA...?
IT TURNS OUT I WASN'T MADE FOR MUSIC.
SO, FINE.
I WON'T TROUBLE MUSIC ANYM-
FLUTTER
...O...

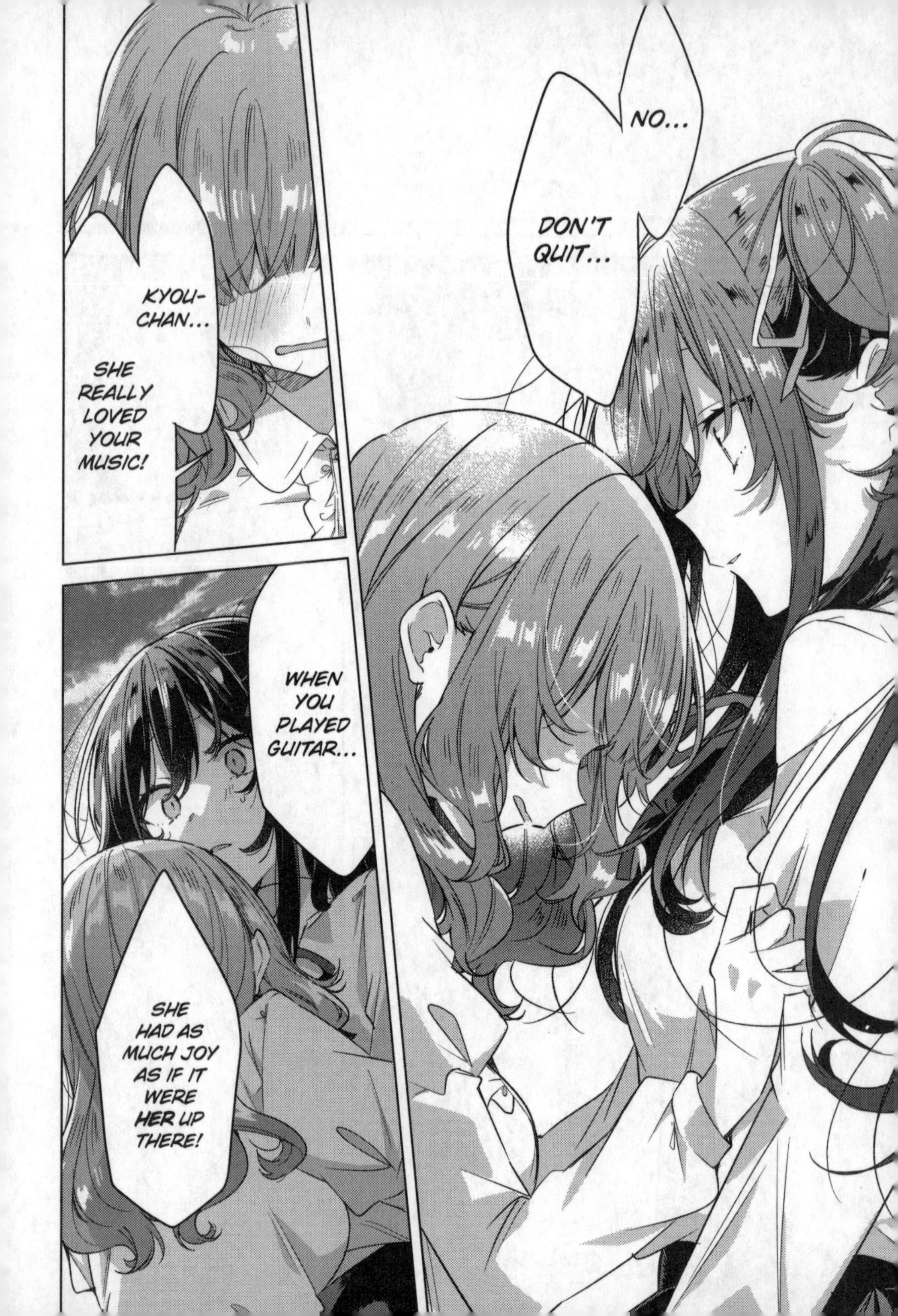
NO...
DON'T QUIT...
KYOU-CHAN...
SHE REALLY LOVED YOUR MUSIC!
WHEN YOU PLAYED GUITAR...
SHE HAD AS MUCH JOY AS IF IT WERE HER UP THERE!

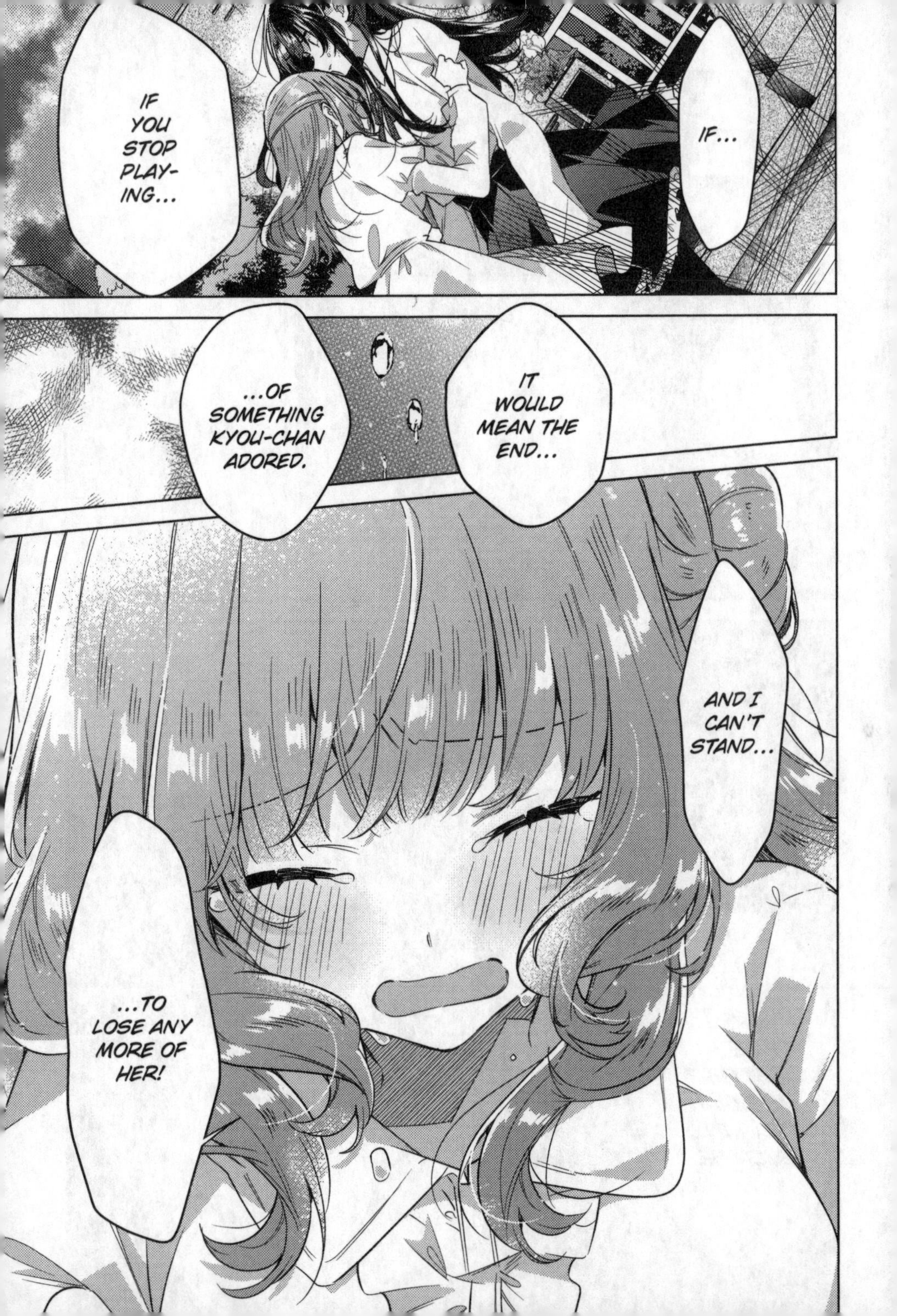
IF...
IF YOU STOP PLAYING...
IT WOULD MEAN THE END...
...OF SOMETHING KYOU-CHAN ADORED.
AND I CAN'T STAND...
...TO LOSE ANY MORE OF HER!

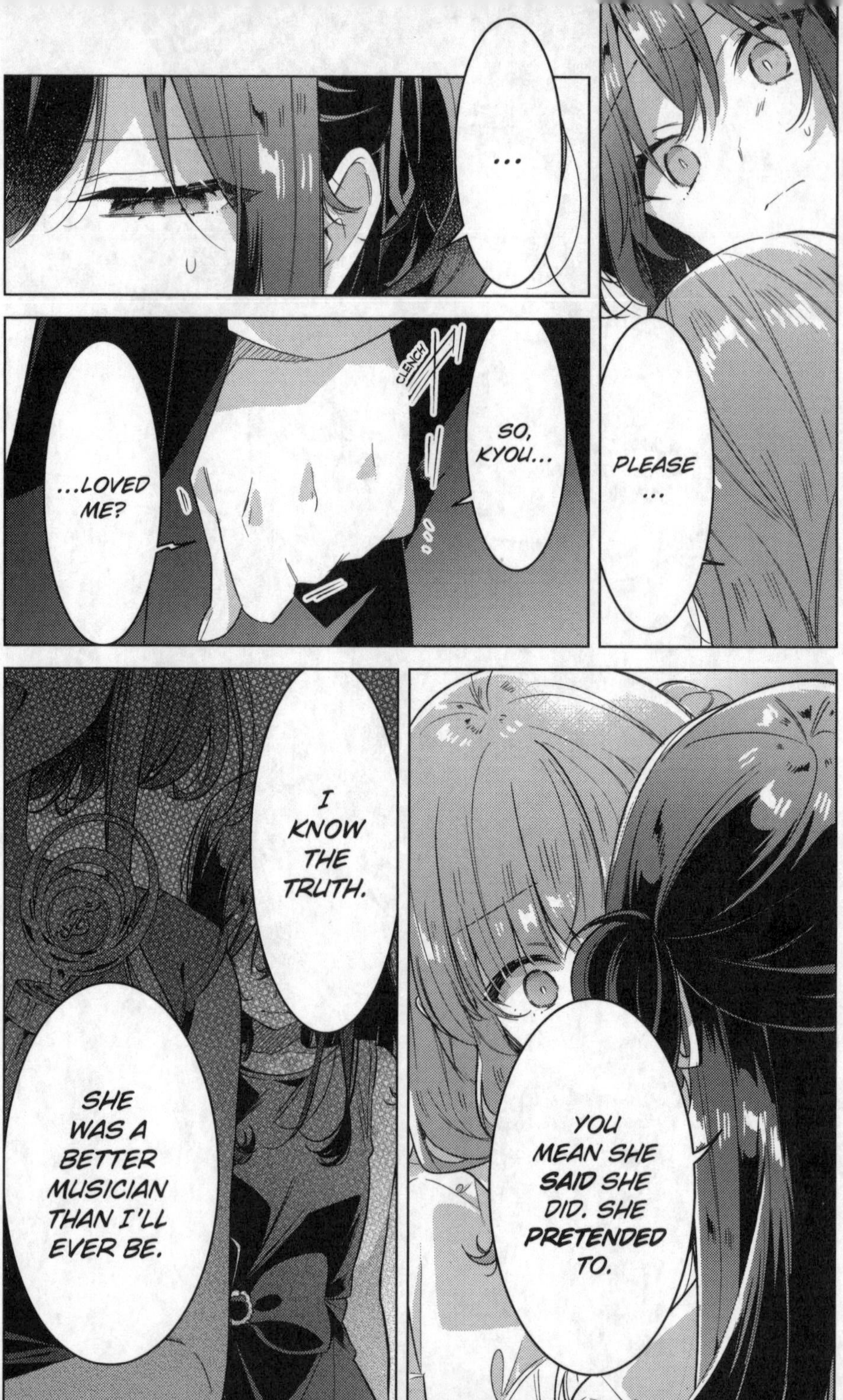
PLEASE ...
...
CLENCH
SO, KYOU...
...LOVED ME?
YOU MEAN SHE SAID SHE DID. SHE PRETENDED TO.
I KNOW THE TRUTH.
SHE WAS A BETTER MUSICIAN THAN I'LL EVER BE.

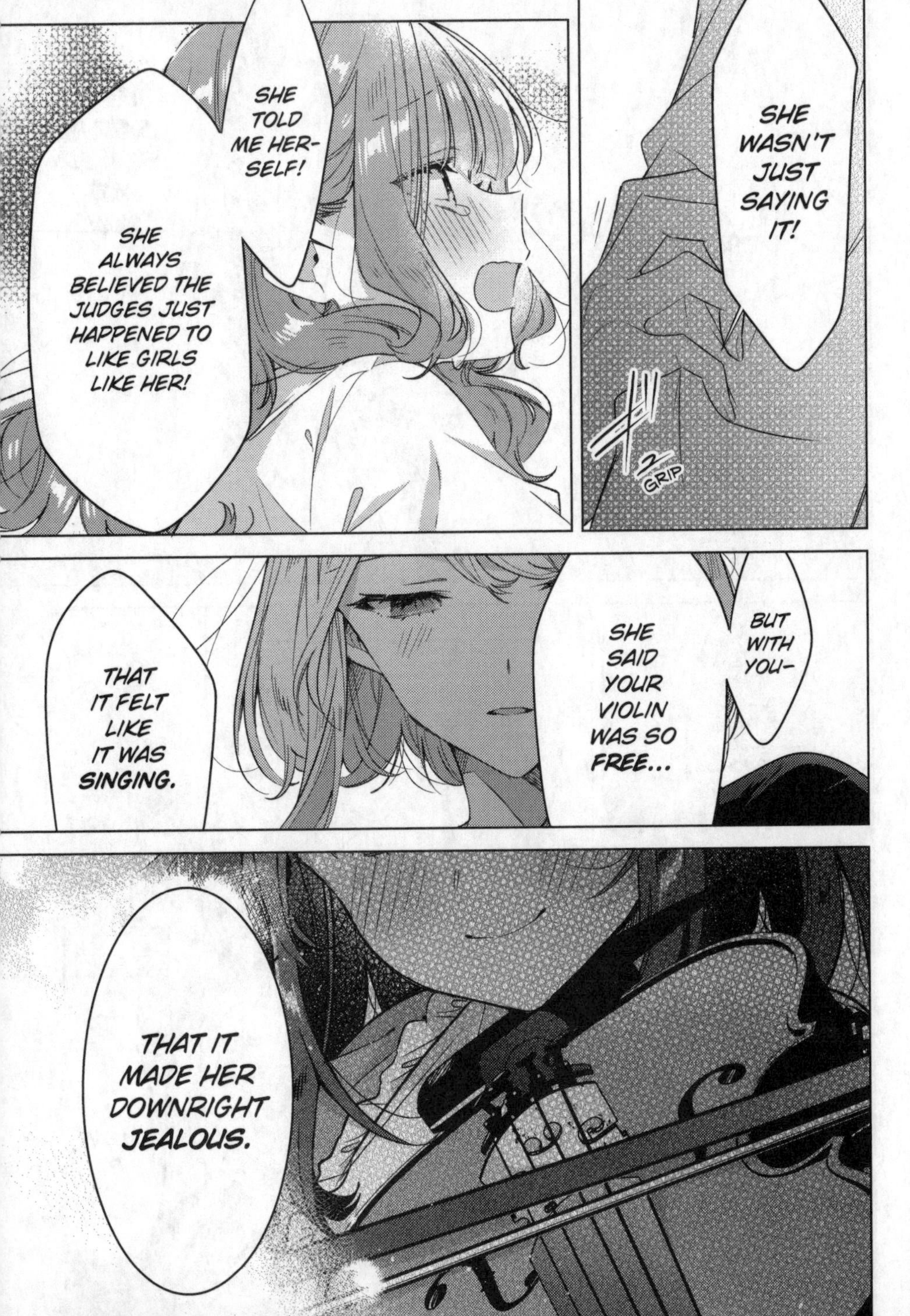
SHE WASN'T JUST SAYING IT!
GRIP
SHE TOLD ME HER-SELF!
SHE ALWAYS BELIEVED THE JUDGES JUST HAPPENED TO LIKE GIRLS LIKE HER!
BUT WITH YOU-
SHE SAID YOUR VIOLIN WAS SO FREE...
THAT IT FELT LIKE IT WAS SINGING.
THAT IT MADE HER DOWNRIGHT JEALOUS.

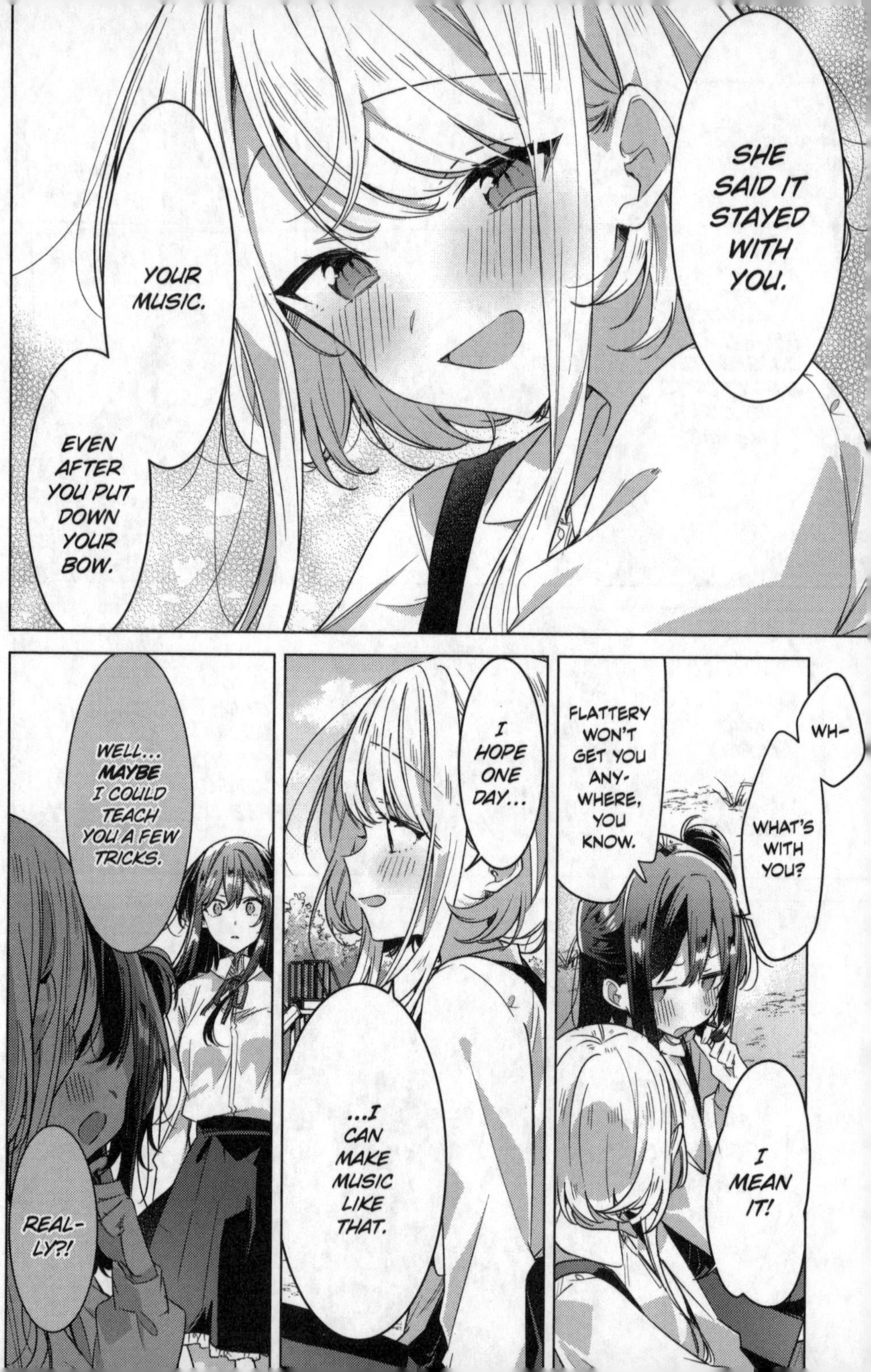
SHE SAID IT STAYED WITH YOU.
YOUR MUSIC.
EVEN AFTER YOU PUT DOWN YOUR BOW.
WH-
WHAT'S WITH YOU?
FLATTERY WON'T GET YOU ANY-WHERE, YOU KNOW.
I MEAN IT!
I HOPE ONE DAY...
...I CAN MAKE MUSIC LIKE THAT.
WELL... MAYBE I COULD TEACH YOU A FEW TRICKS.
REAL-LY?!

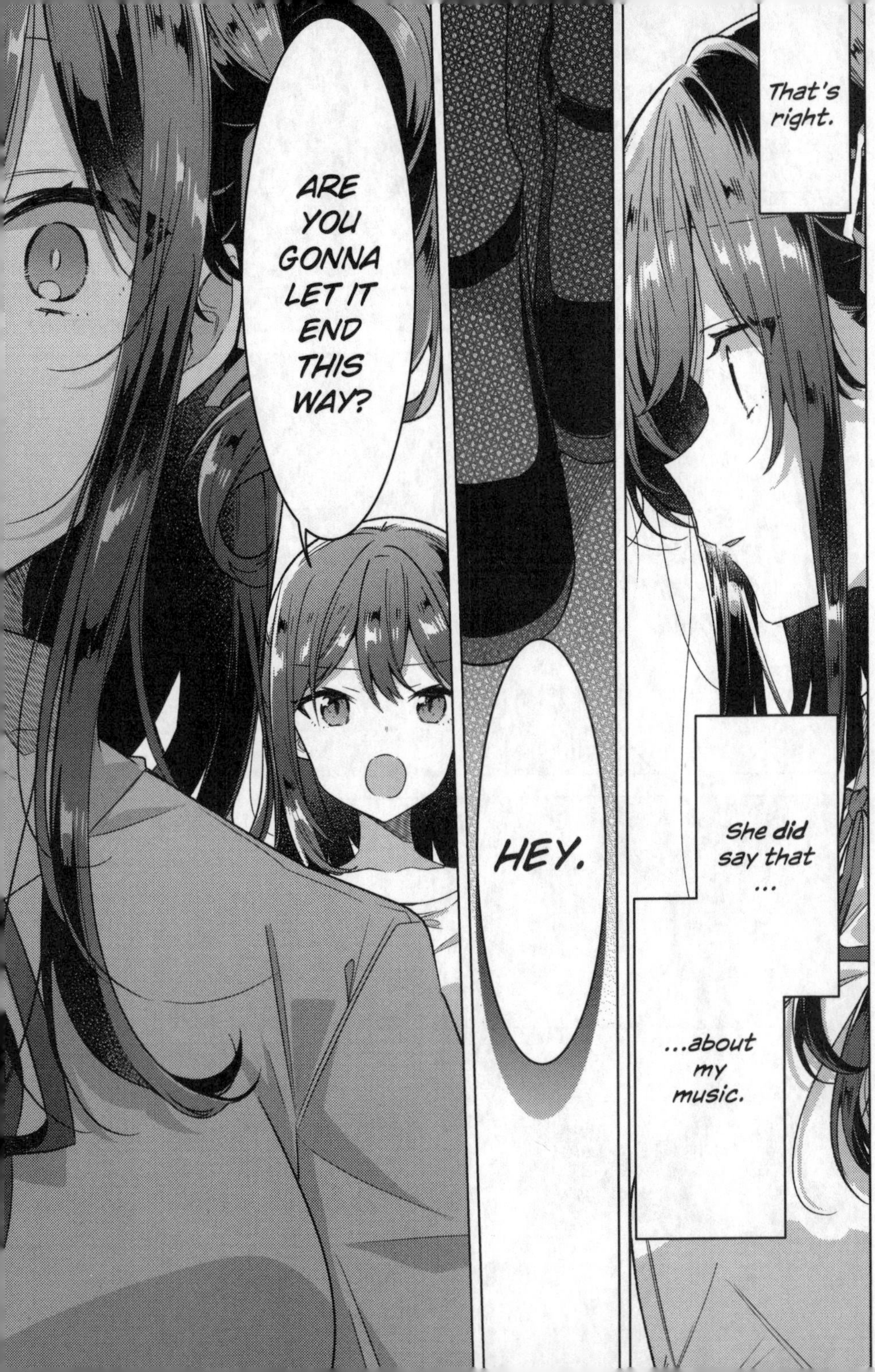
That's right.
She did say that ...
...about my music.
HEY.
ARE YOU GONNA LET IT END THIS WAY?

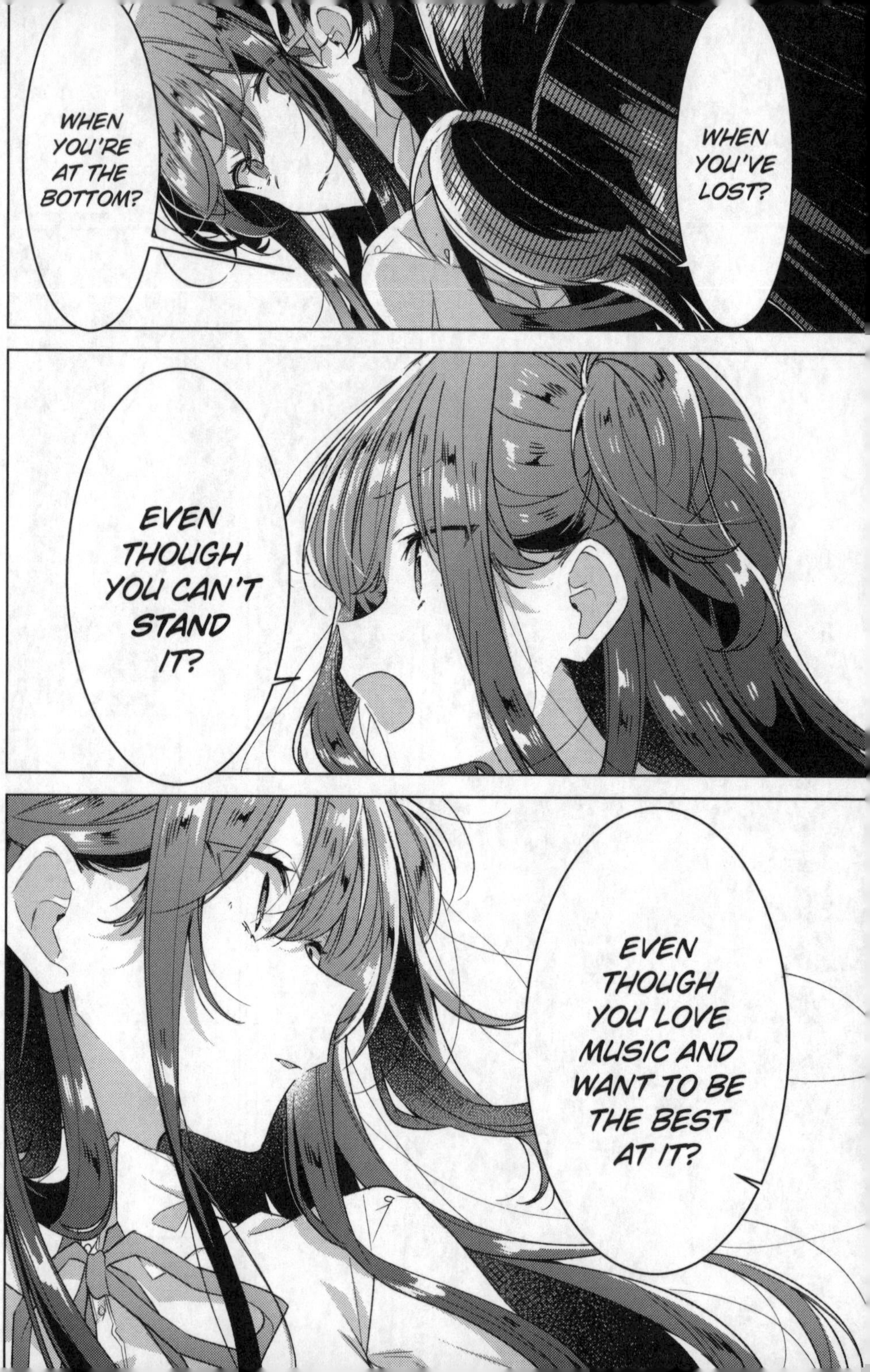
WHEN YOU'VE LOST?
WHEN YOU'RE AT THE BOTTOM?
EVEN THOUGH YOU CAN'T STAND IT?
EVEN THOUGH YOU LOVE MUSIC AND WANT TO BE THE BEST AT IT?

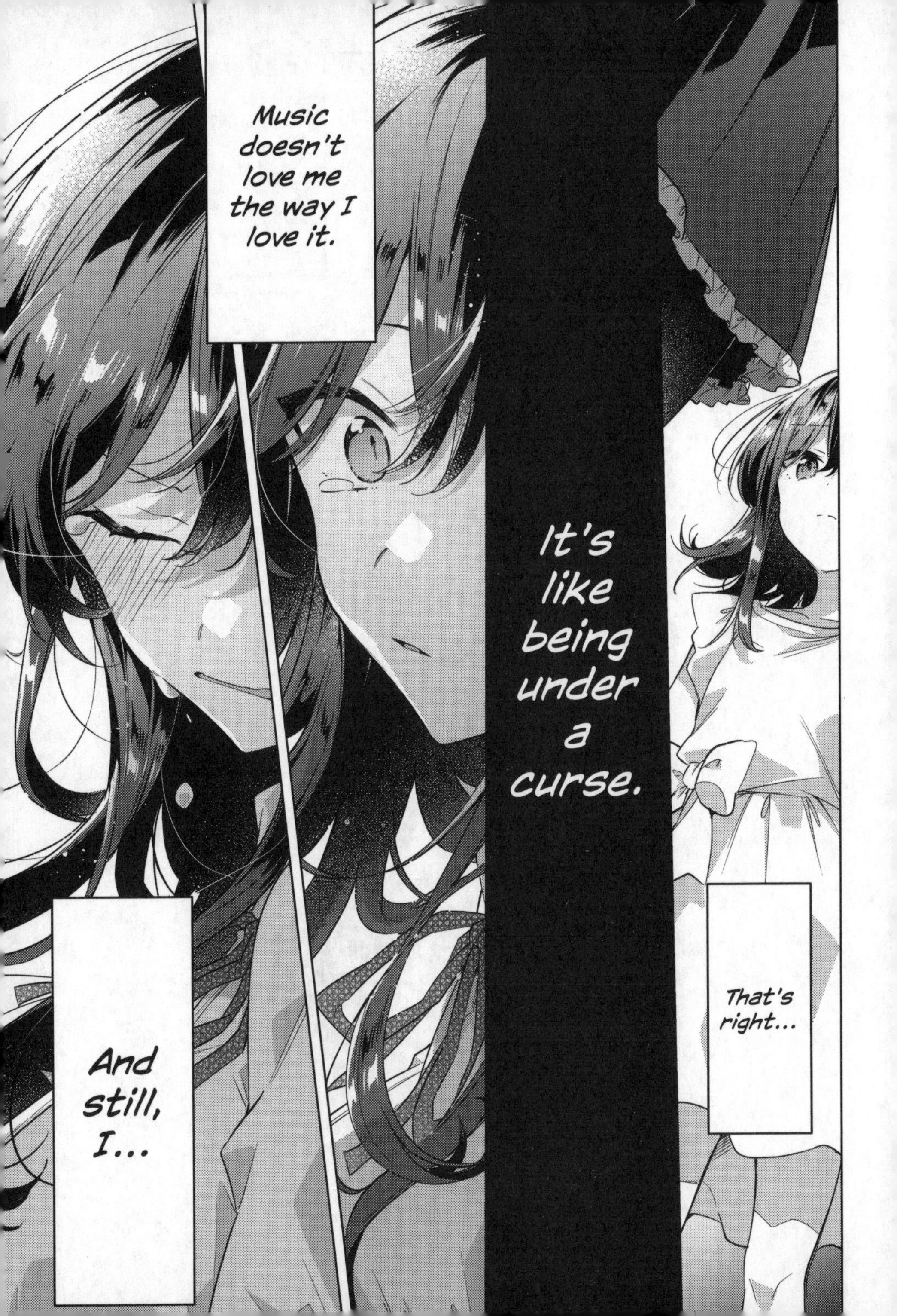
That's right...
It's like being under a curse.
Music doesn't love me the way I love it.
And still, I...

I can never let it go.

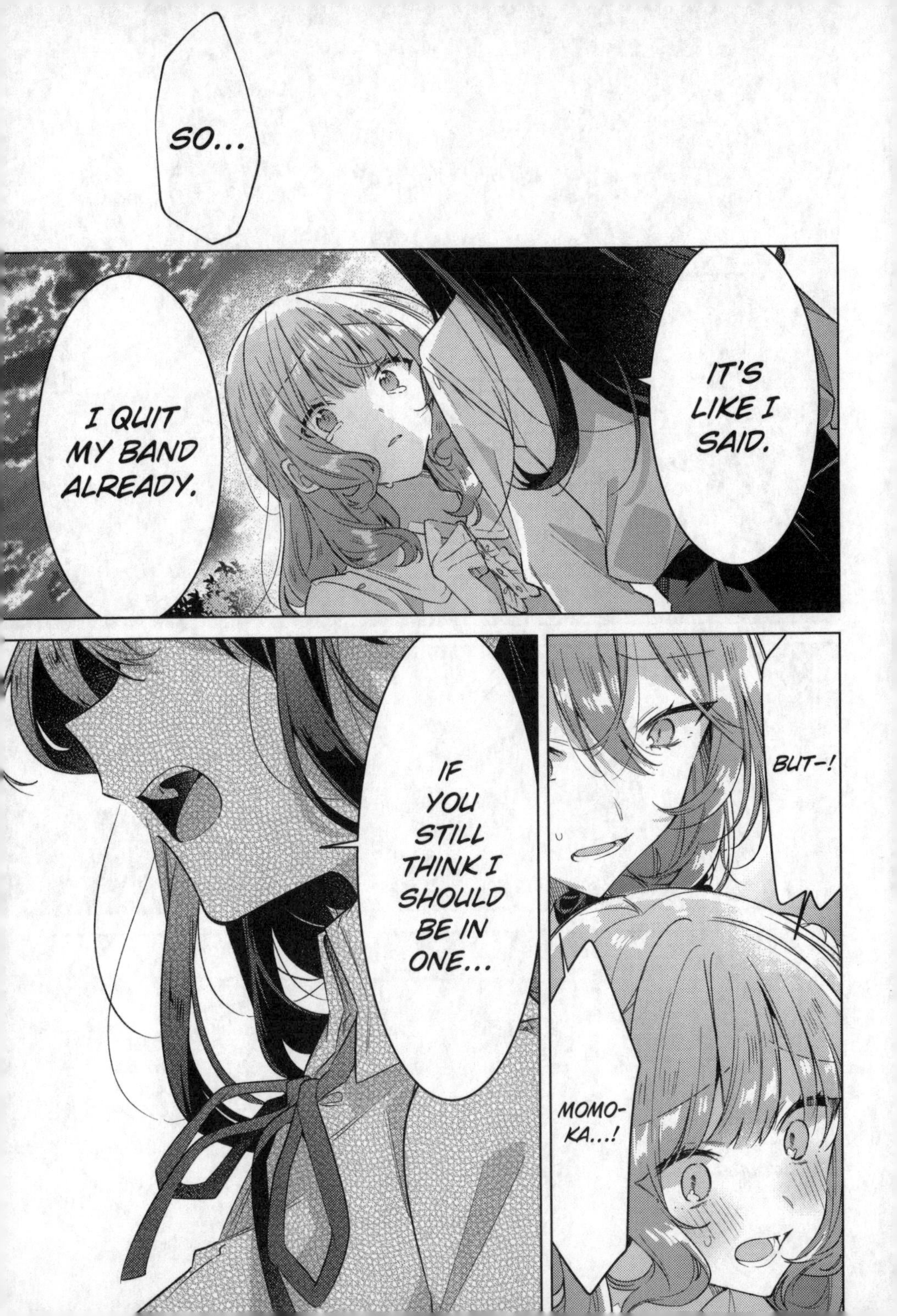
SO...
IT'S LIKE I SAID.
I QUIT MY BAND ALREADY.
BUT-!
MOMO-KA...!
IF YOU STILL THINK I SHOULD BE IN ONE...

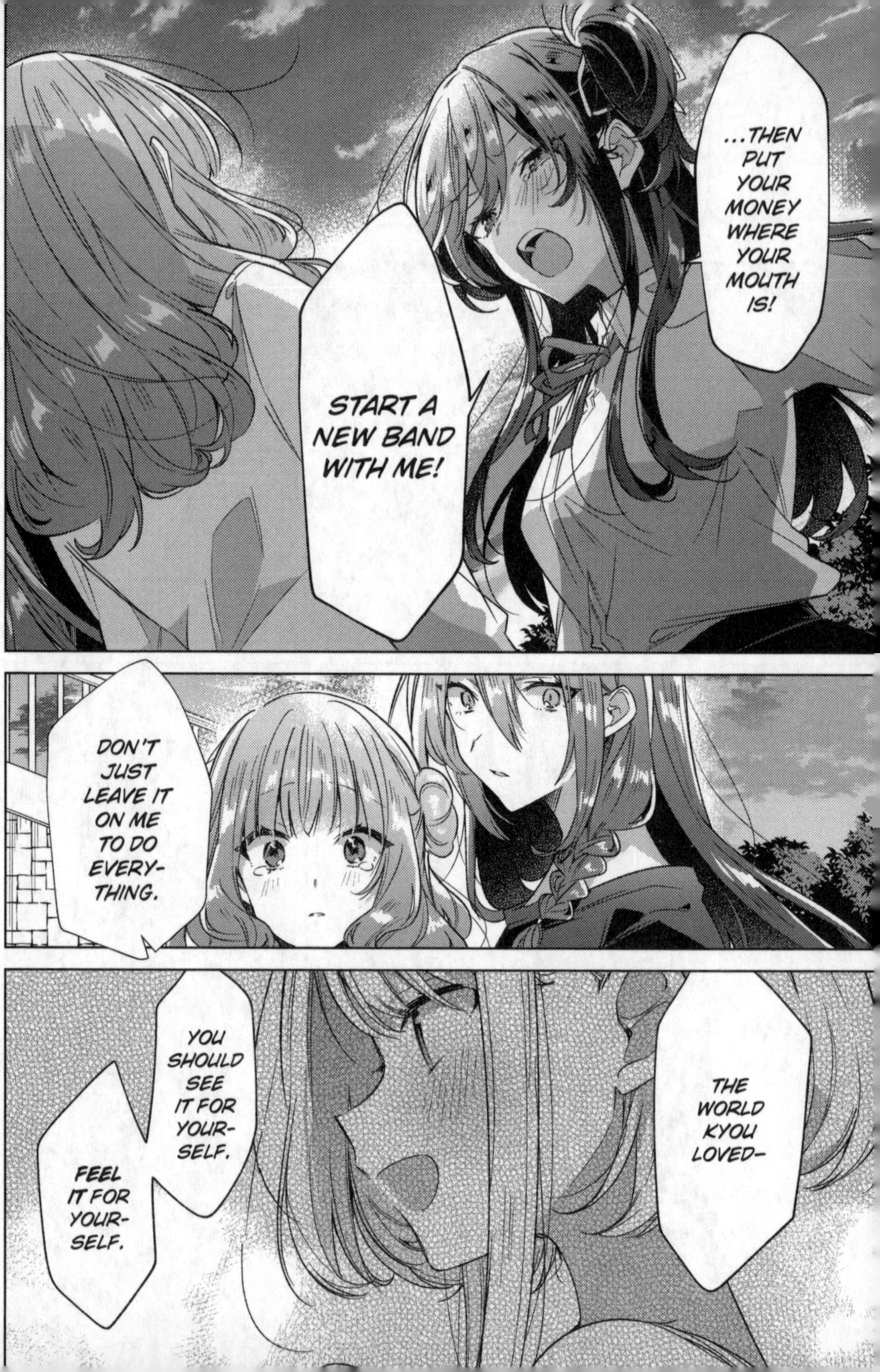
...THEN PUT YOUR MONEY WHERE YOUR MOUTH IS!
START A NEW BAND WITH ME!
DON'T JUST LEAVE IT ON ME TO DO EVERY-THING.
THE WORLD KYOU LOVED–
YOU SHOULD SEE IT FOR YOUR-SELF.
FEEL IT FOR YOUR-SELF.

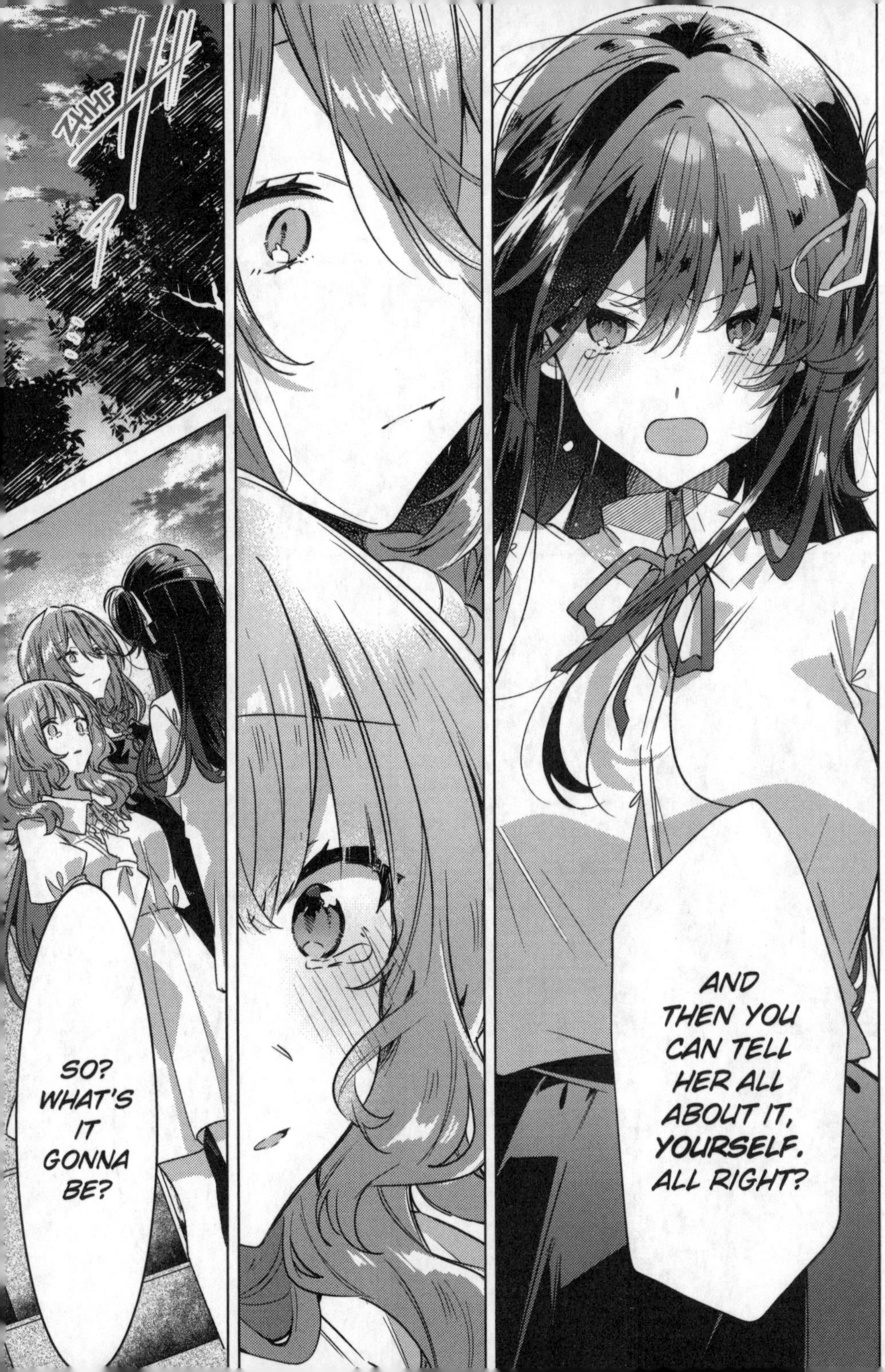
AND THEN YOU CAN TELL HER ALL ABOUT IT, YOURSELF. ALL RIGHT?
ZHHF
SO? WHAT'S IT GONNA BE?

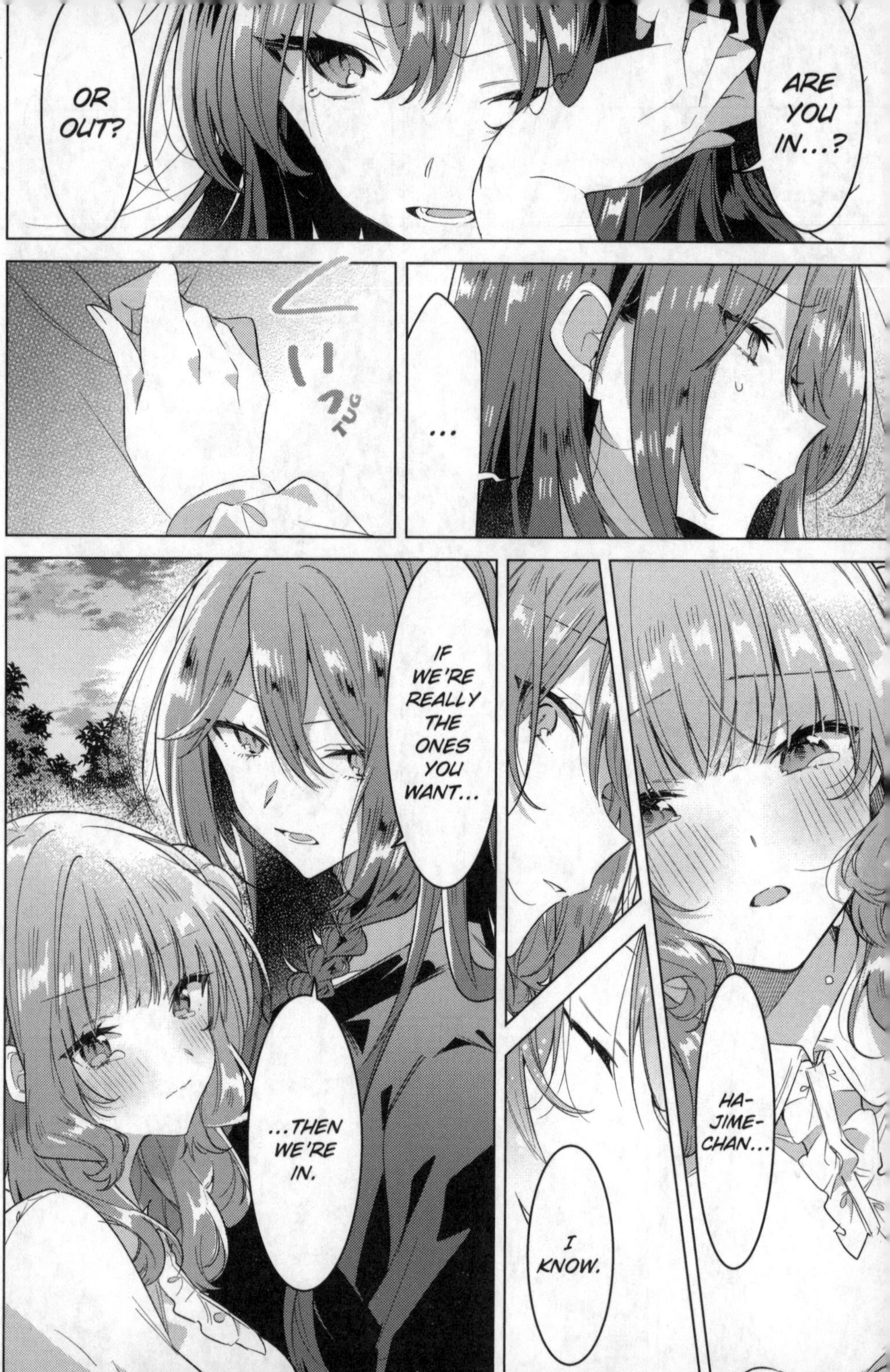
ARE YOU IN...?
OR OUT?
...
TUG
HAJIME-CHAN...
I KNOW.
IF WE'RE REALLY THE ONES YOU WANT...
...THEN WE'RE IN.

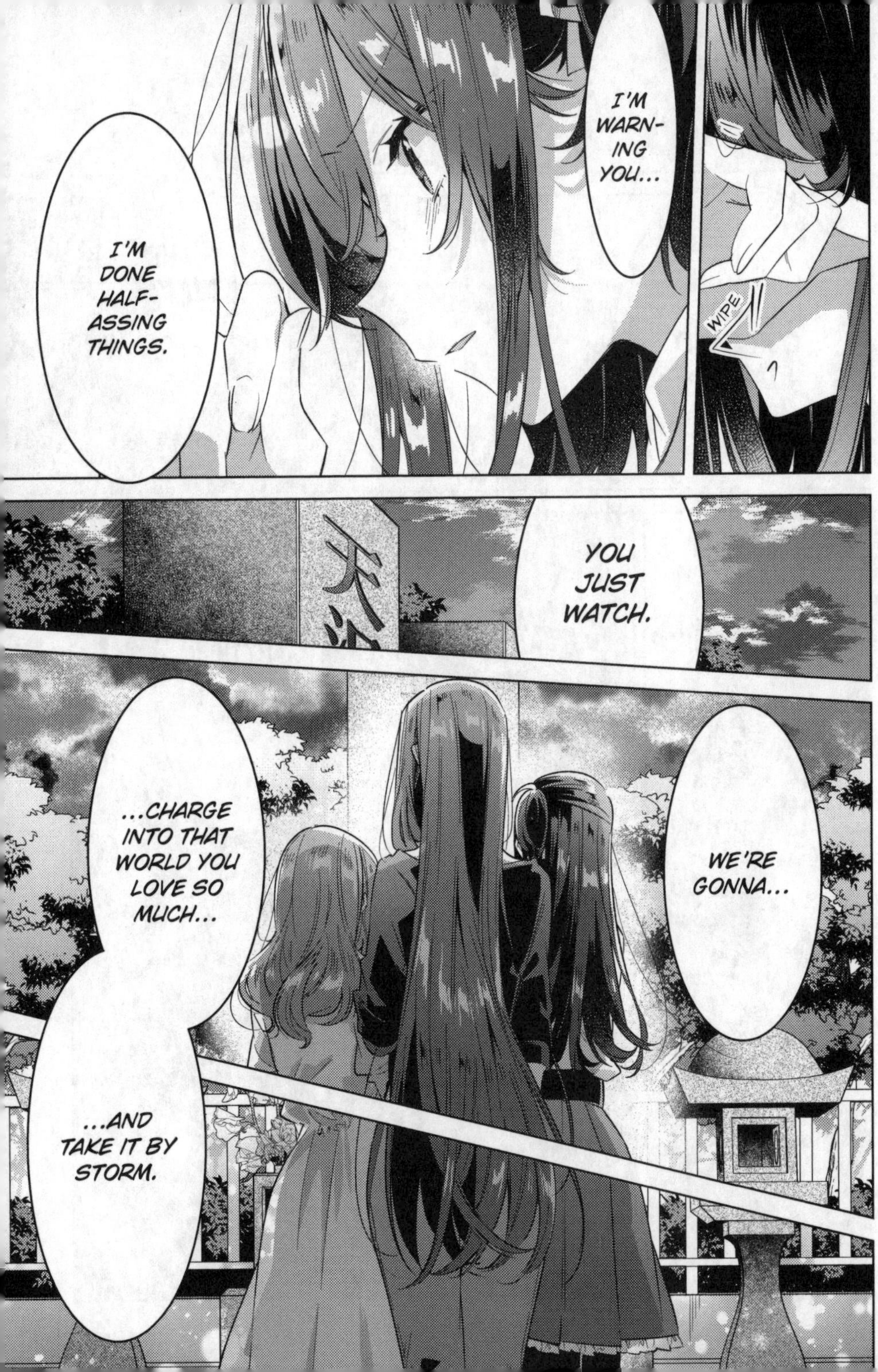
I'M WARNING YOU...
WIPE
I'M DONE HALF-ASSING THINGS.
YOU JUST WATCH.
WE'RE GONNA...
...CHARGE INTO THAT WORLD YOU LOVE SO MUCH...
...AND TAKE IT BY STORM.

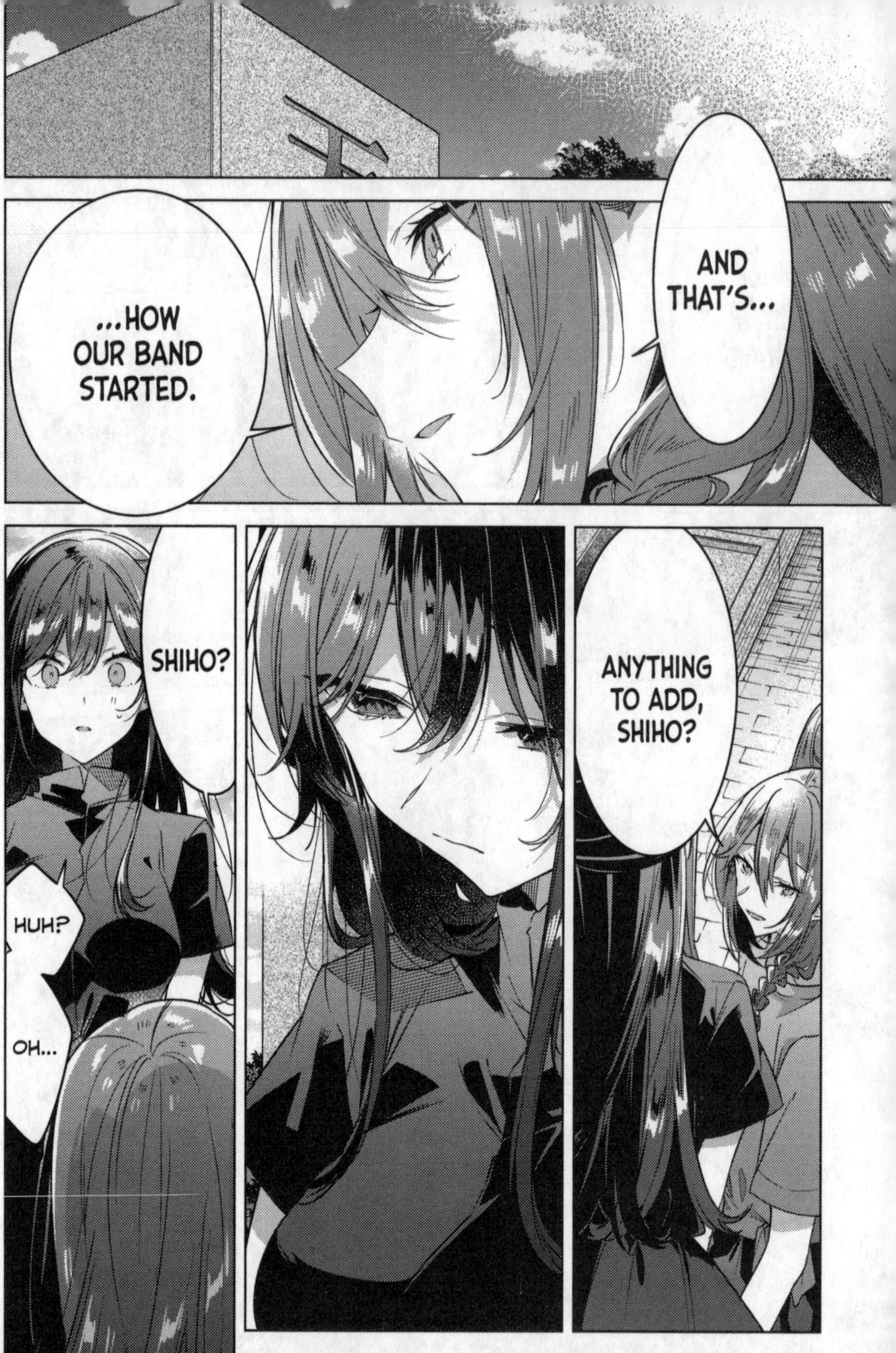
AND THAT'S...
...HOW OUR BAND STARTED.
ANYTHING TO ADD, SHIHO?
SHIHO?
HUH?
OH...

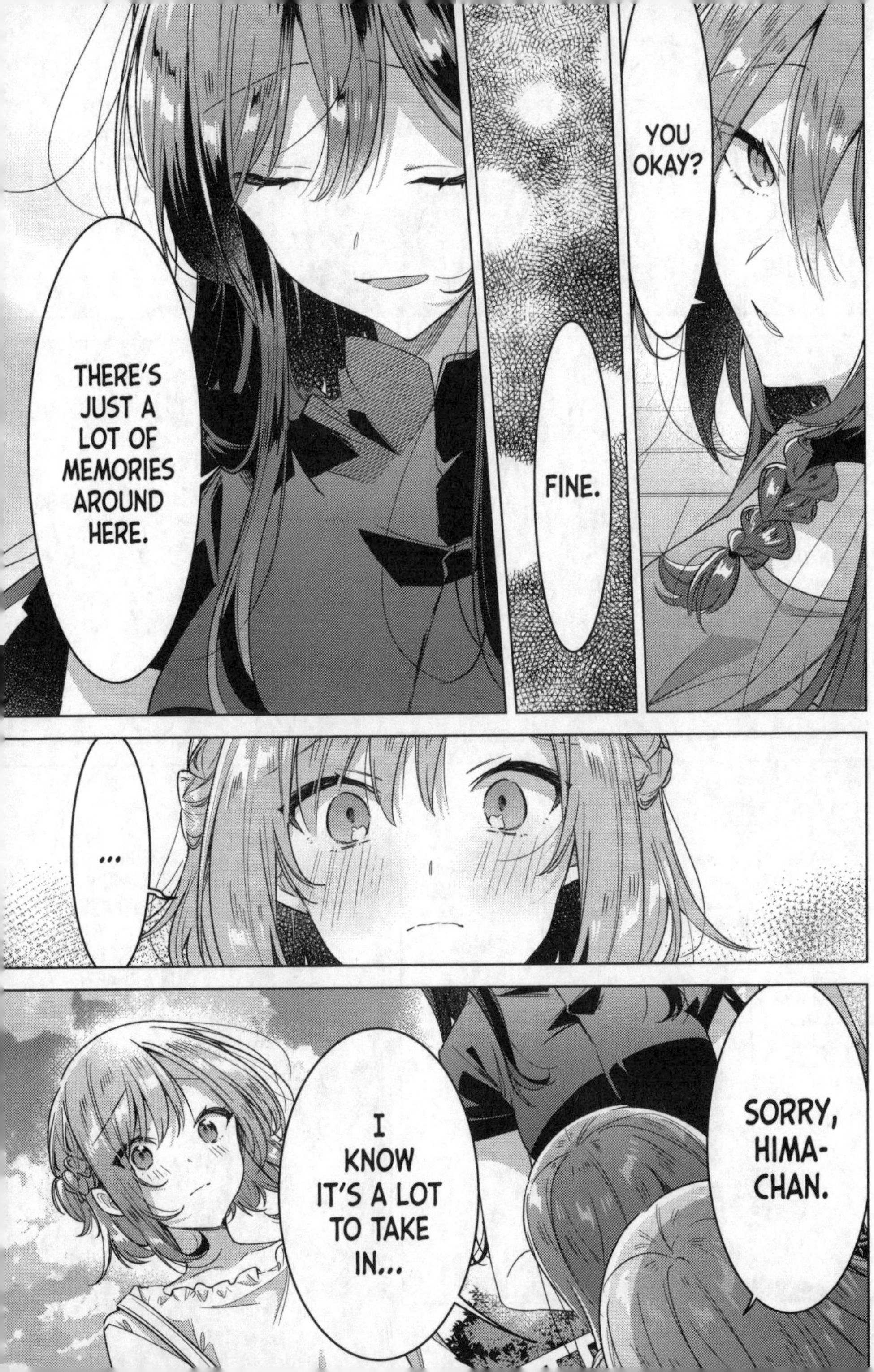
YOU OKAY?
FINE.
THERE'S JUST A LOT OF MEMORIES AROUND HERE.
...
SORRY, HIMA-CHAN.
I KNOW IT'S A LOT TO TAKE IN...

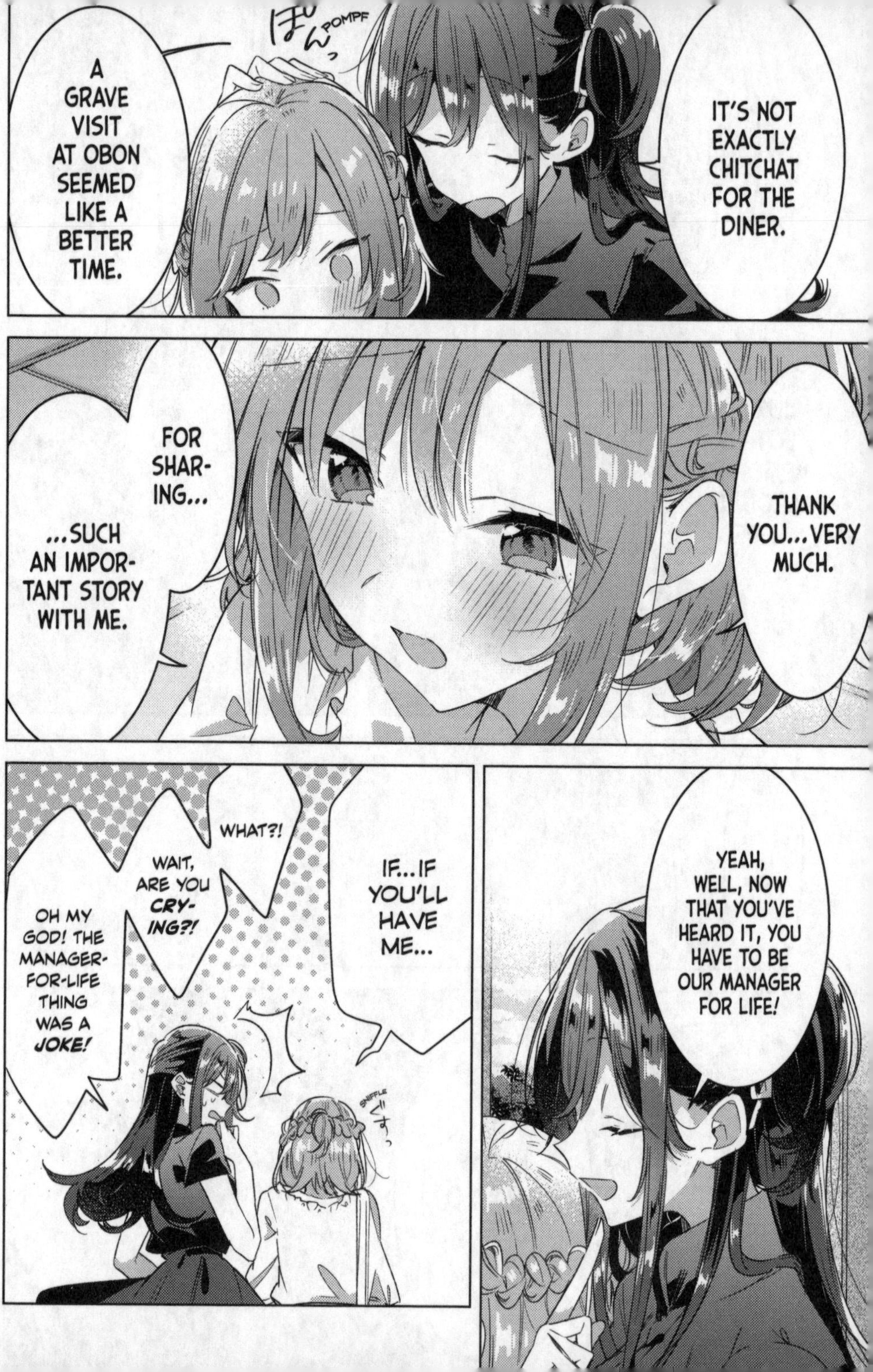
IT'S NOT EXACTLY CHITCHAT FOR THE DINER.
ぽんっ POMPF
A GRAVE VISIT AT OBON SEEMED LIKE A BETTER TIME.
THANK YOU...VERY MUCH.
FOR SHARING...
...SUCH AN IMPORTANT STORY WITH ME.
YEAH, WELL, NOW THAT YOU'VE HEARD IT, YOU HAVE TO BE OUR MANAGER FOR LIFE!
IF...IF YOU'LL HAVE ME...
SNIFFLE ぐすっ
WHAT?!
WAIT, ARE YOU *CRYING*?!
OH MY GOD! THE MANAGER-FOR-LIFE THING WAS A *JOKE!*

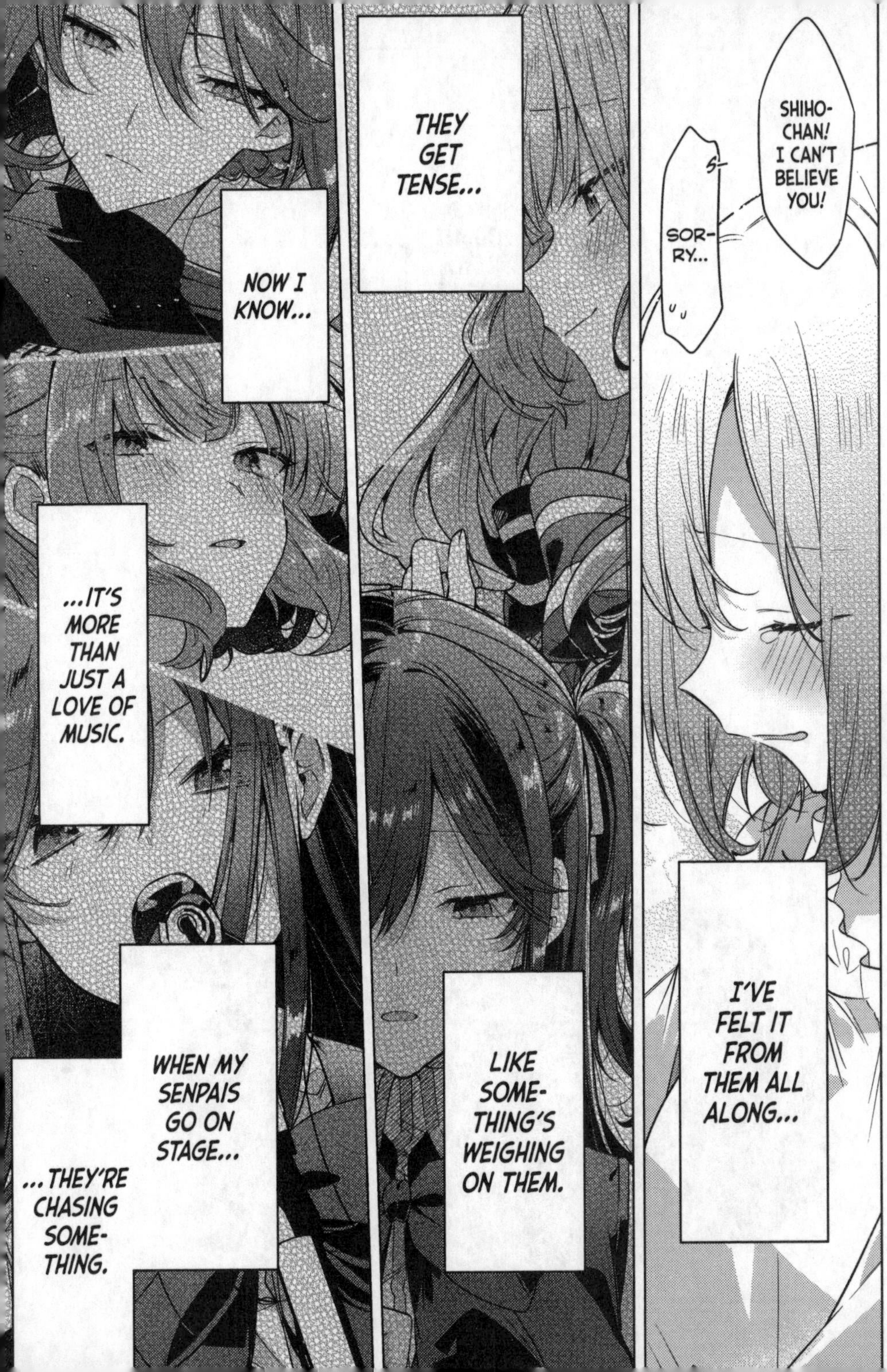
SHIHO-CHAN! I CAN'T BELIEVE YOU!
S- SOR-RY...
I'VE FELT IT FROM THEM ALL ALONG...
THEY GET TENSE...
LIKE SOME-THING'S WEIGHING ON THEM.
NOW I KNOW...
...IT'S MORE THAN JUST A LOVE OF MUSIC.
WHEN MY SENPAIS GO ON STAGE...
...THEY'RE CHASING SOME-THING.

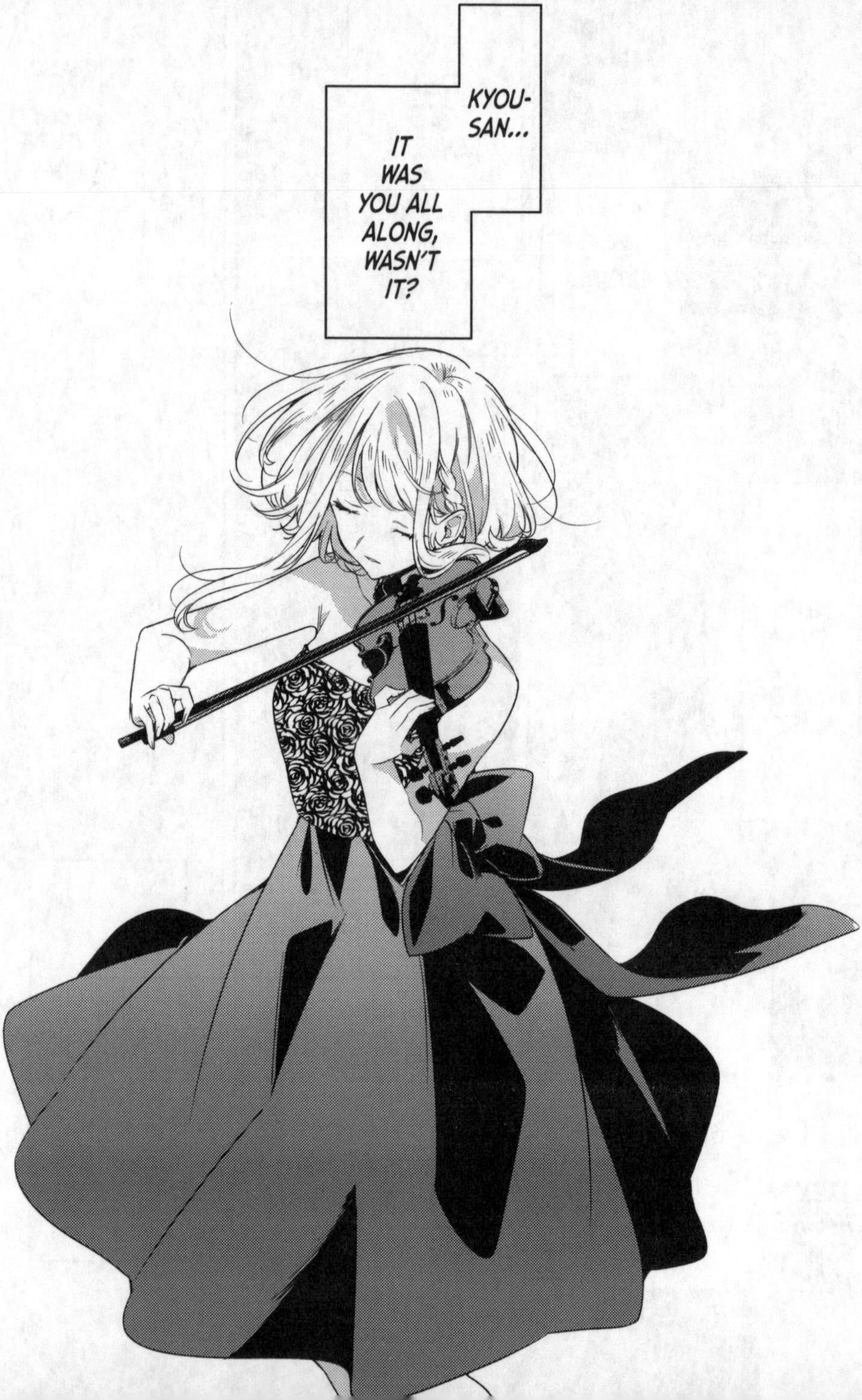
KYOU-SAN...
IT WAS YOU ALL ALONG, WASN'T IT?

Whisper Me
A Love Song

Eku
Takeshima

Whisper Me
A Love Song
Eku
Takeshima

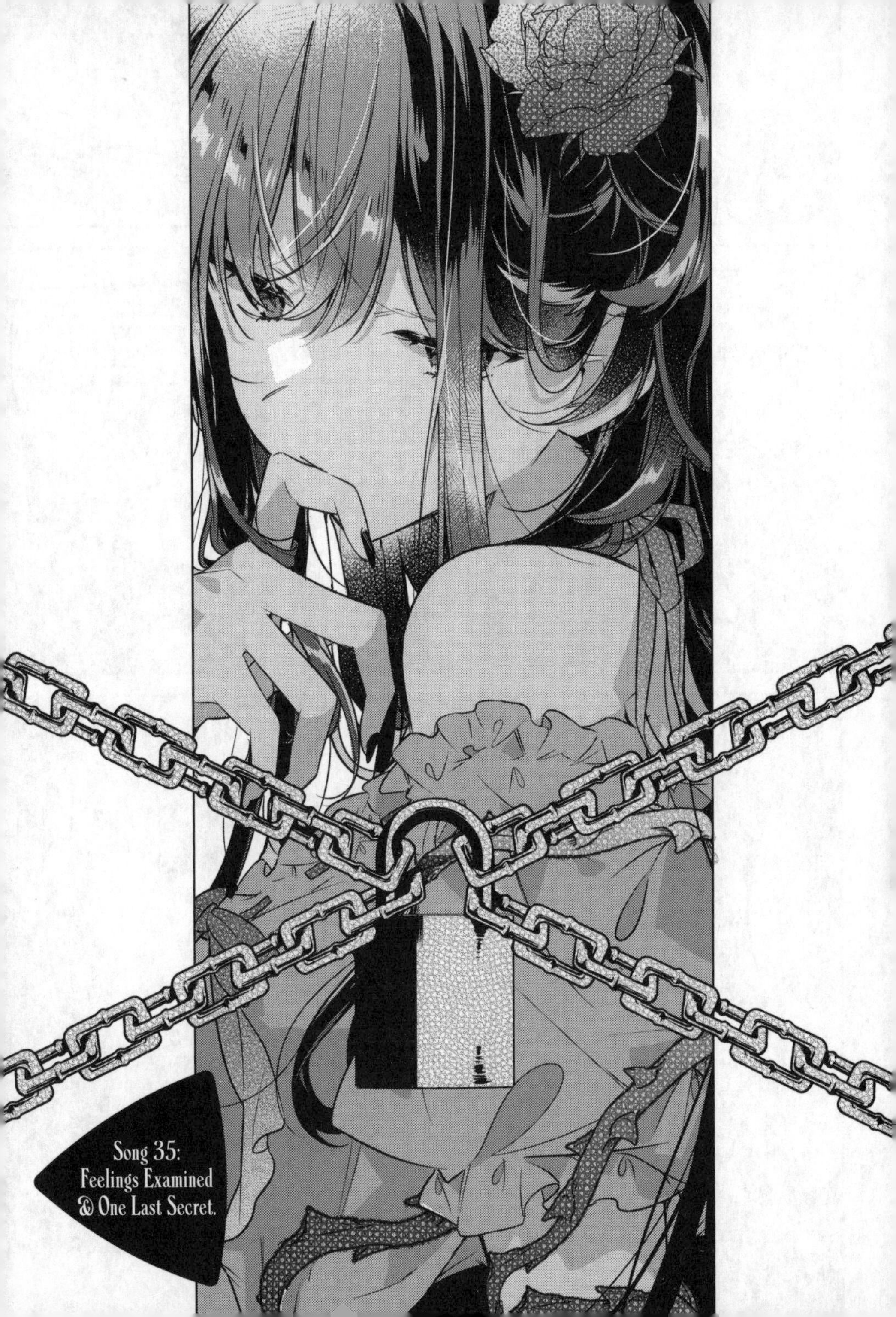
Song 35:
Feelings Examined
& One Last Secret.

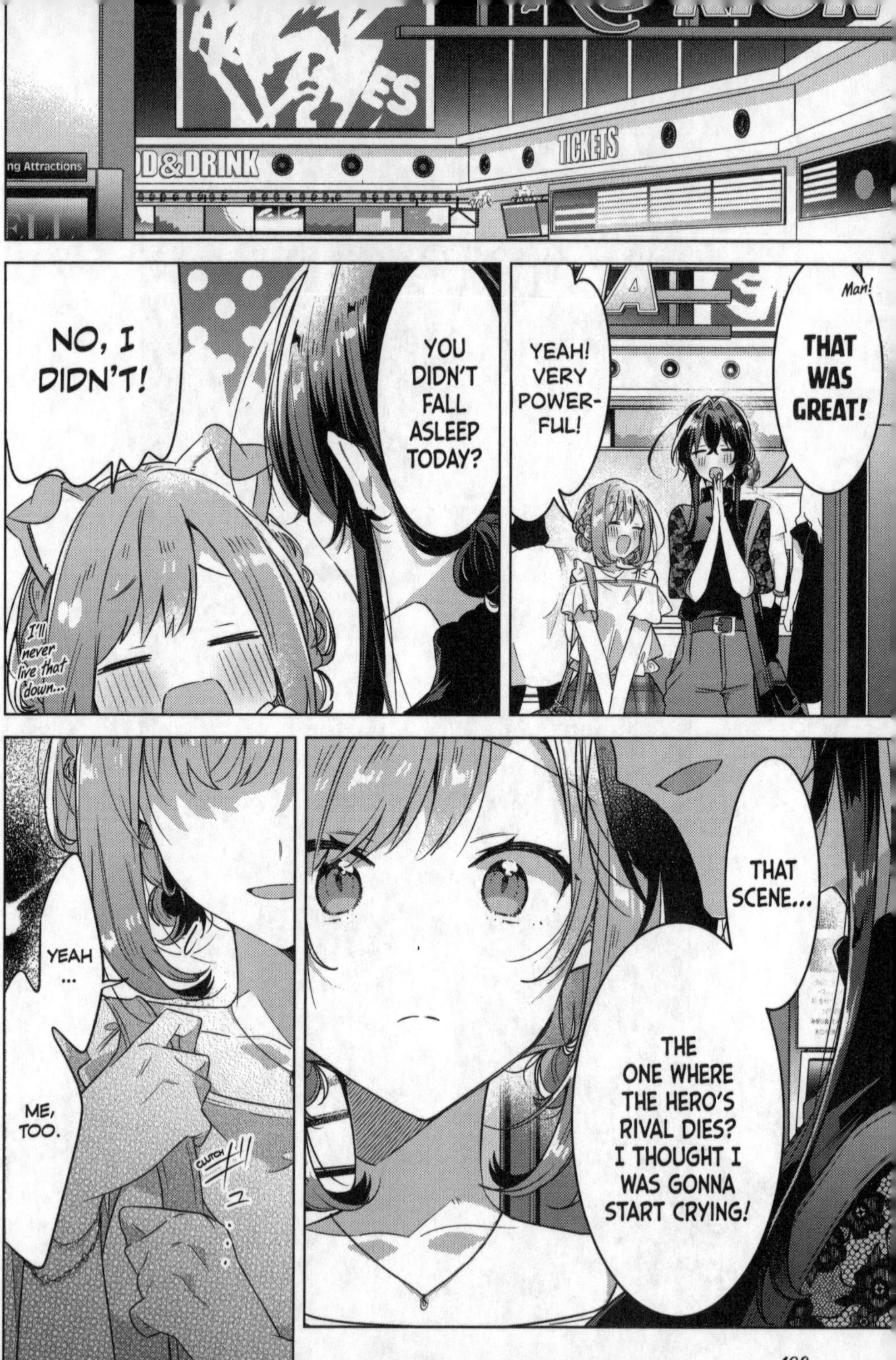
TICKETS
Man!
THAT WAS GREAT!
YEAH! VERY POWER-FUL!
YOU DIDN'T FALL ASLEEP TODAY?
NO, I DIDN'T!
I'll never live that down...
THAT SCENE...
THE ONE WHERE THE HERO'S RIVAL DIES? I THOUGHT I WAS GONNA START CRYING!
YEAH...
ME, TOO.
CLUTCH

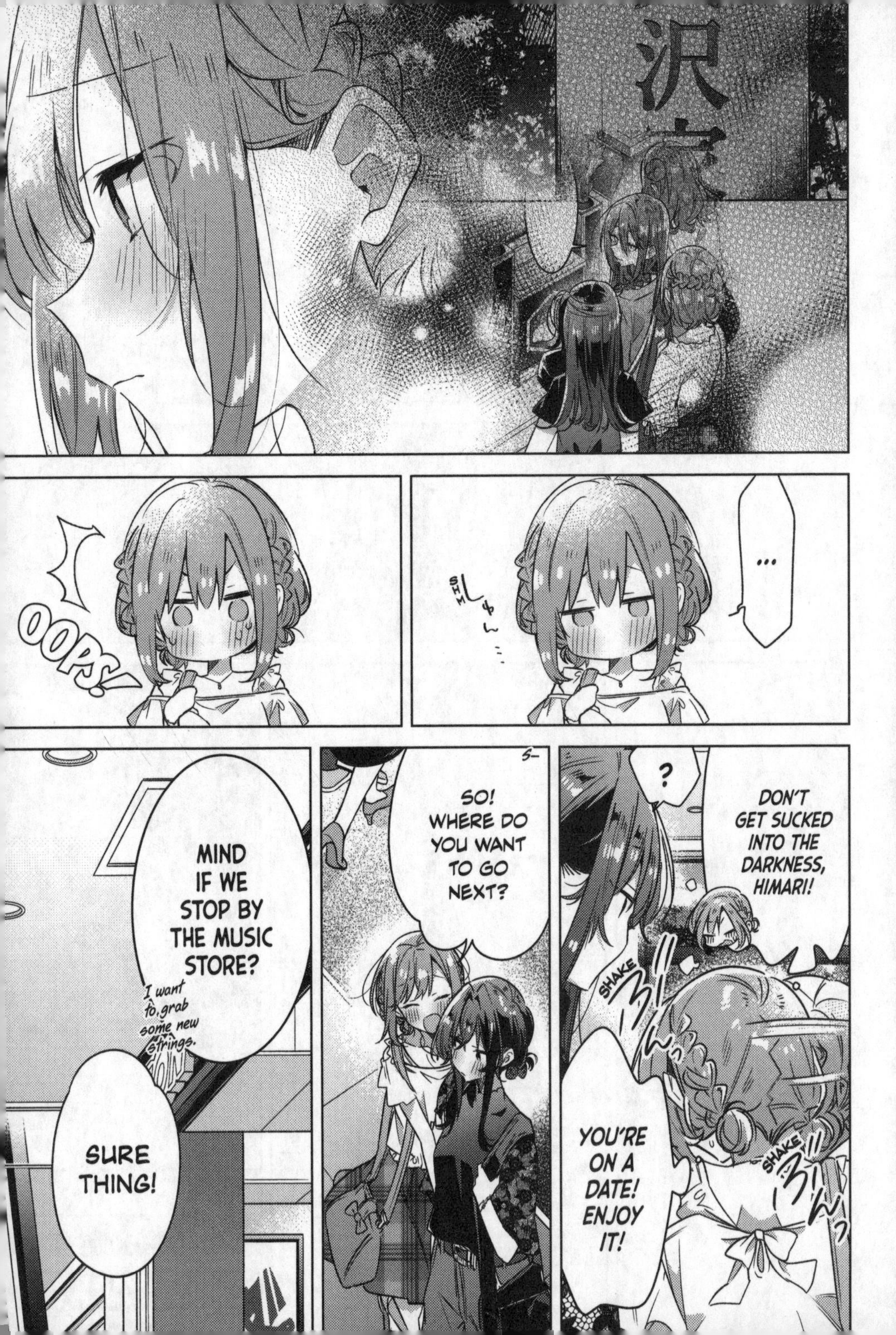
...
SHM
OOPS!
?
DON'T GET SUCKED INTO THE DARKNESS, HIMARI!
SHAKE
YOU'RE ON A DATE! ENJOY IT!
SHAKE
S–
SO! WHERE DO YOU WANT TO GO NEXT?
MIND IF WE STOP BY THE MUSIC STORE?
I want to grab some new strings.
SURE THING!

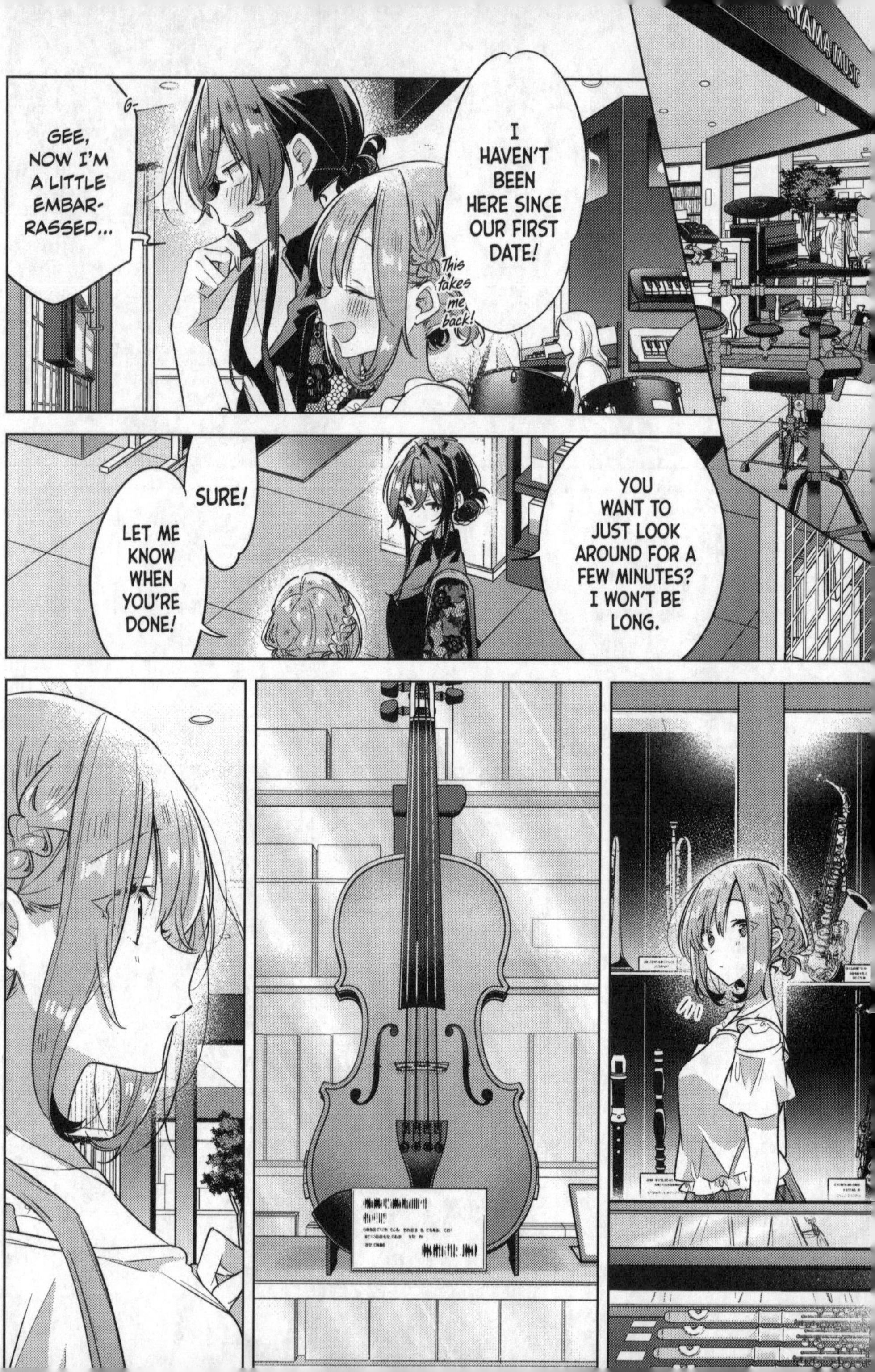
I HAVEN'T BEEN HERE SINCE OUR FIRST DATE!
This takes me back!
G-
GEE, NOW I'M A LITTLE EMBAR-RASSED...
YOU WANT TO JUST LOOK AROUND FOR A FEW MINUTES? I WON'T BE LONG.
SURE!
LET ME KNOW WHEN YOU'RE DONE!

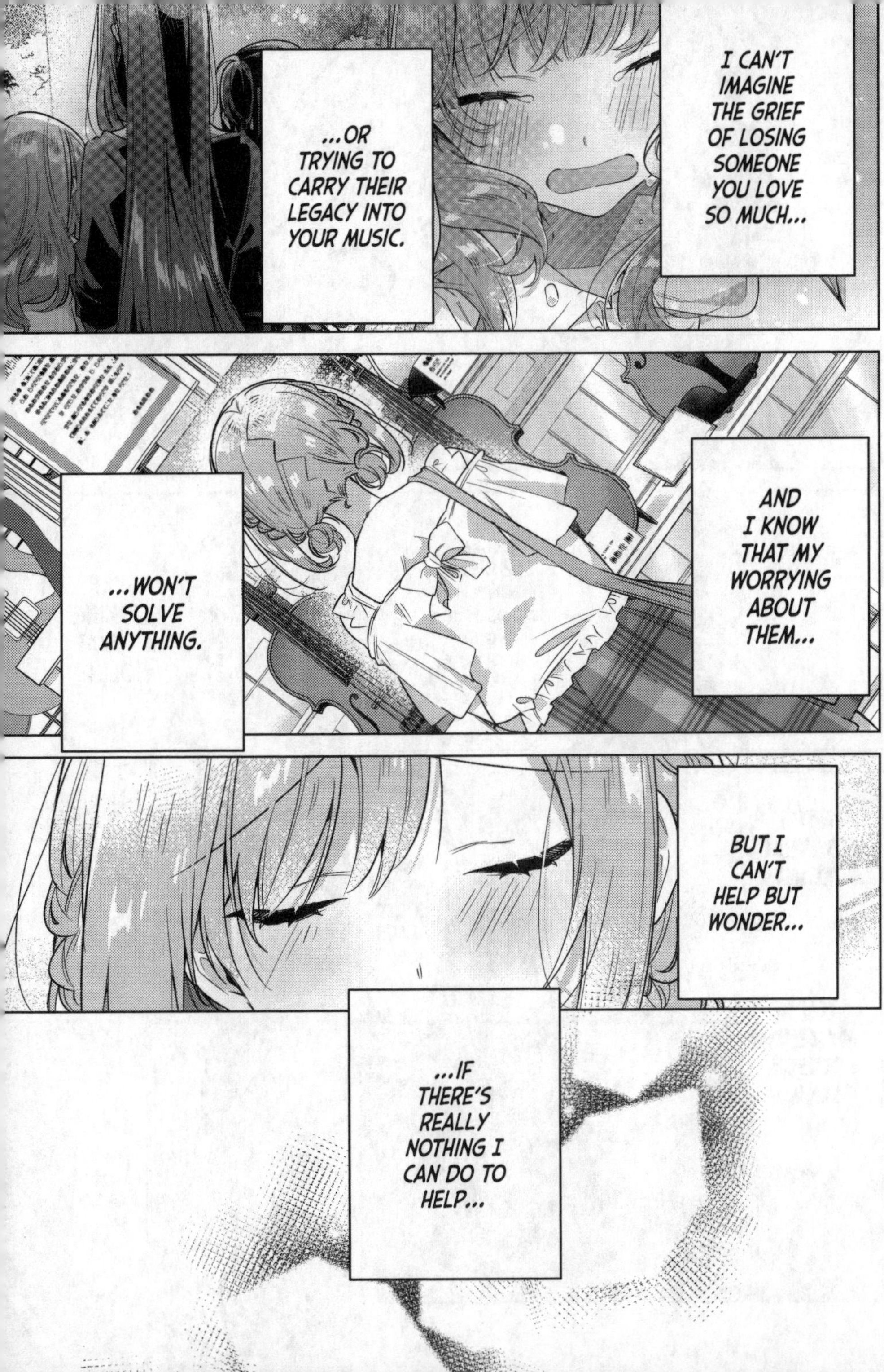
I CAN'T IMAGINE THE GRIEF OF LOSING SOMEONE YOU LOVE SO MUCH...
...OR TRYING TO CARRY THEIR LEGACY INTO YOUR MUSIC.
AND I KNOW THAT MY WORRYING ABOUT THEM...
...WON'T SOLVE ANYTHING.
BUT I CAN'T HELP BUT WONDER...
...IF THERE'S REALLY NOTHING I CAN DO TO HELP...

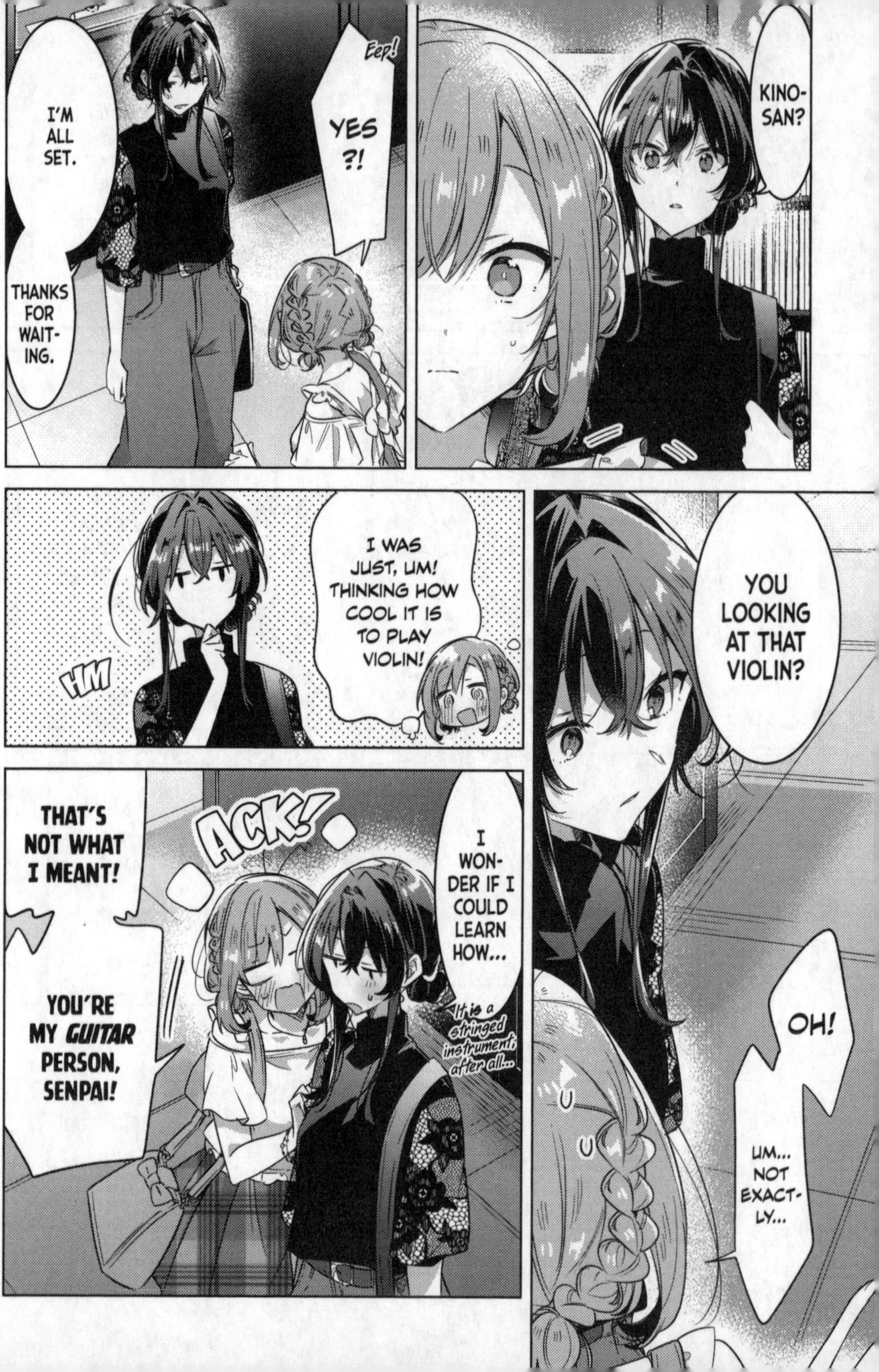
KINO-SAN?
Eep!
YES ?!
I'M ALL SET.
THANKS FOR WAITING.
YOU LOOKING AT THAT VIOLIN?
OH!
UM... NOT EXACTLY...
I WAS JUST, UM! THINKING HOW COOL IT IS TO PLAY VIOLIN!
HM
I WONDER IF I COULD LEARN HOW...
It is a stringed instrument, after all...
ACK!
THAT'S NOT WHAT I MEANT!
YOU'RE MY GUITAR PERSON, SENPAI!

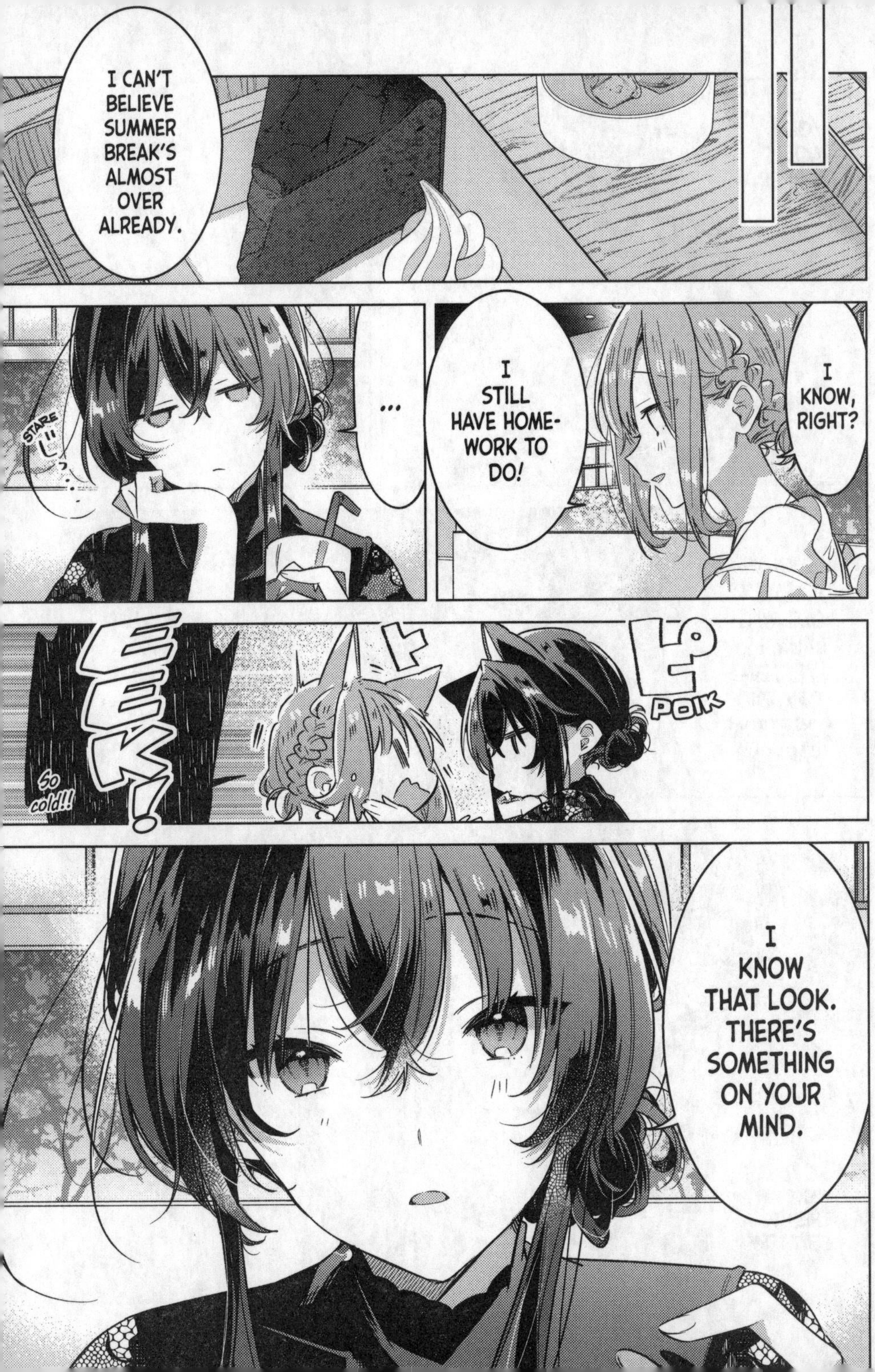
I CAN'T BELIEVE SUMMER BREAK'S ALMOST OVER ALREADY.
I KNOW, RIGHT?
I STILL HAVE HOME-WORK TO DO!
...
STARE
POIK
EEK!
So cold!!
I KNOW THAT LOOK. THERE'S SOMETHING ON YOUR MIND.

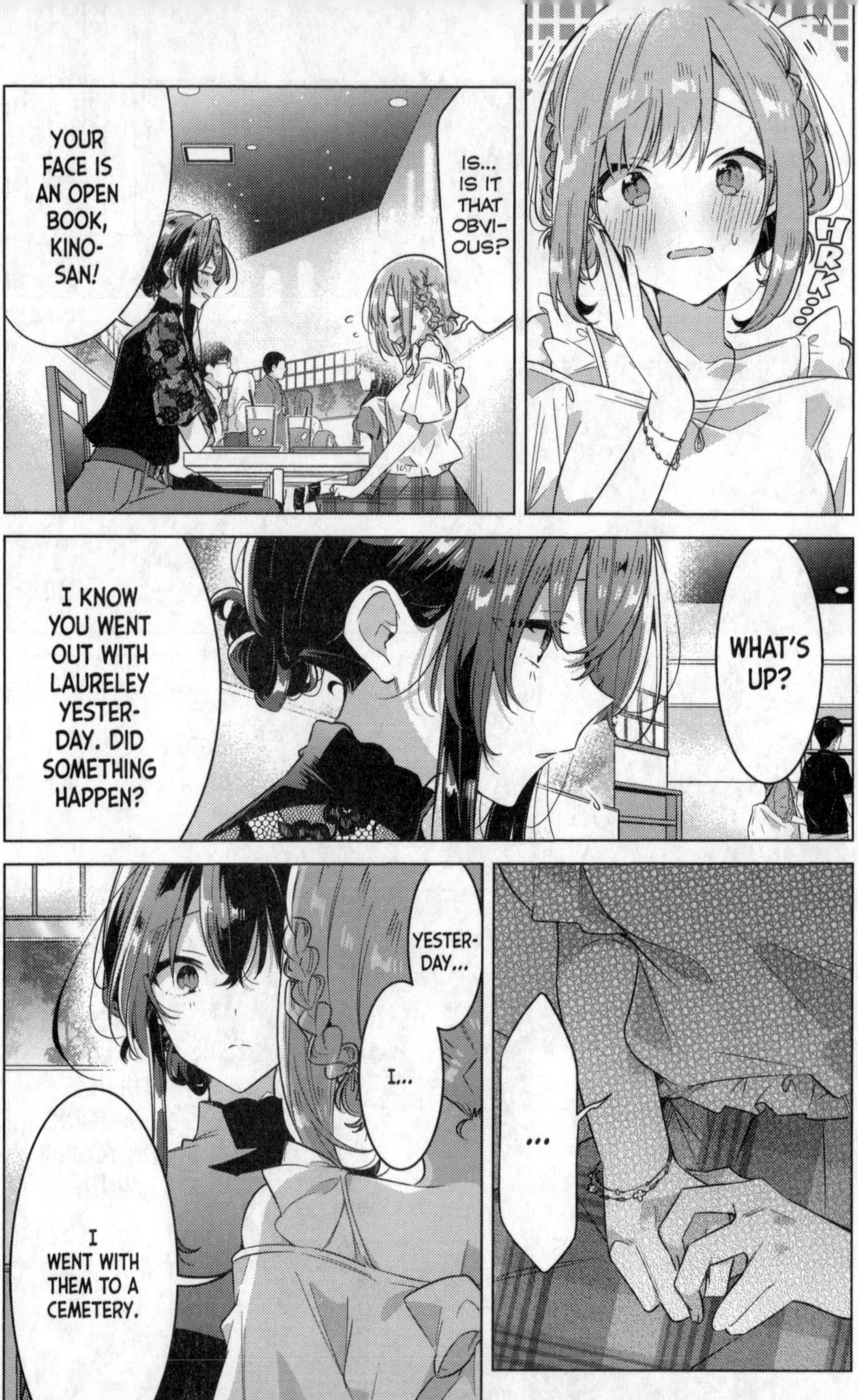
HRK...
YOUR FACE IS AN OPEN BOOK, KINO-SAN!
IS... IS IT THAT OBVIOUS?
WHAT'S UP?
I KNOW YOU WENT OUT WITH LAURELEY YESTERDAY. DID SOMETHING HAPPEN?
...
YESTERDAY...
I...
I WENT WITH THEM TO A CEMETERY.

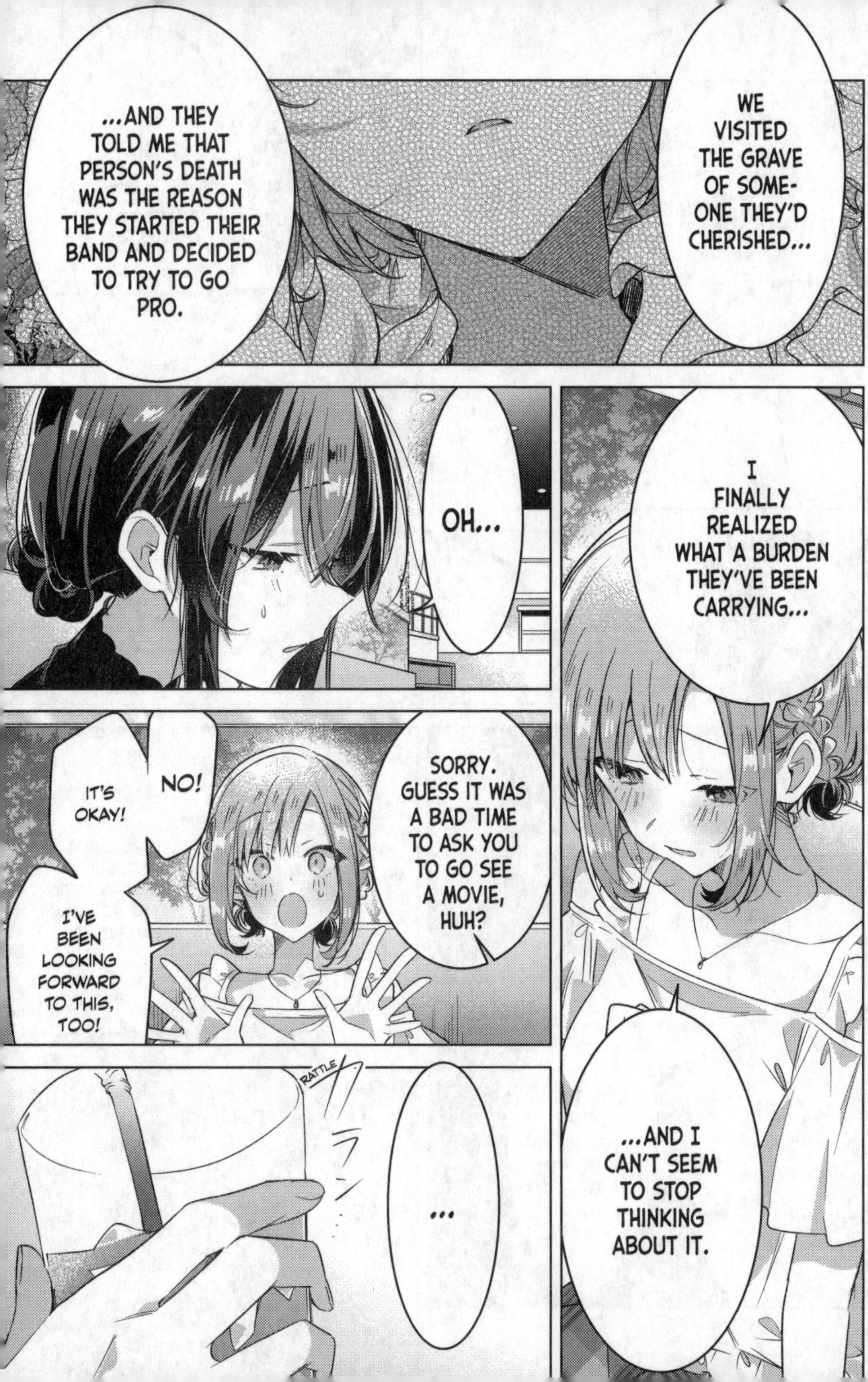
WE VISITED THE GRAVE OF SOME-ONE THEY'D CHERISHED...
...AND THEY TOLD ME THAT PERSON'S DEATH WAS THE REASON THEY STARTED THEIR BAND AND DECIDED TO TRY TO GO PRO.
I FINALLY REALIZED WHAT A BURDEN THEY'VE BEEN CARRYING...
...AND I CAN'T SEEM TO STOP THINKING ABOUT IT.
OH...
SORRY. GUESS IT WAS A BAD TIME TO ASK YOU TO GO SEE A MOVIE, HUH?
NO!
IT'S OKAY!
I'VE BEEN LOOKING FORWARD TO THIS, TOO!
RATTLE
...

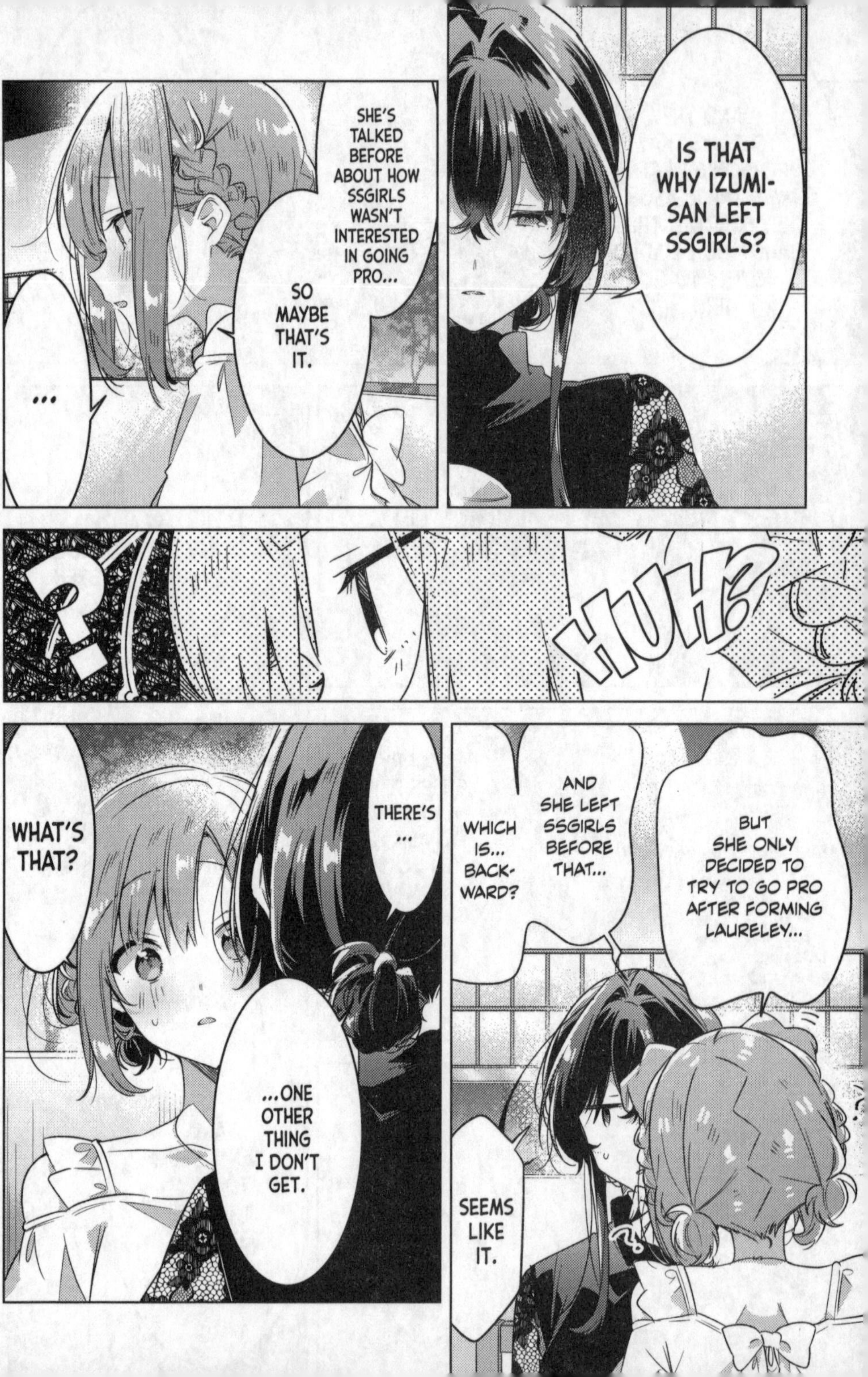
IS THAT WHY IZUMI-SAN LEFT SSGIRLS?
SHE'S TALKED BEFORE ABOUT HOW SSGIRLS WASN'T INTERESTED IN GOING PRO...
SO MAYBE THAT'S IT.
...
HUH?
?!
BUT SHE ONLY DECIDED TO TRY TO GO PRO AFTER FORMING LAURELEY...
AND SHE LEFT SSGIRLS BEFORE THAT...
WHICH IS... BACKWARD?
SEEMS LIKE IT.
THERE'S...
WHAT'S THAT?
...ONE OTHER THING I DON'T GET.

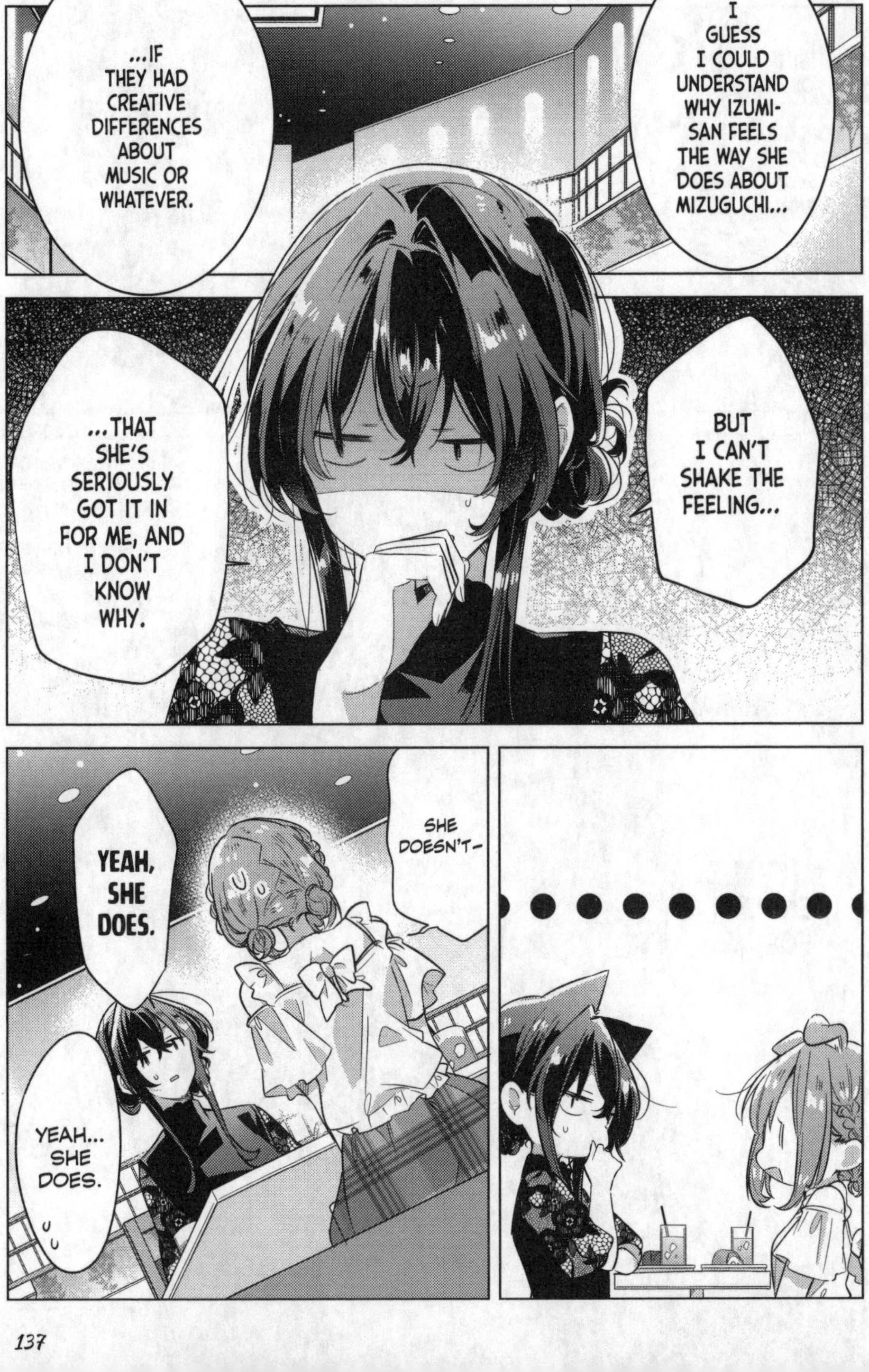
I GUESS I COULD UNDERSTAND WHY IZUMI-SAN FEELS THE WAY SHE DOES ABOUT MIZUGUCHI...
...IF THEY HAD CREATIVE DIFFERENCES ABOUT MUSIC OR WHATEVER.
BUT I CAN'T SHAKE THE FEELING...
...THAT SHE'S SERIOUSLY GOT IT IN FOR ME, AND I DON'T KNOW WHY.
• • • • • • • •
SHE DOESN'T-
YEAH, SHE DOES.
YEAH... SHE DOES.

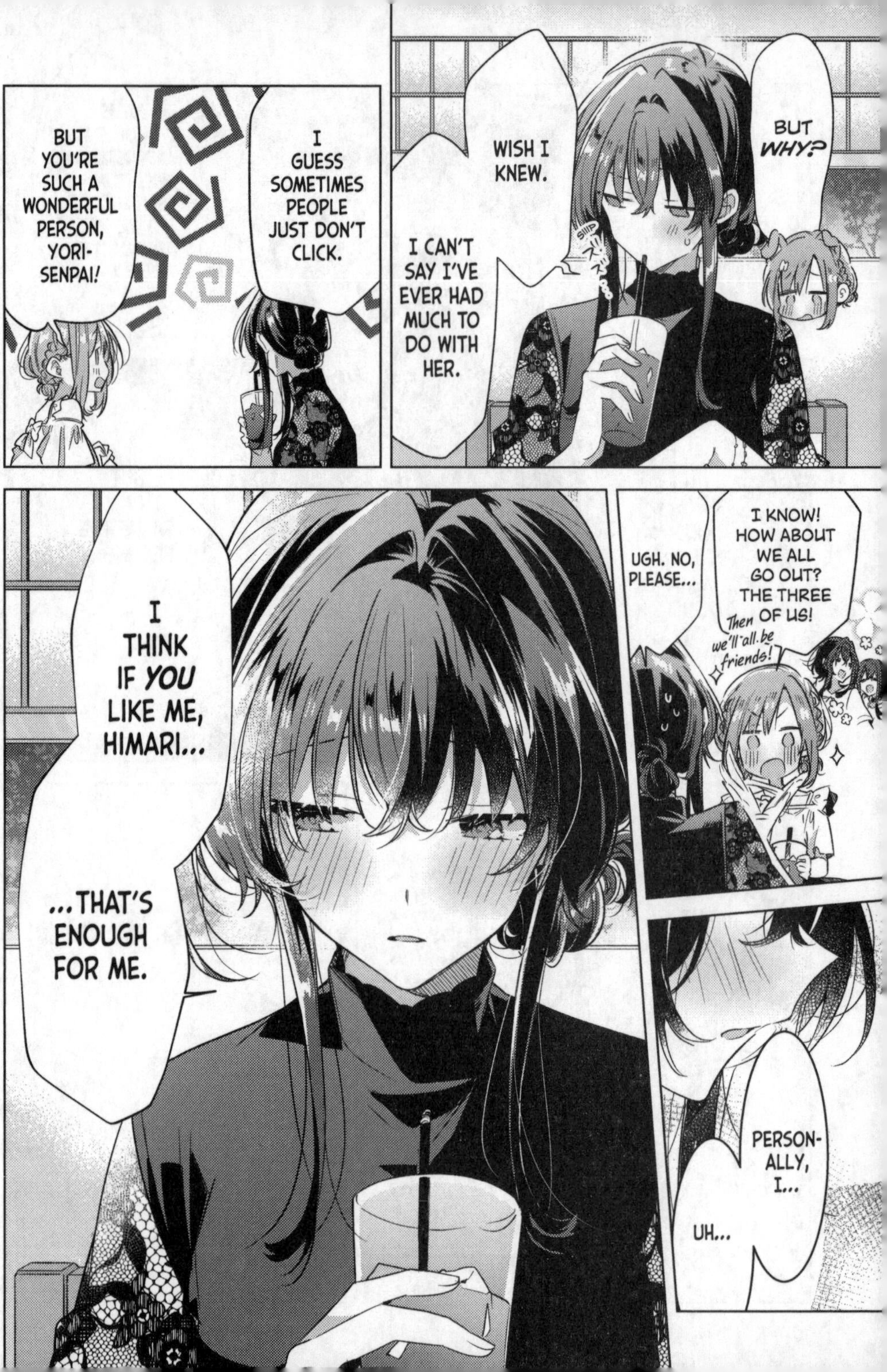
BUT *WHY?*
WISH I KNEW.
I CAN'T SAY I'VE EVER HAD MUCH TO DO WITH HER.
I GUESS SOMETIMES PEOPLE JUST DON'T CLICK.
BUT YOU'RE SUCH A WONDERFUL PERSON, YORI-SENPAI!
I KNOW! HOW ABOUT WE ALL GO OUT? THE THREE OF US!
Then we'll all be friends!
UGH. NO, PLEASE...
PERSON-ALLY, I...
UH...
I THINK IF *YOU* LIKE ME, HIMARI...
...THAT'S ENOUGH FOR ME.

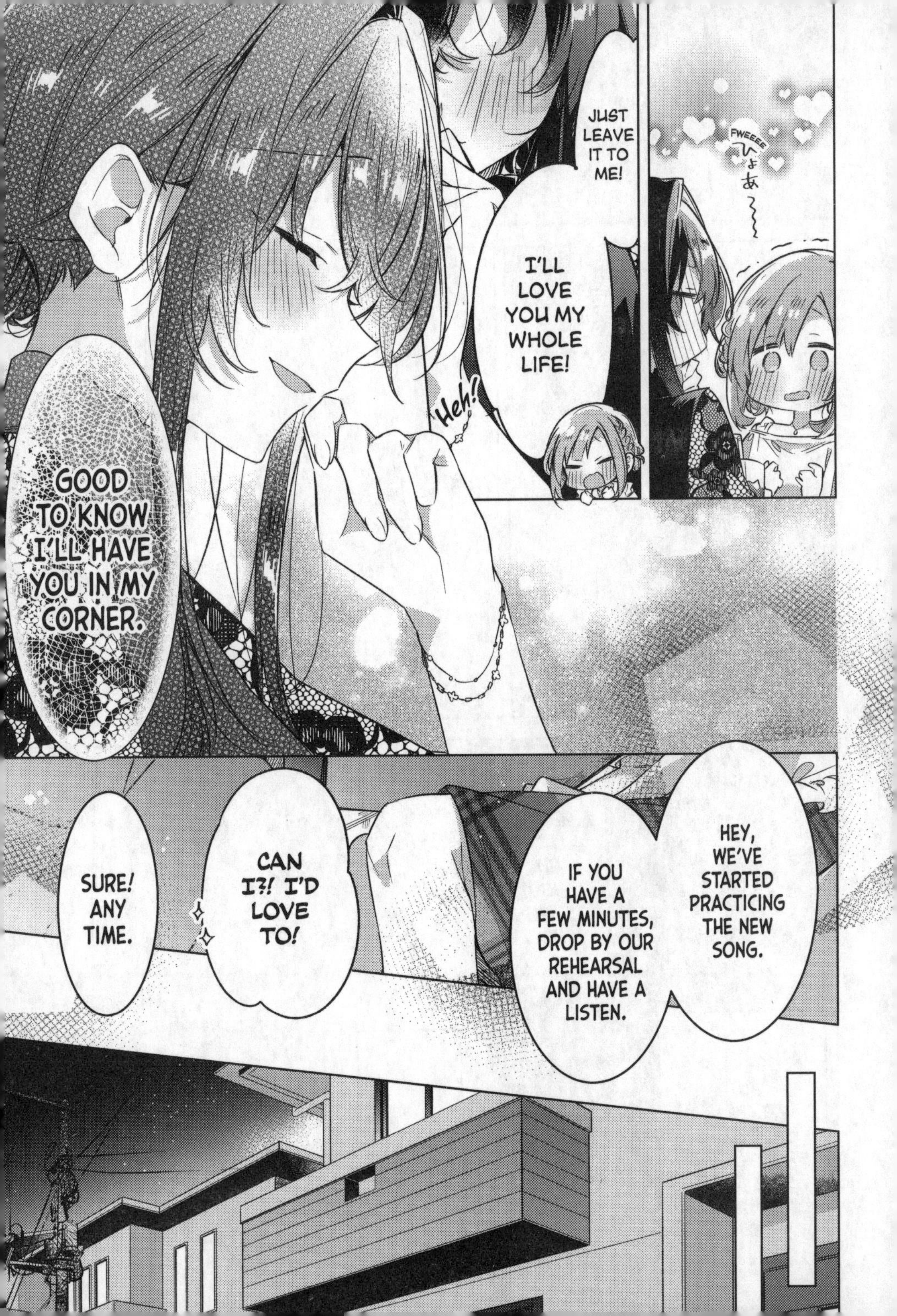
FWEEEE
ひょあ～～～
JUST LEAVE IT TO ME!
I'LL LOVE YOU MY WHOLE LIFE!
Heh!
GOOD TO KNOW I'LL HAVE YOU IN MY CORNER.
HEY, WE'VE STARTED PRACTICING THE NEW SONG.
IF YOU HAVE A FEW MINUTES, DROP BY OUR REHEARSAL AND HAVE A LISTEN.
CAN I?! I'D LOVE TO!
SURE! ANY TIME.

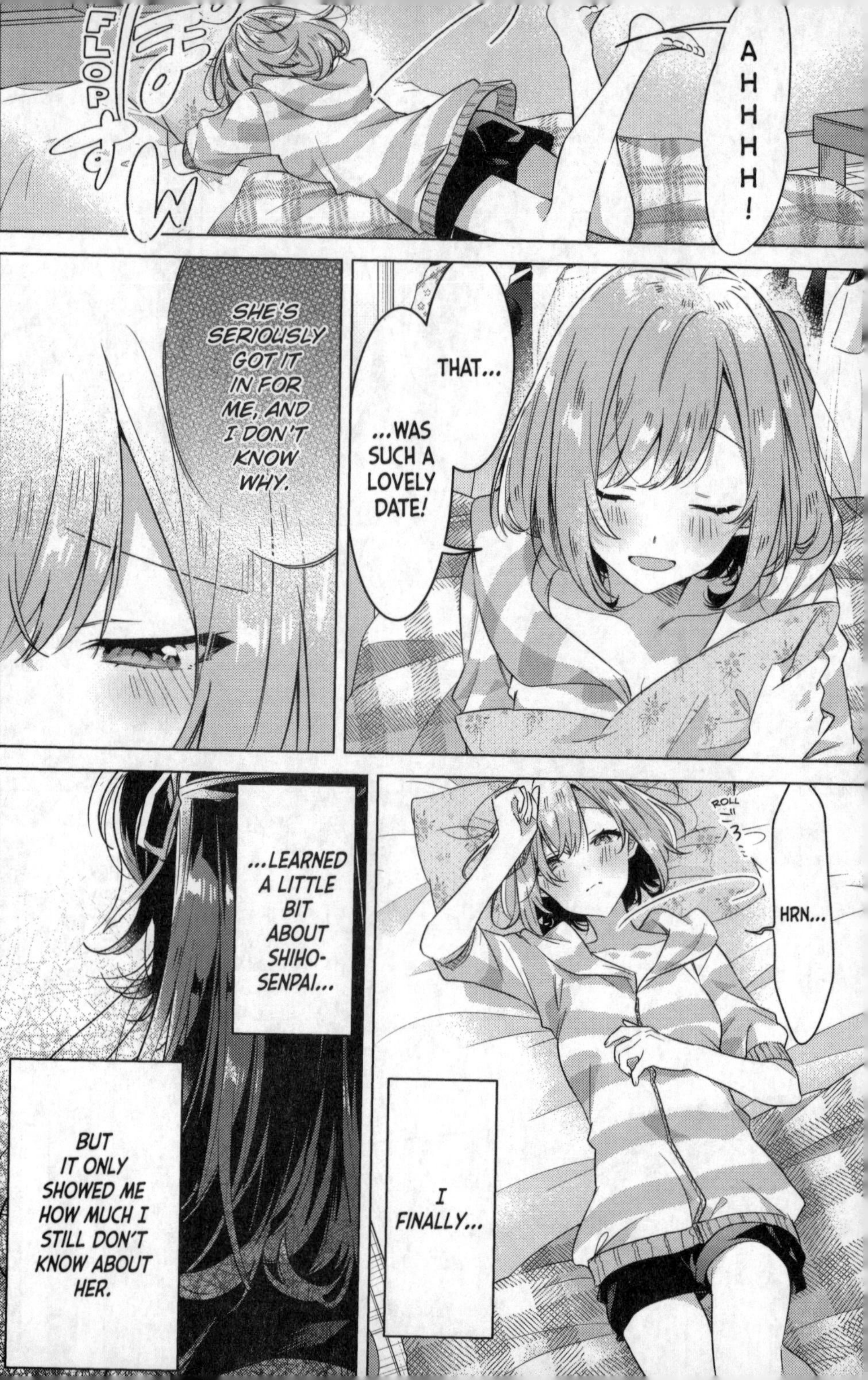
AHHHH!
FLOP
THAT...
...WAS SUCH A LOVELY DATE!
SHE'S SERIOUSLY GOT IT IN FOR ME, AND I DON'T KNOW WHY.
ROLL
HRN...
I FINALLY...
...LEARNED A LITTLE BIT ABOUT SHIHO-SENPAI...
BUT IT ONLY SHOWED ME HOW MUCH I STILL DON'T KNOW ABOUT HER.

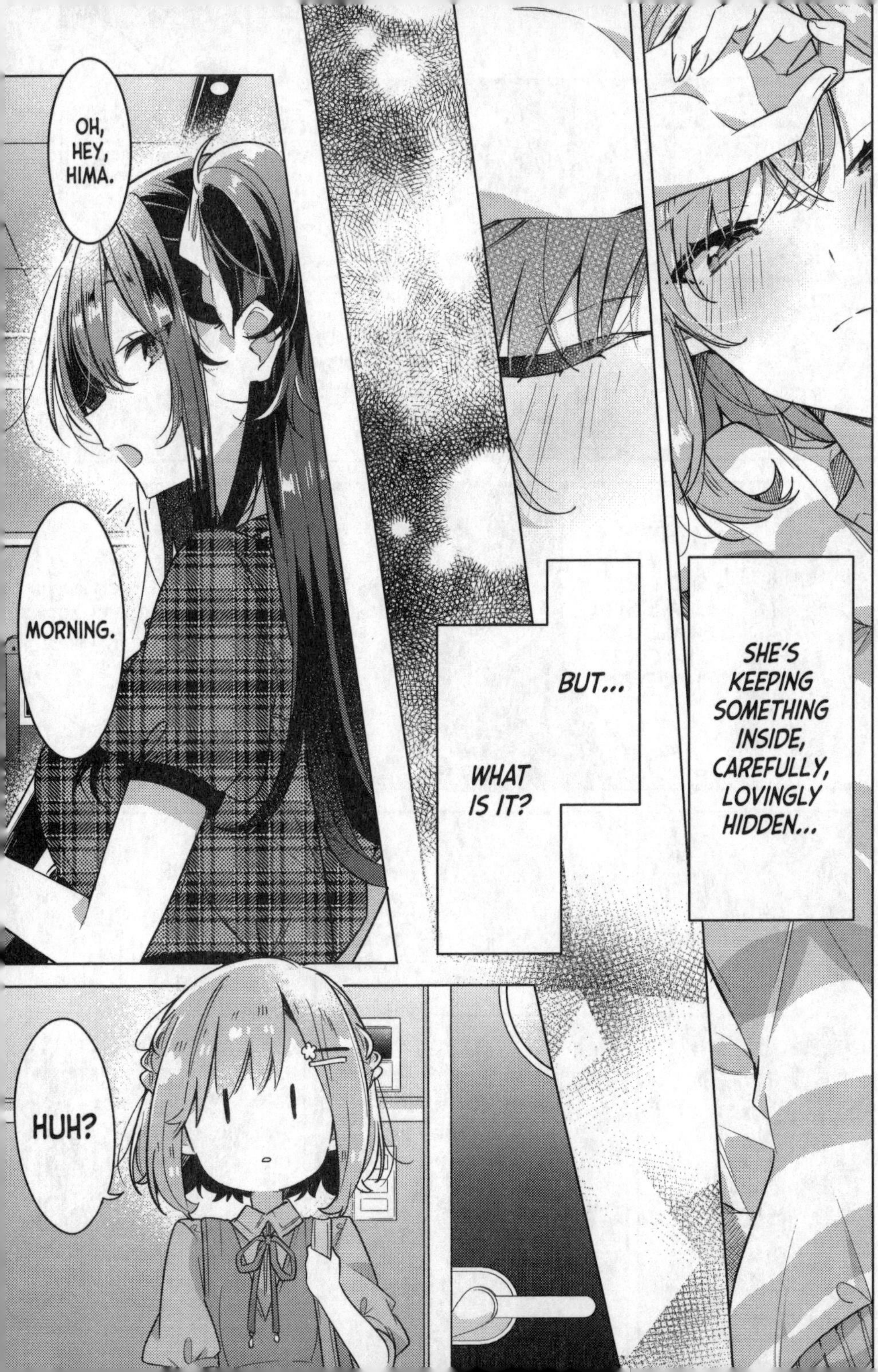
SHE'S KEEPING SOMETHING INSIDE, CAREFULLY, LOVINGLY HIDDEN...
BUT... WHAT IS IT?
OH, HEY, HIMA.
MORNING.
HUH?

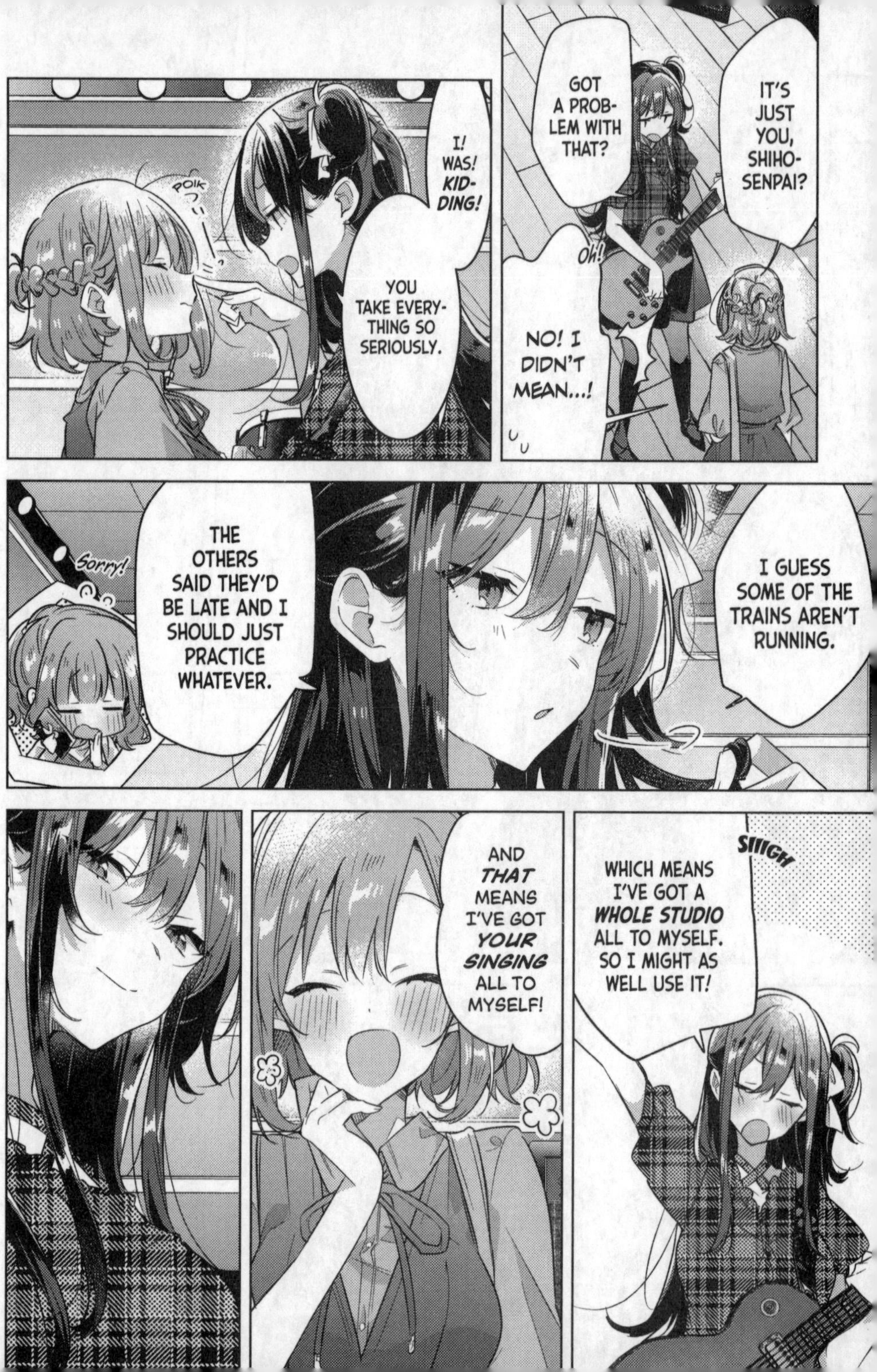
IT'S JUST YOU, SHIHO-SENPAI?
GOT A PROBLEM WITH THAT?
Oh!
NO! I DIDN'T MEAN...!
I! WAS! KIDDING!
POIK
YOU TAKE EVERYTHING SO SERIOUSLY.
I GUESS SOME OF THE TRAINS AREN'T RUNNING.
THE OTHERS SAID THEY'D BE LATE AND I SHOULD JUST PRACTICE WHATEVER.
Sorry!
SIIIGH
WHICH MEANS I'VE GOT A *WHOLE STUDIO* ALL TO MYSELF. SO I MIGHT AS WELL USE IT!
AND *THAT* MEANS I'VE GOT *YOUR SINGING* ALL TO MYSELF!

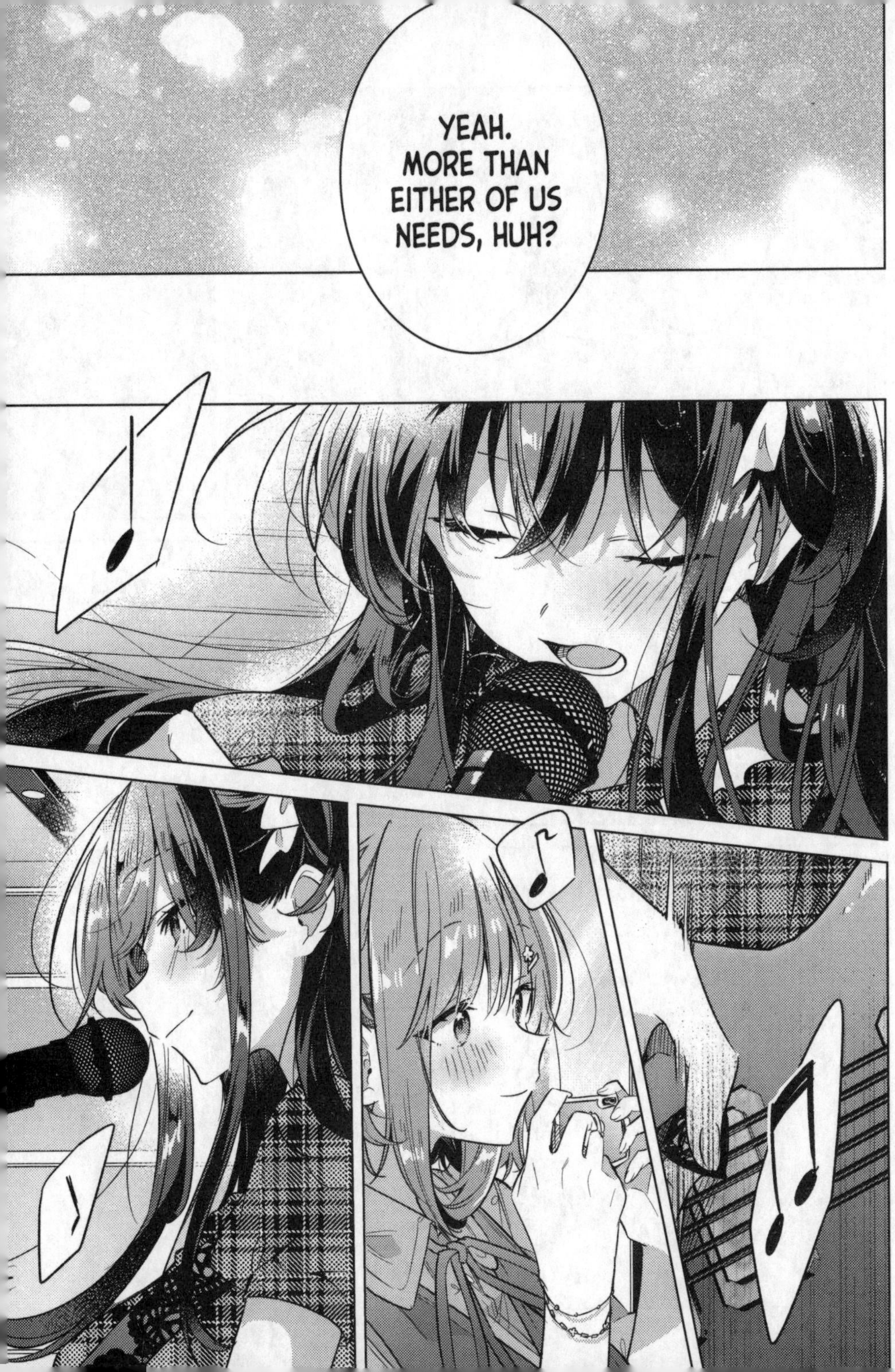
YEAH. MORE THAN EITHER OF US NEEDS, HUH?

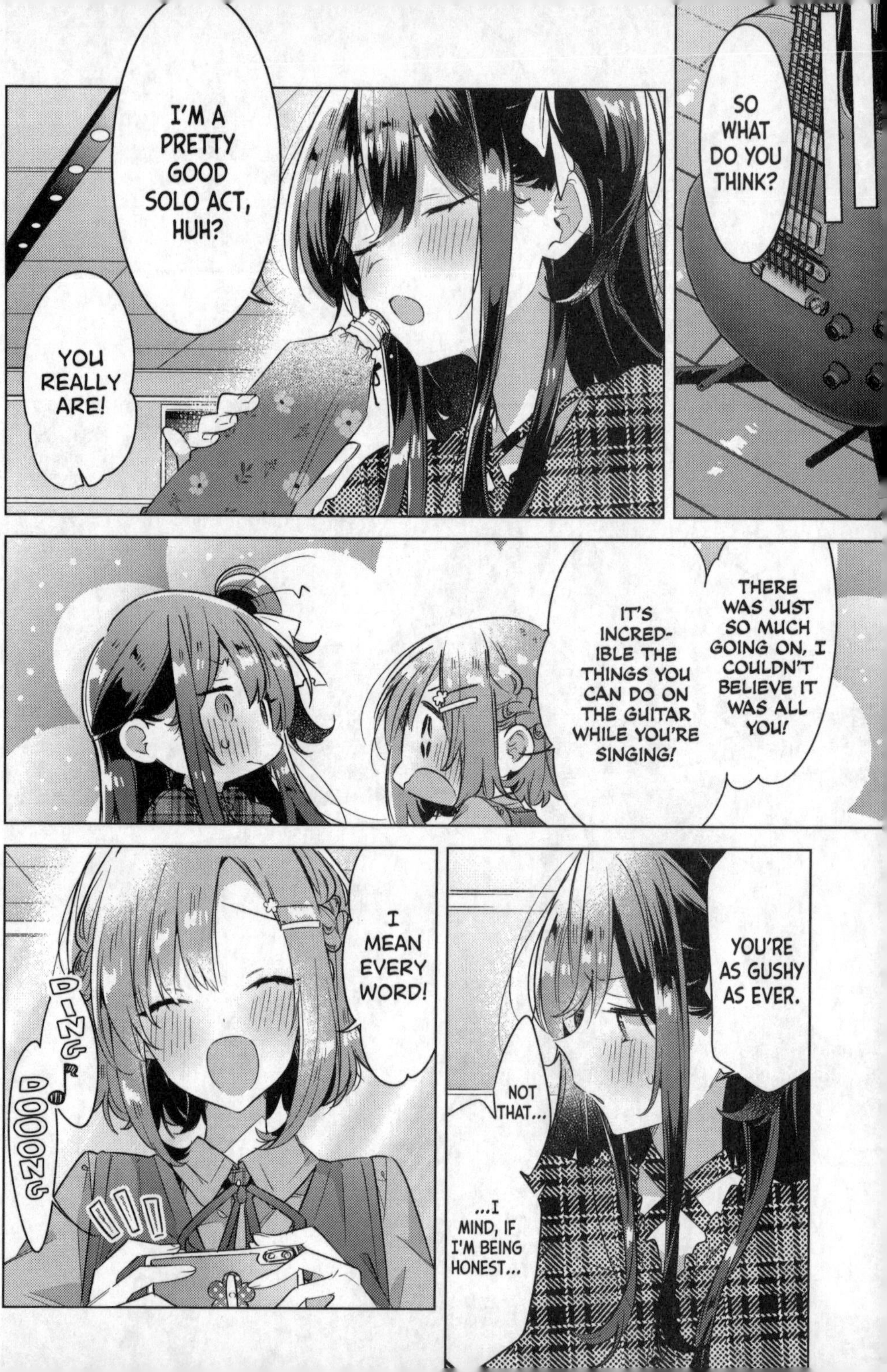
SO WHAT DO YOU THINK?
I'M A PRETTY GOOD SOLO ACT, HUH?
YOU REALLY ARE!
THERE WAS JUST SO MUCH GOING ON, I COULDN'T BELIEVE IT WAS ALL YOU!
IT'S INCRED-IBLE THE THINGS YOU CAN DO ON THE GUITAR WHILE YOU'RE SINGING!
YOU'RE AS GUSHY AS EVER.
NOT THAT...
...I MIND, IF I'M BEING HONEST...
I MEAN EVERY WORD!
DING DOOONG
!!!

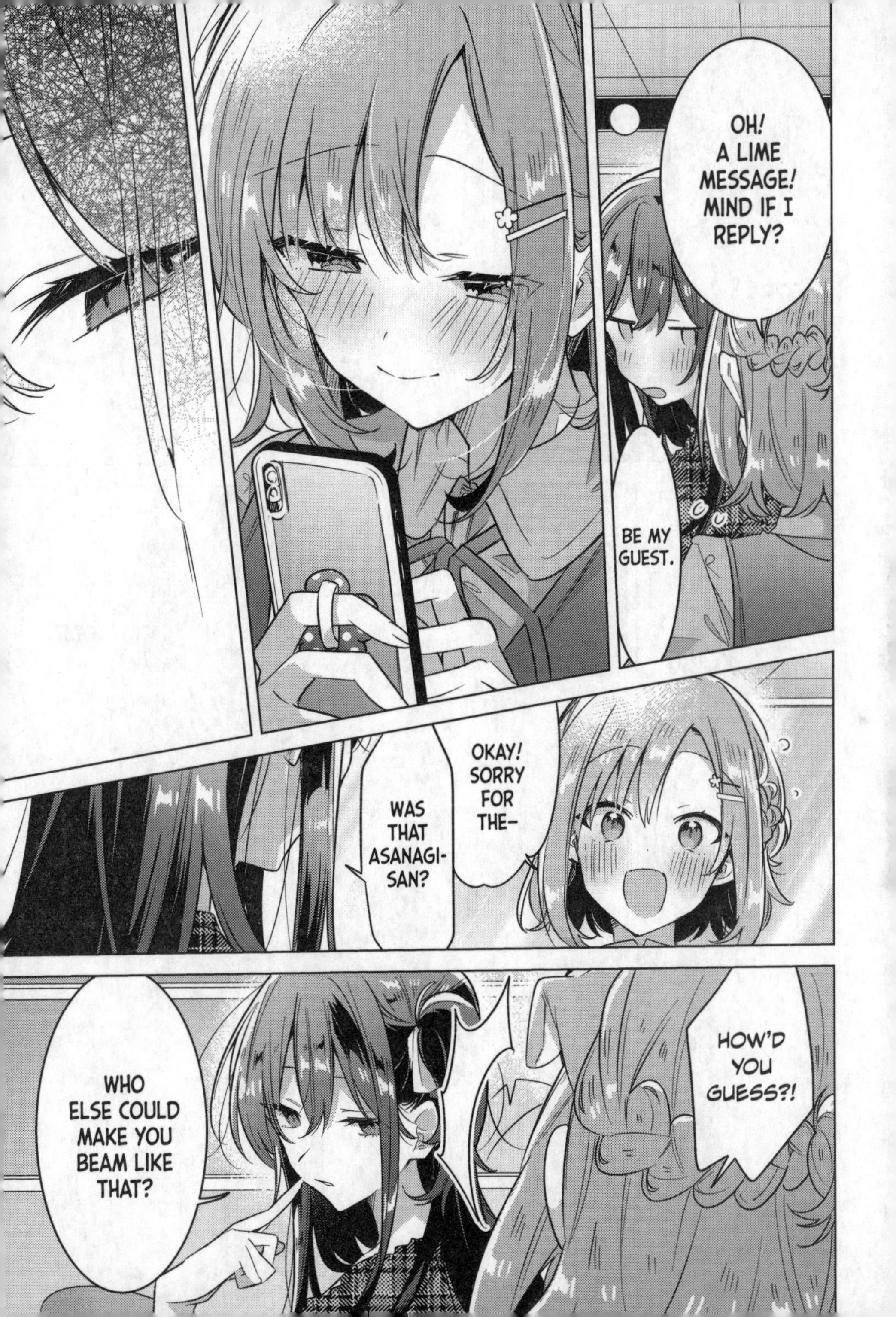
OH! A LIME MESSAGE! MIND IF I REPLY?
BE MY GUEST.
OKAY! SORRY FOR THE-
WAS THAT ASANAGI-SAN?
HOW'D YOU GUESS?!
WHO ELSE COULD MAKE YOU BEAM LIKE THAT?

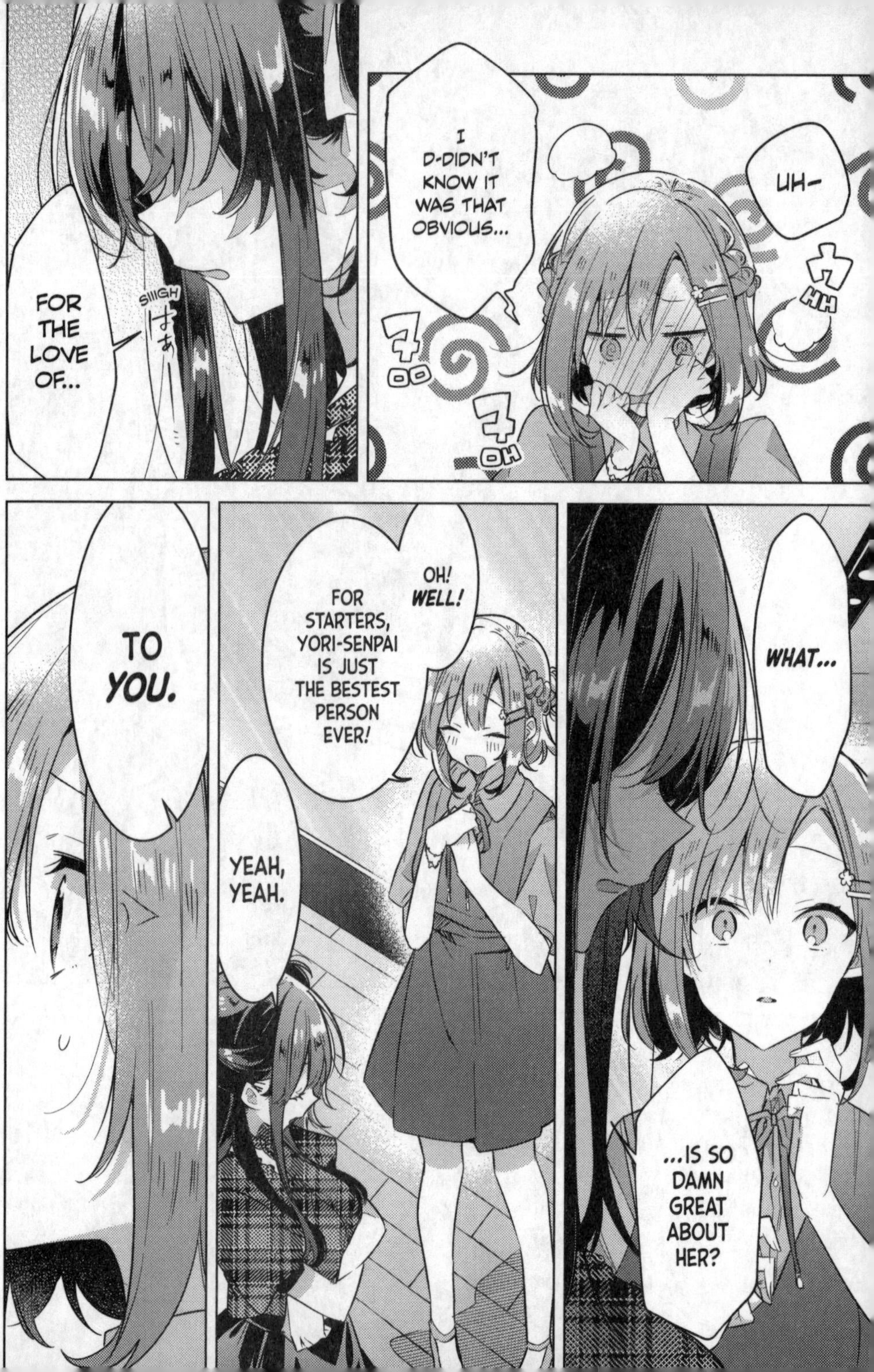
UH-
ウ
HH
I D-DIDN'T KNOW IT WAS THAT OBVIOUS...
OO
OH
SIIIGH
はぁ
FOR THE LOVE OF...
WHAT...
...IS SO DAMN GREAT ABOUT HER?
OH! WELL!
FOR STARTERS, YORI-SENPAI IS JUST THE BESTEST PERSON EVER!
YEAH, YEAH.
TO YOU.

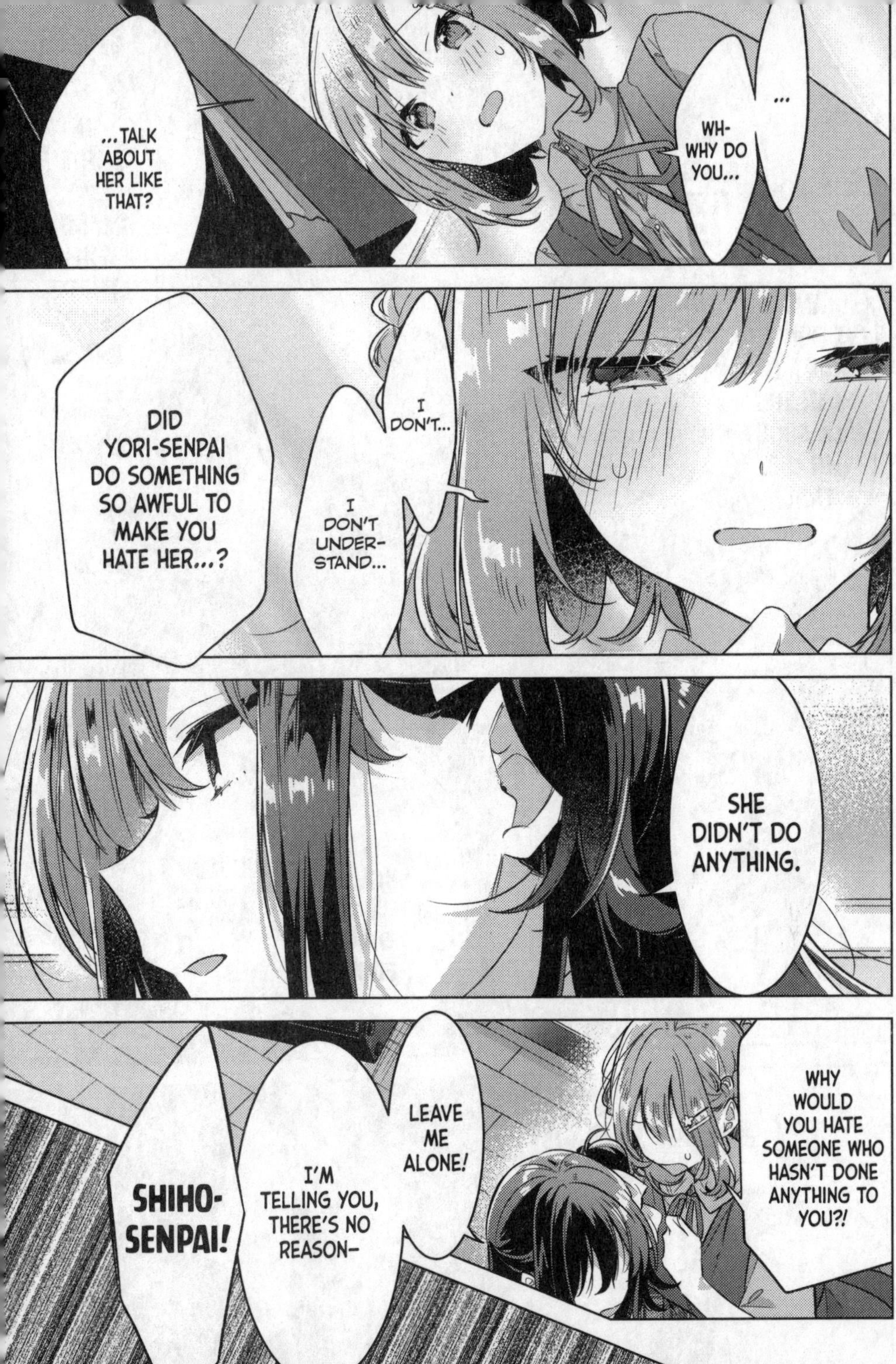
...
WH- WHY DO YOU...
...TALK ABOUT HER LIKE THAT?
I DON'T...
I DON'T UNDER-STAND...
DID YORI-SENPAI DO SOMETHING SO AWFUL TO MAKE YOU HATE HER...?
SHE DIDN'T DO ANYTHING.
WHY WOULD YOU HATE SOMEONE WHO HASN'T DONE ANYTHING TO YOU?!
LEAVE ME ALONE!
I'M TELLING YOU, THERE'S NO REASON–
SHIHO-SENPAI!

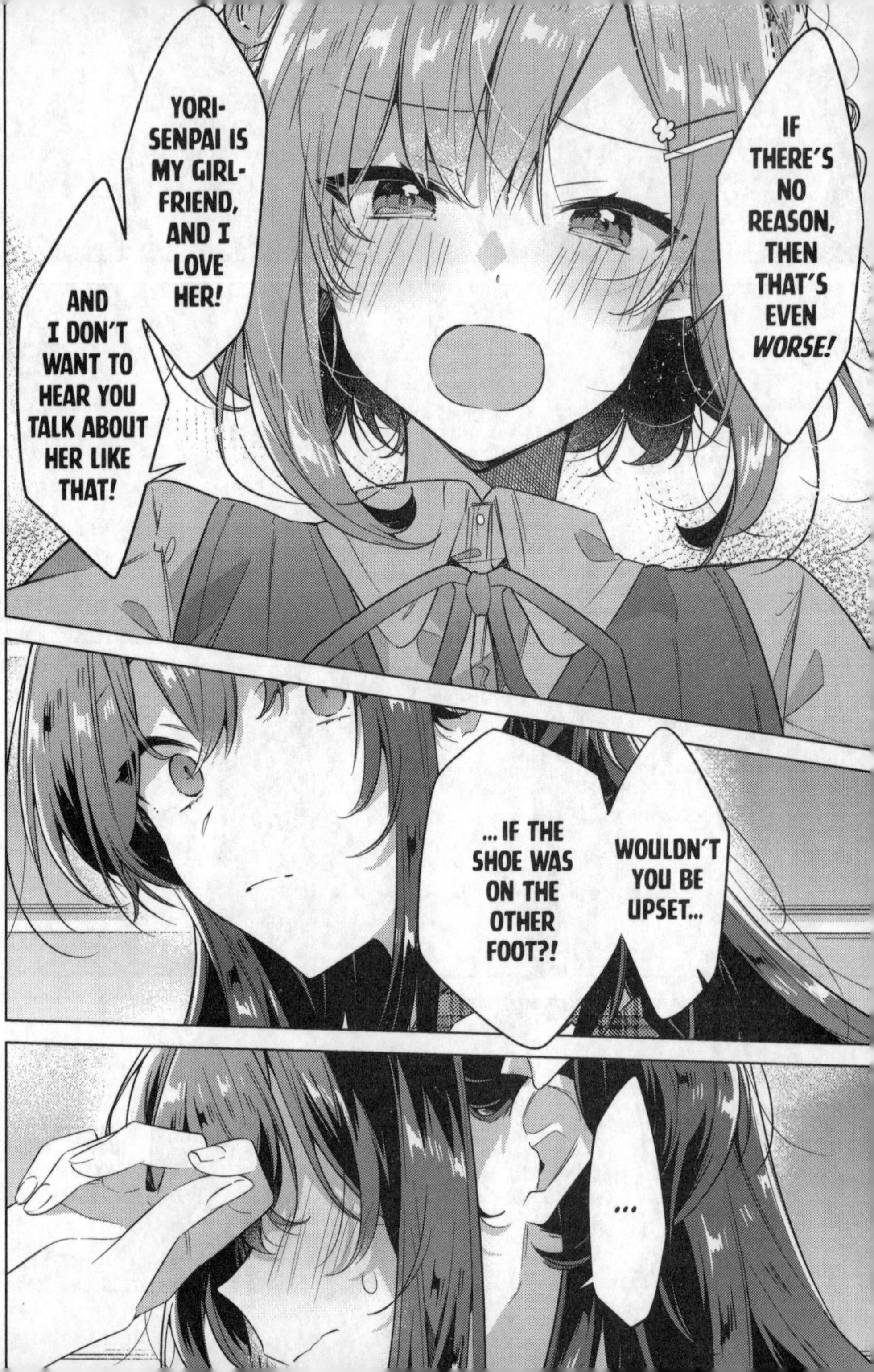
IF THERE'S NO REASON, THEN THAT'S EVEN *WORSE!*
YORI-SENPAI IS MY GIRLFRIEND, AND I LOVE HER!
AND I DON'T WANT TO HEAR YOU TALK ABOUT HER LIKE THAT!
WOULDN'T YOU BE UPSET...
...IF THE SHOE WAS ON THE OTHER FOOT?!
...

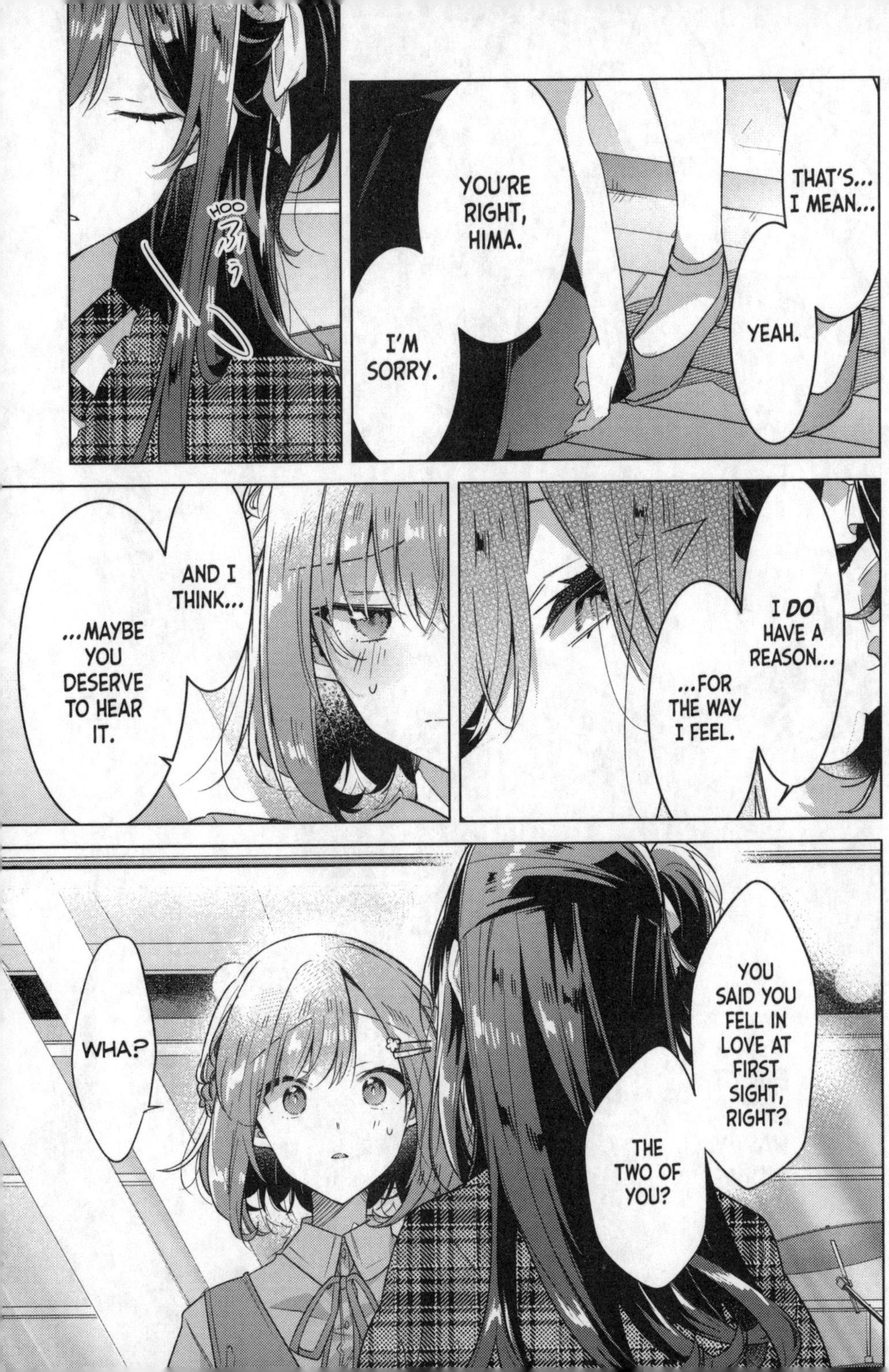
THAT'S... I MEAN...
YEAH.
YOU'RE RIGHT, HIMA.
I'M SORRY.
HOO ふぅ
I *DO* HAVE A REASON...
...FOR THE WAY I FEEL.
AND I THINK...
...MAYBE YOU DESERVE TO HEAR IT.
YOU SAID YOU FELL IN LOVE AT FIRST SIGHT, RIGHT?
THE TWO OF YOU?
WHA?

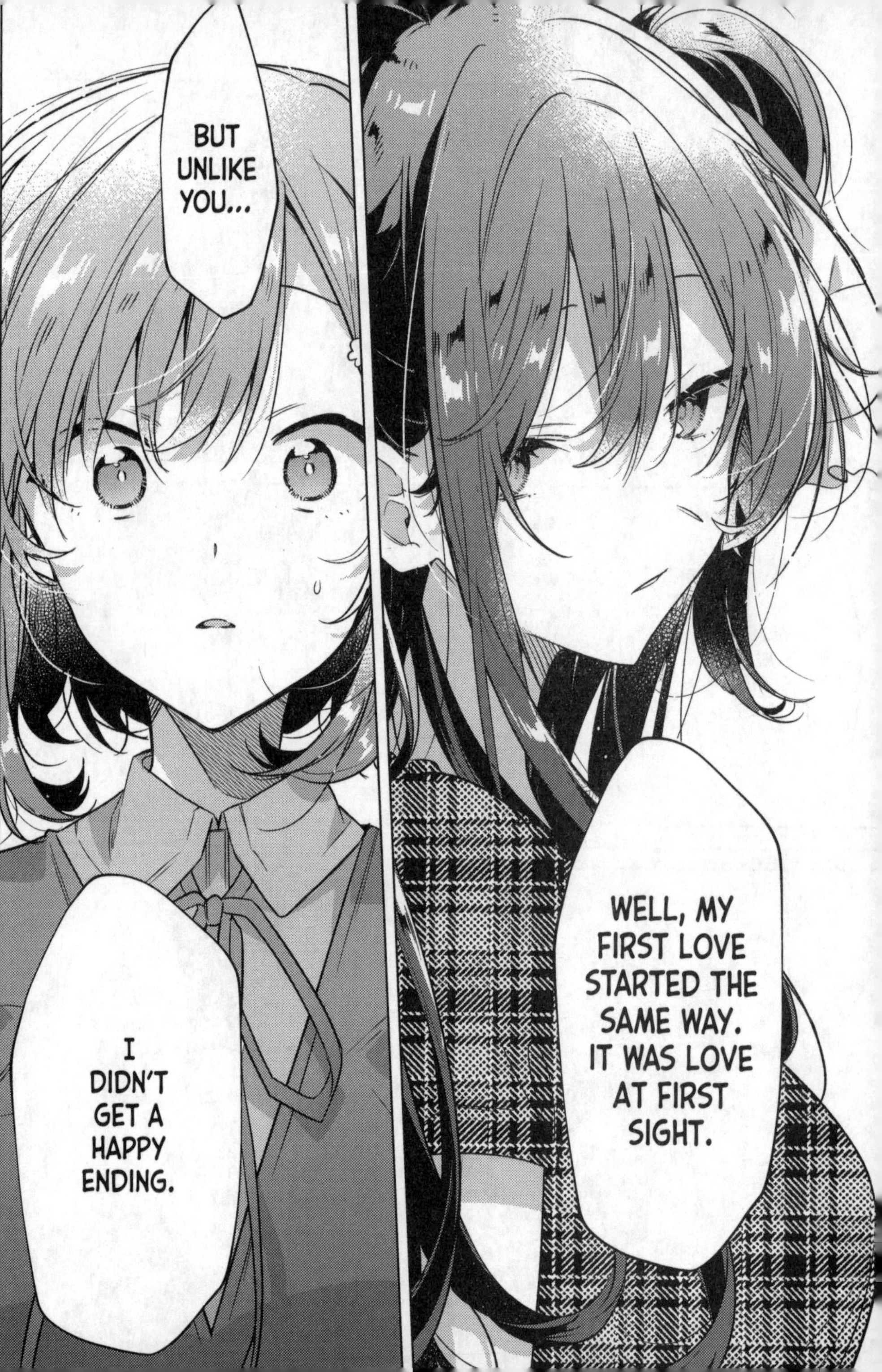
WELL, MY FIRST LOVE STARTED THE SAME WAY. IT WAS LOVE AT FIRST SIGHT.
BUT UNLIKE YOU...
I DIDN'T GET A HAPPY ENDING.

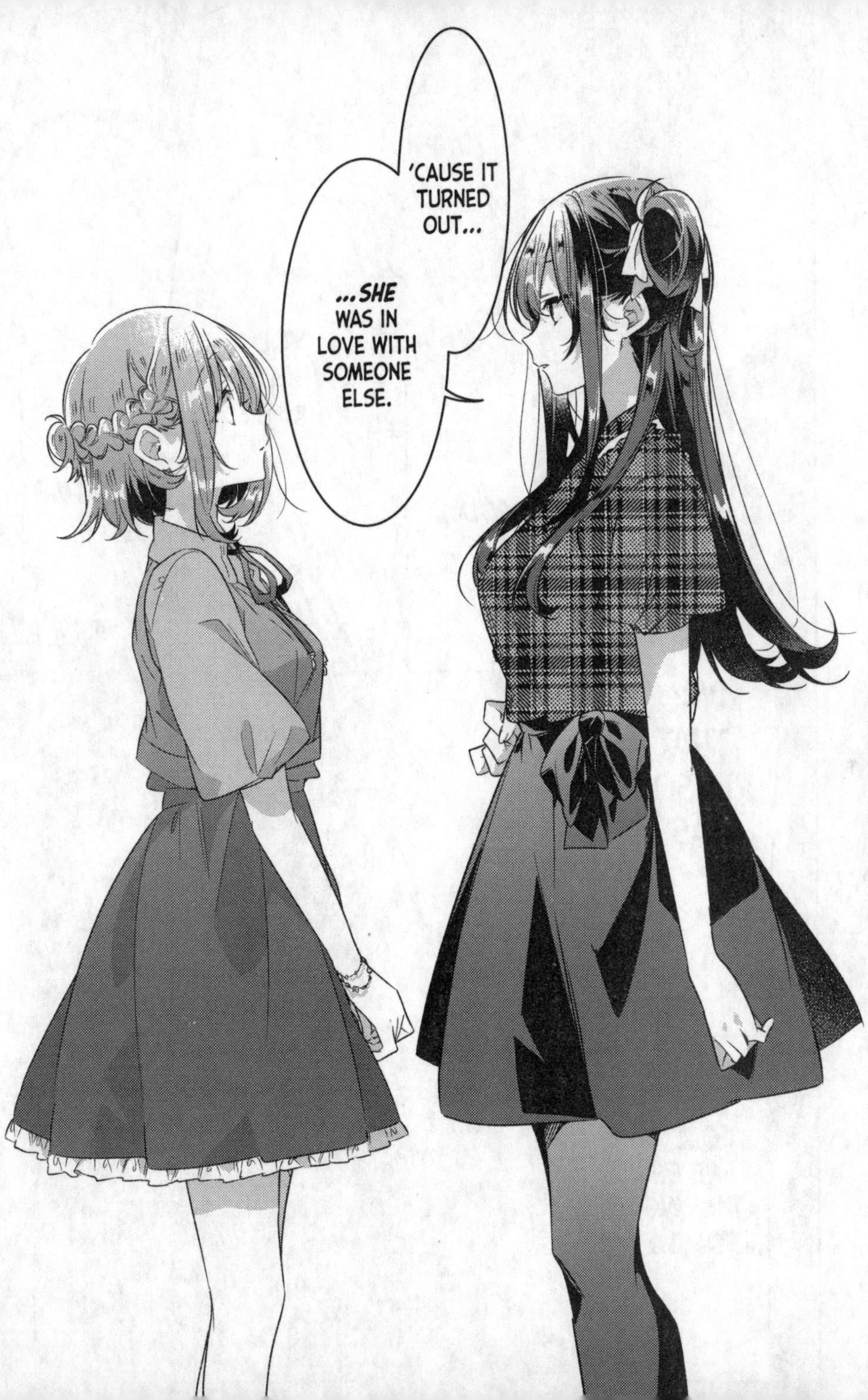
'CAUSE IT TURNED OUT... ...*SHE* WAS IN LOVE WITH SOMEONE ELSE.

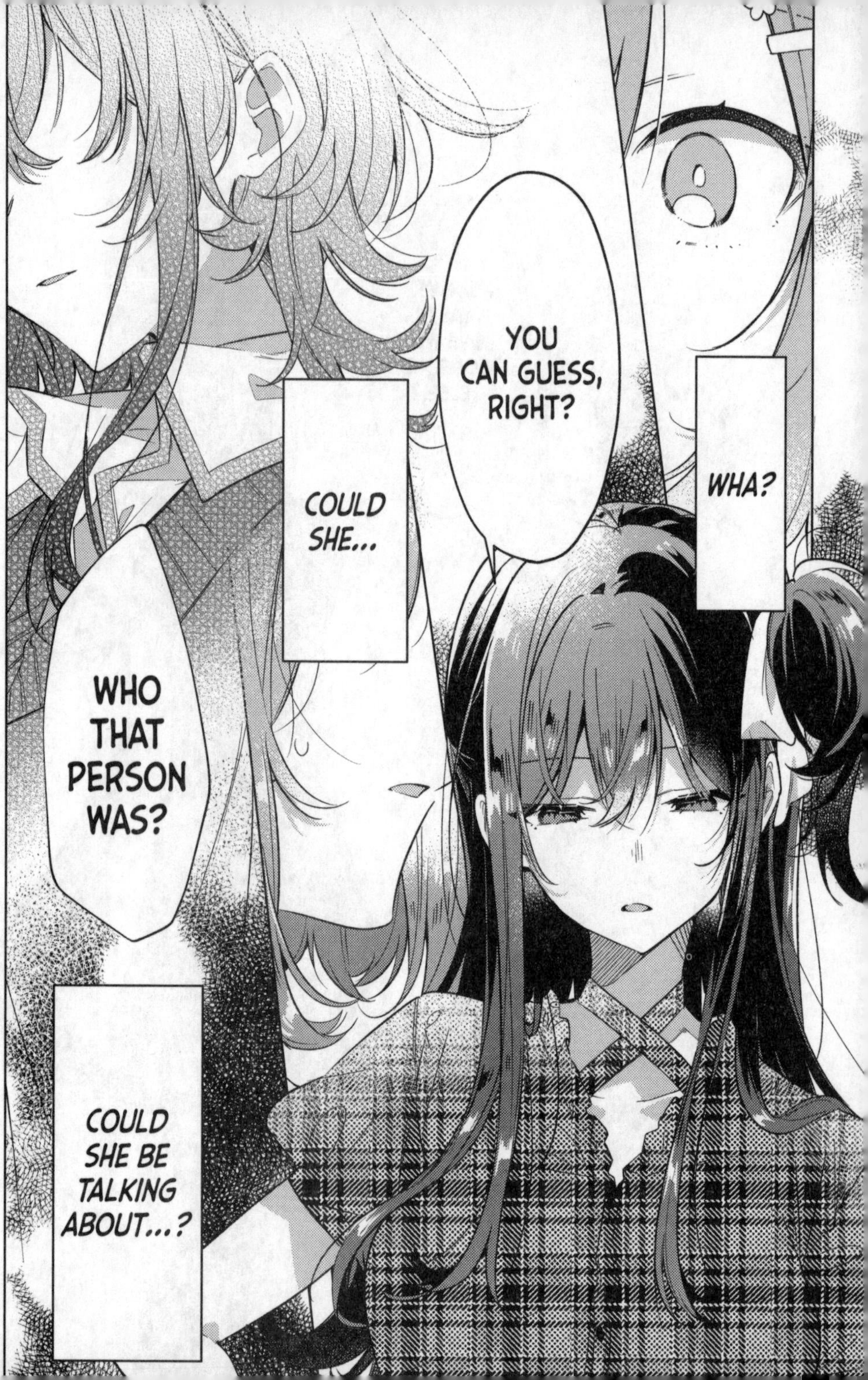
WHA?
YOU CAN GUESS, RIGHT?
COULD SHE...
WHO THAT PERSON WAS?
COULD SHE BE TALKING ABOUT...?

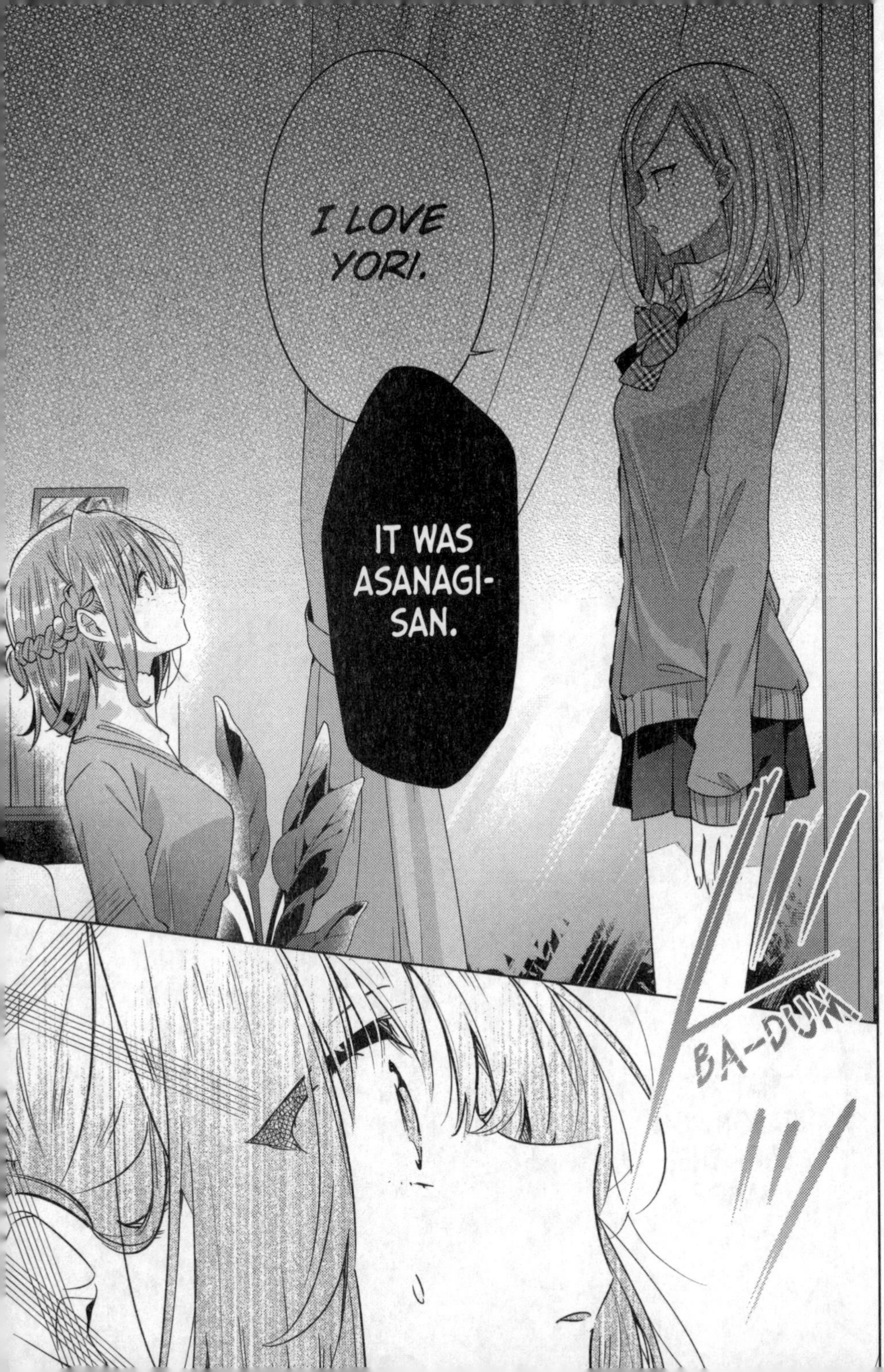
I LOVE YORI.
IT WAS ASANAGI-SAN.
BA-DUM

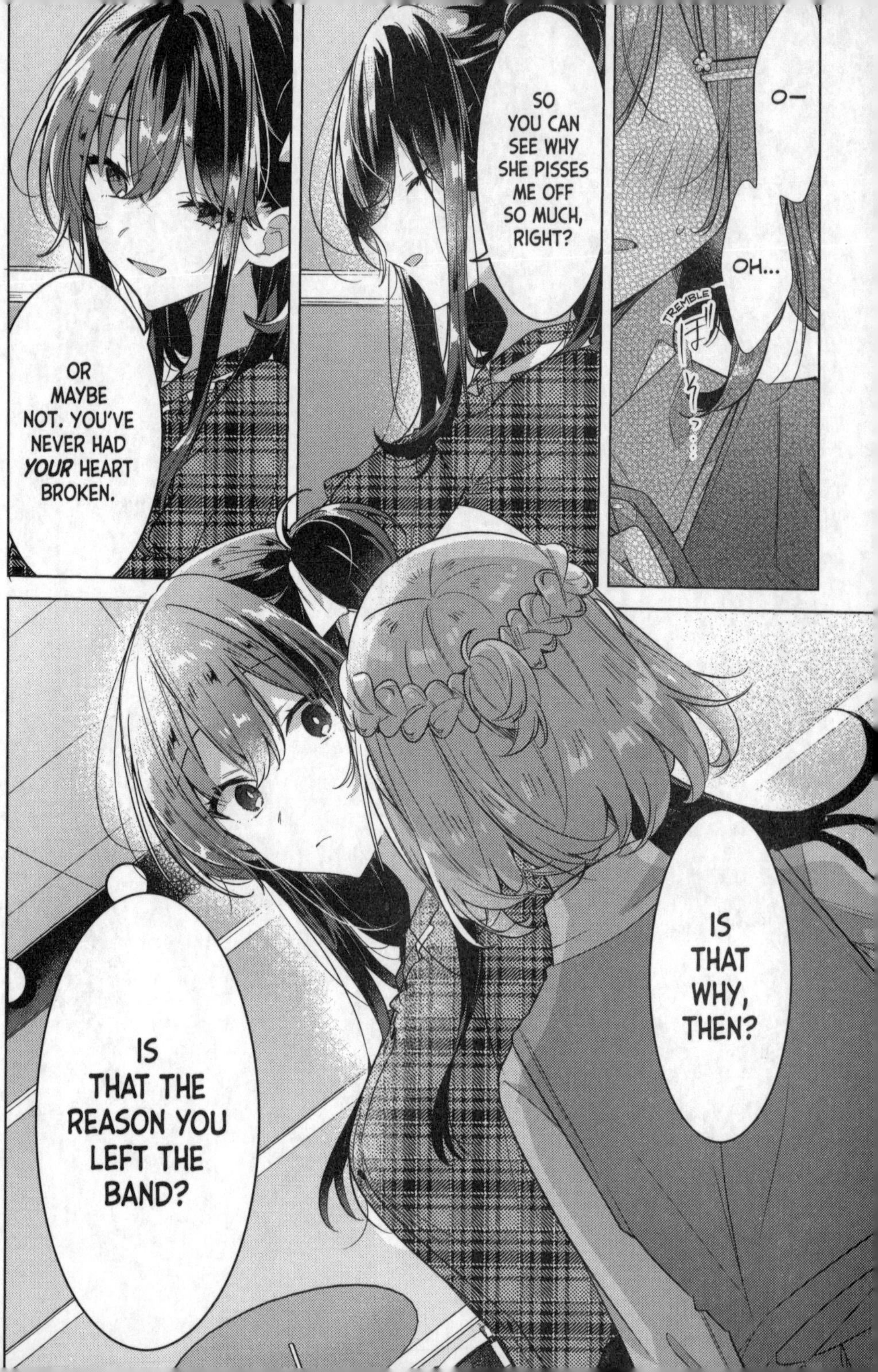
O—
OH...
TREMBLE
SO YOU CAN SEE WHY SHE PISSES ME OFF SO MUCH, RIGHT?
OR MAYBE NOT. YOU'VE NEVER HAD *YOUR* HEART BROKEN.
IS THAT WHY, THEN?
IS THAT THE REASON YOU LEFT THE BAND?

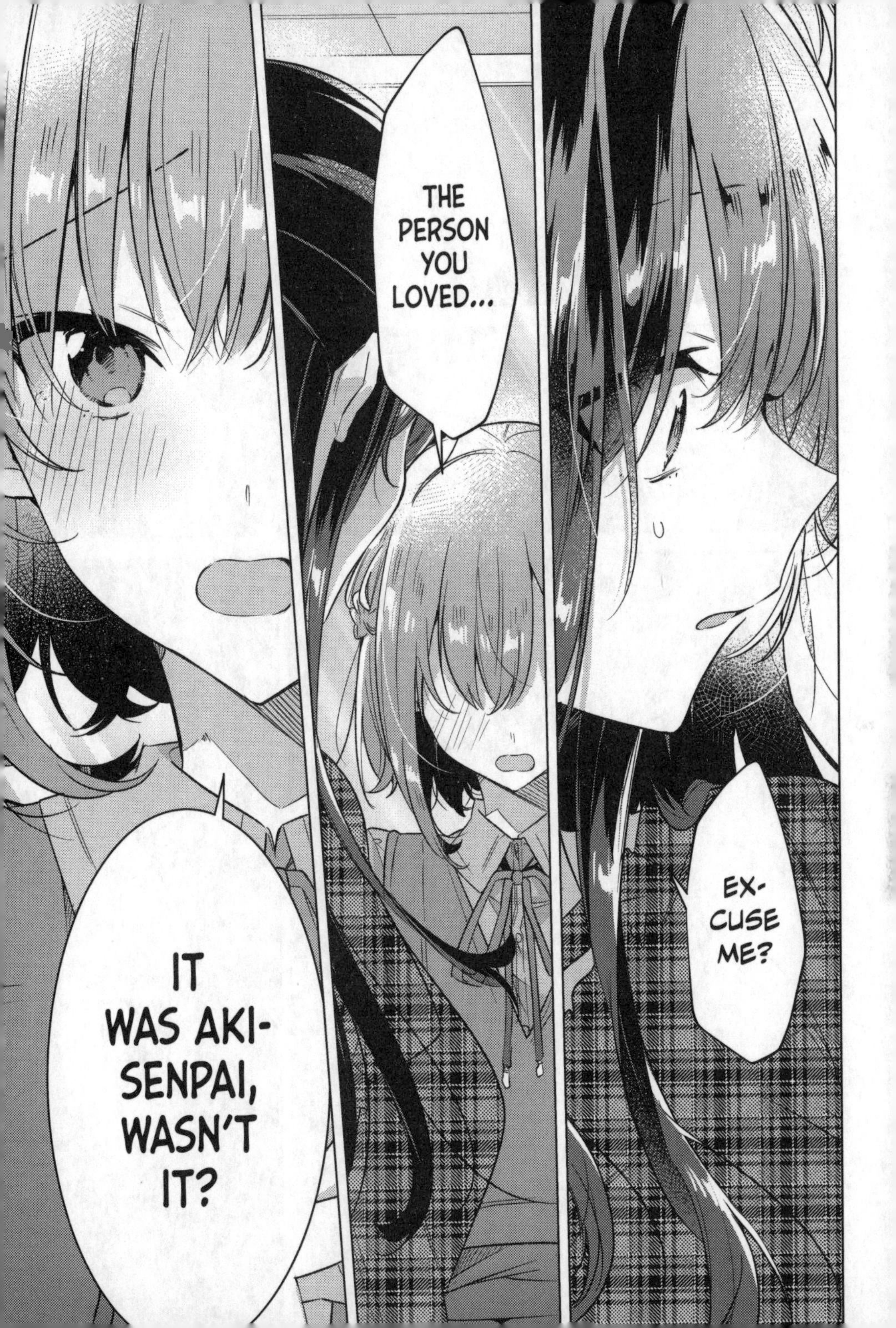
EX-CUSE ME?
THE PERSON YOU LOVED...
IT WAS AKI-SENPAI, WASN'T IT?

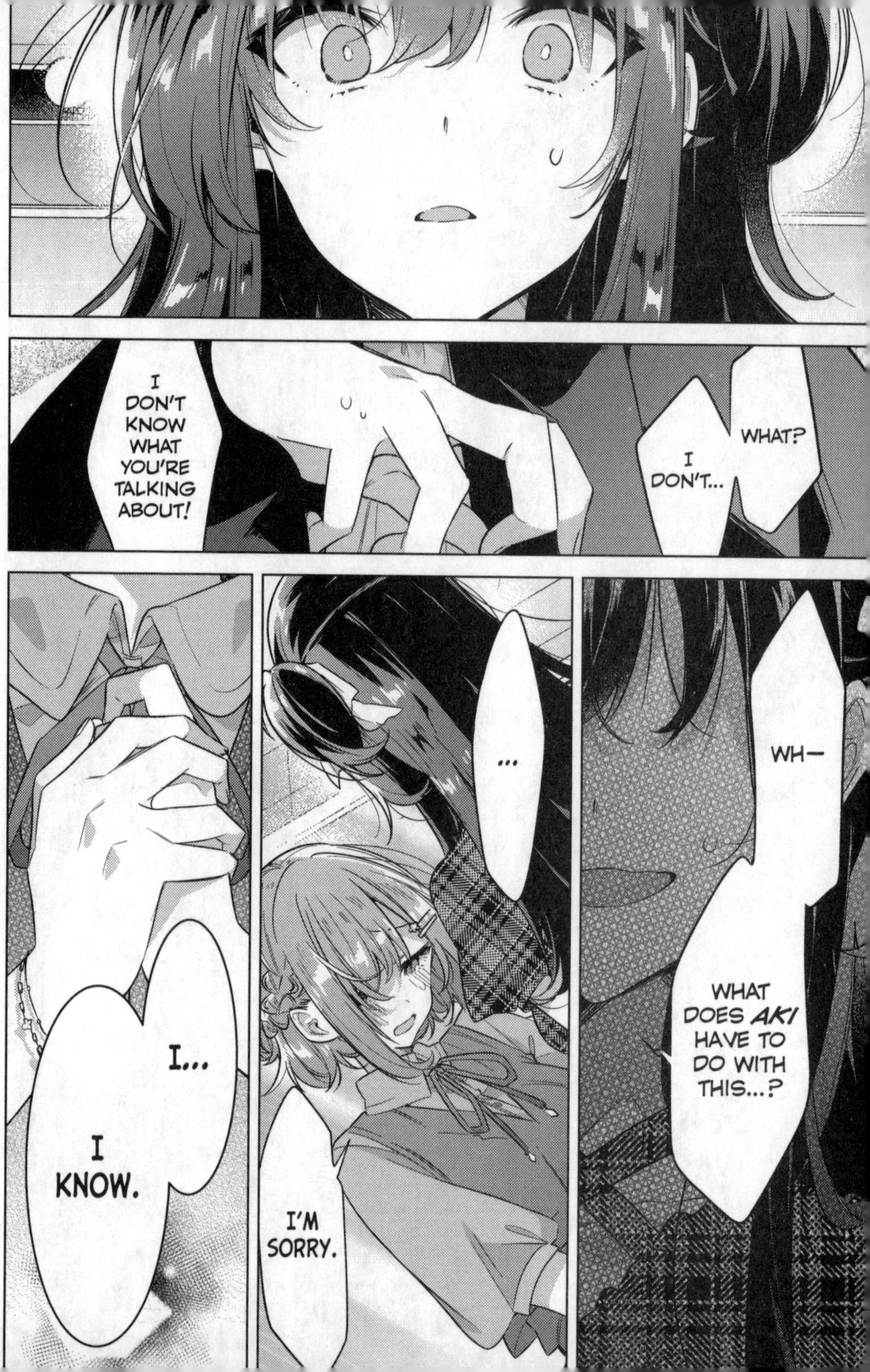
WHAT? I DON'T...
I DON'T KNOW WHAT YOU'RE TALKING ABOUT!
WH—
WHAT DOES *AKI* HAVE TO DO WITH THIS...?
...
I'M SORRY.
I...
I KNOW.

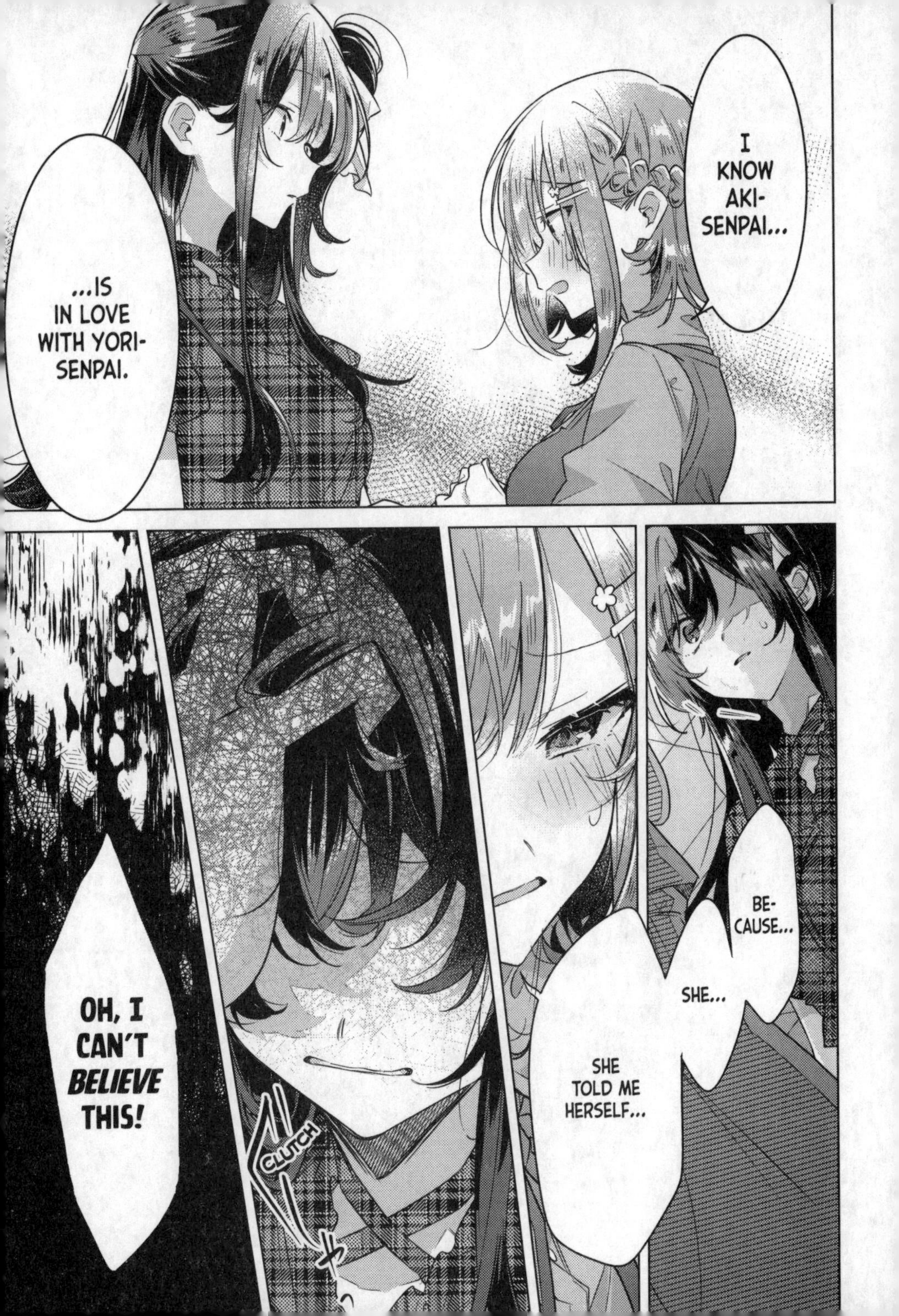
I KNOW AKI-SENPAI...
...IS IN LOVE WITH YORI-SENPAI.
BE-CAUSE...
SHE...
SHE TOLD ME HERSELF...
CLUTCH
OH, I CAN'T BELIEVE THIS!

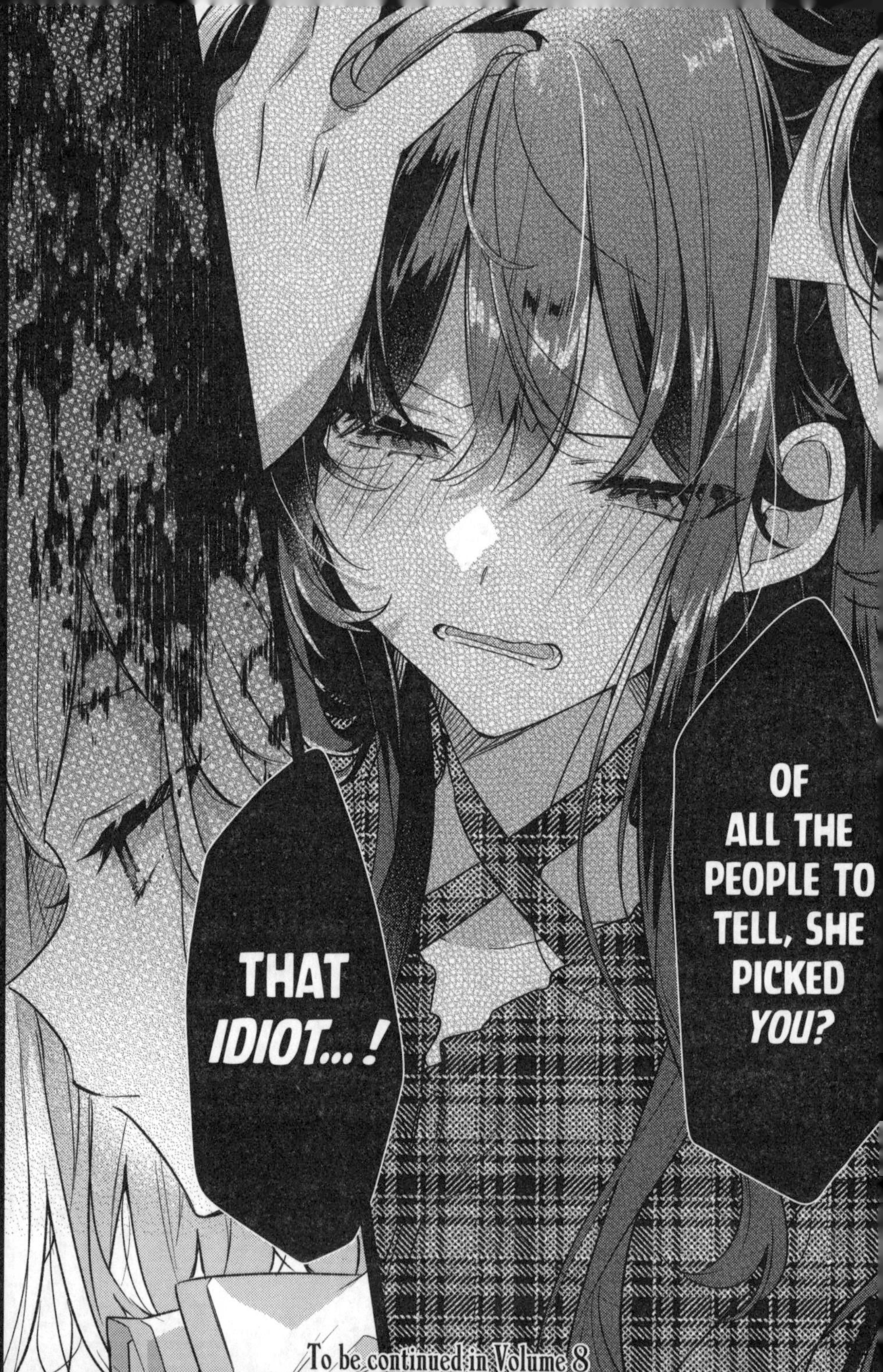
OF ALL THE PEOPLE TO TELL, SHE PICKED *YOU?*
THAT *IDIOT...!*

To be continued in Volume 8

Whisper Me
A Love Song
Eku Takeshima

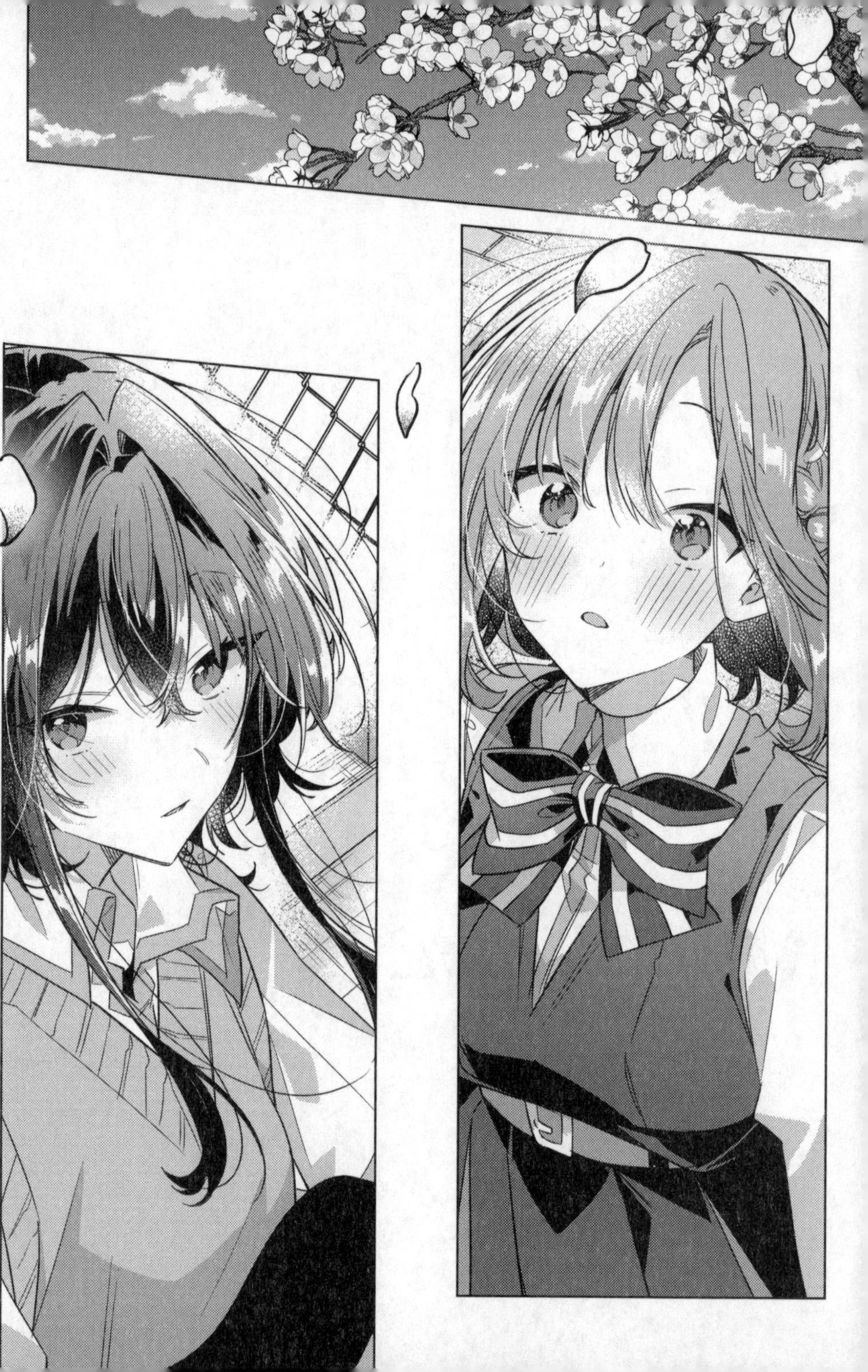

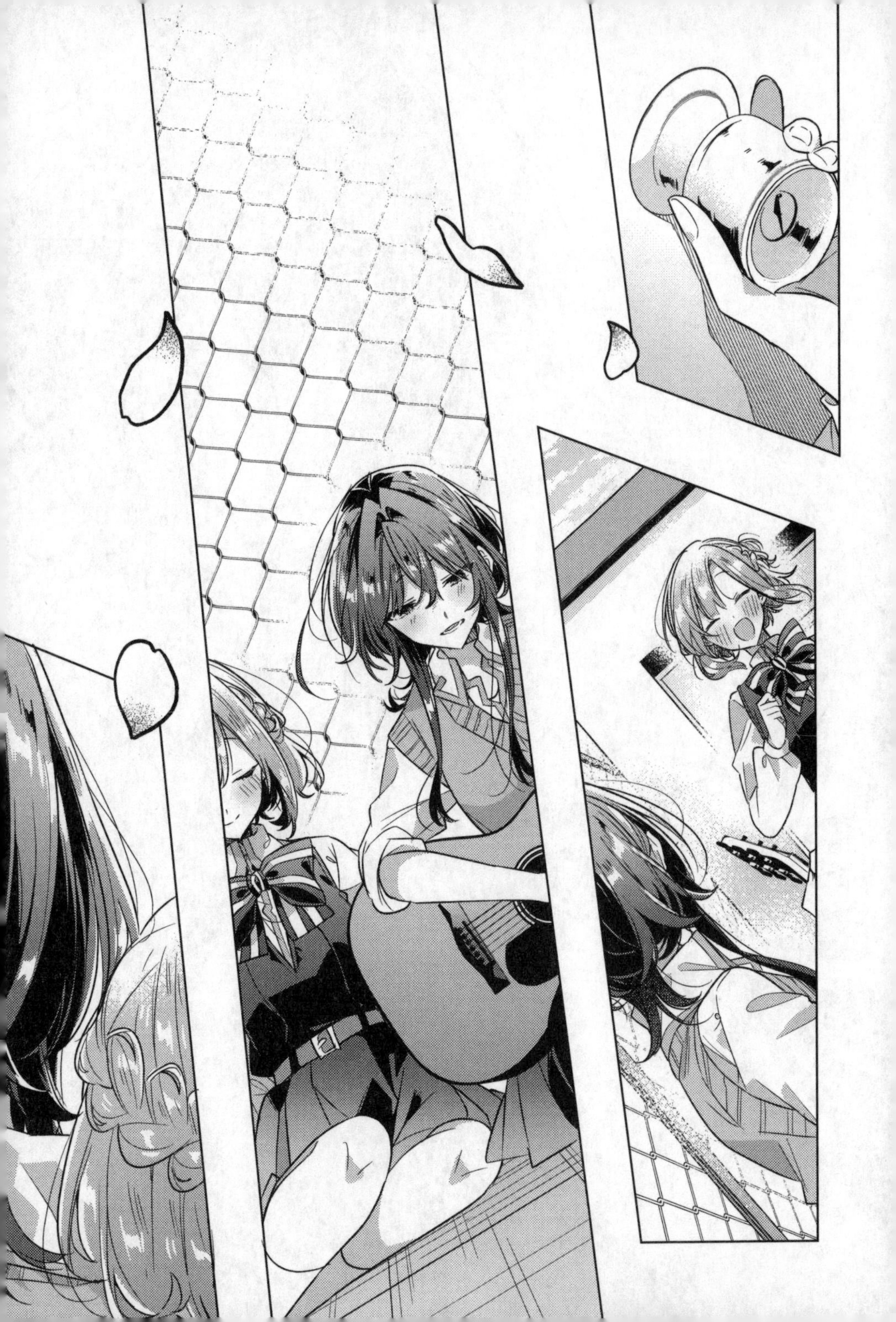

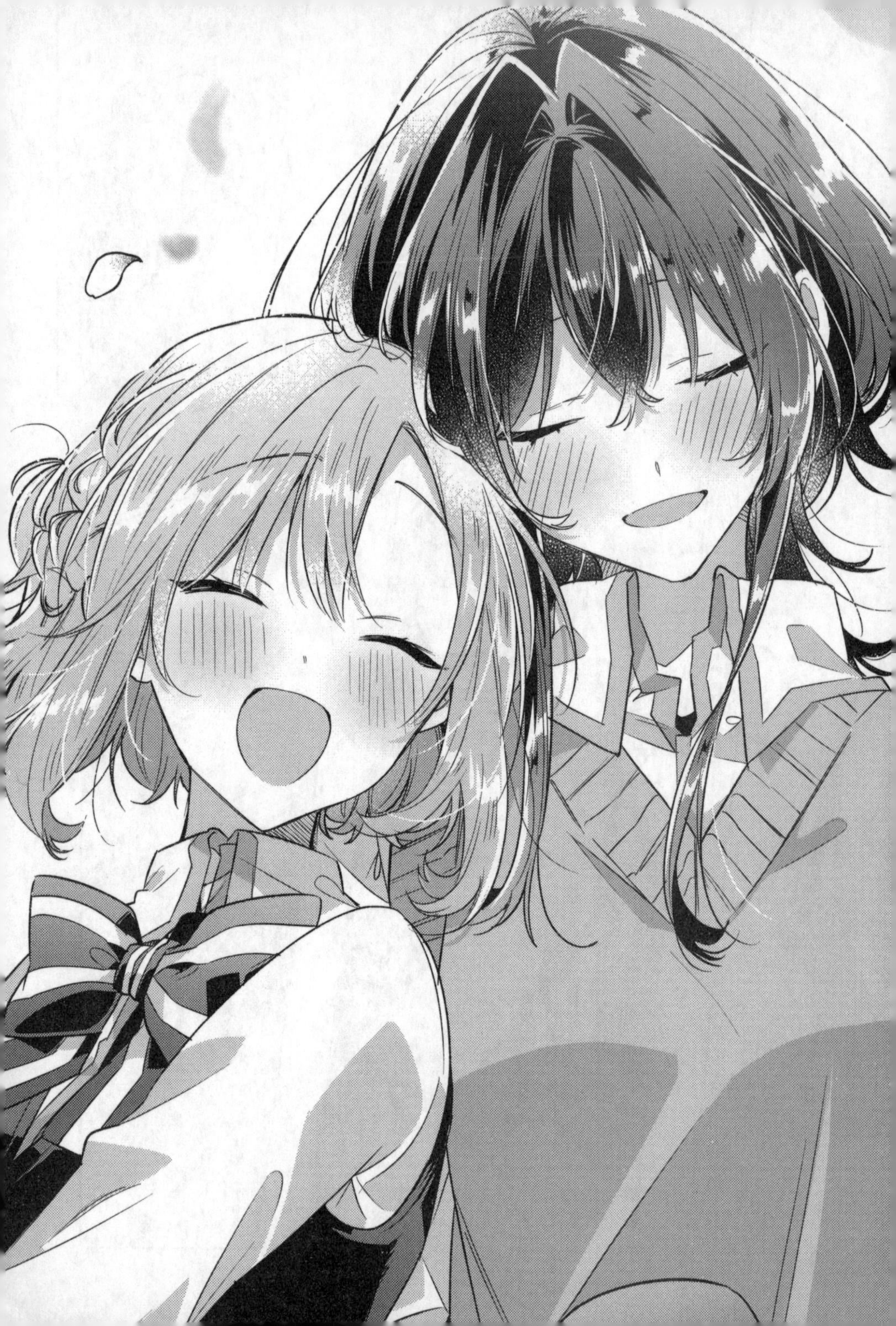

Thanks for all your support, everyone!
The Whisper Me a Love Song anime was just
announced! The thought of seeing characters
I created move and talk feels like a dream!
I'm especially excited to hear the songs, and
I keep wondering, which of Yori-chan's songs
will they include? This one? Or maybe that one?

My gratitude goes out to all the readers who
have come with me this far. I swear I can't
thank you enough! I hope you're as excited
for the anime as I am!

SPECIAL THANKS
Editor – Ten-san
Design – SALIDAS-sama
Assistants – Kaeru-san, Yuki Kuwabara-san
&
Everyone who picked up this book!

TRANSLATION NOTES

Mattress, page 19
Yori says she'll look for a *shiki-buton,* or bedroll, a thin mattress that can go on the ground and then be rolled up when not in use.

Obon, page 71
Obon, also known as simply Bon, is the Buddhist season for remembering the dead (although it's widely observed in Japan regardless of religion). It takes place over a few days in August, during which many people go home to be with their families and commemorate lost loved ones, often by visiting their graves. (In 2023, when this book was published, Obon did indeed begin on August 13th.)

Whisper Me
A Love Song

Eku
Takeshima

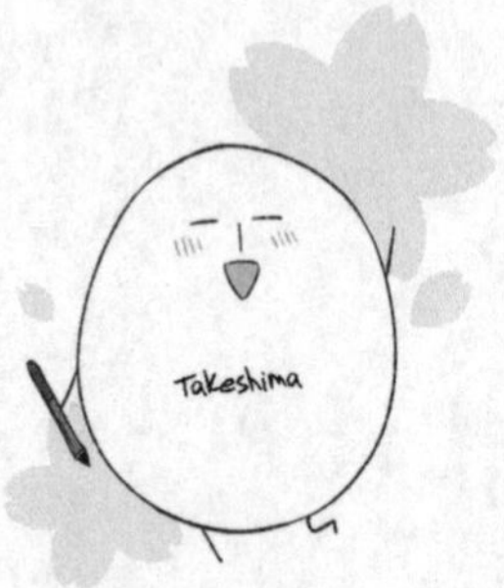
Takeshima

Writing volume 7 was an emotional roller coaster!
I hope you'll watch over my girls as they move forward.
I'm also full of gratitude to be able to bring very happy news to the people who have supported me for so long.
Thank you all so much!

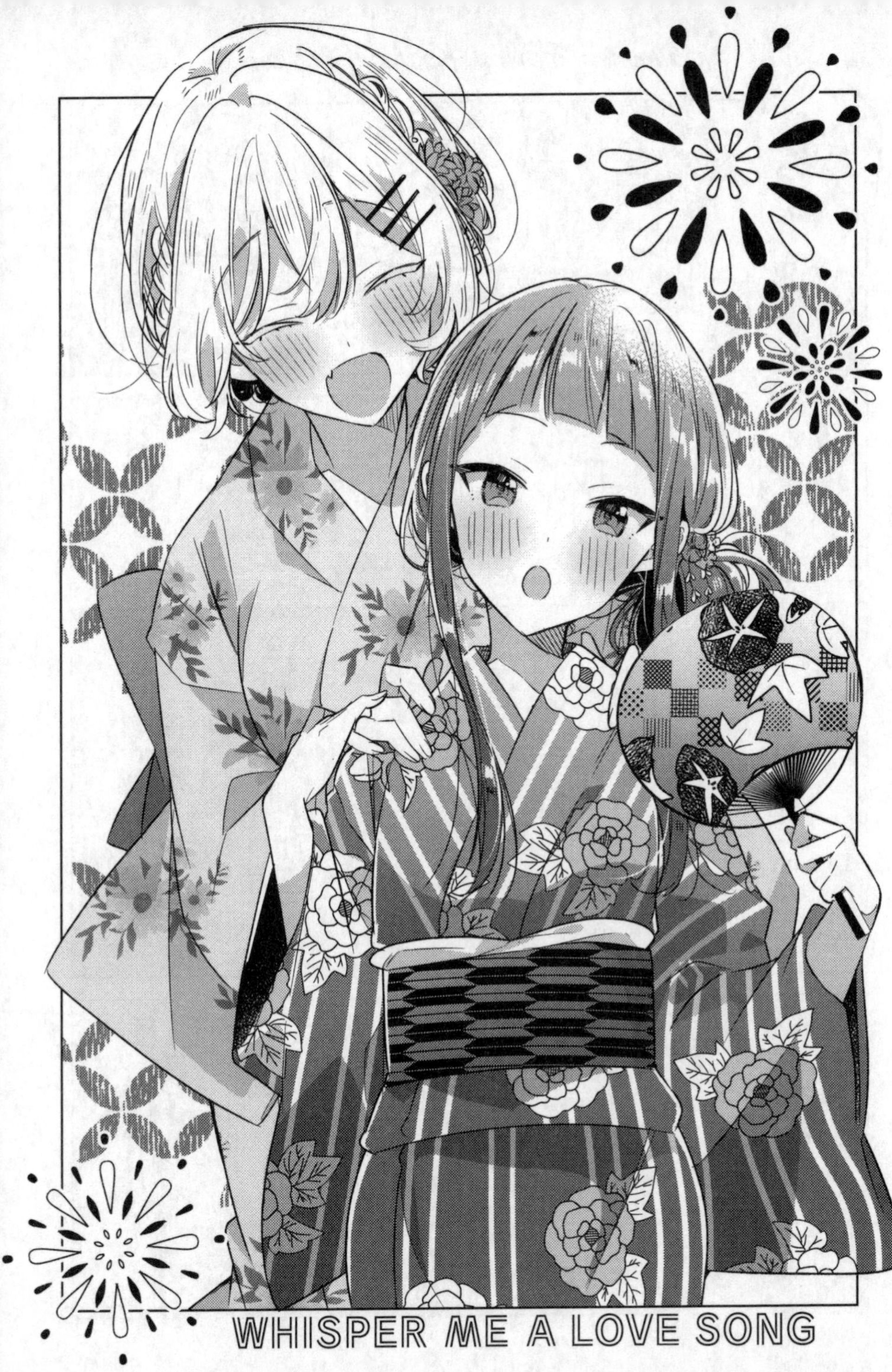
WHISPER ME A LOVE SONG

Summer Festival: KaoMari Edition

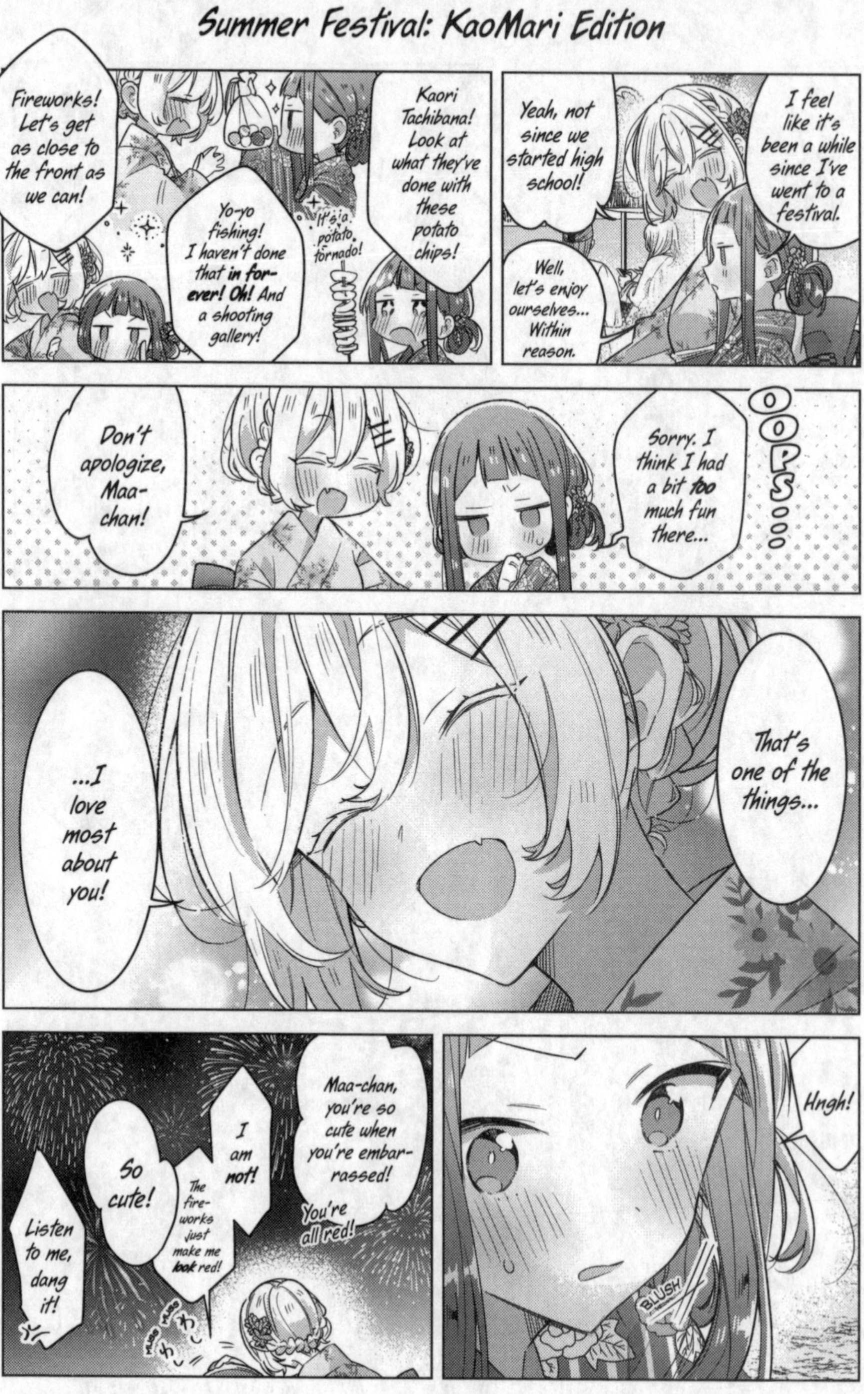
I feel like it's been a while since I've went to a festival.
Yeah, not since we started high school!
Well, let's enjoy ourselves... Within reason.
Kaori Tachibana! Look at what they've done with these potato chips!
Fireworks! Let's get as close to the front as we can!
It's a potato tornado!
Yo-yo fishing! I haven't done that **in forever! Oh!** And a shooting gallery!
OOPS...
Sorry. I think I had a bit **too** much fun there...
Don't apologize, Maa-chan!
That's one of the things...
...I love most about you!
Hngh!
BLUSH
Maa-chan, you're so cute when you're embarrassed!
I am **not!**
You're all red!
So cute!
The fireworks just make me ***look*** red!
Listen to me, dang it!

Whisper Me
A Love Song

Eku
Takeshima

Wandance

Created by
Coffee

Get up and join the Wandance!

A boy named Kaboku sees a girl named Wanda dance, and suddenly burns with a need to join in. A new, inspirational manga for fans of *Blue Period* and *Your Lie in April*.

RATED: 13+

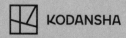

In the Clear Moonlit Dusk

Created by
Mika Yamamori

Push past appearances in this teen romance!

Yoi Takiguchi is resigned to being the hero—not heroine—in her life, until Ichimura-sempai shows her what it feels like to be seen for her true beauty...

RATED: 13+

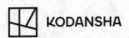 KODANSHA

The Seven Deadly Sins: Four Knights of the Apocalypse

Created by
Nakaba Suzuki

End of the world of the Sins?!
Return to the magical and thrilling
world of Britannia with this new
adventure from the creator of *The
Seven Deadly Sins*, the manga
that inspired the No. 1 hit
Netflix Original Anime!

RATED: 16+

Peach Boy Riverside

Story by Coolkyousinnjya
Art by Johanne

The bloody fantasy that inspired the anime!

There's demon-slaying action galore in this stylish update to a Japanese folktale from the creator of *Miss Kobayashi's Dragon Maid*! A rambunctious princess is fed up being trapped behind walls. But walls keep out monsters...

RATED: 16+

KODANSHA

READ THE MANGA

KODANSHA.US

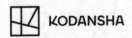

Fire Force Omnibus

Created by
Atsushi Ohkubo

600 pages each—blaze past the anime!
In the year 198 of the Solar Era, the
city of Tokyo is plagued by a deadly
phenomenon: spontaneous human
combustion! The only ones who
can stop it are the Fire Force!

RATED: 16+

KODANSHA

Go! Go! Loser Ranger!

Created by
Negi Haruba

A new "anti-ranger" action-comedy!

The monsters invading earth were subjugated
under the cruel thumbs of the Ranger Force
years ago, but one monster has had enough.
He'll rebel against the Rangers' might and
destroy them all...from the inside!

RATED: 13+

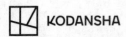

Parasyte Full Color Collection

Created by
Hitoshi Iwaaki

The sci-fi horror classic returns in color!

They infest human hosts and consume them.
The parasites are everywhere, but no one knows
their secret except high schooler Shinichi. After
preventing his own infection, can he find a way
to warn humanity?

RATED: 16+

KODANSHA

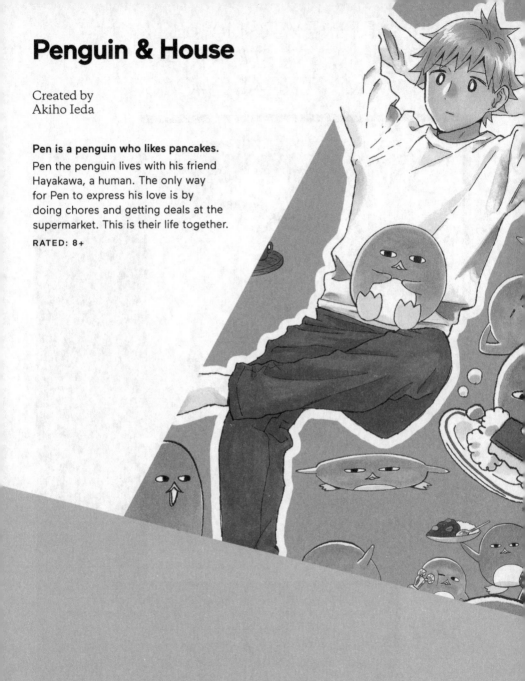

Penguin & House

Created by
Akiho Ieda

Pen is a penguin who likes pancakes.
Pen the penguin lives with his friend
Hayakawa, a human. The only way
for Pen to express his love is by
doing chores and getting deals at the
supermarket. This is their life together.

RATED: 8+

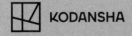 **KODANSHA**

A SMART, NEW ROMANTIC COMEDY FOR FANS OF *SHORTCAKE CAKE* AND *TERRACE HOUSE!*

LIVING ROOM

MATSUNAGA-SAN

Keiko Iwashita

KC KODANSHA COMICS

A romance manga starring high school girl Meeko, who learns to live on her own in a boarding house whose living room is home to the odd (but handsome) Matsunaga-san. She begins to adjust to her new life away from her parents, but Meeko soon learns that no matter how far away from home she is, she's still a young girl at heart — especially when she finds herself falling for Matsunaga-san.